BLACK MARKET BRITAIN

Black Market Britain

1939–1955

MARK ROODHOUSE

OXFORD
UNIVERSITY PRESS

OXFORD
UNIVERSITY PRESS

Great Clarendon Street, Oxford, OX2 6DP,
United Kingdom

Oxford University Press is a department of the University of Oxford.
It furthers the University's objective of excellence in research, scholarship,
and education by publishing worldwide. Oxford is a registered trade mark of
Oxford University Press in the UK and in certain other countries

British Library Cataloguing in Publication Data

Data available

ISBN 978–0–19–958845–9

Printed in Great Britain by the
MPG Printgroup, UK

Contents

List of Figures

List of Tables

List of Abbreviations

BIPO	British Institute of Public Opinion
BL	British Library
BoT	Board of Trade
CEIB	Central Enforcement Intelligence Bureau
CID	Criminal Investigation Department
CPGB	Communist Party of Great Britain
FCC	Food Control Committee
FCES	Food Control Enforcement Subcommittee
IWM	Imperial War Museum
LMA	London Metropolitan Archives
LoN	League of Nations
MAF	Ministry of Agriculture and Fisheries
M-O	Mass-Observation
MoF	Ministry of Food
MoFP	Ministry of Fuel and Power
MoI	Ministry of Information
MoL	Ministry of Labour (and National Service)
OPA	Office of Price Administration
PRO	Public Record Office
TNA	The National Archives
WAC	Written Archives Centre

Preface

This book is born of curiosity and frustration: curiosity about why some individuals chose to participate in illegal 'black' markets while others did not, and frustration with established approaches for understanding such choices. The underdevelopment of black markets in price-controlled and rationed goods during the austerity years was a celebrated economic failure, heralded by former policymakers and contemporary commentators as proof of Whitehall's administrative genius and the superiority of British national character. These boosters believed that the British resisted the lure of black markets, unlike their American cousins and continental neighbours, thanks to their patriotism and law-abiding character.

This self-congratulatory account challenged contemporary ideas about economic behaviour. Compliance with economic controls was not in the self-interest of traders seeking a profit or consumers trying to fulfil their desires. According to the theory of supply and demand, people would buy and sell illegal goods and services to achieve these ends given the means, motive, and opportunity. Contemporary economists, and latterly historians, found it hard to accept that British experience of price control and rationing during the 1940s and 1950s contradicted the fundamental proposition of neoclassical economics that bad things happen in the absence of unfettered competitive markets. Pointing to milder shortages limiting demand, tighter controls restricting opportunities for evasion, and tougher enforcement increasing the risk and cost of being caught, economists argued that Britons were no more virtuous than anyone else.

Stubbornly resisting the well-meaning attempts of Amartya Sen and others to reform him, *Homo economicus*, the central actor in this and many other historical dramas, remains a rational fool: an amoral and self-interested individual out to maximize his utility at others' expense. For him, who feels no shame or guilt, the moral obloquy and legal sanctions associated with illegal dealing are additional costs of doing business. If potential gains outweigh potential losses, black markets thrive. Despite mounting experimental evidence of cognitive biases that make humans poor decision makers, economists cling to their model of man. Believing there is nothing of equal explanatory power to replace it, allowances are made for inadequate information and limited mental capacity. But is this new 'behavioural economics' enough?

Whether such an economic tale provides a satisfactory explanation is partly a question of taste—a preference for a simple, elegant argument that explains a lot with a little over a complex, confused one, or a fondness for a 'thick description' that reveals the richness of our actions over a 'thin' one that does not. 'Matters of taste', as Thomas Kuhn noted, 'are the most difficult of all to define or debate'. Yet a story that does not take into account participants' reported motives, focusing on behaviour alone, cannot be wholly satisfactory. By ignoring these accounts, the tales we tell about economic life risk turning into just-so stories. Incorporating them into our narratives makes them more credible, capturing something important and vital about economic life. After all, the historian's task is to make the complex comprehensible, not simplify it.

Understanding the moral and social dimensions of black markets requires a flexible approach to the study of past choices—one that does not make assumptions about the rationality, or irrationality, of economic actors. If individuals were to use black markets, they needed to overcome their moral inhibitions to illegal dealing first. Only then could they make an 'economic' decision. This understanding of the relationship between norms and rational choice, explained in more detail in the introduction, underpins the book's central argument about fairness. It views rational choice as one of many social mechanisms that can explain human behaviour. Such an approach, associated with the tradition of analytical sociology, has yet to impact on historical research despite its potential usefulness for those seeking to integrate social and cultural approaches to the study of economic life into economic and social history.

Although previous writers disagree about why people obeyed or disobeyed the regulations, they agree that non-compliance with rationing and price regulations was nominal. In the absence of a detailed study describing the pattern of evasion and the operation of black markets, the evidence for this view is slight. Part I addresses these issues by gauging the extent of non-compliance and describing its pattern. Drawing upon economic anthropology and sociology, it develops a model of Britain's underground economy at mid-century that testifies to the persistence and significance of non-market exchange. No control scheme was watertight; all were avoided or evaded to a greater or lesser degree. Reviewing the available evidence, the conclusion reached is that black markets did not fulfil their potential even when economic factors such as supply and demand and the structure of controls are taken into account.

Distilling ten years' experience of clothes and petrol rationing, Brian Reddaway expressed the view of many former government economists when he wrote: 'The successful enforcement of a rationing system and the avoidance of a black market is not primarily a matter of test shopping, flying squads and the like, but rather of devising a rationing system which will be relatively easy to enforce, and which will, indeed, to a large extent enforce itself.' Subsequent generations of scholars have been more sceptical of this view, challenging the idea that enforcement and prosecution did not affect non-compliance. The second part of the book tackles this issue by examining 'test shopping, flying squads, and the like'. Detailed examination of the rationing ministries' compliance strategies, street-level policing, and the criminal-justice system reveals a confused and confusing approach to enforcing the regulations that undermined attempts to make enforcement transparent, predictable, and proportionate. The priorities of hard-pressed law enforcement agencies and the courts frustrated centrally determined enforcement policies. Their staffs were also loath to alienate the public upon whose goodwill they relied.

The third and final part of the book develops an alternative explanation of the pattern of non-compliance. Starting with a close reading of several hundred self-justificatory accounts collected by the research organization Mass-Observation, Part III follows the evidence to create a new explanation of evasion. People obeyed the law, albeit selectively, not because of coercion or fear of coercion—enforcement was too haphazard for that—but because they thought the regulations both necessary and fair. The people who individuals associated with and the nature of the representations of black market activity to which they were exposed shaped what they considered fair and necessary. Patriotism—a powerful but ephemeral emotion—may have inspired but it did not sustain high levels of quasi-voluntary compliance throughout the austerity period.

Evasion centred on regulations that people considered unnecessary or unfair. The government rhetoric of 'fair shares for all' connected with popular notions of justice, which assumed renewed significance in a time of dearth and austerity, only to recede with the advent of the post-war economic boom. Although civilians might disagree with the official definition of what constituted a fair profit, a fair price, or a fair share, how these definitions were arrived at, and how they were implemented, they accepted the idea that the distribution should be fair. But what they considered fair could differ dramatically from official definitions. Nevertheless, offenders limited their black marketing to getting what they considered their true fair share but no more.

Attempting to describe and explain black market activity took far longer than I anticipated at the outset of the project. During that time I have studied at two universities and worked for two employers, incurring numerous intellectual debts along the way. The quiet encouragement of the late Charles Feinstein convinced me that black markets were a feasible and worthwhile topic, while a Cambridge apprenticeship with Peter Clarke helped me to realize its potential. This book benefited greatly from Peter's help and advice. Making tea for Peter's seminar brought me into contact with Martin Daunton and Frank Trentmann, both of whom provided invaluable comments on my work, helping make an idiosyncratic project part of the historical main. Clive Emsley and Ken Mouré supported the project from afar. Their enthusiasm for the topic and astute criticism was priceless. I have also benefited from probing questions after delivering papers in Cambridge, Esbjerg, Ghent, London, The Hague, and Wolverhampton. The Department of History at the University of York, where I completed this book, has been a supportive environment. My York colleagues—notably Stuart Carroll, David Clayton, Alex Goodall, Hannah Greig, Catriona Kennedy, Mark Ormrod, Bill Sheils, and Miles Taylor—gave me the confidence to finish it, and I thank them all. Thanks are also due to Seth Cayley, Stephanie Ireland, Emma Barber, Bob Marriott, and Andrew Hawkey for patiently guiding me through the publishing process.

Finding evidence of past crimes presents historians with a conundrum: only the crimes of the unlucky or the incompetent are recorded in government archives. Fortunately, I have had the assistance of many excellent librarians and archivists when trying to solve this problem. The National Archives staff helped me to use the provisions of the Freedom of Information Act to good effect. Mary Gower and Stuart Stone were cheery guides to the riches of the Radzinowicz Library in Cambridge, while Dorothy Sheridan shared her knowledge of the Mass-Observation collection with me.

A series of awards and grants, both large and small, from the Arts and Humanities Research Council, the Economic and Social Research Council, Trinity College, Cambridge, and the University of York made it possible to research and write this book. I am particularly grateful to Jim Bamberg for providing me with academic out-relief in the form of a research post at the BP History Project. I hope my working papers on the history of petrochemicals were recompense.

Thanks are also due to the following people and institutions who have granted me permission to quote from work or reproduce images for which they hold the copyright: the BBC, the Board of Deputies of British Jews, the Bodleian Library, Oxford, the Centre for South Asian Studies, Cambridge, Getty Images, IPC Media, Deirdre McLellan, and Curtis Brown Group Ltd, London on behalf of the Trustees of the Mass-Observation Archive. Every effort has been made to trace and contact copyright holders, but this has not been possible in every case. If notified, the publisher will undertake to rectify any errors or omissions at the earliest opportunity.

Friends and family endured this project for many years, especially my friends Joe Bord and Neil Rushton, my parents Simon and Liz, and my children Matthew, Seth, and Freya, but none more so than my wife Madeleine. Without her love and support, I would never have brought this project to book.

York, January 2013

Introduction: the 'unethical' consumer

At 11.10 am on Friday 24 March 1944 Detective Sergeant Bert Hannam of the London Metropolitan Police knocked on the front door of Ivor Novello's Aldwych flat. The composer, actor, and playwright lay in bed reading the paper. He had not been awake for long, as he had appeared on stage at The Adelphi in his musical *The Dancing Years* the night before. His secretary Captain Lloyd-Williams opened the door and showed Hannam through to Novello's bedroom. There, the detective served Novello with a summons for conspiring with one of his most ardent fans and a frequent back-stage visitor, Dora Constable, to avoid petrol rationing and evade the motor fuel regulations.

Constable, then working as a junior filing clerk for a venture capitalist, had helped Novello obtain a license to convert his chauffeur-driven maroon Rolls Royce from petrol to gas. Novello used the car to commute between his London flat and his country house in Berkshire, but the withdrawal of the basic petrol ration for private motorists in 1942 had forced him to commute by train. He detested the commute from Paddington to Maidenhead, and tried unsuccessfully to obtain a licence to convert his car to gas. When Constable heard him complain about the situation in his dressing room after a performance on Christmas Eve 1943, she promised to help him.

Without her superiors' knowledge, but with Novello's connivance, Constable arranged for the car's ownership to be transferred to her employer's firm. She then applied for a licence to convert the car, claiming that it would be used by company executives to visit the firm's factories. Having successfully obtained a licence, Constable provided Novello's chauffeur with a letter explaining that he worked for the firm. Armed with this letter, the chauffeur resumed driving Novello between London and Berkshire. The scam was not discovered until Constable confessed all to her employer after being accused of embezzling more than £1,000 of company cash. A police investigation followed, unravelling the conspiracy and bringing Hannam to Novello's door.

On being handed the summons, Novello exclaimed:

> Going to take me to Court! I did hope they would believe my statement and forget this. Inspector, probably persons in my profession overrate their importance but really you know I am engaged on very, very important war work for morale and my licence should not have been refused. The War Ministry have caused all this trouble. The suggestion of me conspiring with a person of Constable's type is repugnant.

After reading a few lines of Constable's statement, Novello slumped back into his pillows and delivered the lines that would later irritate and amuse newspaper readers by turns.

This is terrible. Oh! The publicity it will mean. I don't mind myself but I detest causing
a stain on the theatrical profession. You know inspector I used the car on numerous
occasions to get to my home. My health would not stand the strain of train travel.
I really thought Mr Haywood [Constable's employer] knew all about the arrangement
and that he was being kind to me.[1]

A month later, the journalists sitting in Bow Street Magistrates' Court listening to
the case seized upon Novello's words, reporting his 'verbal' in full. This was possible
because the editors of the national dailies devoted several scarce column inches to
the case, as it had all the elements of a great news story: crime, celebrity, hypocrisy,
selfishness, and ungentlemanly conduct. According to one diarist, even *The Times*,
the august paper of record, gave the case 'quite a lot of publicity', quoting what
both sides said 'with considerable gusto for such an organ'.[2] The coverage showed
Novello in an unsympathetic light. The fact of his conviction and sentencing to
eight weeks' imprisonment when combined with selective reporting of statements
made in court gave the impression that Novello exploited a vulnerable and unstable woman, for whom he had no regard, in order to achieve his own selfish ends
at the expense of the national war effort.

His fellow thespian Noël Coward, who also fell foul of wartime regulations,
shared the public's opinion, recording in a diary entry a conversation that took
place over dinner at Novello's house in Berkshire early in 1946.

> …we embarked on Ivor's trial and the injustice, etc. I became a little uneasy but he
> has no qualms whatever. He told me how he evaded fire watching and flew to the
> shelter whenever danger threatened.

Novello's 'selfish, pathetic triviality' rankled with Coward, who threw himself
behind the war effort.[3] Although Novello and Constable were not black marketeers
dealing in rationed or price-controlled goods, they had evaded the regulations,
and, in the eyes of many, disregarded the principle of 'fair shares for all' that under-
wrote the system of consumer regulation.

The price and rationing regulations, evaded by Novello amongst others, were an
important part of a system of controls on economic activity. Imposed during the
Second World War and dismantled from the late 1940s onwards, the aim of
control was to restrain consumption, prevent inflation, and ensure orderly distribution. Interest rates and taxation were the principal methods of indirect control,
which worked in tandem with a range of direct or physical controls. Contemporary economists distinguished between seven types of direct control: labour con-
trol, import control, exchange control, export control, raw materials control, price
control, and consumer rationing. Only the last two impacted directly on consumers, and it was non-compliance with these that came to be labelled 'black market'.

---

[1] The National Archives (TNA): Public Record Office (PRO), Kew, MEPO 3/2354, 'Statement of
Detective Sergeant Herbert Hannam', 27 March 1944.

[2] Mass-Observation Archive (M-OA), University of Sussex, Falmer, Diaries, 1944, April, Women,
D5349, 25 April 1944.

[3] Noël Coward diary, 27 January 1946, in Graham Payn and Sheridan Morley (eds.), *The Noël
Coward Diaries* (2nd edn., London, 1998), 50.

By diverting economic activity into official channels, policymakers and administrators simplified supply chains, which made it easier for them to control the flow of goods and services around the economy. But ironing out the meanders of existing chains and diverting resources into new untested channels created unexpected problems. Controls criminalized some customary practices, such as the conditional sale, and created new ones, such as coupon trafficking. Most of these related to rationing, which introduced a second currency in the form of ration coupons, placing similar demands in terms of banking and accounting procedures on consumers and suppliers as the existing monetary currency did. Canalizing economic activity took time. The system of control was not fully formed until 1943. By then, three government departments—the Board of Trade, the Ministry of Food, and the Ministry of Fuel and Power—or the rationing ministries, controlled the price of clothing, household goods, food, petrol, and domestic fuel as well as rationed clothing, food, and petrol.[4] Control reached its greatest extent in 1948 when 31% of consumer expenditure went on rationed goods.[5] Not only did these official channels determine what was legal, but they also created new criminal opportunities as the forces of supply and demand found out weaknesses in the channels' banks.

Invited to deliver the Marshall Lectures in 1947, the economist Lionel Robbins, who had acquired an unrivalled overview of the war effort while directing the War Cabinet's Economic Section, chose to outline the economic problem of war. According to Robbins, the Second World War was a 'total war' that required the British government to direct all available resources to the war effort. Having determined the minimum standard of living necessary to maintain the health and morale of the population, and securing the resources to deliver this, everything else could be directed to the war effort. Only direct controls backed by indirect ones could achieve these ends, as an uncontrolled free-market economy could not achieve them with the same speed or attention to detail.[6] A high level of import dependence before the war exacerbated the problem facing the country as limitations on shipping space and foreign currency imposed additional constraints on civilian supplies.

In a more sober paper for a Whitehall seminar, Robbins discussed the role that price control and rationing played in regulating consumer demand. As civilian supplies fell and demand increased due to full employment, prices began to rise. Price control and subsidies stabilized prices of essential and semi-essential goods. This ensured that people on low incomes could afford price-controlled goods, but it did not guarantee that they could buy them. To prevent consumers with time and money from emptying shop shelves of essential goods, rationing was necessary to parcel out supplies, balancing equality with individual need. Financial measures

---

[4] See Ina Zweiniger-Bargielowska, *Austerity in Britain: Rationing, Controls, and Consumption, 1939–1955* (Oxford, 2000), 9–59 for details.

[5] J. C. R. Dow, *The Management of the British Economy 1945–60* (London, 1970), 173.

[6] Lionel Robbins, *The Economic Problem in Peace and War: Some Reflections on Objectives and Mechanisms* (London, 1947).

had an ancillary role in combating inflation, mopping up excess demand through higher taxation and incentives to savers.[7] This vision of war economy, which emerged from Robbins' Economic Section, found expression in the price stabilization policy announced in the Fourth War Budget of April 1941.

Demobilizing the economy would present government with a different problem. With the support of colleagues at the Board of Trade, Treasury officials persuaded politicians of all parties to retain direct controls during the transition from war to peace.[8] This was necessary in order to avoid mass unemployment and an inflationary boom as demobbed servicemen swamped the labour market while businesses restocked and shoppers scrambled to get their hands on decontrolled goods. Post-war control was also necessary to avoid a balance-of-payments crisis as the release of pent-up domestic demand sucked in dollar imports that the country could ill afford while its export industries struggled to recover and it serviced its debts. As the balance of payments righted itself and the supply situation improved, officials planned to first relax and then remove regulations within a few years of Japan's defeat.[9] Events such as the cancellation of US Lend-Lease aid in 1945, the harsh winter of 1947, and the Korean War reversed this process temporarily.[10] As a result, price control and rationing continued for nine years after the war, ending in 1954, many years after decontrol in Canada, the USA, and Germany.

The effects of control on civilians were dramatic. By the time a detective called at Novello's flat in 1944, Britons' standard of living and quality of life had fallen dramatically. Civilians saw their diet decline in quality and variety. Each week the food ration book entitled an ordinary adult to buy 4 oz of bacon and ham, 1s 2d-worth of meat, 3 oz of tea, 8 oz of sugar, and 4 oz of preserves, which could be exchanged for an extra 4 oz of sugar and 8 oz of fats. Non-priority consumers like Novello received two pints of milk a week, a pack of dried eggs every two weeks, and four fresh eggs a quarter.[11] Every four weeks, adults received food points worth 2s 6d each to spend on biscuits, breakfast cereals, canned foods, and dried foods, plus personal points for 12 oz of sweets and chocolate.[12] Fillers such as bread and potatoes were coupon-free, as were offal and fruit and vegetables. Subject to price control, they were costly and sometimes unobtainable. Thanks to the gendered division of labour, the burden of meal planning, food shopping, and cooking fell heaviest on women.[13]

People's personal appearance also deteriorated under control. With twenty-four clothing coupons to last six months, Novello could buy a new two-piece woollen suit for court hearings. He would have to wait a further six months to complete the

---

[7] Lionel Robbins, 'Economic Policy in War Time', in Robbins, *The Economist in the Twentieth Century and other Lectures in Political Economy* (London, 1954), 201–25.

[8] George Peden, *The Treasury and British Public Policy 1906–1959* (Oxford, 2000), 346; Correlli Barnett, *The Audit of War: The Illusion and Reality of Britain as a Great Nation* (London, 1986), 265.

[9] Employment Policy (PP 1943–4 Cmd.6527 viii, 119), 6–10.

[10] Zweiniger-Bargielowska, *Austerity*, 9–59.

[11] R. J. Hammond, *Food*, 3 vols. (London, 1951–62), i, 402–3; Hammond, *Food*, ii, 799.

[12] *Manchester Guardian*, 1 December 1943.

[13] Zweiniger-Bargielowska, *Austerity*, 99–150.

look with a new shirt, collar, pair of cuffs, tie, and small pocket square. If Constable had the money, she could buy a single outfit with her coupons.[14] The lipstick and powder that Constable pulled out of her handbag during her court appearances were scarce luxuries. Rationed by price and subject to a punitive purchase tax of 33⅓ or 100%, women paid a fortune for cosmetics.[15] The same was true of many other luxuries and home comforts. A stiff purchase tax, steep income tax increases, and reduced supplies had eroded civilians' ability to enjoy a drink and a smoke in the local pub. Home provided no refuge from these and other austerities. Fuel restrictions left Novello with only 4 cwt of coal a month to heat the many rooms of his large country house, which he could not redecorate nor refurnish.[16]

The middle class felt these enforced cuts keenly. Ministers argued that for reasons of equity, people on middle to high incomes had to accept larger falls in their standard of living and quality of life than did the working class. Although large in absolute terms, their personal sacrifices pained them less than the smaller sacrifices made by people on lower incomes. Equalizing the burden of cuts across the civilian population was problematic due to the difficulty of defining and measuring equal sacrifice as well as more mundane resource constraints. Regulators wanted to define equal sacrifice in marginal rather than proportional terms. According to the economist A. C. Pigou, the aim was to ensure that 'the last unit of commodity permitted to any one purchaser shall carry about the same satisfaction as the last permitted to any other', but measuring satisfaction was beyond the regulators' abilities. Instead, they opted to make 'an adjustment of rations based on needs rather than on demands'.[17] When it came to prices, this meant taxing luxury goods heavily and leaving the market to set their price. In contrast, regulators fixed the price of essential and semi-essential goods so as to put them within reach of working-class consumers while securing a reasonable profit for suppliers. The middle class came to resent the 'unfair' principle of equal marginal sacrifice on which administrators based these austerity policies, as its utilitarian focus on minimizing the marginal loss of an unknown and unknowable level of satisfaction ignored the large and measurable cuts in middle-class living standards.

The squeezed middle ignored what they saw as special pleading by wealthy evaders who had the money to avoid the worst effects of control. Worth £146,245 at his death in 1951,[18] Novello was a very rich man for whom control was a costly inconvenience. Cushioned by a high income and large personal wealth, Novello and others like him maintained their social rank despite the wartime levelling of incomes. A large wardrobe insulated Novello from the worst effects of clothes rationing. He could not replace clothes frequently, dressing more shabbily and less fashionably than before the war, but he could afford the highest quality clothing, which lasted longest. Food rationing affected him little. His staff shouldered the

---

[14] E. L. Hargreaves and M. M. Gowing, *Civil Industry and Trade* (London, 1952), 339–40.
[15] Zweiniger-Bargielowska, *Austerity*, 190.
[16] W. H. B. Court, *Coal* (London, 1951), 364; Hargreaves and Gowing, *Civil Industry*, 332–8.
[17] A. C. Pigou, *The Political Economy of War* (London, 1940), 141.
[18] John Snelson, 'Novello, Ivor (1893–1951)', in H. C. G. Matthew and Brian Harrison (eds.), *Oxford Dictionary of National Biography*, 60 vols. (Oxford, 2004), xli, 225–8.

additional burden of putting appetizing meals on the table. They could augment his diet with fruit and vegetables from a large kitchen garden, which they tended. Unlike most civilians, Novello could also eat coupon-free at London's best restaurants whenever he liked.[19] Although they cost him dearly, Novello continued to enjoy his usual luxuries and home comforts, for which his staff had scoured the shops. Petrol rationing was harder to avoid. Taxis and hire cars were few in number and their operation restricted to the local area, which forced Novello to use crowded trains and mingle with his public. Removing his freedom to motor was a personal sacrifice too far.

Those who cheated a system designed to ensure 'fair shares' of scarce goods, especially those imported at considerable human cost during the war, were social pariahs, as their actions denied others a fair share. If caught, public opinion demanded that the authorities dealt harshly with all ration cheats, whatever their social standing. This was why ex-servicemen, including the secretary of the Citizens Union, wrote to the Home Secretary Herbert Morrison protesting at the leniency of Novello's sentence.[20] A few days later a secret summary of police morale reports crossed Morrison's desk confirming the lack of public sympathy for Novello. According to the Chief Constable of Reading, the local populace welcomed the dismissal of Novello's appeal against his sentence.[21] A thirty-six-year-old food packaging manager from Belmont, Surrey, keeping a diary for Mass-Observation, shared this view.

> I am not at all sorry that Ivor Novello has had his sentence confirmed by the London Sessions Court. I often hear indirectly of men in public positions who because of influence get away with breaking wartime regulations. When one is caught it would be a travesty of justice if a heavy conviction is not recorded. He deserves more than he got, and only simpering females have pity for him.[22]

But even 'simpering females' had little time for Novello. Having read about the outcome of the appeal in a London evening paper, Vere Hodgson noted in her diary: 'Poor Ivor Novello. But it is no excuse to say you do not know you are breaking the law.'[23]

Public hostility towards Novello evaporated soon after his release from Wormwood Scrubs. Having served his time, he resumed his role in *The Dancing Years* to great acclaim, and received a standing ovation at the end of his first performance.[24] By the time of his death in March 1951, the conviction was forgotten: it did not

[19] *The Times*, 12 June 1942.

[20] TNA: PRO, HO 45/25153, G. Nicholson to Herbert Morrison, 17 May 1944, and G. Briggs to Morrison, 18 May 1944.

[21] TNA: PRO, HO 45/25153, 'Police Duty Room report', 21 May 1944.

[22] M-OA, Diaries, 1944, May, Men, D5004, 17 May 1944.

[23] Vere Hodgson diary, 16 May 1944, in Vere Hodgson, *Few Eggs and No Oranges: A Diary showing how Unimportant People in London and Birmingham Lived through the War Years, 1940–1945* (London, 1976), 382.

[24] E. Marsh to C. Hassall, June 1944, in Christopher Hassall and John Guest (eds.), *Ambrosia and Small Beer: The Record of a Conversation between Edward Marsh and Christopher Hassall* (London, 1964), 294.

receive a mention in *The Times* obituary nor in the *Daily Mirror*, which championed fair-shares policies throughout the 'People's War' and into the post-war years.[25] As Coward's diary entry from 1946 shows, Novello's actions had been forgotten but not forgiven. Empathy, let alone sympathy, for Novello was a scarce commodity, much like the petrol he tried to wangle. His closest friends were the only people not to cast him as the villain of the piece. The former civil servant and patron of the arts Eddie Marsh, who was one of Novello's character witnesses, felt that Novello 'had certainly been most imprudent and far too happy-go-lucky, but if there's one thing in the world I'm certain of it is that he had neither intention nor consciousness of doing anything wrong, and now he bears his misfortune with exemplary courage and fortitude'.[26] Marsh's fellow character witnesses, the actress Dame Sybil Thorndike and her husband Lewis Casson, president of the actors' union Equity, viewed Novello's actions in a similar fashion.

It is all too easy to dismiss their view of Novello, and that of Novello himself, as special pleading. The actor broke the law and did not have a legitimate excuse for his actions; he was an unethical consumer. While it is the case that ignorance of the regulations was no defence, this misses an important point: like most black market offenders, Novello did not consider himself to have done anything wrong. With Constable's help he obtained a licence to which he believed his 'essential war work' entitled him. Regional officials may not have considered his performances in *The Dancing Years* vital to the war effort, but Novello did. Entertaining civilians and off-duty servicemen and women boosted their morale. The government's action in releasing the actor Barry Sinclair from the RAF to replace Novello in performances of *The Dancing Years* while he served his prison sentence conceded as much. He felt that his war work and the personal sacrifices entitled him to a little comfort. The Regional Transport Commissioner's office did not share his view.

When assessing licence applications, officials decided whom to give a licence to on the basis of desert and need, asking whether the applicant did vital war work, and if so, whether the inability to use a car made it impossible for them to carry out that work. Novello agreed with the criteria while disagreeing with the decision that his work was neither vital to the war effort nor dependent upon the use of a car. Offenders could, and often did, agree with the distributive principles on which officials based price and ration levels while disagreeing with the application of these principles in their case. They might also invoke popular beliefs about distributive justice that official allocations could not, or would not, take into account. These two points are vital to understanding the pattern of non-compliance, as it reveals the ethical dimension of economic life in austerity Britain.

By 1942 the stage was set for a boom in the underground economy as profit-hungry traders tried to capitalize on consumer greed—or at least that was what contemporary supply and demand theory predicted. The steps taken by the War Cabinet to mobilize the economy had reduced total consumer spending by almost 15% compared to figures for 1938, the last full year of peace. Food expenditure

---

[25] *The Times* and *Daily Mirror*, 7 March 1951.
[26] Christopher Hassall, *Edward Marsh, Patron of the Arts: A Biography* (London, 1954), 635.

dropped by the same amount, while expenditure on clothing, furniture and hardware, and petrol tumbled by 39%, 71%, and 87% respectively. At the same time the quality and variety of the goods on offer fell. It took a further six years to return to the pre-war level of total expenditure with consumption of many foods remaining below 1938 levels while consumption of non-food items floated little above until 1954, the year rationing ended.[27] But the dire prognostications of the dismal science proved unfounded. True, the underground economy grew, but not to the extent anticipated by economists.

North American economists developing a theory of price control and black markets in the late 1940s acknowledged their failure. They attributed it to their disregard of an ethical dimension to illegal dealing, but found this hard to incorporate into their theories. Sitting at his desk in Chicago, Martin Bronfenbrenner excluded the moral dimension from his analysis of the relationship between official and black market prices, making the heroic assumption that 'consumers have no repugnance' and producers are 'devoid of scruples' against black marketing. When fellow economists criticized his assumptions as unrealistic, Bronfenbrenner conceded the point but did not see how it could be squared with the notion of amoral economic man.[28] Across the border in Montreal, Kenneth E. Boulding tried to integrate moral calculus into his analysis of black market prices. He assumed that buyers and sellers took 'moral obloquy' into account when deciding whether or not to look for a black market deal. In addition to weighing the benefits of an illegal deal against the likelihood of being caught and the severity of legal penalties, potential buyers and sellers had to consider the severity of social sanctions.[29] The implication was that the greater the social stigma attached to black marketing, the less likely a person would be to evade price and rationing regulations. Boulding was ahead of his time. Nearly two decades later the New York-based economist Gary S. Becker published an influential paper analysing crime and punishment in terms of rational choice for which he later received a Nobel prize.[30] But neither Boulding nor Becker acknowledged that the emotional content of social norms governing the exchange, distribution, and use of resources makes cold calculation difficult if not impossible.[31]

Ivor Novello could have told them that social opprobrium is not just another cost. Through an ongoing dialogue with parents, friends, and others, children internalize norms and experience self-contempt, guilt, shame, and regret after infracting a norm. Of course, the degree to which an individual internalizes these

---

[27] Zweiniger-Bargielowska, *Austerity*, Table 1.6, 53.

[28] M. Bronfenbrenner, 'Price Control under Imperfect Conditions', *American Economic Review*, 37 (1947), 107–20; J. A. Nordin and Wayne R. Moore, 'Bronfenbrenner on the Black Market', *American Economic Review*, 37 (1947), 933–4; M. Bronfenbrenner, 'Regressus in Black Market Demand: A Reply', *American Economic Review*, 37 (1947), 934–6.

[29] K. E. Boulding, 'A Note on the Theory of the Black Market', *Canadian Journal of Economics and Political Science*, 13 (1947), 115–18.

[30] Gary S. Becker, 'Crime and Punishment: An Economic Approach', *Journal of Political Economy*, 76 (1968), 176.

[31] See Jon Elster, *The Cement of Society: A Study of Social Order* (Cambridge, 1989), 119, and Elster, *Nuts and Bolts for the Social Sciences* (Cambridge, 1989), 98 on this issue.

norms varies. A weakly internalized norm has a loose grip on the emotions, making it easier to side-step. Individuals can also be deaf to its emotional tones when faced with a novel situation not covered by society's pre-existing moral code. Until a moral consensus emerges that aligns existing norms with new legal prescriptions, individuals can justify breaking the law without infracting a norm. Even then there is always wriggle room, as it is not always clear how to apply a norm in a particular circumstance. This was the position in which Novello and others found themselves. The fine detail of what constituted a fair share in austerity Britain was unclear, leaving space to evade the regulations while maintaining a non-deviant self-image, but also placing limits on what illegal activities could be justified and hence countenanced.

Despite the theoretical problems involved in Boulding's genuflections to the moral dimension of economic life, economists continue to make obeisance to popular morality in their theories of price control, rationing, and black markets.[32] In a similar vein, economic historians bob their heads to social and cultural factors when studying black markets in mid-twentieth-century Britain: these variables explain away what economic factors cannot. When discussing evasion, Ina Zweiniger-Bargielowska attributes the pattern of illegal dealing to the operation of supply and demand, and the structure of control, but concedes that 'Altruism and commitment to the war effort contributed towards containing the black market' before adding the further qualification that 'voluntary compliance was less forthcoming after the war'.[33] Here she agrees with earlier discussions of evasion of price control and food rationing in wartime Britain.[34]

It is the contention of this book that explanatory variables such as the structure of control do not help us to understand why Ivor Novello broke the law while those in a similar position did not. Although the legal framework of control shaped the opportunities for evasion, the structure of control cannot explain why some did and some did not exploit these opportunities. If we are to understand Novello's behaviour, we need to listen carefully to the accounts of his actions that he gave to detectives and others. Attending to traders' and consumers' accounts of their motives and intentions makes it possible to explore the morality of illegal dealing, especially when they are combined with other sources.

There are obvious problems with this approach. First, how can such testimony be located? And, second, what is the nature of the link between what people said and what they did? Although laborious, finding accounts does not present too much of a challenge. Many individuals and organizations documented everyday life, conscious that they and their fellow citizens were witnessing and taking part in historic events. As the defining experience of what Tom Brokaw dubbed the

---

[32] See John Butterworth, *The Theory of Price Control and Black Markets* (Aldershot, 1994) for a review of this slim literature.

[33] Zweiniger-Bargielowska, *Austerity*, 201–2.

[34] Geofrey Mills and Hugh Rockoff, 'Compliance with Price Controls in the United States and the United Kingdom during World War II', *Journal of Economic History*, 47 (1987), 197–213; Alan S. Milward, *War, Economy and Society, 1939–1945* (1977; Berkeley, 1979), 282–3.

'greatest generation' in the American context—that is to say, the generation that came of age during the depression and the Second World War—there is a vast quantity of life writing about the war and the early post-war years, both published and unpublished. And, of course, there are press reports of remarkable court cases like Novello's.

The second issue about the reliability of such evidence is trickier to deal with. Often traders and consumers were uncertain of the regulations. In his Christmas letter for 1944, a retired bank clerk, who played the organ at his local church, told his sisters that he gave his clothing coupons to his daughter so that she could buy a dress. The former clerk knew very little about 'this coupon business' and was unsure whether or not this was legal.[35] In fact it was legal, but his uncertainty coloured his account of his actions. Even if individuals knew their actions to be illegal they did not always understand or recall their motives. They might also deliberately conceal them. The context in which an account was given might distort it too. The memoirs of career criminals are a useful source, but the conventions of true crime writing and courtroom pleas shape these accounts. Also, members of a group might give the *real* reason for their actions to other members while giving a *good* reason to outsiders.

Although such accounts are self-serving and partial, they are an invaluable source. As Novello's case demonstrates, individual dissatisfaction with official rations and prices could prompt people to break the law. At the same time, the rhetoric of fairness placed limits on evasion as disgruntled individuals had to justify to themselves and others obtaining more than their 'fair share'. Unhappiness with the system of allocation was also a threat to compliance with control schemes. Although the majority of Britons accepted the need for wartime control and its continuation to prevent a post-war inflationary boom during the transition from war to peace, there was considerable political disagreement about its extent and when or if it should end.[36] Initially, support for control rested on collective memory of the experience of the First World War, patriotism, and, most importantly, the government's legitimacy. Support was, however, conditional on control of delivering goods in short supply to those who wanted them, when they wanted them, and in quantities that accorded with popular notions of fair shares. Political disagreements about the future of control, which emerged from 1943 onwards, threatened to destabilize this moral economy.

People's concerns about the fairness or effectiveness of control mattered, as it was easy for traders and consumers to evade price and rationing regulations if they wanted to. Due to the country's dependency on foreign imports, the authorities had near complete control over its supply chains from source to point of sale. Yet the vertically and horizontally integrated control schemes that geography made possible could not stop collusive offences such as overcharging and conditional

[35] P. Chignell to sisters, 15 December 1944, in Philip Chignell, *From Our Home Correspondent: Letters from Hessle in the Second World War* (Beverley, 1989), 51–2.

[36] See Zweiniger-Bargielowska, *Austerity*, 60–98 and 203–55 for detailed discussion of popular attitudes and party politics.

sales, or the transfer of unused rations and ration coupons. Administrators, producers, traders, and consumers learned anew the lesson of the First World War that no price control or rationing scheme, no matter how well designed, was watertight. Britons had plenty of opportunities to evade the regulations, but how many of them followed Novello's lead and took them? And if they did, why did they take them?

PART I

'UNDER THE COUNTER': EVADING ECONOMIC CONTROL

Introduction

Looking back on a criminal career spanning four decades, Billy Hill, the self-proclaimed boss of Britain's underworld, expressed the hope that 'Some day someone should write a treatise on Britain's wartime black market. It was the most fantastic side of civil life in wartime.'[1] Writing four years later in 1959, Lord Woolton, who was the minister responsible for preventing illegal dealing in rationed food between 1940 and 1943, agreed with Hill that this was a theme awaiting its historian, but his reasons for settling on it were very different: 'The fact that, in spite of all the scarcity of supplies and the rigidity of rationing, there was little or no black market in Britain was a tribute to the British people, which I hope the historians of this period will proudly record.'[2] The gangster and the minister could not resolve their disagreement about the extent of evasion by appealing to figures, as reliable data were hard to obtain. Even if they could have done so they were unlikely to agree, as they understood 'black market' to mean quite different things. The conceptual confusion that plagued contemporary discussion of illegal economic behaviour continues to affect historical writing about the black market, which remains deaf to the different meanings of the term.

In the hands of Lord Woolton and his officials, 'black market' referred to 'offences involving illegal transactions in food obtained otherwise than through the authorized channels'—a definition that excluded overcharging, conditional sales, and illegal transfers of rationed foods and food coupons.[3] Evasion, like today's preferred term 'non-compliance', was a broader concept that embraced all contraventions of the regulations. Although the American distinction between avoidance and evasion was known in Britain, it had not yet found favour in official circles. For other agencies 'black market' was a synonym for all evasion of price control and rationing.[4] But this wider definition excluded 'traditional' crimes, such as

---

[1] Billy Hill, *Boss of Britain's Underworld* (London, 1955), 73.
[2] Lord Woolton, *The Memoirs of The Rt Hon The Earl of Woolton* (London, 1959), 231.
[3] Ministry of Food (MoF), *How Britain was Fed in War-time: Food Control, 1939–1945* (London, 1946), 41.
[4] Criminal Statistics: England and Wales, 1939–1945 (PP 1946–7 Cmd.7227 xv, 781), 12; Report of the Commissioner of Police of the Metropolis for the Year 1944 (PP 1944–5 Cmd.6627 v, 427), 5.

adulteration, mislabelling, giving short weight, forgery, fraud, and theft, which were related to black marketing. The public did not understand 'black market' in such narrow terms. For them it covered all evasion and related criminal activity that people deemed both illegal and immoral. A second term, 'grey market', referred to all those offences considered illegal but socially acceptable. Although these folk categories are central to describing illegal economic behaviour—in fact, they are the analytical categories around which Chapters 2 and 3 are organized—it is the evasion of price and rationing regulations as well as all related crimes that are the subject of this part. And it is with this definition in mind that the next chapter sets out to gauge the extent of the black market.

The issue of non-compliance fascinates historians, as they, like Lord Woolton, view the black market as a barometer of social solidarity and popular support for government. Evasion is viewed as an antisocial or political act. From this moral–statistical perspective, as Ina Zweiniger-Bargielowska states, 'The black market casts doubt on the myth of shared sacrifice on the home front'.[5] Despite recent revisions upwards, it is generally accepted that the level of non-compliance never posed a systemic threat to control, although it increased once the war ended. Limited evasion during wartime is taken to indicate high levels of social solidarity and strong support for the Coalition government, while more extensive illegal dealing after 1945 is seen as pointing to weak social ties and shaky support for the post-war Labour government. The evidence for such views is weak, as the black market is more discussed than studied. Unlike previous work, Part I lays out a synoptic vision of illegal dealing. It draws on a much wider range of sources than any previous discussion of this topic has done, including recently declassified material at the National Archives and newly preserved documents from Mass-Observation. By answering two simple questions—namely, how big was the black market and what shape did it take?—Part I suggests that the black market is a poor indicator of social solidarity, and reveals the workings of mid-century Britain's underground economy in unprecedented detail.

[5] Zweiniger-Bargielowska, *Austerity*, 151.

1

'Large enough to cause concern': gauging the extent of non-compliance

In December 1944, readers of the *Daily Mail* learned about life in 'racket town', a 'big, busy, thriving' northern city where locals could buy petrol at 5*s* a gallon, clothing coupons at 2*s* each, or a £5 bottle of whisky from London gangsters seeking refuge from the attentions of the Luftwaffe and the Metropolitan Police. Here, cloth robberies were a nightly occurrence.[1] A month later the *News Chronicle* unmasked 'racket town' as Leeds.[2] These and similar reports led the assistant commissioner in charge of Scotland Yard and the head of enforcement intelligence at the Ministry of Food (MoF) to dub Leeds, Liverpool, and London, the principal centres of black marketeering, as the 'L-triangle'.[3] Fearing the growth of large-scale, organized illegal dealing by criminal gangs, the Home Office asked Scotland Yard to investigate the black market in Leeds. According to the two detectives sent to the city, the London-based journalists found their sources in bars close to Leeds railway station. Cloth robberies aside, they found little evidence of racketeering in Leeds.[4]

The investigation left the Home Secretary 'in no doubt that the allegations were much exaggerated, and in most instances quite unfounded, and that, while Leeds is no more immune than any other large city from black market activities, there is no reason to think that it is, as was suggested, the headquarters of openly practised black market activities'.[5] It also led the Metropolitan Police Commissioner to question 'the somewhat lurid descriptions published in some newspapers of super-criminals controlling a vast organization with widespread tentacles'.[6] Similarly, the findings of committees inquiring into evasion of meat rationing in 1947 and petrol rationing in 1948 would reassure ministers that there was no basis for press panics about black marketeering. Policymakers concluded that price control and rationing, unlike prohibition, had not given rise to racketeers, bootleggers, and speakeasies. Although it required careful monitoring, the black market was a minor irritant.

---

[1] Montague Smith, 'In Racket Town', *Daily Mail*, 6 December 1944.
[2] Vincent Evans, 'The Black Market of Leeds', *News Chronicle*, 11 January 1945.
[3] *Evening Standard*, 4 January 1945.
[4] TNA: PRO, HO 45/23812 863,760/7, R. Macdonald, 'Alleged Black Market at Leeds', 13 February 1945.
[5] HC deb, vol. 409, 12 April 1945, col. 1981.
[6] Report of the Commissioner of Police of the Metropolis for the Year 1944, 5.

This tallied with the crime figures, which the government used to gauge the extent of evasion, and the inflation figures, which it used to judge the success of control.

The public did not share this view. After Lord Woolton gave a speech congratulating British business on the fact that there had been no profiteering in food in June 1943,[7] the *News Chronicle* asked the British Institute of Public Opinion (BIPO) to determine whether the public believed that no black market existed. The poll, conducted in July, found that 71.8% of the 1,792 adults questioned disagreed with the food minister, believing that a black market existed. When interviewers asked those who disagreed what kind of black markets existed, 505 or 39.7% of those who responded mentioned food, citing the traffic in meat, fruit, fish, tomatoes, and eggs. A further 339 or 26.7% talked about illegal dealing in clothing. Just over a fifth of those questioned believed that black markets in most materials and goods existed, and over a tenth cited miscellaneous black markets. They based their beliefs upon personal knowledge and private information. Only 6.4% of those questioned assumed that black markets existed on the evidence of news reports alone.[8] The institute found a similar discrepancy between official and popular perception of evasion in April 1947. When asked 'Do you think that in this country the black market is increasing or decreasing?', 61% of those questioned thought the black market (principally food, petrol, and clothes) was increasing.[9]

Since Angus Calder published *The People's War* in 1969 historians have struggled to reconcile these seemingly contradictory views of the extent of evasion. Thanks to a wartime statistical black-out and a police manpower shortage, there are no records of the number of black market crimes known to the police and the number of arrests made for such offences to which scholars can appeal. While prosecution and conviction data exist, these judicial statistics are ill defined, incomplete, and too far removed from criminal acts to be a reliable indicator of anything other than the behaviour of the criminal justice system. All agree with Ina Zweiniger-Bargielowska that the black market 'defies the statistics' assuming, as Angus Calder does, that 'it was in the nature of a successful black market transaction that it was left out of official statistics and evaded the courts of law'.[10]

In this statistical vacuum, whether the black market was 'extensive throughout the 1940s', as Zweiniger-Bargielowska suggests, or 'relatively unimportant in Britain during and after the war', as Alec Cairncross asserted fifteen years earlier, remains a moot point with anecdotal evidence swaying the debate.[11] Whatever stance is taken, the arguments are flawed, as they use official definitions of 'black market'

[7] *The Times*, 16 June 1943.

[8] UK Data Archive, University of Essex, Colchester, SN: 3331, J. Hinton, P. Thompson and I. Liddell, *British Institute of Public Opinion (Gallup) Polls, 1938–1946*, April 1996.

[9] George H. Gallup (ed.), *The Gallup International Public Opinion Polls: Great Britain 1937–1975*, 2 vols. (New York, 1976), i, 153; Robert J. Wybrow, *Britain Speaks Out, 1937–87: A Social History as seen through the Gallup Data* (Basingstoke, 1989), 24.

[10] Zweiniger-Bargielowska, *Austerity*, 152; Angus Calder, *The People's War: Britain 1939–1945* (1969; London, 1992), 407.

[11] Zweiniger-Bargielowska, *Austerity*, 152; Alec Cairncross, *Years of Recovery: British Economic Policy 1945–51* (London, 1985), 351.

uncritically while assuming that 'black market' meant the same things to the public. Like the government of the day, they also ignore indirect indicators of the level of evasion such as insurance claims, the amount of cash in circulation, and discrepancies between production and consumption figures. Thanks to the interest shown in developing ways to measure the size of the black economy from the 1970s onwards, the potential value of these figures can be realized. Fragmentary though the data are, it is possible to use them to produce a composite picture of the pattern of evasion. While the resultant identikit resembles evasion more closely than either the official or popular pictures do, it still misses important details that are now impossible to recover.

'NO BLACK MARKET ON A CONTINENTAL SCALE'

With thirty minutes to share his experiences with a gathering of exiled government officials preparing to return to liberated Europe, the MoF enforcement director Alex Monro outlined the British approach to policing food control, which he believed had prevented the emergence of a black market on a continental scale. While admitting the existence of a black market in June 1944, which he defined as 'large scale and organized illegal dealing' in food, Monro told his audience that the 'rackets' had never affected national supplies nor interfered with 'the housewives' daily purchases of staple foods'. Thanks to the enforcement division's efforts, British journalists, unlike their counterparts in German-occupied Europe, could not quote black market prices 'on the lines of the Stock Exchange'.[12] Reviewing official publications and public pronouncements about black marketeering, the journalist Angus Maude reached a similar conclusion to Monro in June 1948.

Surveying the British scene at the supposed height of evasion, Maude judged that the black market had 'never become, in this country, a normal part of everyday housekeeping for millions of families'. Britain's black markets were much smaller than their continental counterparts. They had 'never reached such a size that the authorities had almost given up their efforts to control' them. Above all, it had 'never been necessary for people (other than deserters and criminals who could not secure genuine ration-books) to deal in the black market in order to feed and clothe themselves decently'. Nevertheless, illegal dealing in a handful of commodities such as petrol had been 'very bad indeed'. Not because of the volume of goods involved in black market transactions, but because of the large number of individuals involved in small-scale dealing. Although supplies were never threatened, the black market was 'large enough to cause concern' because petty dealing eroded respect for the law.[13]

Enforcement officials shared Maude's view, though this did not stop them worrying about abuse of individual control schemes. In February 1948 an internal

[12] A. Monro, 'Enforcement', in MoF, *Lectures on the Administration of Food Control, Rationing and Distribution* (London, 1944), 263–70 at 267.

[13] Angus Maude, *The Black Market*, Current Affairs 56 (London, 1948), 2–13.

MoF inquiry concluded that there was 'no extensive black market in pigs, pork, and bacon'. The same was true of other red meat.[14] Evasion was only 'widespread and open' when it came to home supplies of poultry, rabbits, and eggs. Eggs aside, these were not staple foods. A parallel Ministry of Fuel and Power (MoFP) inquiry found no 'evidence of "master minds" at work organizing a black market on a colossal scale, or of large quantities of petrol by-passing the rationing scheme'.[15] What evasion took place involved a secondary market in ration coupons. The 'three Cs' of clothing *coupons*, stolen and illicitly manufactured *clothing*, and illicitly manufactured *cosmetics* posed the biggest challenges to the Board of Trade (BoT) Investigation Section.[16] While irritating, the board believed that the proportion of controlled goods involved in these black markets was low.

Although enforcement officials held firm views about the historical development of black markets, the official histories failed to record them. Evasion receives cursory treatment in the Civil Histories of the Second World War, which downplay the size and significance of black markets in petrol, food, clothing, and cosmetics. In their synoptic volume *British War Economy*, Sir Keith Hancock and Margaret Gowing mention black markets twice in 629 pages of text. Their considered opinion was that black markets 'never threatened serious obstruction to the war economy nor did they engender the social bitterness that had marked the First World War'. They conceded that 'There were queues, sales "under-the-counter" and black markets', but maintained that 'these symptoms never became really alarming. The Government succeeded in its efforts to hold the economy steady under immense inflationary pressure.'[17] The absence of rampant wartime inflation, which pointed to limited evasion of price control and rationing, proved their point. If large numbers of people had evaded price and rationing regulations, prices and wages would have risen alarmingly.[18] The official historians of civil industry and trade, financial policy, food, inland transport, and oil shared this view.[19]

With this in mind, Richard Hammond, official historian of food, saw little point in spending time extracting a coherent story from the 'voluminous' and 'amorphous' enforcement records. 'An official historian, surrounded as he is by his own *dramatis personae* as critics, is ill advised to attempt the making of bricks without straw. It seems fair to claim that the filling of these gaps would not alter the general picture, for all that they might be of interest to specialists.'[20] Enforcement officials did, however, possess clear views about the development of black markets

---

[14] TNA: PRO, MAF 83/46, 'Interim Report on Pigs', 16 December 1947.
[15] Report of the Committee of Enquiry on the Evasions of Petrol Rationing Control (PP 1947–8 Cmd.7372 xiv, 187), 5.
[16] G. W. Yandell, 'The Black Market', *The Magistrate*, 6 (1942), viii–x and id., 'The "Harry Limes" of Britain', *Sunday Dispatch*, 14 May 1950.
[17] W. K. Hancock and M. M. Gowing, *British War Economy* (London, 1949), 511.
[18] Hancock and Gowing, *War Economy*, 342 n. 2.
[19] Hammond, *Food*, ii, 93–5, 665–6, and iii, 294–8, 721–6; C. I. Savage, *Inland Transport* (London, 1957), 431–2; D. J. Payton-Smith, *Oil* (London, 1971), 217–19, 397; R. S. Sayers, *Financial Policy, 1939–45* (London, 1956), 122, 129; and Hargreaves and Gowing, *Civil Industry*, 98, 111–12, 327–8, 536.
[20] Hammond, *Food*, iii, xi.

that informed the official histories and which, as Zweiniger-Bargielowska shows, can be found in government publications and unpublished internal histories.

According to Monro—one of Hammond's *dramatis personae*—profiteering in uncontrolled foods preceded black marketeering. Anticipating shortages and further economic regulation, traders stockpiled uncontrolled foods, which drove prices up by creating artificial shortages. This attracted speculators whose activities exacerbated the problem. The Central Price Regulation Committee faced similar problems with non-food goods. As food control extended, the speculators began to manufacture worthless food substitutes such as a milk substitute made of flour, salt, and baking powder that sold at 5s a pound. The racket collapsed in November 1941 when the MoF required all traders to apply for a licence to manufacture substitutes.[21] For the BoT the main challenge during the first two years of the war was the textiles 'quota racket'. Manufacturers paid traders to use 'spare' quotas— quotas that the traders had obtained fraudulently—to evade regulations limiting supplies to the home market.[22]

From 1941, profiteering gave way to black marketeering as government extended control. Throughout the war and beyond, the majority of black market food came from British farms. With 893 food inspectors in 1944, the MoF could not ensure that the 300,000 farmers in Great Britain took all their fat livestock to ministry collecting centres, all their eggs to approved packing stations, and all their cereals and potatoes to licensed merchants. The ministry also placed no limits on the amount of milk, butter, cheese, poultry, fruit, vegetables, or cereals that producers could retain for home consumption. Farmers and growers seldom abused this privilege. According to one official, there was no indication of black markets in meat and livestock, cereals, potatoes, milk, and milk products in 1944.

Eggs were the only important home produced food in which officials admitted black marketeering was rife. The MoF estimated that 30% of all hen eggs produced commercially escaped control during 1943/44. The uncontrolled market for hatching eggs provided cover for many of these transactions. According to the Bodinnar committee, the figure had risen to 38% of commercial production by the war's end, which represented a loss to rationed consumption of three million boxes of eggs. By this point, dealers, caterers, and consumers bought most of their black market eggs at the farm gate. There were also thriving wartime black markets in table poultry and wild rabbits. Although the ministry controlled their price, it did not canalize their distribution. As a result, the market in price-controlled table poultry collapsed while the uncontrolled trade in poultry for laying and breeding boomed. As with eggs, undeclared private sales of poultry soared. The same was true of wild rabbits. Although large in proportion to total supplies, both black markets had little impact on the British diet, as few people ate rabbit or chicken regularly before the war.[23] The Christmas trade in turkeys and the year-round trade in Kosher poultry were the worst affected.

---

[21] Hammond, *Food*, i, 310.
[22] Hargreaves and Gowing, *Civil Industry*, 111.
[23] Hammond, *Food*, iii, 721.

When it came to imported foods, black marketeers had to acquire their supplies through theft and fraud as the MoF controlled the entire distribution chain from dockside to salespoint. Manufacturers who misused food allocations were an important source of black market food in wartime. Typically, a trader received the necessary sugar or fat to manufacture a food product according to an established recipe. If the recipe changed or production ceased, the trader had to notify the authorities and return any unused ingredients. Of course, the unscrupulous sold the food. In some cases they continued to draw supplies for months. Officials, however, believed that shop-breakers, warehouse-breakers, and lorry hijackers posed a bigger threat to control than business fraudsters.[24] Unlike pilferage, a chronic condition affecting the controlled economy, theft threatened orderly food distribution as losing a consignment left local suppliers temporarily short. Police blamed military deserters for the rapid increase in crimes of theft from autumn 1943 onwards.[25]

BoT inspectors faced similar problems to food inspectors. Illicit manufacturing of cosmetics was a chronic problem throughout control. Backyard producers dominated the black market as the industry required little or no machinery, used small quantities of raw materials, and produced goods that were easy to transport and hide.[26] The theft and illicit manufacture of cloth were acute problems by comparison. Towards the end of the war, thieves and receivers operating in textile districts such as Leeds supplied retailers and manufacturers as far afield as London with stolen cloth. This was not a problem earlier, as it took until 1943 for traders to dispose of stocks, which they had hoarded during spring 1941 in anticipation of clothes rationing.[27] Illicit manufacture was also a problem in these districts. By stretching cloth, textile mills could produce more cloth than accounted for in their raw materials quotas. The extra cloth, which did not exist officially, went to the black market. While these activities worried clothes inspectors, they paid more attention to the secondary market in coupons.

Secondary markets in coupons posed the biggest threats to clothing and petrol rationing in wartime. Although pilfering of petrol was widespread, a black market in petrol, which was bulky and difficult to store safely, did not emerge in wartime. Instead, 'a small but demoralizing black market in petrol coupons' developed during the second half of 1941 after cuts in the basic petrol ration for private motorists.[28] Hauliers and farmers with surplus coupons to sell supplied this market with garage owners acting as intermediaries. This 'was causing serious concern to the Government' in October 1941. The problem disappeared after the MoFP withdrew the basic ration in July 1942. Unless they received an essential or supplementary allowance, private motorists—the principal buyers of black market

---

[24] H. Jaegar, 'Warehousing', in MoF, *Administration of Food Control*, 158–9.

[25] Edward Smithies, *Crime in Wartime: A Social History of Crime in World War II* (London, 1982), 51; Report of the Commissioner of Police of the Metropolis for the Years 1943–5 (PP 1943–4 Cmd.6536 iv, 507) 4–5, (PP 1944–5 Cmd.6627 v, 427) 4, (PP 1945–6 Cmd.6871 xiv, 215) 4.

[26] Hargreaves and Gowing, *Civil Industry*, 535–6.

[27] TNA: PRO, BT 64/3032, C. C. J. Simmonds, 'Note', 3 September 1942.

[28] Payton-Smith, *Oil*, 217.

petrol—received no petrol ration with which to disguise illegal purchases. Demand for coupons collapsed until the restoration of the basic ration in June 1945.[29]

Trafficking in clothing coupons worried the BoT from the start of clothes rationing. Accepted in all clothes shops and valid for twelve months, clothing coupons were more valuable than food or petrol coupons. Within weeks of its introduction in June 1941, the Board discovered that many retailers accepted loose coupons rather than clipping them from ration books.[30] Customers did not have to prove that the coupons they offered were theirs, which made it possible to pass forged, stolen, or washed coupons. Before the introduction of coupon banking in June 1942, it was also impossible to check the billions of coupons passed up the supply chain. Unscrupulous traders exploited the situation by submitting envelopes of 'coupons' padded with waste paper or claiming replacements for 'lost' coupons that found their way back into circulation.[31] Consumers exploited the system for replacing 'lost' coupons too, but this was a minor problem, with replacement books accounting for less than 0.5% of total coupon issues in 1942–43.[32]

Officials believed that black marketeering increased once victory appeared inevitable. According to an internal history of food enforcement, 'the determination to win, and general unselfishness resulting from patriotism', which ensured 'a considerable measure of cooperation from the public' evaporated. At the war's end, 'black market operators on a larger scale came into existence', while 'the public tired of controls and withdrew, to a great extent, their cooperation with the Enforcement inspectorates'.[33] The extension and tightening of post-war food control made the situation worse. Although strained, the system continued to work as the MoF allowed black markets in price-controlled luxury foods to develop, surrendering the 'ice cream outposts' in order to better protect rationed staples, the 'citadels of the rationing system'. Black markets in ice creams and wafers joined those in poultry and rabbits while the egg black market held steady and the meat black market expanded slightly.

Despite mounting public concern about black market meat, the Bodinnar committee found little evidence of black marketeering in 1948. What illegal trade existed in 1948 centred on knackers' yards, which disposed of livestock deemed unfit for human consumption. Despite regulations to the contrary, knackers continued to slaughter low-grade animals, mainly old cows, as well as diseased and injured beasts. Knackers—many of whom were also butchers and horseflesh dealers—disposed of the meat illegally, selling it for human consumption. This lucrative trade attracted new entrants, with the number of yards doubling from 200 in 1939

---

[29] TNA: PRO, MT 55/493, A. W. Clarke, 'History of fuel rationing of commercial motor vehicles 1939–1950', November 1950.

[30] TNA: PRO, BT 64/871, 'Publicity Committee minutes', 5 August 1941; Zweiniger-Bargielowska, *Austerity*, 178.

[31] Hargreaves and Gowing, *Civil Industry*, 325–6.

[32] Hargreaves and Gowing, *Civil Industry*, 328–9; TNA: PRO, BT 64/1519, 'The history of the lost ration document', August 1948.

[33] TNA: PRO, MAF 75/40, Enforcement.

to 400 in 1948. Most were slaughterers whose businesses closed after the MoF took control of slaughtering fatstock in 1940. Over 11,500 slaughterhouses closed as the ministry concentrated operations in 500 of the 12,000 premises used in 1939. The uncontrolled market in store pigs for fattening was another source of black market meat between 1944 and 1948. Tempted by higher prices, pig farmers sold fat pigs destined for government collecting centres as store pigs. Bought as 'stores' at farms or auctions, these fat pigs were slaughtered immediately by or on behalf of pig clubs after falsely declaring that they had kept the pig for four months in order to secure a licence to kill it.

The petrol black market—the most widely publicized of all post-war black markets—mushroomed after the restoration of a basic ration in June 1945. With private motorists back on the roads, effective demand for black market petrol leapt. 'Attempts at evasion of petrol rationing regulations fell into three main categories, namely, the misuse of petrol or coupons by individuals; the persistent transfer to private cars of supplies intended for commercial use and, to a much lesser extent, the use of forged, stolen or "washed" coupons.'[34] Of these, the traffic in commercial coupons was the most serious: officials estimated that the trade accounted for more than 3% of total petrol consumption in 1947.[35] The market collapsed suddenly in October 1947 after the need to economize on dollar imports forced the Labour government to withdraw the basic ration. The government restored basic in June 1948 after deciding to dye commercial petrol supplies red. This simple measure, which made it possible to detect commercial petrol in a fuel tank, prevented a black market boom, as it deterred motorists from buying red petrol coupons. For the remaining twenty-three months of rationing—control ended in May 1950—ration fraud was the main source of supply for a smaller black market.

Like food and petrol officials, BoT staff found themselves administering controls 'in an atmosphere increasingly hostile to regulations and restrictions' after VE Day.[36] Yet, evasion of clothes rationing and price control occasioned less comment than black marketeering in food and petrol. The illicit market in clothing coupons flourished in the immediate post-war period. When the Labour government removed subsidies for cotton, wool, and leather in 1948, the black market crumpled. As a result, footwear and clothing increased in cost. With consumers unable or unwilling to pay high prices for poor quality or unfashionable garments, unsold stock and unused coupons built up, which made decontrol possible. It began with footwear in May and was followed by gloves and knitted swimwear. By October the black market price of a clothing coupon had tumbled from 1s 6d or 2s a coupon to 6d per hundred.[37] The board continued its striptease throughout the second half of 1948 and into 1949, decontrolling individual items of clothing before ending clothes rationing in March 1949.

---

[34] TNA: PRO, MT 55/493, A. Franklyn Williams, 'Motor fuel rationing in the UK', November 1950.
[35] Evasions of Petrol Rationing, 7.
[36] Hargreaves and Gowing, Civil Industry, 637.
[37] Financial Times, 12 October 1948.

The second half of 1945 witnessed a further surge in recorded theft, which had been increasing since 1943. According to the Metropolitan Police Commissioner, deserters and demobilized servicemen exploited the longer autumn and winter nights to steal goods and coupons, which they sold for ready money to unscrupulous businesses and greedy consumers.[38] The surge in theft peaked in 1946, abating somewhat in 1947 and 1948, before falling away in 1949. The Home Office and the Northern Irish Ministry of Home Affairs believed black market demand drove this trend.[39] Independent research supported by the Home Office supported this view. Crimes of theft grew 'very rapidly' between 1938 and 1947, with the sharpest increases involving shop and warehouse breaking and theft from railways, which rose by 172% and 315% respectively. While theft increased across England and Wales, it grew faster outside London. It was also more serious, with the value of property stolen jumping from £2.5 million in 1938 to £13 million in 1947.[40]

Despite worries about bribery and corruption, officials did not believe that a British version of the Soviet economy of *blat* emerged. While inquiries into corruption in Newcastle, Leeds, and Brighton in 1944, 1945, and 1947–8 uncovered personal misconduct, investigators found no indications of institutional corruption.[41] None of these inquiries produced enough proof to warrant the prosecution of the councillors and local officials involved. There were even fewer indications of corruption in central government. In 1948 the worst that an investigation into corruption at the BoT could discover was evidence of a junior minister acting improperly.[42] Small and medium-sized firms seeking supplies relied upon their local MP to represent them. This was rarely successful, as policymakers were inundated with letters from MPs querying decisions about applications for buying permits and licences.[43] In 1948–49 the MoFP, which processed 4.2 million petrol allowance applications that year, received more than 13,000 letters from MPs about petrol rationing. There was clearly scope for private intermediaries to make money by helping firms secure petrol, but the MoFP knew of only two 'contact men' operating in 1949. Together, they handled five cases.[44]

Evasion receded further into the background when surveying the economy from the Cabinet Office. The various Cabinet committees responsible for overseeing and coordinating economic policy judged the success of control against inflation and public opinion. If controls reduced civilian consumption while keeping inflation in check and delivering a standard of living that was publicly acceptable, then

---

[38] Report of the Commissioner of Police of the Metropolis for 1945, 4–5.

[39] TNA: PRO, HO 326/68, Advisory Council on the Treatment of Offenders, 'The effect of war on criminality', 1950.

[40] H. Silcock, *The Increase in Crimes of Theft, 1938–1947* (Liverpool, 1949), 32–3.

[41] Report of the Newcastle-upon-Tyne Inquiry (PP 1943–4 Cmd.6522 iv, 315); TNA: PRO, HO 45/23812, 863760/7, 'Alleged black market at Leeds', 13 February 1945; TNA: PRO, MAF 150/661, 'Report of the committee of enquiry on alleged irregularities at Brighton', 1948.

[42] Report of the Tribunal appointed to inquire into Allegations reflecting on the Official Conduct of Ministers of the Crown and Other Public Servants (PP 1948–9 Cmd.7617 xviii, 425).

[43] TNA: PRO, T 167/3, 'Report on personal applications to ministers and to senior officials of government departments', 16 June 1949.

[44] Report of the Committee on Intermediaries (PP 1950 Cmd.7904 xii, 391).

they had achieved their aims. There was no need to pay close attention to crime, as widespread evasion would lead to rapid inflation and public disquiet. The working-class cost of living index, which served as the standard measure of inflation, caused little concern after 1941 and 1947 due to price stabilization policy.

Assessments of public opinion were much less precise, with Cabinet ministers relying on the press, political meetings, constituency correspondence, and political 'surgeries' to judge the public mood. Between 1940 and 1944 ministers also received weekly morale reports from the Home Intelligence division of the Ministry of Information (MoI), which were based on BBC Listener Research reports, published BIPO poll results, M-O file reports, police duty-room reports, the views of party whips, Postal and Telephone Censorship reports, and the Wartime Social Survey findings.[45] Public concern about black marketeering, as reflected in these sources, peaked twice—first in 1941–42 and then in 1947–48. On both occasions ministers judged this a problem of perception, as internal figures suggested that they had crime and inflation under control. Nevertheless, they took steps to reassure the public by tightening enforcement and thus avoiding a self-fulfilling prophecy.

INVISIBLE CRIMES

In their memoirs, politicians and senior civil servants reiterated the official view that black marketeering was not a threat to control, and dismissed popular beliefs about widespread evasion. The nutritionist Lord John Boyd Orr, a former MoF adviser, agreed with his former boss Lord Woolton that 'there was little or no black market in Britain'.[46] Many of Boyd Orr's ministry colleagues would have shared his view:

> The British public approved of Lord Woolton's plan and, though there was a little black marketeering by 'spivs', it worked well. The rich people got less to eat, which did them no harm and the poor, so far as the supply would allow, got a diet adequate for health, with free orange juice, cod-liver oil, extra milk, and other things for mothers and children.[47]

Former government economists did much to popularize this view, which the Cabinet Secretary Sir Edward Bridges ensured was entombed in the Civil Histories of the Second World War.[48] In 1947, Lionel Robbins, who had recently stepped down as Director of the Cabinet Office's Economic Section, attributed the 'comparative infrequency of black-market activities' during the war to 'the will to cooperate and the sense of responsibility of the majority of those to whom these regulations applied'.[49] Writing in 1951, Alec Cairncross, a wartime member of the Economic

---

[45] TNA: PRO, INF 1/292, 'Home Intel. weekly report no. 79', 8 April 1942.

[46] Woolton, *Memoirs*, 231.

[47] John Boyd Orr, *As I Recall* (London, 1966), 121–2.

[48] José Harris, 'Thucydides amongst the Mandarins: Hancock and the World War II Civil Histories', in D. A. Low (ed.), *Keith Hancock: Legacies of a Historian* (Melbourne, 2001), 122–48 at 138.

[49] Robbins, *Economic Problem*, 45.

Section and the BoT, believed control was successful, and attributed this to popular support for the war effort too.[50] A former BoT colleague Brian Reddaway, who played an important role in designing and refining the clothes rationing scheme, seconded Cairncross's view. Reflecting on his experiences, Reddaway concluded that 'automatic enforcement' through the passing back of coupons kept black market activity within bounds.[51] Whether or not these champions of control shared the narrow understanding of the black market current in Whitehall, they relied upon official evidence of black marketeering that excluded what Alex Monro classed as 'the more ordinary type of offences'. Only the MoFP defined the black market broadly as involving 'all unlawful transactions in petrol or petrol coupons'.[52]

For Monro and other food officials a black market offence was 'an offence involving illegal transactions in food obtained otherwise than through the authorized channels'. He judged a butcher who sold meat from an illicitly slaughtered animal guilty of a black market offence.[53] By extension, officials defined a black market as 'a market where goods illicitly acquired are illegal disposed of'.[54] Doing so excluded two important ways in which people obtained goods illegally. According to this definition, a shopkeeper who overcharged a customer for an article that he obtained legitimately from his wholesaler was not participating in the black market. Overcharging along with conditional sales by wholesalers were 'collusive offences'. A third category of 'minor offences' existed. Given official sanction in spring 1944, this grouping embraced the innocent mistakes and honest misunderstandings of overworked traders. Inspectors handled these technical offences by ignoring them or issuing a warning.[55] Consumers transferring their unused coupons or unwanted rations illegally—the commonest offences by far—did not fall into any category.

Although the definitions used at the MoF excluded many illegal economic transactions, they acknowledged that the black market was an economic entity. This was not the case elsewhere. The Home Office, the Northern Irish Ministry of Home Affairs, the Scottish Home Department, and the police had a legalistic understanding of the black market, reflected in the criminal and judicial statistics that they compiled. Only contraventions of defence regulations 55 and 56A as well as violations of the finance regulations constituted black market offences.[56] This definition excluded adulteration, mislabelling, and giving short weight as the police brought prosecutions for these offences under existing legislation. It also discounted crimes of theft and forgery dealt with under the criminal law. Cross-border smuggling—a

---

[50] Alec Cairncross, *Introduction to Economics* (2nd edn., London, 1951), 532.

[51] W. B. Reddaway, 'Rationing', in D. N. Chester (ed.), *Lessons of the British War Economy* (Cambridge, 1951), 182–99 at 192.

[52] Evasions of Petrol Rationing, 5.

[53] Monro, 'Enforcement', 267.

[54] Dexter M. Keezer, 'Observations on Rationing and Price Control in Great Britain', *American Economic Review*, 33 (1943), 264–82 at 281.

[55] TNA: PRO, MAF 100/32, 'Divisional food officers circular', 6 April 1944; HC deb, vol. 400, 9 June 1944, col.1669.

[56] Criminal Statistics: England and Wales, 1939–1945, 12; Report of the Commissioner of Police of the Metropolis for the Year 1944, 5.

problem in Northern Ireland throughout control—and the post-war problems of maritime and aerial smuggling did not feature at all, as countering them was the responsibility of HM Customs and Excise. Officials conceded that these were 'black market related offences', but the law-and-order bureaucracy continued to understand them as 'traditional crimes'.

Overlooking much evasion as they did, these narrow and legalistic definitions hampered official understanding of illegal markets. There was, however, no incentive to study evasion and revise definitions of black markets as the cost-of-living index indicated that control was effective. Reliance on the index to judge control's success blinded the economic high command to the problem that non-compliance posed. The manner in which the Ministry of Labour (MoL) Statistics Branch constructed the index meant that it could not accurately reflect the wartime cost of living. Every month, local employment exchange officials collected information on food prices and forwarded the data to the ministry. A clerk from the exchange visited five food retailers who the clerk thought catered to a predominantly working-class clientele, noting prices openly. Ideally, one of the shops would be a branch of the local Co-op, and another would be a branch of a national chain store. Food prices apart, the ministry statisticians relied upon monthly returns from suppliers of various goods and services.[57] The chances of an official visit or a postal survey capturing black market prices were minuscule. The Statistics Branch did not collect black market price data, and would not have known if it had done so, as it did not compare its data to official price lists. The statisticians felt that any attempt to collect such data would make suppliers reluctant to co-operate with the Statistics Branch. The Technical Committee appointed to consider the creation of a new cost-of-living index stated the official position in its report.

> No special attempt is made to allow for 'black market' prices. Insofar as any of the selected retailers openly sell goods above the permitted or list prices (whether inadvertently or deliberately) those prices are taken for the index, but it is impracticable to ascertain prices charged for clandestine transactions, even where these are legal.

The Technical Committee did not consider that 'the effect of such transactions, when averaged with the open ones would be significant'.[58] Thus the government's single most important measure of the success of price control and rationing did not take evasion into account.

Public opinion was the second most important measure of the success of economic control, but official methods for gauging popular attitudes towards control and black markets were unreliable. Despite the work of the Wartime Social Survey and Home Intelligence, ministers and senior civil servants did not fully appreciate the value of government surveys of public attitudes. Independent opinion research

---

[57] On data collection methods during period 1914–47 see 'Retail Prices Statistics: Scope and Method of Compilation', *Labour Gazette*, 29 (February 1921), 69–72 on data collection from 1914 to 1947; and Ministry of Labour and National Service (MoL), *Industrial Relations Handbook, 1944, Supplement No. 2, January 1948* (London, 1948), 7–10 for the period 1947–55.

[58] MoL, *Industrial Relations Handbook, 1944, Supplement No. 2*, 13.

was not highly regarded either. Winston Churchill ignored BIPO findings.[59] Conservative politicians' pre-war suspicions about the left-wing bias of independent opinion researchers plus a ferocious press campaign against the MoI 'spying' on the public meant that policymakers paid little attention to survey results.[60] Although the MoI sent copies of Home Intelligence weekly reports to most departments, they went unread. The rationing departments did not put the reports on file, and the various government committees responsible for the war economy never discussed them. Even if they had read them, 'Home Intelligence was in fact propaganda in reverse'. Contributors to the reports, such as the historian A. J. P. Taylor, 'merely put down what I myself thought at the time or wanted to advocate'.[61] Instead, policymakers relied upon traditional sources of information: editorials, letters columns and commentaries in the press, parliamentary questions and debates, contacts with representative bodies, correspondence from the public, and personal experience. Selection biases meant that colourful or comforting information from these predominantly middle-class sources was likely to register with policymakers. With economic indicators suggesting inflation was under control policymakers concluded that periodic concern about black markets had little or no connection with the level of evasion. From the economy's commanding heights, public perception of evasion seemed to pose a greater threat to economic control than the reality of illegal dealing.

Undisturbed by the level of non-compliance, central government did not seek further information about evasion. Neither the Lord President's Committee nor the Economic Policy Committee discussed black markets at length. During a Cabinet debate about petrol rationing it became apparent that the Labour Prime Minister Clement Attlee, who as former Lord President of the Council coordinated the domestic policies of the Coalition Government between 1943 and 1945, had no idea about the extent of the petrol black market, asking colleagues 'Is it true there is widespread evasion?' Later in the same meeting, Attlee asked 'What proportion does actual consumption bear to what it should be on ration? Can't this be ascertained, as [a] check on [the] allegation re [the] black market?'[62] Emmanuel Shinwell, the Minister of Fuel and Power, could not answer Attlee's questions nor could the ministry's statistical branch. When a senior official reviewed the evidence a year later, the 'paucity of information' impressed him. He concluded:

> There is a lot of talk, but much of it is like bomb damage talk in war time; it is more interesting to have a story to tell than not. The stories are very nearly always about someone else's experiences; few people can vouch for the alleged black market dealings by their own personal experience.[63]

[59] Robert M. Worcester, *British Public Opinion: A Guide to the History and Methodology of Political Opinion Polling* (Oxford, 1991), 6.

[60] See Laura Beers, 'Whose Opinion? Changing Attitudes towards Opinion Polling in British Politics, 1937–1964', *Twentieth Century British History*, 17 (2006), 177–205.

[61] A. J. P. Taylor, 'Alarm in High Places', *The Observer*, 8 April 1979.

[62] TNA: PRO, CAB 195/4, 'Cabinet Secretary's notebook', 8 July 1946.

[63] TNA: PRO, POWE 33/1500, Alfred Rake to Sir Laurence Watkinson, 17 December 1947.

He was not alone in his ignorance. Economists and statisticians working for the Cabinet Office, the Treasury, and the other rationing departments were in a similar position. The Economic Section, the Central Statistical Office, and the Central Economic Planning Staff did not produce a single paper examining black markets throughout the austerity period.

Without consistent pressure from the centre for information about evasion, the individual departments responsible for control made little effort to monitor the level of non-compliance. Their only gauges of the extent of illegal dealing were statistics produced by enforcement activity. From 1941 the MoF Statistics and Intelligence Division included figures for prosecutions, convictions, and sentences in weekly and monthly reports to the Minister of Food and the monthly report sent to the Cabinet Office.[64] The ministry released the headline figures every month, which the papers reported sporadically. For internal use, ministry statisticians broke these data down by type of offence. Figures for the number of persons prosecuted, as opposed to the number of offences prosecuted, by type of offender and the commodity involved, were also compiled. Only the data from January 1944 to November 1951 survive (see Table 1.1).[65]

Studying annual summaries of the figures that the Minister of Food made available to his fellow ministers, it is soon apparent why enforcement data did not alter official perception of the challenge that non-compliance posed. The ministry statistics for the period 1944–51 showed the number of successful prosecutions peaking at 25,667 in 1944 and falling dramatically to 17,256 in 1945 before climbing rapidly back to the 1944 level between 1946 and 1948 when the number of cases peaked at 25,609. Comparable data for the war ending in August of every year show that successful prosecutions reached similar levels between September 1941 and August 1944, with 1941/42 as the worst year for black market prosecutions, with courts prosecuting 26,403 offences successfully.[66] From this perspective the figures for 1946–49 should not have worried ministers and senior officials unduly. In fact, the peaks reflect the expansion of control and the toughening of enforcement policy during the periods 1941–42, 1944, and 1946–49. The breakdown was also reassuring, as most offences involved first-time offenders who received a suspended sentence or a small fine.

The Central Price Regulation Committee supplied the BoT with similar data, but these were for internal consumption. Prosecutions for price offences were rarer than prosecutions for food offences. Judging by the figures in Table 1.2, the prosecutions that the BoT solicitor brought were usually successful. Like MoF data, these reassuring figures are an artefact of government policy. During the period 1944–46 the Board closed loopholes in price control and tightened enforcement—a policy initiated by Hugh Dalton and continued by his successors. It also collected

---

[64] TNA: PRO, MAF 75/80, 'Record of Statistics and Intelligence Division', 15 December 1950.

[65] The monthly 'Summary of prosecutions and penalties imposed' can be found in MAF 100/5 and MAF 156/289. See Tables 4.4–4.7 in Zweiniger-Bargielowska, *Austerity*, 163–8, for a handy summary of the data.

[66] Zweiniger-Bargielowska, *Austerity*, 163.

Table 1.1. Outcomes of successful prosecutions for food offences in the UK, 1944–51

Year	Successful prosecutions	Cases with previous successful prosecutions	Cases dismissed under the Probation of Offenders Act	Number of penalties					
				£1 and under	Over £1 and up to £5	Over £5 and up to £10	Over £10 and up to £20	Over £20	Imprisonment
1944	25,667	1,122	1,146	8,828	11,191	2,207	852	1,065	429
1945	17,256	1,032	878	5,581	7,607	1,580	705	779	326
1946	20,466	1,090	933	6,889	8,180	1,964	874	1,172	454
1947	24,265	1,234	781	7,690	9,625	2,420	1,276	1,525	848
1948	25,609	1,007	958	7,348	10,391	2,834	1,527	1,719	824
1949	22,517	1,064	548	6,622	9,653	2,737	1,170	1,355	432
1950	14,383	564	487	4,602	6,426	1,378	625	685	180
1951	12,343	379	464	4,484	5,111	1,087	503	552	142

Notes

1. The data for 1946 and 1951 are for the eleven months from January to November only.
2. The figure for cases with previous successful convictions in 1948 is for the eleven months from January to November only.
3. The figure for cases with previous successful convictions in 1951 is for the ten months from January to October only.

Sources: Data are from 'Summary of prosecutions and penalties imposed' in MAF 100/5 and MAF 156/289 at TNA.

Table 1.2. Outcomes of all prosecutions for price control offences in the UK, 1940–50

Year	Prosecutions	Convictions	Dismissals	Dismissals under the Probation of Offenders Act	Not proven
1940	31	23	4	3	1
1941	153	139	5	9	0
1942	448	383	29	31	0
1943	836	741	55	32	8
1944	980	898	46	31	5
1945	1,069	1,005	32	28	4
1946	973	917	28	25	3
1947	705	669	20	16	0
1948	696	667	21	6	2
1949	400	395	5	0	0
1950	537	523	12	2	0

Notes

a. Total fines imposed amounted to £124,407 in 1940–46.

b. The number of cases in which terms of imprisonment were imposed during 1940–46 was 32.

c. The Board of Trade did not submit these figures to Parliament. On a handful of occasions partial data were presented.

Sources: Data for 1940–46 from Hargreaves and Gowing, *Civil Industry*, 91. Data for 1947–50 from the Minutes of the Central Price Regulation Committee in BT 94/8–12 at TNA.

data about clothes rationing offences for internal use, but these figures appear to have been lost or destroyed. Parliamentary questions requesting statistics and press criticism of enforcement forced the BoT to make some of these data public.[67] But even these figures did not capture the whole picture. Black market prosecutions brought under the criminal law or by other agencies were not included in the rationing departments' figures.

The criminal statistics published by the Home Office, the Scottish Home Department, and the Northern Irish Ministry of Home Affairs provided an overview of the problem based on figures for court proceedings. But the categories used did more to obscure the issue than illuminate it. Police and court returns distinguished between criminal offences and offences against Defence Regulations. The police prosecuted thieves and receivers of stolen goods destined for black markets as ordinary criminals, while government departments prosecuted evaders for offences against Defence Regulations. As far as the police were concerned, only offences against Defence Regulations counted as black market offences. Police in England and Wales labelled offences against Defence Regulation 55, Defence Regulation 56A, and Finance Regulations as black market.[68] Police in Scotland and Northern Ireland did not provide a breakdown of the figures for offences against Defence

[67] HC deb, vol. 460, 3 February 1949, cols. 243–4, w.a.
[68] Criminal Statistics: England and Wales, 1939–1945, 12.

Regulations. As an indicator of enforcement activity, these figures were worthless. Almost 73% of people convicted of offences against Defence Regulations at English and Welsh magistrates' courts between 1939 and 1945 were guilty of breaking blackout restrictions, and the pattern elsewhere in the UK was probably the same.

These data did little to shape official perception of non-compliance, as the Home Office and its counterparts in Scotland and Northern Ireland had no interest in monitoring black market offences. In 1940 the government stopped collating, analysing, and publishing crime figures. Publication resumed in 1947 with the release of the annual statistics for 1946 and summary figures for the war years. When the Home Secretary showed an interest in black market offences during Spring 1942, the Statistical Branch prepared a graph charting the number of convictions, but his interest was not sustained.[69] The Scottish Home Department did keep a close eye on the judicial statistics between 1942 and 1953, but only in order to counter accusations from Whitehall bureaucrats that Scottish courts were soft on black marketeers.[70] This lack of interest in black market offences meant that the authors of the official Home Office account of the effect that the war had on crime acknowledged but could not describe how illicit demand affected crime.[71]

Today, criminologists regularly criticize politicians and social commentators who use crime figures as an indicator of the level of crime. The numbers of people prosecuted and convicted are more a reflection of police activity and court processes than the amount of crime. In private, civil servants held a similar view and used figures for black market offences and sentences as performance indicators. In a letter to the Scottish Secretary urging him to communicate to the Scottish courts the need to enforce food regulations rigorously, Lord Woolton cited the low conviction rate and lenient sentences in Scotland compared to England and Wales.[72] MoFP officials used enforcement statistics in a similar way. Ministry headquarters at Millbank instructed the North East regional enforcement officer to confront Chief Constables whose forces were not enforcing petrol rationing stringently. Tynemouth police, for example, failed to test any vehicles for black market petrol during the four-month period from July to October 1949.[73] Enforcement data were also used to convince the public that the regulations were being enforced rigorously. In the first official newsreel talk about black markets, the food minister Major Lloyd George reassured cinema-goers that the ministry was doing all it could to stop evasion, citing the figure of 22,000 convictions for food offences since control began.[74]

[69] TNA: PRO, HO 329/42, 'Graphs prepared by Dr R. M. Jackson from 4 monthly returns', 4 April 1942.

[70] National Archives of Scotland, Edinburgh, HH 60/61, 'Defence Regulations 55 and 90', 1942–53.

[71] Home Office Advisory Council on the Treatment of Offenders, 'The War and Criminality in England and Wales', in International Penal and Penitentiary Commission (IPPC), *The Effects of War on Criminality* (Berne, 1951), 85–123.

[72] TNA: PRO, MAF 100/41, Woolton to Tom Johnston, 24 July 1943.

[73] TNA: PRO, POWE 33/1511, A. E. Jones to A. V. Lindsay, 9 January 1950.

[74] ITN Source, BGU408130105, 'Major Gwilym Lloyd George makes speech about "Black Market"', *Gaumont British*, 11 August 1941.

Rationing statistics proved to be a more reliable indicator of the level of non-compliance. On a handful of occasions, statisticians analysing the figures concluded that fluctuations in the figures could only be attributed to illegal dealing. A sudden drop in the number of fat pigs sold to the MoF and a dramatic increase in auction prices for store pigs during the summer and autumn of 1947 prompted the Minister of Food to appoint a committee to investigate meat black markets. Having been alerted to worrying trends like this, senior civil servants directed their enforcement staffs to concentrate on the problem commodity. For example, the MoF Enforcement Division looked out for unusual patterns in throughput at collecting centres and slaughterhouses, launching enforcement drives in areas with unusually low collection rates.[75] Similarly, BoT officials became concerned about the rising number of claims for replacement ration books during the war. They feared that many of the claimants sold their 'lost' books.[76] As a result, inspectors targeted districts with an unusually high number of claims.[77] The bureaucrats also worried about retailers accepting loose clothing coupons instead of clipping coupons from ration books, as this allowed customers to use surplus or used coupons. As a result, the Wartime Social Survey conducted a study of the prevalence of the practice for the BoT in 1941.[78]

Civil servants and politicians failed to recognize the importance of rationing statistics when it came to monitoring non-compliance. Surprisingly, headquarters staff did not ask regional coupon checking offices to compile statistical returns about frauds and forgeries, which would have provided them with invaluable information about black market dealing. For officials, an unexpected fluctuation in the figures was a warning that evasion was becoming a problem. Unlike their colleagues involved in the administration of the British occupation zone in Germany, they did not attempt to use these data or collect price data to track the extent of evasion.[79] No attempt was made to track black market prices or to calculate the volume of material being traded. When contemplating ending clothes rationing in 1948, Harold Wilson asked his officials for information about black market prices. As they proved unable to provide him with price data, Wilson relied upon information from a detective superintendent at Scotland Yard.[80] On occasion, departments' reluctance to share information frustrated attempts to monitor evasion. It took two years' lobbying before food inspectors secured permission from the Ministry of Agriculture to compare returns from its quarterly census returns of livestock with MoF marketing data.[81]

[75] Hammond, *Food*, ii, 92–7.

[76] TNA: PRO, BT 64/1519, 'The history of the lost ration document', August 1948.

[77] *Sunday Dispatch*, 14 May 1950.

[78] TNA: PRO, RG 23/1, 'Investigation into retailers' difficulties', August 1941.

[79] See John E. Farquharson, *The Western Allies and the Politics of Food: Agrarian Management in Postwar Germany* (Leamington Spa, 1985), esp. ch. 12, and Alan Kramer, 'Law-abiding Germans? Social Disintegration, Crime and the Reimposition of Order in Post-War Western Germany, 1945–9', in Richard J. Evans (ed.), *The German Underworld: Deviants and Outcasts in German History* (London, 1988), 238–61.

[80] Harold Wilson, *Memoirs: The Making of a Prime Minister 1916–1964* (London, 1986), 103–4.

[81] Hammond, *Food*, ii, 92.

Statisticians at the MoFP and other departments viewed rationing figures as indicator lights, not gauges. As the indicator lights winked on so infrequently, the case for monitoring black markets was weak. But why divert resources to researching a 'problem' that did not exist? The Whitehall view of illegal dealing as mainly a problem of perception meant officials relied upon national newspaper coverage of black markets when the warning lights came on. This had significant consequences for the pattern of enforcement. This attitude towards monitoring and researching non-compliance ensured that many useful data went unanalysed. Although some officials, economists, and journalists recognized the potential value of black market prices quoted in court reports and of figures for the number of bank-notes in circulation, they were not encouraged to develop their insights further, as received opinion suggested that evasion was not serious enough to justify the effort. By analysing these data retrospectively using ideas developed to measure the black economy from the 1970s onwards, it is possible to make the invisible visible.

MAKING THE INVISIBLE VISIBLE

Public perception of widespread black market dealing as captured in the polls does not conflict with the Cabinet Office view that illegal activity was economically insignificant or the rationing departments' belief that evasion posed an occasional threat to a small number of control schemes. 'Black market' did not mean the same thing to officials as it did to the public. For the public it was as much a moral category as it was an economic or legal one. Embracing profiteering and misuse of controlled goods—activities that were not always illegal—the authorities tended to dismiss popular knowledge as anecdote and hearsay. Based on personal experience and private knowledge, popular beliefs about the extent and pattern of black market dealing deserved more credence in Whitehall. Equally, civil servants should have questioned their assumption that black market dealing would have a noticeable effect on official measures of inflation. This would have led them to develop ways of measuring black market activity using commodity and rationing statistics.

In the absence of an official black market index, and with a handful of point estimates of black markets in individual commodities, several scholars believe the question of measurement to be unanswerable. As Zweiniger-Bargielowska puts it, 'it is possible to construct some quantitative data of the extent of the black market for particular commodities for limited periods or to estimate changes over time in black market activity from a range of sources, ultimately the black market—in line with the black or informal economy more generally—defies the statistics'.[82] Ultimately, black markets may defy the statistics, but a rough estimate based on all the available evidence is better than a guess. There is also a greater wealth of evidence available to historians than to contemporaries. Insurance claims for goods lost in transit can be set alongside ministry enforcement statistics. Commodity and

---

[82] Zweiniger-Bargielowska, *Austerity*, 152.

rationing figures can be used to gauge illegal production and consumption of controlled goods. Insights gained from statisticians' attempts to measure informal economies make it possible to use financial statistics to track the development of black markets too.[83] Wedding this quantitative evidence to qualitative evidence makes it possible to triangulate the size and pattern of black market activity.

From a macro-economic perspective, black market dealing did not pose a serious threat to economic policy. Although the official cost-of-living index could not capture black market prices, the idea that evasion of price control and rationing boosted the rate of inflation was a good one. In order to capitalize on their insight, officials needed to compare the official index with price indices constructed from other sources. Economists have constructed alternative price indices that enable such comparisons to be made. When constructing a price index for their study of American and British monetary history, the economists Milton Friedman and Anna Schwartz adjusted their index numbers for the period 1940–46 to take evasion of price control into account, which they concluded peaked in 1943. The Friedman–Schwartz adjustment, which used nominal income data to interpolate prices, is an unreliable indicator of non-compliance, as changes in income had more to do with wartime output growth than evasion.[84] The economic historians Geofrey Mills and Hugh Rockoff refined this econometric technique and came up with their own evasion adjustment to the Friedman–Schwartz index. Mills and Rockoff used nominal wage data to interpolate prices, choosing to ignore the fact that the MoL controlled wages informally through agreements with the trade unions. They concluded that evasion of price control was limited, peaking in 1946.[85] The Mills–Rockoff index, which is based on the implicit NNP deflator used by Charles Feinstein in his historical study of UK national income, is lower than the official composite price index which links Feinstein's implicit consumer expenditure deflator to the retail prices index.

Comparing these various measures of inflation, all broadly track the official cost-of-living index (see Fig. 1.1). This picture tallies with popular memory. In stark contrast to memory of the First World War, inflation was not central to memory of the austerity period. Inflation did not cause the same problems in the 1940s as it did in the 1910s. Of course, the focus on inflation ignores illegal transactions that did not contravene price regulations such as swaps, gifts, and cash payments at or below the fixed price. None of these transactions fed inflation and affected the general price level. Nevertheless, comparing the indices, each with their own bias, provides some support for the view that evasion did not pose a systemic threat to control—at least as far as evasion of price control was concerned—and that control succeeded in checking inflation.

The demand for cash—another indicator of the extent of black market activity—also supports the perception that illegal dealing did not pose a serious threat to

[83] See Stephen Smith, *Britain's Shadow Economy* (Oxford, 1986) for an accessible introduction to the most basic of these techniques.

[84] Milton Friedman and Anna Schwartz, *Monetary Trends in the United States and the United Kingdom* (Chicago, 1982), 101–4, 115–19.

[85] Mills and Rockoff, 'Compliance'.

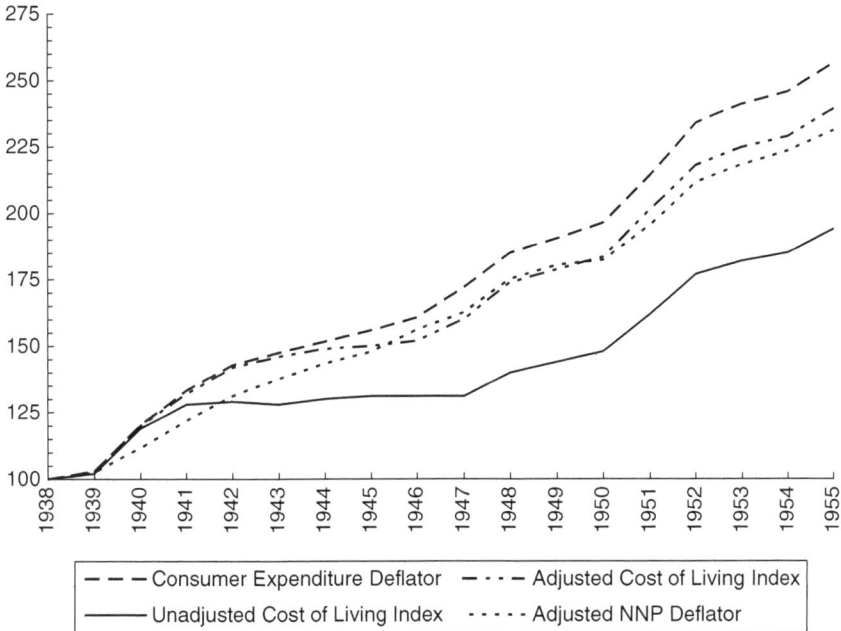

Fig. 1.1. UK cost of living, 1938–55 (1938 = 100).

Source: Cost-of-living index from *Annual Abstract of Statistics*, composite price index from *Economic Trends*, adjusted cost-of-living index from G. D. Allen, 'Prices', *London and Cambridge Economic Service Monthly Bulletin*, 27 (1949), 15–17, and adjusted NNP deflator from Mills and Rockoff, 'Compliance'.

economic control. There was an appreciable increase in the demand for cash during the 1940s. Assuming that black marketeers used cash to avoid detection, bankers and financial journalists attributed this growth to evasion.[86] Of particular concern to Bank of England officials were the figures for the number and value of high-denomination bank-notes in circulation. The bankers believed that black marketeers used high denomination bank-notes to transact their business, and one of the supposed benefits of the Bank's decision to stop issuing 'tenners' and higher-denomination banknotes from April 1943 was that black marketeers and tax evaders would find it difficult to carry and store large amounts of cash. Bankers used the same argument to defend their decision to withdraw all notes worth £10 or more from circulation in April 1945.[87]

If it did make illegal dealing harder, it did not hinder the growth in the demand for cash (see Fig. 1.2). Between 1930 and 1960 the real value of cash held by the public rose sevenfold, with a distinct bulge in the value of notes and coins in the hands of the public during the period 1941–1950 that peaked in 1947. That year, the public held a total of £1,342,355,000 in cash, or £8 18s per capita. This is a

---

[86] *The Times*, 6 February 1942.

[87] A. D. Mackenzie, *The Bank of England Note* (Cambridge, 1953), 151–2; Elizabeth Hennessy, *A Domestic History of the Bank of England, 1930–1960* (Cambridge, 1992), 134–5.

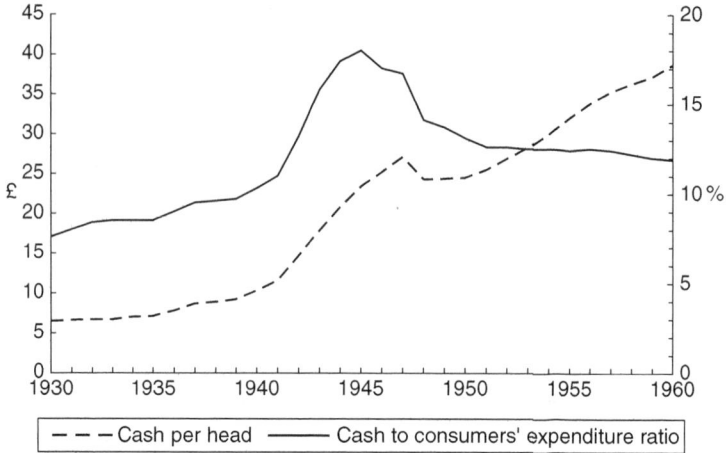

Fig. 1.2. UK demand for cash, 1930–60.

Sources: Currency in the hands of the public—Forrest Capie and Alan Webber, *A Monetary History of the United Kingdom, 1870–1982, i: Data, Sources, Methods* (London, 1985), 153–4, table ii.(2), col. ii. UK population—David Butler and Gareth Butler, *Twentieth Century British Political Facts 1900–2000* (Basingstoke, 2000), 347. Consumer expenditure—C. H. Feinstein, *Statistical Tables of National Income, Expenditure and Output of the United Kingdom 1855–1965* (Cambridge, 1976), Table 2, column 1, T9.

very high figure, given that the average working-class household spent £4 3s 7d per week in 1938.[88]

Assuming that the public used all this cash to pay for black market goods and that it changed hands once a week, a *New York Times* correspondent estimated that together British black marketeers could expect an annual turnover of £156 million per year in March 1942.[89] The correspondent overestimated turnover, as the £3 million that the authorities estimated never returned to the banks would have changed hands only nine times during 1941.[90] With an annual turnover of £27 million, black markets were worth less than 0.3% of GDP—small beer indeed. But was all this cash needed to pay for black market goods?

Wartime studies of saving and spending habits confirm that middle-class and working-class families held surprisingly large amounts of cash. In Glasgow this money served as a store of value, not a means of payment for legally and illegally obtained goods. Full employment and overtime payments revolutionized working-class household budgets. For the first time, weekly wages exceeded weekly outgoings regularly. Social investigators discovered that working-class Glaswegians hoarded their money, hiding cash in stockings, under mattresses, and up chimneys, rather than opening a savings account. The extent of the practice became clear when bombing threatened to destroy these hoards. The Glasgow Savings Bank was inun-

---

[88] Dudley Seers, *Changes in the Cost of Living and the Distribution of Income since 1938* (Oxford, 1949), 36–8.

[89] Craig Thompson, 'Britain alarmed at Black Markets', *New York Times*, 5 March 1942.

[90] In 1941 narrow money velocity (nominal income divided by nominal money balances) was 8.9.

dated with applications to open savings accounts after the city experienced a series of bombing raids.[91] The social investigators found similar behaviour and attitudes elsewhere in Britain. Interviewed during the first German invasion of France in May 1940, a Coventry factory worker explained his motives and those of his colleagues for keeping cash to one of these investigators:

> It's a little bit of solid comfort. You need it by you for emergencies. I remember the last war, and I'm afraid of the terrible inflation there will be after this one. So I'm keeping the money by, and if I see a good pair of shoes I shall buy them. It may help to keep my feet dry when I'm in the bread line later on.[92]

Uncertainty about the future, combined with pre-war savings patterns and increased mobility, explains much of the growth in the demand for cash. Large sums of cash did not change hands in black market deals, as illegal transfers of controlled goods involved barter as well as money, and gifting as well as trading.

Officials appreciated that consumers would trade and gift unused coupons, or the goods to which they entitled the bearer, from the start of control. Pre-war planners had never considered allowing consumers to transfer unwanted ration coupons, as they felt it would undermine the principle of equality of sacrifice and could not be persuaded to change this policy.[93] The authorities would only tolerate pooling of rations within a household; any other exchanges were illegal. From 1940 until 1948 the Oxford economist Miss T. Schulz compared the amounts of various rationed foods bought per person per week in a sample of grocery shops. Schulz's survey revealed that civilians did not consume their entire rations. Shoppers at the grocery stores in Schulz's sample never bought their full ration of dried eggs, fats, tea, sugar, and jam, and rarely bought all the cheese and bacon to which they were entitled.[94] The British Market Research Bureau recorded underconsumption of rationed goods in the MoF Points Rationing Survey and the BoT Clothing Consumer Panel Survey.[95] MoFP statisticians observed the same phenomena when comparing deliveries of petrol into civilian consumption with petrol coupon issues.[96]

Evidence of under-consumption of rationed goods demonstrates that the black markets in these goods never reached their full potential. If consumers had transferred all their unwanted coupons to other consumers who wanted them, then researchers would not have recorded under-consumption in their surveys. The requirement that consumers register with food retailers to receive specific rations limited the number of opportunities for the illegal transfer of coupons, but this was not the case for foods rationed by points and the rationing schemes for non-food products. In fact, the figures for petrol coupons reveal that private motorists—the

[91] Charles Madge, *War-time Patterns of Saving and Spending* (Cambridge, 1943).

[92] Cited in Charles Madge, 'War-time Saving and Spending—A District Survey', *Economic Journal*, 50 (1940), 334.

[93] See Hammond, *Food*, i, 280, and iii, 210–11.

[94] See articles by T. Schulz in *Bulletin of the Oxford Institute of Statistics* from 1941 to 1948.

[95] John Downham, *BMRB International: The First Sixty Years, 1933–1993* (London, 1993), 42–7.

[96] TNA: PRO, POWE 33/2207, C. C. Lucas, 'Historical statement—coupon issues v. consumption of motor spirit', n.d. [1949].

group believed to consume black market petrol—returned a significant amount of unused coupons to the authorities throughout the period of control.[97] On closer examination, consumer surveys and retail audits reveal that middle-class households in urban areas bought most of their ration entitlement and spent a considerable amount on price-controlled and uncontrolled foodstuffs, while urban working-class households did not. Urban middle-class households were also more likely to supplement their diet with home-grown produce, as they could afford a house with a garden or pay for an allotment.[98] Women employed in middle-class households as domestic helps, shopkeepers with a mixed clientele, co-workers and employees, as well as black market dealers, met the middle-class demand for coupons. The domestic help trading spare clothing coupons for secondhand clothes, food, or cash was a stock figure in public discussion of the trade.[99]

Bartering and giving away spare coupons and goods did not pose a threat to control, as it did not greatly increase civilian consumption at the expense of the war effort or the balance of payments. No money changed hands, so there was no inflationary risk. In rural areas the gift economy and the barter economy increased in importance, and they made startling comebacks in Britain's urban areas. A researcher working for Mass-Observation noted the prevalence of barter in London. Housewives gave shopkeepers rationed foods in return for assured supplies of price-controlled and uncontrolled goods. One fifty-year-old housewife gave her butcher sugar in return for tins of corned beef, and gave cigarettes to the shop assistants in the local Co-op in return for under-the-counter goods.[100] If money changed hands, the amounts involved were small. Paying a few pennies for an unused coupon or tipping a shop assistant or shopkeeper for price-controlled goods did not pose a great problem for the Treasury. Yet coupon trading remained illegal and constituted the main source of black market supply.

From the commanding heights of the economy, black market dealing looks insignificant, but evasion did pose a significant threat to individual control schemes from time to time. Black markets in home-produced foods proved to be the biggest challenge to food control. The black market in fresh eggs was the largest of these, and the first year of egg control proved the most difficult. A variety of exemptions for small producers and producers in remote rural areas meant that almost 20% of eggs produced fell outside the egg scheme. The remaining 80% should have passed through licensed packing stations, but the MoF estimated that only two-thirds of these eggs did so. These figures panicked officials into revising the scheme, but the situation was worse than thought.[101] When the UK agricultural departments revised their estimate of the average rate of egg laying for hens in 1953, it became clear that egg packing stations received 41.1% of fresh eggs

[97] TNA: PRO, POWE 28/105, 'Coupon availability in Great Britain', August 1950.
[98] MoF, *The Urban Working-Class Household Diet: First Report of the National Food Survey Committee* (London, 1951), 33–5, 71–2; MoF, *Studies in Urban Household Diets: Second Report of the National Food Survey Committee* (London, 1956), 14–18.
[99] *The Times*, 16 November 1942.
[100] M-OA, Topic Collections (TC), Food 6/E, 'Black Market and Barter', 12 May 1947.
[101] Hammond, *Food*, ii, 86–7.

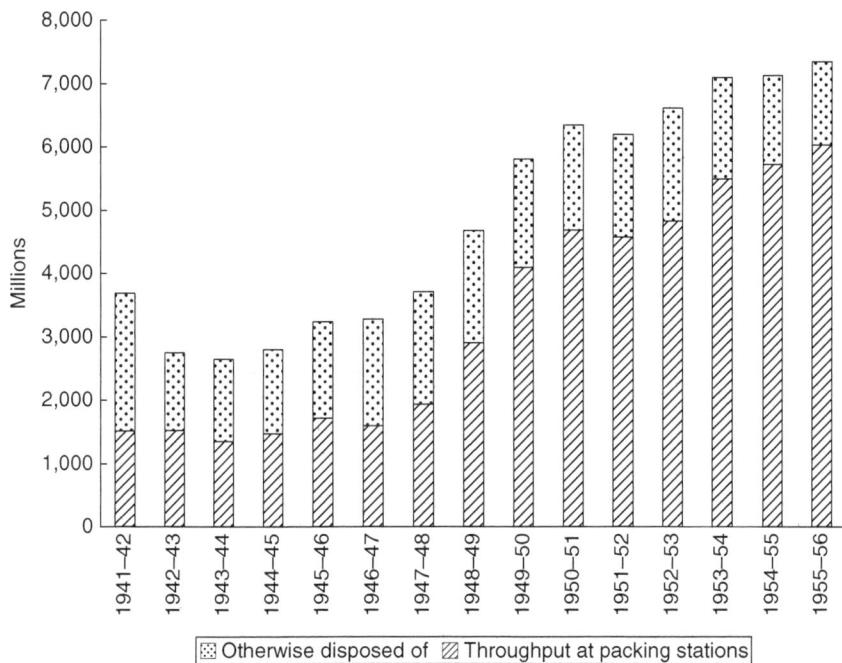

Fig. 1.3. Hen eggs available for food from UK agricultural holdings, 1941–42 to 1955–56.

Source: 1941–42 to 1945–46—*Agricultural Statistics: United Kingdom, ii: Output and Utilisation of Farm Produce in the Agricultural Years 1943–1944 to 1949–1950* (London, 1953), Table 21; 1946–47 to 1955–56—*Output and Utilization of Farm Produce in the United Kingdom 1946–47 to 1955–56* (London, 1958), Table 24.

produced on agricultural holdings. The situation improved slightly the following year, but the packing stations received little over half of all eggs produced until 1946/47. That year only 48.5% of all eggs laid passed through official channels. The figures improved dramatically in 1947/48, and continued to do so until the MoF decontrolled eggs in March 1953. During 1951/52—the last full year of egg control—packing stations processed 73.8% of all eggs laid. This compares favourably with the figure of 77.4% for 1953/54—the first full year after decontrol (see Fig. 1.3). Yet the Minister of Food Gwilym Lloyd George stated publicly his belief that the egg control scheme had broken down completely. If this constituted a breakdown in orderly distribution then the system had broken down long before November 1952.[102]

Price control of poultry was more often broken than observed. Throughout the period of control, the market in stock poultry provided a legal cover for illicit dealing. The MoF chose not to control the price of poultry sold for breeding, laying, or rearing. Black market dealers could obtain birds using the cover of buying 'stock poultry', and poultry farmers could realize a very high and legal profit.[103]

---

[102] HC deb, vol. 508, 26 November 1952, col. 433.
[103] HC deb, vol. 389, 26 May 1943, cols. 1571–2.

Unsurprisingly, the prices paid for stock poultry outstripped the official price for live poultry. The volume of sales and the prices realized attracted auction marts into the market. Stock poultry sales were rare during the inter-war years, but became commonplace during the 1940s while traditional Christmas sales of fat poultry collapsed.[104] In 1944 the number of fat turkeys, ducks, geese, and chickens sold at the Christmas poultry sales in Diss, Norfolk, fell dramatically. Auctioneers expected to sell 20,000 birds at the sales, but sold only twenty hens at the controlled price ten days before Christmas.[105] The three local firms that held auctions reported poor sales throughout the 1940s, with their sales hitting rock bottom in 1947 and recovering to pre-war levels in 1950.[106] Most poultry keepers sold their birds direct to buyers from outside the area for more than the official price. In 1944 reporters discovered unofficial sales of turkeys and geese taking place at farm gates, on village greens, and in village pubs outside Diss. By 1948, buyers took to placing advertisements in the local paper offering to buy turkeys direct from farmers for good prices.

Milk and dairy products proved difficult to control too. The MoF did not force dairy farmers to sell all their milk through marketing schemes. There was a noticeable increase in the amount of milk consumed in farm households during the period of control. During the inter-war period farms kept 5.2% of all milk production for their own use. By 1942/43, UK farmers consumed 7.9% of all milk produced that year, or 142.4% of the annual average of 92 million gallons consumed on UK farms during the inter-war years. Ostensibly, farming households consumed this milk, but the increase in farm consumption offset the fall in direct farm sales. Prior to the war, UK farmers sold an average of 74 million gallons of milk per year outside of marketing schemes. In the war's first year this fell by slightly less than half to 38 million gallons, and in 1940/41 it fell even further to 19 million gallons. The increase in sales through marketing schemes more than made up for this decline. It would be tempting to argue that the milkman from the local dairy replaced the local farmer as the main supplier of milk in rural communities, but the increase in the amount of milk retained for home consumption suggests that farmers did not desert their customers. In 1942/43, farm households consumed 131 million gallons of milk—39 million gallons more than their pre-war average.[107] Some farmers sold this 'extra' milk locally on the black market, or used it to make butter and cheeses, which they sold illegally.

Evasion of the bacon and meat rationing schemes was a greater problem for the MoF than evasion of the milk distribution scheme, but not as serious or persistent as evasion of egg control. The rapid growth in the number of slaughter licences issued to pig clubs in 1947, and the high prices that store pigs fetched at auction compared to the official price for finished pigs, were indicative of avoidance and

[104] Hammond, *Food*, iii, 722.

[105] *The Times*, 16 December 1944.

[106] *Norfolk and Suffolk Journal and Diss Express*, 15 December 1950.

[107] Calculated using figures in *Agricultural Statistics* and *Output and Utilization of Farm Produce in the United Kingdom*.

Table 1.3. Pigs slaughtered for year ending 31 August, 1941–49 (in 000s)

	Self-suppliers	Ministry of Food
1941–1942	409	1,601
1942–1943	479	1,496
1943–1944	513	1,158
1944–1945	467	1,586
1945–1946	544	1,563
1946–1947	551	936
1947–1948	637	776
1948–1949	740	1,990

Source: Hammond, *Food*, iii, 794–6.

evasion of meat and bacon rationing. Pig clubs proved a major headache for ministry officials, as few self-suppliers of meat followed the finer points of the regulations. These increased in popularity in the late 1940s, with some pig farmers stabling large numbers of pigs for 'self-suppliers' (see Table 1.3). During autumn 1947, journalists and MPs questioned ministers and official spokesmen about the suspicious jump in store pig prices. The price data collected by market reporters show that prices realized at auction leapt in 1947 (see Fig. 1.4). Neither Ministry of Agriculture and Fisheries (MAF) nor MoF officials anticipated this development, and privately agreed with their critics that this was due to black market activity.

People who lived in the countryside during the 1940s did not complain about food shortages. When interviewed, country dwellers said that rationing did not affect their diet, and tended to stress the problems faced by friends and relatives living in urban areas. Farmers, small-holders and people with large gardens could augment their rations, gifting or trading any surplus produce with scant regard for the regulations. Throughout the war, Margaret Holland's father, who lived in Shropshire, sent her eggs and bacon produced on his smallholding.

> He made two wooden boxes, each with twelve compartments, which he lined with felt. In these he placed twelve eggs, each wrapped in greaseproof paper so that if any cracked in transit the egg could be emptied into a basin without loss. These two boxes did a shuttle service in the post to keep us supplied with eggs. When he got the butcher to kill a pig and cure the meat, my father would also send us a piece of bacon through the post.[108]

The Royal Mail carried a surprisingly large and varied quantity of food from the countryside to the town during rationing, but fresh eggs were an unlikely staple of the mails. Like Margaret Holland's father, the Briggs family—London evacuees— sent eggs to relatives who stayed in the city. Dennis Briggs remembers 'a constant exchange of parcels' between south London and Daylesford, Worcestershire. 'We actually used to wrap eggs up in newspaper, and then wrap that up in some box,

[108] Margaret Holland cited in Jonathan Croall, *Don't You know there's a War on? The People's Voice 1939–45* (London, 1988), 268–9.

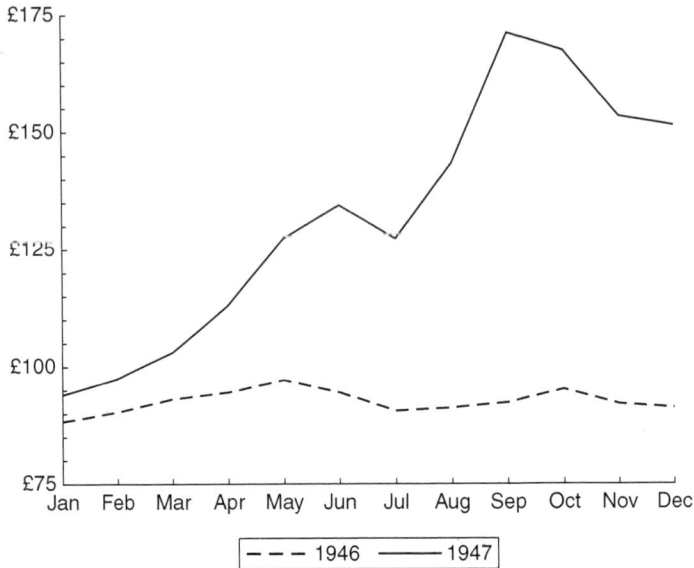

Fig. 1.4. Monthly average price of store pigs marketed in England and Wales, 1946–47 (in £ per head).

Source: Agricultural Statistics: England and Wales.

and post a dozen eggs to my uncle in Bermondsey, and we'd get a letter back four days later, saying, "That was lovely, only five were smashed".'[109]

Resource limitations made policing the rural economy difficult. Local officials tolerated low-level dealing for the same reason that the MoL and the MoFP chose not to look into miners' use of their 'concessionary coal' allowance too closely. To do so risked alienating workers who were central to the war effort and post-war reconstruction. MAF and MoF officials recognized that food producers' first concern was that they and their families should not go short of food. To secure the willing cooperation of farmers and growers, the joint Home Agricultural Supplies Committee placed no limit on the quantity of their own produce, which they could keep for home consumption. The only exception was livestock—especially pigs, which could be killed only under licence. In private, one senior MoF official admitted that 'we frankly accept the impossibility of preventing producers from living better than the general population'.[110] This concession made it easy to conceal illegal gifting, bartering, and sale of milk, butter, cheese, eggs, poultry, fruit, vegetables, and cereals. As a result, the underground economy flourished in rural areas such the Soar Valley, and attracted visitors from towns and cities.[111]

---

[109] Dennis Briggs cited in Croall, *Don't You Know*, 53–4.

[110] C. H. Blagburn, 'Control of Marketing and Utilisation of Home-produced Foods', in MoF, *Administration of Food Control*, 72.

[111] Stephen Joyce, 'The Black Economy in the Soar Valley, 1945–1971', *Transactions of the Leicestershire Archaeological and Historical Society*, 82 (2008), 245–54.

Illegal dealing in home-produced foods was a perennial problem for the MoF, but the MoFP encountered similar problems in rationing commercial motorists. Hauliers, bus and coach operators, taxi drivers, and other commercial drivers had to be issued with enough petrol to allow them to complete their journeys in the foulest of driving conditions. Despite the bitter winters during the 1940s, drivers rarely encountered hazardous conditions such as strong winds and driving rain. Unused commercial petrol coupons passed into the hands of private motorists, who used them to augment their basic ration. Petrol controllers feared that the leakage of petrol from commercial to private use had reached a significant level in autumn 1941, and plugged the leak in 1942 when they withdrew the basic ration. The problem re-emerged after the restoration of basic ration for private motorists in 1945. In 1947 the government dyed all commercial petrol red to enable police to detect the presence of commercial petrol in private motor vehicles. Comparing civilian consumption of petrol during 1947 with civilian consumption in 1948, it is possible to gauge the size of the most notorious black market of the post-war years.

In October 1948 the MoFP Statistical Branch did just that, calculating the amount of petrol saved by the red-petrol scheme. They compared figures for monthly averages of weekly deliveries of petrol into consumption in 1947 with the same figures for 1948. They calculated that the red-petrol scheme was saving the ministry 5,000 tons of motor spirit per week—250,000 tons per year.[112] In fact, the red-petrol scheme saved 11,150 tons per week during the ten months from May 1948 to February 1949 (see Table 1.4). Although some of the change may be accounted for by changes in rationing and consumption patterns, Statistical Branch was convinced that most savings came from suppressing the black market.[113] If the rate of saving remained constant, then the red-petrol scheme would have saved 579,800 tons of petrol during the twelve months from May 1948 to April 1949. If this represented savings from suppressing the black market, then approximately 12.6% of all petrol delivered into inland consumption in the UK leaked onto the black market during 1947.

The red-petrol scheme put an end to the petrol black market. Other methods of evading the regulations, such as filtering commercial petrol through bread, removed the red dye but did not remove the trace chemical for which the police tested. Although the activated carbon filters in civilian gas masks could remove the dye and the trace chemical, one gas mask could filter a negligible amount of petrol. Random tests for the presence of red petrol conducted by the police confirmed that private motorists no longer used red. The results of these routine checks showed that by June 1948 less than 1% of private motorists were using illicitly obtained commercial petrol (see Table 1.5). This is not too surprising given extensive publicity of police enforcement. The chance of being caught was increasing, just as the incentive to take a risk was decreasing. Gradual increases in civilian supplies of petrol meant that motorists were able to meet their demands with their ration.

---

[112] TNA: PRO, PREM 8/1060, CP (48) 233, 15 October 1948.
[113] TNA: PRO, POWE 33/2207, 'Note on estimated saving from the black market', 2 March 1949.

Table 1.4. Estimated savings of petrol after introduction of the red-petrol scheme (in 000 tons)

Month	Deliveries into consumption		Saving
	1947	1948	
May	91.0	83.3	7.7
June	97.4	82.8	14.6
July	104.1	91.5	12.6
August	98.6	84.8	13.8
September	103.4	90.0	13.4
October	94.8	82.4	12.4
November	80.8	82.9	-2.1
December	92.4	81.6	10.8
January	93.1	76.9	16.2
February	93.9	81.8	12.1
Total	949.5	838.0	111.5
Monthly average	95.0	83.8	11.2

Notes

a. Figures for May are for the ten weeks ended 20 May.

b. Figures for February are for the two weeks ended 17 February.

Source: TNA: PRO, POWE 33/2207, 'Note on estimated savings from the black market', March 1949.

Table 1.5. Results of routine tests for red petrol in England and Wales, 1949–50

Month	No. of cars routinely tested	Positive results	
		No.	%
June	12,688	44	0.35
July	17,037	82	0.48
August	24,799	77	0.31
September	18,202	77	0.42
October	15,725	93	0.59
November	12,658	82	0.65
December	11,045	39	0.35
January	10,686	48	0.45

Notes

a. Routine tests do not included tests carried out on information received.

b. The figures include the London Metropolitan Police and City of London Police Forces.

c. The Statistical Branch of the London Metropolitan Police was unable to separate tests based on information received from routine tests for June and July 1949.

Source: Monthly red petrol returns in POWE 33/1511 at TNA.

If the petrol black market was the most notorious of illegal markets, dealing in clothing coupons came a close second. BoT officials assumed that 5% of clothing coupons and vouchers would pass through the black market once during the first year of control, and that their black market value would be 10% of their retail purchasing power. With a retail purchasing power of at least 2*s* per coupon, each coupon would be worth a minimum of 2½*d*. Given that the BoT expected to issue 3,000 million coupons and 2,000 million vouchers during the first year of clothes rationing, the annual turnover of the black market would be at least £52 million.[114] The figures for the number of replacement clothing coupons issued and the number of retail outlets willing to accept loose coupons led senior officials to worry that their original estimate might have been too low. During the first year of control, the BoT received 781,900 applications for replacement coupons and issued 29.9 million replacements, while a Wartime Social Survey report concluded that 6.4% of clothing retailers received mainly loose coupons from their customers and a further 11.2% received some loose coupons. The problem was particularly bad in Liverpool, where 39.2% of clothing retailers estimated that more than 20% of their customers brought loose coupons.[115]

Independent surveys of the number of unused coupons available to trade confirm the potential for a sizeable black market in coupons. BIPO interviewers asked civilians whether they had any clothing coupons left in August 1944 and February 1945 when the rationing period ended. On both occasions, 40% of those interviewed had coupons left, 35% had none left, and 5% did not know.[116] The British Market Research Bureau's monthly panel survey of clothing coupon expenditure for the BoT provided a more detailed picture of the situation. Studying the monthly returns, the Bureau's analysts noticed that women's average expenditure during the first two years of rationing was higher than their average coupon allotment. Commenting on the figures in the bulletin of the Oxford Institute of Statistics, the economist Peter Ady concluded that this 'has clearly taken place at the expense of other groups...actual coupon income therefore is not determined solely by the official allocation and cannot be accurately assessed'.[117] Household pooling of clothing coupons as well as gifting and trading of coupons allowed women to consume more than their allocation of coupons. The BoT sanctioned pooling of clothing coupons within families, but it discouraged people gifting or trading the family surplus. Women supplied the black market too, selling other family members' unused coupons. Some working-class mothers sold their children's spare coupons. Ritchie White, a London schoolboy during the war, remembered this well and understood the rationale: 'You swapped the clothes coupons for food because you could do without clothes. The richer people would give you money for them so

---

[114] TNA: PRO, BT 64/869, W. E. Parker, 'Black market in coupons and vouchers', 10 June 1942.

[115] TNA: PRO, BT 64/1519, 'The history of the lost ration document', August 1948; TNA: PRO, RG 23/1, 'Investigation into retailers' difficulties', August 1941.

[116] Gallup, *Public Opinion Polls*, i, 93, 105.

[117] P. H. Ady, 'The Statistical Background of Clothes Rationing 1941–1944', *Bulletin of the Institute of Statistics Oxford*, 6 (1944), 213.

you could go and buy.'[118] Schoolteachers deplored the practice, which they attributed to greed. The National Association of Head Teachers lobbied the BoT about the problem, writing to Hugh Dalton about the issue in 1943 and 1944.[119]

Coupon offences, overcharging for price-controlled goods, and leakages of home-produced foodstuffs from British farms and market gardens were the main ways in which consumers obtained black market goods. These invisible crimes did not feed an inflationary spiral, as many black market transactions involved gifting or bartering. When money did change hands, the sums involved were small. Coupon trading and overcharging did not threaten the orderly distribution of rationed and price-controlled goods, as they did not increase civilian consumption at the expense of the war effort or post-war reconstruction. This was true of the petrol black market too. Officials wanted to boost rationed supplies by squeezing the black market. Leakages of home-produced foods from official channels could have undermined several food control schemes, as they did in the British occupation zone in northern Germany, but only did so in the case of the control schemes for eggs and poultry.

Despite differences in their use of the term 'black market', it is clear that the popular and official views of the extent and pattern of non-compliance are complementary. Large-scale black market operations involving big sums of money and large quantities of controlled goods were few and far between, but petty transactions involving large numbers of people and little or no money were commonplace. Illegal dealing increased rapidly during 1941 as the number of control schemes increased and shortages became acute. Black markets experienced another period of rapid growth from 1945 through to 1947 as controls reached their greatest extent and shortages worsened. From 1948, black market activity declined due to targeted enforcement drives and decontrol. The end of clothes rationing in 1949 and petrol rationing in 1950 killed two major black markets, but black marketeering in controlled foods continued until the decontrol of meat in 1954.

Writing about black market activity shortly after it peaked in 1947, Angus Maude summed up the situation accurately: 'We may perhaps conclude that the British black market has never reached such dimensions—except in the case of petrol—as to have any appreciable effect on supplies of important products to legitimate consumers.'[120] Maude's assessment of the extent of non-compliance, based as it was upon a review of all the publicly available evidence, is the most compelling contemporary survey of Britain's black markets. Maude—then deputy director of the independent think-tank Political and Economic Planning—hoped his pamphlet for the Bureau of Current Affairs would inform public debate about evasion of rationing and price control. Sadly for Maude, it did not. Contemporary commentators did not read his pamphlet, which went to schools that subscribed to the

---

[118] Ritchie White cited in Jess Steale (ed.), *A Working Class War: Tales from Two Families* (London, 1995), 110.
[119] *The Times*, 16 September 1943 and 29 June 1944.
[120] Maude, *Black Market*, 8.

series, or weigh the available evidence as carefully as Maude had done. Instead they chose to emphasize either the absence of large-scale dealing or the ubiquity of small-scale dealing. Government ministers and senior officials, who looked for signs of extensive large-scale evasion, downplayed the economic significance of black markets, while newspaper columnists, who sought to express their readers' common anxieties and frustrations, drew attention to the morally corrupting effects of widespread small-scale dealing.

2

'A matter of friendship': the grey market

Asked by Mass-Observation to define 'Black Market dealings' in January 1948, a middle-aged commercial traveller joked that it was 'the way the bloke down the road gets what he wants' before reflecting that 'when the issues become more personal one notes a tendency for the colour of the transaction to become Grey or even only Slightly Dirty White'. Nevertheless, he felt 'most people seem to make a difference between the bloke who gets hold of half-a-dozen eggs, and he who corners the market in pears (for instance), and make[s] tens of thousands in the process'.[1] The self-serving nature of such definitions did not escape the attention of others. Offering advice to teachers leading discussions about black marketing later that year, the editor of *Current Affairs* warned that 'it is a natural human tendency to think of the black market as what the *other* fellow does, and to class our transactions among the lighter shades of grey'.[2]

The 'Grey Market', far larger than the 'Black Market', straddled the boundary between legal and illegal markets, encompassing avoidance as well as evasion of the regulations. Like 'Black Market', the term 'Grey Market' had its origins in the world of inter-war commerce and finance where traders used it to refer to legal currency dealing that took place outside official channels.[3] When the term was applied to dealings in controlled goods, the distinction drawn between the legal dodge that avoided the regulations and illegal evasion frequently disappeared. The 'Grey Market' stretched to cover petty evasions that lay in the middle ground between legal dealings that society considered morally acceptable and illegal dealings that it did not.

'Grey Market' and 'Black Market' are the most important linguistic remains of the underground economy's mid-century boom.[4] Although the meaning of these concepts is ambiguous, they are no less precise than the terms coined to describe the underground economy since the 1970s. Unlike anachronistic ideas about a 'black' or 'hidden' economy, and 'compliance' and 'non-compliance', these terms meant something to contemporaries. They were not concepts coined by academics and policymakers seeking to understand economic crime so that they could better control it. Although official references to the 'contravention', 'breach', or 'evasion' of regulation were comprehensible, these legalistic terms were not part of everyday

---

[1] M-OA, DR January 1948, DR 161.
[2] Maude, *Black Market*, 14.
[3] 'Money Market', *Economist*, 23 December 1933.
[4] R. W. Zandvoort, *Wartime English: Materials for A Linguistic History of World War II* (Groningen, 1957), 34–5.

talk about non-compliance. The difference between a 'Grey Market' deal and a 'Black Market' deal mirrored the legal distinction drawn between acts that were illegal, and acts that were illegal and wrong in themselves. Although the authorities exerted some influence over the categorization of an offence through its approach to its enforcement, colour coding was ultimately in the hands of the public.

Not only did these contemporary terms structure people's economic choices, they also shaped the meanings that they attached to them. Describing the structure and operation of the underground economy by offence or commodity misses the shared characteristics that led people to lump together swapping coupons and tipping, and to distinguish between illegal cash sales conducted for profit or for more than profit.[5] The grey market—the subject of this chapter—grew out of local exchange networks that formed the basis of the underground economy between the wars. Largely legal, but including some illegal economic activities such as pilfering, these communal networks became illegal as economic control criminalized informal exchanges of controlled goods.

SHADES OF GREY

When asked what she understood 'Black Market dealings' to be, the novelist and poet Naomi Mitchison told M-O that she defined them as 'Any dealing in rationed or controlled supplies contrary to the law'. Like most M-O contributors who replied to the monthly postal survey in January 1948, her reply shows that Mitchison was familiar with the official definition of a black market transaction. But she refused to accept that all evasion was black market. 'I feel it is Black when the object is money, and Grey when it is an obligement or [a] matter of friendship.'[6] This was a common distinction to make. Grey market dealing was not conducted for profit alone. Gifting and swapping of surplus coupons, rations, home-grown produce, and home-made goods—the most common types of evasion—were grey market, as was the practice of banking coupons with retailers. Another directive respondent characterized them as 'dirty white'. This was not unique to Britain's underground economy. It featured prominently in continental black markets as well.[7] It was, however, proportionately larger in the UK than elsewhere in Western Europe. Greyer still, shading into black, were the paid favour, the tip, the fiddle, and the

---

[5] Smithies focuses on the type of offences in *Crime in Wartime* and *The Black Economy in England since 1914* (Dublin, 1984). In *Austerity* Zweiniger-Bargielowska considers offences by commodity. This hybrid approach is found in other national historiographies, starting with *The Black Market: A Study of White Collar Crime* (New York, 1952), Marshall B. Clinard's study of the USA.

[6] M-OA, DR January 1948, DR 65.

[7] See Polymeris Voglis, 'Surviving Hunger', in Robert Gildea, Olivier Wieviorka, and Anette Warring (eds.), *Surviving Hitler and Mussolini: Daily Life in Occupied Europe* (Oxford, 2007), 27–31; Kenneth Mouré and Paula Schwartz, 'On vit mal: Food Shortages and Popular Culture in Occupied France, 1940–1944', *Food, Culture and Society*, 10 (2007), 277; Paul Steege, *Black Market, Cold War: Everyday Life in Berlin, 1946–1949* (Cambridge, 2007), 49–63; and Ralf Futselaar, *Lard, Lice and Longevity: A Comparative Study of the Standard of Living in Occupied Denmark and the Netherlands, 1940–1945* (Amsterdam, 2008), 158–90.

'homer'. Some common dodges sat at this end of the spectrum too—especially eating coupon-free in clubs, hotels, and restaurants. Like jumble sales and prize draws, eating out was a legal but morally dubious way of avoiding the regulations.

The exchanges classed as 'grey market' had many but not all properties in common, as the category embraced a diverse array of wheezes and fiddles. Often the partners in a grey market deal knew each other, with the result that a deal was rarely a one-off. The quantity of goods involved in each exchange was small, and little or no money changed hands. Profit was not the object of a deal, though one was sometimes taken. These features point to an underlying characteristic of every deal in the grey market's eclectic repertoire of exchanges: they respected the re-source allocations that the government made between and within sectors of the economy. Consumers considered surplus goods, ration coupons, home-grown pro-duce, and handicrafts—the principal grey market goods—as their personal prop-erty. Traders viewed their spare stock in a similar light, while workers in some trades considered pilfered goods as part of their pay. None of them saw how trans-ferring this personal property caused direct or indirect harm to third parties, as it did not divert goods from one sector to another. In some cases a deal could even increase the volume of goods circulating in the economy. Given the personal in-vestment in growing flowers, fruit, and vegetables, rearing poultry or pigs, and making clothes, toys, and other handicrafts, feelings of ownership towards such tangible goods are readily explicable, as are those towards rationed goods that had been bought and paid for. Property law bore out these feelings. As their personal property, people could dispose of these goods as they saw fit. Proprietary attitudes towards ration coupons—bits of paper given people by government—require a little more explanation.

Throughout austerity the legal position was that ration coupons remained the property of the relevant ministry, which retained the right to determine how the public used them and to reclaim any unused coupons. Officials, who aimed to re-strict individual consumption of rationed goods, wanted to claw back unused ra-tions for the common pool. In fact, their calculations of ration levels factored in unused rations. For this reason the rationing ministries prohibited the sale or ex-change of ration coupons and rationed goods. Despite criticism from economists who thought free coupon transfers would maximize utility by evening out dispari-ties in individual tastes and preferences, the ministries refused to allow coupon transfers. Although they did not have the resources to enforce their policy or refine it by creating a system for collecting unused coupons, the ministries stood firm.[8] The rationing ministries banned such transfers, arguing publicly that the exchange of coupons, especially if money changed hands, undermined equality of sacrifice, the moral basis for control.[9] There was one exception. Acknowledging the realities

[8] Hammond, *Food*, ii, 286, and iii, 210–11; M. Kalecki, 'Notes on General Rationing', *Bulletin of the Oxford Institute of Statistics*, 3 (1941), 103–5; F. Burchardt, 'Shipping—The Bottleneck', *Bulletin of the Oxford Institute of Statistics*, 4 (1942), 193–7; M. Kalecki, 'Differential Rationing', *Bulletin of the Oxford Institute of Statistics*, 4 (1942), 215–17; Fuel Rationing (PP 1941–2 Cmd.6352 iv, 275), 282.
[9] *Manchester Guardian*, 10 January (food) and 1 June 1940 (petrol).

of household budgeting, the ministries permitted families to pool coupons, but this was the only concession that officials countenanced.

This policy on coupon transfers did not accord with common-sense notions of property. A ration book and the coupons in it were yours by right. You could gift them or swap them, and some felt that you had the right to sell them. Initial publicity did little to disabuse the public of such notions. When, during a radio discussion in January 1940, a London housewife asked a ministry official whether she could swap bacon coupons for extra butter, the official told her that she could not, as it was an offence to exchange her coupons. 'There was nothing, however, to prevent the friendly exchange of commodities with a neighbour.'[10] Such statements made it clear that the goods but not the coupons were yours to do with as you will. The public did not, or would not, understand such fine distinctions. If the goods that you obtained by surrendering coupons were yours to do with as you pleased, why was this not the case for the coupons themselves?

Attempts to explain points rationing confused the issue further. Government propaganda encouraged consumers to think of food and clothing points as a second currency to spend on rationed goods. By giving individuals and households the opportunity to save their points, to 'bank' them with a retailer, to pool points within a household, and to choose from a limited range of goods, there seemed little difference between points and pounds sterling. If points coupons, and by extension all ration coupons, were a form of currency with the number in circulation under government control, then there was nothing wrong with transferring points or exchanging them for other coupons. Economists thought so too.

Given the intricacies of rationing, it is not surprising that people latched onto the cash analogy. But such comparisons obscured two fundamental differences between coupons and cash. Cash was the property of the bearer, not the Bank of England, while coupons remained government property.[11] Cash was a general-purpose currency that could be used to purchase goods, pay debts, and compare the value of goods, while the various types of coupon were special-purpose currencies that could be used only to purchase a much narrower range of goods in conjunction with cash. The restrictions placed on coupon use underscored this point. In addition to being non-transferable, coupons were inconvertible: they could not be exchanged legally for cash or other types of coupon. The cash analogy which elided these differences undermined the integrity of rationing, as it led people to believe that they could use coupons as freely as they could cash.

In November 1942 the strength of people's proprietary feelings towards spare coupons, rations, home-grown produce, and handicrafts became clear. As civilians began their seasonal trawl of the shops for Christmas gifts, the MoF reminded consumers that it was illegal to give food coupons or rationed foodstuffs as presents. The announcement came as news to civilians, many of whom gave coupons and

---

[10] *Manchester Guardian*, 10 January 1940.
[11] David Fox, 'Bona Fide Purchase and the Currency of Money', *Cambridge Law Journal*, 55 (1996), 547–65.

rationed goods as gifts. It prompted outraged readers to write to the editor of *The Times*. In their letters they denounced the Minister of Food Lord Woolton for creating a new crime. Others sought advice about the rights and wrongs of giving food to servants, children, or tramps. *The Times* food correspondent answered their queries. As servants living in counted as members of the household, giving them coupons or rations was legal. Inviting a tramp into one's home and feeding them was legal, but giving them food to take away was not. Offering sweets to a child or saving chocolate to send to a prisoner of war was also permissible, as the MoF classified the sweets ration as a personal ration. This was a unique category that allowed consumers to do as they wished with their entitlement.[12]

In the face of public hostility the ministry appeared to retreat, restating its earlier policy that all transfers were illegal while reassuring civilians that it would not prosecute people for making innocent gifts—a position it maintained for the duration of food control.[13] This concession created more confusion as people disputed what counted as a gift, and dragged the ministry into regulating gifts.[14] Three months after the initial furore, a M-O investigator, soliciting views on food rationing, found that two out of twenty-four interviewees continued to express strong, unprompted views on the topic. One, a thirty-five-year-old man, told the investigator: 'It's silly to make a fuss when people exchange their rations...If people want more of one thing and are prepared to have less of another, why shouldn't they?'[15] Neither the BoT nor the MoFP followed suit. All transfers of clothing and petrol coupons outside the household remained illegal, gift or not.

Unused coupons and spare rations proved a major source of grey market supply, taxing the minds of civil servants who considered them intractable problems. Clawing back unused coupons was too expensive, as was enforcing the rule that coupons were not transferable. The BoT made a half-hearted attempt to prevent coupon transfers by forbidding retailers to accept loose coupons. Like the MoF, the board retreated within a few months, ignoring the issue publicly while legitimizing related practices such as leaving your ration book with a retailer. The MoFP did not concern itself with transfers between private motorists, as they tended to consume their full ration. Officials worried more about unused commercial petrol coupons finding their way into the hands of private motorists.[16] This was not a problem when the ministry withdrew the basic petrol ration between 1942 and 1945 and from 1947 to 1948. During these periods, no car driver received petrol for shopping trips, days out, or motor tours. Anyone doing so had to be misusing petrol which they had received for other purposes, or were running on 'black' petrol obtained illegally.

The attitude of traders towards their stock bears comparison with the proprietorial feelings that consumers bore towards ration coupons. Like spare coupons or rations,

---

[12] *The Times*, 21 and 30 November 1942.
[13] HC deb, vol. 385, 2 December 1942, cols. 1152–4; HC deb, vol. 397, 23 February 1944, col. 838, w.a.
[14] Zweiniger-Bargielowska, *Austerity*, 174–5.
[15] M-OA, FR 1594, J. F., 'Food Indirects', 6 February 1943.
[16] Payton-Smith, *Oil*, 219.

surplus stock was theirs to dispose of. It was an important source of grey market food as rationing regularly left retailers with surplus bacon and ham, sugar, butter and margarine, cooking fats, preserves, cheese, and meat. Customers had to register with retailers to receive these rations, and many chose to leave the relevant coupons with them too. Although shopkeepers cancelled coupons, they did not have to pass them back to wholesalers or local food offices to receive replacement stocks. Instead, the MoF issued retailers with permits to buy enough food to meet every customer's ration in full. Of course, some customers did not buy their full ration, which left traders with surplus stock and unused coupons. An annual survey of grocers' turnover found that civilians never consumed their full allowances of dried egg and dried milk, though they took all the fresh eggs and liquid milk they could obtain. Grocers found themselves with surplus butter and cheese whenever the weekly ration exceeded 2 oz per person. The same was true of sugar if the weekly sugar ration topped 8 oz. Margarine and cooking-fat rations were never consumed in full, and the same was true of preserves.[17] If any of these retailers declared a surplus, the local food office deducted them from their next buying permit. With a limited shelf life and unused coupons to cover overconsumption by some customers, retailers made such declarations rarely, preferring to give away or sell any surplus.

The allowances granted to distributors to cover processing and storage losses constituted another source of illicit supply. The relationship between the points value of articles of clothing and the cloth used to make them was the principal weakness of clothes rationing. The BoT found it difficult to equate the points value of made-up goods and cloth. Officials decided a yard of woollen cloth 36 inches wide was worth three coupons, and a yard of any other material was worth two coupons. Officials fixed the points value of an article of clothing according to the estimated amount of cloth needed to make a garment of average size. The assumption was that the differences between smaller and larger sizes would cancel out each other.[18] But this formula meant that it was possible for makers-up to accumulate large surpluses of clothing coupons if they made fewer large sizes or used simpler designs that economized on cloth. Utility schemes specifying clothing designs and materials minimized but did not resolve the problem.[19]

Throughout austerity, food retailers and their customers benefited from MoF allowances for wastage and shrinkage when preparing or processing food. In their stores, retail grocers displayed wheels of cheese and boxes of butter from which they cut portions for their customers. Some losses due to cutting or evaporation were inevitable, but a skilled grocer with good storage facilities and a high turnover could keep them to a minimum. The reward for the careful cutter who avoided waste was 'extra' butter and cheese that could be sold coupon-free or given away. The allowances made for cutting losses when dressing meat and preparing meat products were more generous than those for butter and cheese due to the greater

---

[17] See T. Schulz in *Oxford Bulletin of Statistics*: 3 (1941), 213–23; 4 (1942), 57–66; 6 (1944), 49–57; 7 (1945), 116–23; 8 (1946), 97–107; 9 (1947), 261–73; and 10 (1948), 105–16.
[18] Hargreaves and Gowing, *Civil Industry*, 308.
[19] Hargreaves and Gowing, *Civil Industry*, 310–11.

variability of the product. This allowed experienced retail butchers to build up size-able 'invisible' surpluses that could be sold off-ration as raw or cooked meat.[20] The most liberal allowances related to bacon and ham. Due to evaporation the weight of a ham or a box of cured bacon could fall by as much as 6% before it reached consumers. But ministry officials did not take into account quicker turnover under rationing, which minimized the evaporation problem.[21]

The perks and fiddles of miners, factory workers, and transport workers were another significant source of grey market goods. Miners' coal was the most well-known and controversial perk. If he was a householder, a miner received an allow-ance of house-coal on top of his wages. This was a longstanding practice to limit pilferage.[22] On occasion, agricultural and forestry workers received food and timber from their employers, but this was on a more informal basis than miners' coal. Although the size of the allowance varied from county to county and colliery to colliery, it tended to work out as just under 1 ton of coal every six weeks. This made the miners' allowance roughly four times greater than that of the average household allowance.[23] With coal to spare, miners gave it to friends or swapped it for other goods once the government outlawed its sale in 1943.[24] Their repeated refusal to accept higher wages in return for a cut in their coal allocation testified to its exchange value at a time when it was quasi-rationed.

Pilferage from factories and workshops producing controlled goods was more widespread but less well documented, as private employers preferred to deal with the problem internally.[25] Before clothes rationing began, textile workers pilfered cloth regularly, and taking home off-cuts and using them to make clothes was commonplace in Lancashire's textile districts before the war.[26] Workers in east Lon-don's rag trade smuggled cloth out of the workplace by wrapping lengths of ma-terial around their bodies. Wearing pilfered clothes under a worker's clothes was another common practice.[27] Pilfering of textiles continued under clothes ration-ing, increasing despite rising pay which it had supposedly subsidized. Other indus-tries producing controlled and uncontrolled goods suffered too, as workers stole raw materials and finished goods. Losses of cigarettes, matches, batteries, and proc-essed foods increased, alarming manufacturers.[28] With falling turnover due to pro-duction restrictions, pilferage presented a serious threat to the bottom line. Yet an employer's ability to take disciplinary action was constrained by the need to retain staff at a time when labour was scarce. The result was that they found themselves

[20] Hammond, *Food*, iii, 289–304.

[21] Hammond, *Food*, iii, 410–14.

[22] Jason Ditton, 'Perks, Pilferage and the Fiddle: The Historical Structure of Invisible Wages', *Theory and Society*, 4 (1977), 46.

[23] HC deb, vol. 436, 1 May 1947, col. 2184.

[24] Ferdynand Zweig, *Men in the Pits* (London, 1948), 129–32.

[25] J. P. Martin, *Offenders as Employees* (London, 1962), 85–7.

[26] Elizabeth Roberts, *A Woman's Place: An Oral History of Working-Class Women, 1890–1940* (Oxford, 1984), 48, 68.

[27] Smithies, *Black Economy*, 59–63.

[28] Smithies, *Black Economy*, 79–83, 107–9; Donald Thomas, *The Underworld at War: Spivs, Deserters, Racketeers and Civilians in the Second World War* (London, 2003), 122–6.

incapable of challenging practices that they had tolerated before the war. Unable to staunch this wound, goods continued to seep out of workshops and warehouses. This flow increased as austerity gave way to affluence judging by the experience of the Soar Valley, where workers took advantage of slacker surveillance to steal tools and raw materials as well as footwear from boot and shoe factories in Mountsorrel and Sileby.[29]

Like miners and factory hands, transport workers viewed petty fiddles as a customary addition to their wage packets. Dockers were notorious for their predatory behaviour prior to the war. This was borne out in Liverpool, where pilfered cargo was a regular and welcome supplement to dockers' income.[30] The same was true of their counterparts across the Mersey in Birkenhead.[31] War did not alter this pattern. The loss of goods in transit was the most well documented facet of the pilferage problem due to the readiness of firms to make insurance claims for such losses. As sole importer of many controlled goods and latterly owner of many transport industries, the government took a keen interest in the problem too. The government suppressed information about Hull dockers pilfering Red Cross supplies destined for their Soviet 'comrades', while merchant sailors stripped lifeboats of emergency supplies and equipment to prevent theft.[32] At the height of the Battle of the Atlantic, M-O investigators working for naval intelligence noted rampant pilfering by dockers in Glasgow and Liverpool. Anyone walking home purposefully and at a steady pace was very unlikely to be stopped and searched by the dock police.[33] Social investigators returning to Liverpool after the war found that pilferage continued to be an important addition to household income.[34] The post-war revival of London's docklands saw a resurgence in pilfering that reasserted the port's status as working-class London's larder.[35]

Petty theft was also a problem for the nationalized British Railways and its predecessors. When speaking to the social investigator Seebohm Rowntree after the war, a senior British Railways executive bemoaned the number of light bulbs, mirrors, ash trays, window-blinds, spoons, and cups stolen by passengers, but this was a minor irritant compared to pilferage by railway workers.[36] An inspector handling claims made against the Great Western Railway for goods lost in the Cirencester area spent much of her war chasing stolen cigarettes and clothes that went missing from cartons and crates as they were loaded and unloaded from goods wagons in

---

[29] Joyce, 'Black Economy', 249–53.

[30] Pat Ayers, 'The Hidden Economy of Dockland Families: Liverpool in the 1930s', in Pat Hudson and W. R. Lee (eds.), *Women's Work and the Family Economy in Historical Perspective* (Manchester, 1990), 286.

[31] Smithies, *Black Economy*, 35–6, 44–5, 61.

[32] Imperial War Museum (IWM), Lambeth, Sound Archive, tape ref. 10304/4/3, 'Interview with Captain Geoffrey Habesch', 29 July 1988; TNA: PRO, FO 371/29652 and FO 371/32957.

[33] M-OA, FR 600, 'Preliminary report on morale in Glasgow', 7 March 1941 and FR 1245, Tom Harrisson, 'Merseyside shipping situation', 7 May 1942; Croall, *Don't You Know*, 11.

[34] Madeline Kerr, *The People of Ship Street* (London, 1958), 125; John Barron Mays, *Growing up in the City: A Study of Juvenile Delinquency in an Urban Neighbourhood* (1954; rev. edn. Liverpool, 1964), 117–18, 122–3.

[35] Bill Gibson, cited in Rib Davies and Pam Schweitzer (eds.), *Southwark at War* (London, 1996), 16.

[36] B. Seebohm Rowntree and G. R. Lavers, *English Life and Leisure: A Social Study* (London, 1951), 222.

sidings and on station platforms.[37] Faced with a dramatic rise in the number and value of claims made for goods lost in transit, the railway companies took special precautions to prevent pilfering.[38] From 1944 onwards, supervisors ensured that staff kept vans locked at all times, concentrated valuable freight for loading so as to monitor it more carefully, instituted earlier collections to allow same-day despatch before the black-out, minimized transfers from road to rail, removed descriptions of goods and advertisements from packaging that revealed their contents, and increased checks and supervision.[39]

Of all the workers whose customary perks and fiddles weakened control, the depredations of delivery drivers and long-distance lorry drivers were the most serious. Many of the losses attributed to workers in railway goods yards were actually the fault of delivery drivers employed by the railways who ferried loads to and from the yards. Once out of the depot it was easy for a driver and his mate to stop, 'drag' the van, and stash the pilfered goods.[40] This was not a problem confined to the railways. Hauliers competing with the railway companies found it difficult to control the behaviour of long-distance lorry drivers who had more time to pilfer their loads in lorry parks and at wayside cafés than did railway delivery drivers.[41] Deliberately damaging goods to get into a package or to ensure they had to be given away was a longstanding fiddle. This practice achieved notoriety after the war, as evidenced by the popularity of the phrase 'It fell off the back of a lorry'.[42] The short delivery—deliberately unloading only part of an order so as to leave the driver with goods to sell—was another scam practised by roundsmen.[43] This was one of the ways by which drivers of petrol tankers pilfered fuel.[44] From an employer's perspective, overloading was more worrying than 'shorting' customers. Unlike 'shorting', overloading pointed to problems in the depot, as a driver needed the help of loaders and checkers to load extra goods that went unrecorded and could be sold at a discounted price to new and existing customers.

Unlike their fellow transport workers, drivers could also fiddle expenses. If a driver travelled any distance from his depot, his employer needed to give him enough money and petrol coupons to complete a journey in the worst driving conditions. Naturally, drivers found themselves with surplus coupons, as they rarely encountered the foulest weather.[45] Economical driving could reduce petrol consumption further and add to this surplus. Coupons acquired in this way were considered a perk of the job. Haulage contractors were in no position to object.

---

[37] Croall, *Don't You Know*, 61–2.

[38] George C. Nash, *The LMS at War* (London, 1946), 37.

[39] TNA: PRO, AN 3/54/61, 'Joint report of goods, passenger and police committees', 22 April 1944.

[40] TNA: PRO, AN 3/45, 'Police Committee minutes', 23 February 1943.

[41] TNA: PRO, MT 33/400, 'National Road Transport Federation minutes', 16 October 1947.

[42] Eric Partridge and Paul Beale (eds.), *A Dictionary of Catch Phrases: from the Sixteenth Century to the Present Day* (2nd edn., London, 2005), 93.

[43] See Bill Naughton, *A Roof Over Your Head* (London, 1945), 102–9 for a semi-autobiographical account of coal roundsmen 'shorting' customers in Bolton.

[44] Evasions of Petrol Rationing.

[45] Evasions of Petrol Rationing.

The owner of one of Coventry's largest haulage firms expressed the problem succinctly to his MP: 'Drivers are extremely difficult to get and even more difficult to keep. I don't mind if they make a little extra on the side by selling petrol to the Black Market if it keeps them quiet.'[46]

Individual households were a source of grey market goods as important as workers' perks and fiddles. Shortages of controlled goods and official encouragement of 'self-suppliers' had reversed the inter-war trend of a gradual decline in domestic production, which prompted a boom in home-grown produce and home-made goods. A house with gardens was much desired, and failing that, an allotment.[47] Demand for plots increased during the 1940s, and in London, parkland was turned over to allotments to cater for it.[48] The effect of the MAF 'Dig for Victory' and 'Dig for Plenty' campaigns can be seen in the statistics produced by the National Food Survey. During the summer of 1941, 49% of urban households consumed fruit and vegetables grown in gardens and allotments. The contribution of these 'free' supplies to urban larders peaked during the summer of 1943. That summer, home-grown potatoes accounted for 11.5% of the total value consumed within working-class households, while 25% of the value of other fruits and vegetables consumed came from gardens and allotments.[49] In some years self-suppliers found themselves with more fruit and vegetables than they could eat. The sugar ration and a shortage of glass jars placed a limit on what they could preserve, which left them with a surplus to give away or trade.[50]

Some of those people who were not wealthy enough or fortunate enough to have access to a vegetable plot resented this fact while coveting the self-suppliers' garden produce. Unsurprisingly, scrumping of fruit and pilfering of vegetables increased, which prompted the National Allotments Society to complain to the Lord Chancellor about an 'epidemic of pilfering'.[51] In Ipswich, allotment holders formed a crop protection society to patrol their holdings at night.[52] Most of the complaints about pilfering of allotments that the MoF received came from Essex.[53] The perceived seriousness of the problem in urban areas led the government to amend the defence regulations, making it possible to prosecute trespassers who might be looking for produce to steal.[54]

In rural areas, poaching provided a ready supply of food and entertainment. Naomi Mitchison relished furtive night fishing expeditions around the coast of

[46] TNA: PRO, MT 55/233, Richard Crossman to Hugh Gaitskell, 17 November 1947.

[47] Stephen Constantine, 'Amateur Gardening and Popular Recreation in the 19th and 20th Centuries', *Journal of Social History*, 14 (1981), 397.

[48] Kevin Ducker, 'Growing Pains: Allotment Gardening and the East End', *Rising East*, 4 (2000–1), 68–9.

[49] Ministry of Food, *Urban Working-Class Household Diet*, 33–5, 71–2.

[50] Paul Brassley and Angela Potter, 'A View from the Top: Social Elites and Food Consumption in Britain, 1930s–1940s', in Frank Trentmann and Flemming Just (eds.), *Food and Conflict in the Age of the Two World Wars* (Basingstoke, 2006), 223–42.

[51] TNA: PRO, MAF 48/759, G. W. Giles to Viscount Simon, 17 October 1941.

[52] *Daily Mirror*, 7 October 1942.

[53] TNA: PRO, MAF 48/759, S. J. Merrells to D. H. Chalk, 4 August 1941 and D. Swaffer to Chalk, 27 August 1941.

[54] HC deb, vol. 391, 14 July 1943, cols. 313–34.

Kintyre.[55] Taking fish, rabbits, partridges, and pheasants from other people's land was an accepted part of life in Leicestershire's Soar Valley throughout austerity and well into the 1960s. The men who 'went out' and had meat to spare were well known to locals.[56] In Merionethshire there was a nationalistic edge to the practice. Local Welsh speakers took great pleasure in poaching salmon, augmenting their families' diets while depriving English visitors of their fishing.[57] In East Anglia, American airmen swelled local poachers' ranks.[58] The object of the airmen's hunting expeditions and most poaching by locals was to bag a few rabbits. Farmers and landowners tolerated such trips. Although they disliked trespassers on their land, they disliked rabbits, which they considered a pest, and had little time to catch and kill the rabbits themselves.[59]

Rustling of poultry and livestock was rarer than poaching of game. Farmed animals belonged to someone who had invested considerable time and money in rearing each beast. Naturally, farmers' tended to have stronger feelings of ownership towards their animals than rabbits and other wild game—a proprietorial claim that rural communities recognized and respected. When the police caught rustlers, the culprits were most likely servicemen on manoeuvres raiding a hen coop or downing a sheep on a fellside.[60] The actions of Canadian troops in the southern counties attracted most comment as they were dealt with in British courts, unlike American GIs.[61] Gangs of rustlers stealing animals to feed black market demand were rarer still, as petrol rationing restricted the use of lorries on which the interwar gangs had depended.[62] Turkey farmers suffered the most from their depredations during the run up to Christmas, due to high demand and the comparative ease of slaughtering, plucking, and cleaning the birds.[63]

Less important but noteworthy sources of supply were goods from overseas received as unsolicited gifts, bought through mail-order firms, or smuggled into the country. Of these three sources, gifts were the most significant. By February 1948 the MoF estimated that Britons received in excess of 900 tons of rationed and unrationed food each month from friends living overseas.[64] Irish mail-order firms were also an important source of grey market goods from the start of control.[65] By the 1950s the mail-order business had grown so large that it affected commodity

---

[55] Naomi Mitchison diary, 5 June and 11 July 1941 in Dorothy Sheridan (ed.), *Among You taking Notes: The Wartime Diary of Naomi Mitchison 1939–1945* (London, 1985), 150–1, 155–8.

[56] Joyce, 'Black Economy', 246–7.

[57] Isabel Emmett, *A North Wales Village: A Social Anthropological Study* (London, 1964), 69–89.

[58] Roger A. Freeman, *The Friendly Invasion* (Norwich, 1992), 51.

[59] Hammond, *Food*, iii, 721–6; *Country Life*, January 1941 cited in Sadie Ward, *War in the Countryside, 1939–45* (London, 1988), 78.

[60] Ward, *War in the Countryside*, 79.

[61] C. P. Stacey and Barbara M. Wilson, *The Half Million: The Canadians in Britain, 1939–1946* (London, 1987), 164–5.

[62] *The Times*, 2 March 1939; *Manchester Guardian*, 4 July 1939.

[63] John Martin, 'The Commercialisation of British Turkey Production', *Rural History*, 20 (2009), 214–15; *Manchester Guardian*, 11 December 1945 and 22 December 1946.

[64] HC deb, vol. 447, 16 February 1948, col. 153 w.a.

[65] TNA: PRO, MEPO 2/3434, Home Office, 'Summary of reports received from Chief Officers of Police and Regional Police Staff Officers', 23 December 1939–6 January 1940.

markets. Ministry agents trying to buy South African fruit began to complain that they could not compete with the buyers working for the Irish firms. As a result, the British government banned all food imports from Éire.[66] Some of these now illegal mail-order purchases had been gifts, as Irish firms encouraged customers to give their goods as gifts. The mail-order gift was a useful fiction for others who wanted to circumvent the regulations. Once postal censorship ended in 1945 it was much harder to control the flow of gifts and mail-order goods though the post, as Customs opened very few letters and parcels. By comparison to gifting and mail order, smuggling was a minor source of supply outside of Northern Ireland. Limited opportunities for overseas travel during and after the war meant that it was the preserve of service personnel, merchant sailors, and the wealthy. The quantities involved were small: a few pairs of nylon stockings, a coat, a ham, or some tinned food.[67]

All these sources of supply respected the allocations made by government between economic sectors. The illegal transfer of spare coupons and unwanted rations did not encroach on supplies for the military or latterly the export sector of the economy. Although some civilians might consume 'a little bit extra' over their official entitlement, doing so involved goods that were earmarked for domestic consumption. Obtaining goods from overseas did not seem to deprive anyone else of their fair share either. Growing your own fruit and vegetables or turning unwanted raw materials into something else was seen in the same way. Pilfering, however, did not always respect the Chinese walls between economic sectors. Workers did not consider perks and fiddles in this light, considering them a customary part of their wages to which they were entitled. Here, popular ideas of fairness worked against control, as pilfering ensured that workers received a fair day's pay for a fair day's work. People outside these occupations did not always agree, seeing no difference between pilferage and petty theft.

EXPANDING THE REPERTOIRE

Gifting of coupons and controlled goods was the most common and most acceptable kind of grey market exchange, as it allowed people to maintain some semblance of inter-war gift-giving practices. As a landowner and farmer, the writer Naomi Mitchison was in the privileged position of being able to give fish, game, and home-grown produce as gifts to friends and neighbours throughout the year. Like many, the housewife Nella Last took pleasure in giving and receiving presents, but she did not enjoy Mitchison's privileges, and struggled to maintain a practice that she felt was under threat, birthdays and Christmases apart.

> There is so little to give nowadays. It often gives me a sadness. Somehow so much of the 'sweet' of life has passed. How can we teach children to be unselfish, to 'pass the sweeties', 'give a bite of their apple' or 'break a piece of cake off and give a bit to the

---

[66] PRO: CUST 49/4338, Notes of meeting, 7 March 1951.
[67] Betty Jones cited in Croall, *Don't You Know*, 86; Marina Moore cited in Steale, *Working Class War*, 66; M-OA, DR January 1948, DR 217.

poor doggie'? It used to be said of a greedy adolescent, 'Well, he was the only one and there was no one to share things with'. A generation is growing up who don't know what it is to have many little goodies themselves, and even tiny tots know the value of points and what is rationed.[68]

Last need not have worried. Shortages did not end the habit of taking a present when visiting other people, but it did change the type of thing offered as a gift. Cut flowers, chocolates, cakes, puddings, and alcoholic beverages gave way to more mundane items such as a lump of cheese, a few ounces of sugar, or a jar of dripping.[69]

Rationing had also created a new type of gift voucher in the form of the ration coupon, which soon found its place alongside Boots tokens, book tokens, and record tokens in the gift economy.[70] Couples setting up or moving house might receive a gift of coupons, while illness was often a spur for illegal dealing as friends and relatives tried to obtain 'health' foods to build up the patient. When a Pembrokeshire estate agent went into hospital with a duodenal ulcer, one of his local friends, a farmer, brought him eggs to eat. After his discharge, another local farmer with whom the estate agent was acquainted gave him three eggs. The farmer would not take any money for them, but the estate agent expected that he would have to give him some cigarettes in return.[71] With goods in short supply, civilians might give ration coupons as well as cash in lieu of a gift. Before a wedding, friends and family might present the couple with coupons, rations, or second-hand goods in addition to a wedding present. The couple could spend the clothing coupons on a bridal dress or a new suit, while gifts of food coupons and rations might be used to bake a cake or lay on a good spread at a wedding breakfast. Gifts of second-hand furniture meant that furniture dockets could go further.[72] Saving one's coupons or rations and presenting them as a birthday or Christmas gift was not an uncommon thing to do either.[73] Preparing for Christmas, which was stressful enough in peacetime, now became a trial. Housewives who received gifts from friends and acquaintances did not enquire too closely as to their provenance.[74] A social investigator noted that women received presents of sugar, tea, and margarine with rapture at Christmas—presents they would not have sent in peacetime.[75]

Barter was closely associated with gift-giving. Not only were the goods obtained from similar sources, but the parties to a swap were also known to one another.

---

[68] Nella Last diary, 1 March 1946, in Patricia Malcolmson and Robert Malcolmson (eds.), *Nella Last's Peace: The Post-war Diaries of Housewife 49* (London, 2008), 84–5.

[69] Last diary, 3 November 1945, 30 December 1945, in *Nella Last's Peace*, 39, 61.

[70] Boots introduced a gift token scheme *c.*1900. In November 1932, just in time for Christmas, the National Book Council introduced the book token. Picking up on the popularity of this trend, the subject of much social commentary, HMV introduced its record voucher seven years later.

[71] M-OA, DR January 1948, DR 274.

[72] Louise Purbrick, 'Wedding Presents: Marriage Gifts and the Limits of Consumption, Britain, 1945–2000', *Journal of Design History*, 16 (2003), 219; Chris Neale, *Cardboard Wedding Cakes: the Lives of the Ordinary People of Fife during the Second World War* (Kirkcaldy, 2005), 85.

[73] Mitchison diary, 25 December 1942, in Sheridan, *Among You Taking Notes*, 222.

[74] Nina Mansell, 'Peace on Earth', in Maria Hubert and Andrew Hubert (eds.), *A Wartime Christmas* (Stroud, 1995), 142–4; Mike Brown, *Christmas on the Home Front 1939–1945* (Stroud, 2004).

[75] M-OA, FR 1030, 'Christmas and New Year's Eve 1941', January 1942.

Fig. 2.1. 'The Housewife's Dream' market, Croydon, 9 August 1941. National Science and Society Picture Library.

Delayed barter of home-grown produce and handicrafts blurred the boundary between the gift and the swap further. There was one major difference between the gift and the swap: barter required people to agree upon the terms of trade. Establishing an exchange rate between different types of goods can be very time-consuming, but this did not hinder the mushroom-growth of barter networks. Barter was thriving in London and other urban areas from as early as 1941.[76] In Croydon, the Food Office even tolerated an open-air barter market. Local gardeners with a surfeit of fruit and vegetables could exchange their surplus for vouchers that entitled them to clothes, shoes, furniture, and other goods. It was popular with shoppers, 300 of whom descended on the makeshift stalls erected in a local store's car park (see Fig. 2.1).[77]

Inter-war experience of bartering and pawning goods made this overnight growth possible. In rural areas some retailers allowed farmers, crofters, and labourers to swap their produce for goods instead of paying cash or buying things on

---

[76] Anne Valery, *Talking about the War: A Personal View of the War in Britain* (London, 1991), 61–5.

[77] *The Observer*, 10 August 1941.

credit.[78] Barter was not unknown in urban areas either. Fish friers bartered with children, swapping free chips or cinema tickets for used newspapers.[79] Pawnbroking also meant that the poorest had a good idea of what the exchange value of goods was, and invested in them for this reason.[80] Although pawnbroking was of declining significance as hire purchase increased in popularity, it was still something which people understood until well into the second half of the century.[81] For the cash-rich with no experience of bartering or pawning goods, the ration coupon served as a ready measure of value.

An M-O investigator sketched the contours of this economic landscape in handwritten notes summarizing the findings of a series of interviews with middle-aged Londoners in spring 1947. The investigator's predominantly female interviewees recounted giving shop assistants and proprietors rationed goods in return for other rationed goods or goods in short supply. One fifty-year-old housewife gave sugar to her butcher in return for tins of corned beef, and cigarettes to shop assistants in the Co-op in return for under-the-counter goods. She initiated these relationships and kept a mental record of the terms of trade. Towards the end of each rationing period, when she had the opportunity to reregister with her food retailers or register with their local competitors, she reflected on whether what she had received in return for her rations matched her expectations. If it did not, she took her custom elsewhere. She had recently changed greengrocer for this reason, telling the M-O investigator that 'I was very good to her but she never kept things for me—like bananas or oranges'.[82]

Retailers and their employees acted as intermediaries in many barter networks, and were just as likely as the entrepreneurial housewife to initiate swaps. Another London housewife speaking to the M-O investigator in 1947 recalled an incident several months earlier when a new assistant at her butchers told her openly: 'If you look after me, I'll look after you.' After that she began to notice other customers slipping cigarettes into their ration books before handing them over to the assistant.[83] Anecdotal evidence from across urban Britain suggests that retailers played a central role in this barter economy. The testimony of one shop assistant working in a Hull store during the war is typical. She recalled poorer customers who could not afford to buy their full ration handing over their unused coupons in exchange for a little more of their official entitlement.[84]

---

[78] Margot C. Finn, *The Character of Credit: Personal Debt in English Culture, 1740–1914* (Cambridge, 2003), 77–8; Sam Mullins and David Stockdale, *Talking Shop: An Oral History of Retailing in the Harborough Area during the Twentieth Century* (Stroud, 1994), 19; P. Mathias, *Retailing Revolution* (Harlow, 1967), 47–8.

[79] John K. Walton, *Fish and Chips and the British Working Class, 1870–1940* (Leicester, 1992), 161.

[80] Paul Johnson, *Saving and Spending: The Working-Class Economy in Britain, 1870–1939* (Oxford, 1985), 177.

[81] David Vincent, *Poor Citizens: The State and the Poor in Twentieth Century Britain* (Harlow, 1991), 146.

[82] M-OA, TC Food 6E, D. H., 'Black Market and Barter', 12 May 1947.

[83] 'Black Market and Barter'.

[84] IWM, Sound Archive, tape ref. 11850/2, 'Interview with Irene Brewster', 1986.

The grey market encompassed monetary exchanges as well as gifting and barter-ing. Secret Home Intelligence reports drew attention to persistent grumbling about shopkeeper favouritism from 1941 onwards.[85] M-O had recorded similar feelings about under-the-counter trading in its file reports, noting that when questioned, one in five people accused shopkeepers of favouritism in August 1941, as opposed to one in eight six months earlier.[86] Reserving price-controlled goods for regular customers or letting them have a little extra of a rationed good coupon-free aroused feelings of anger and jealousy in those excluded from such deals. Unsurprisingly, shopkeepers and their valued customers had a more positive view of these 'paid favours', which were an expression of a shopkeeper's regard for a customer. A teacher told M-O how his 'garage sometimes lets me have two or four gallons coupon free at the usual price', while 'A grocer who has hens sells me eggs at the packing station price instead of sending all to the packing station'. The teacher was adamant that this was 'out of kindness because I live alone'.[87]

Like the paid favour, the practice of tipping shadowed the formal economy. Traditional recipients of tips such as taxi-drivers, waiters, porters, and deliverymen found that gratuities increased in size and frequency once the war began. At the same time, occupational groups who had previously eschewed tips began to receive them. According to a retired civil servant, shop assistants working in Leeds re-ceived tips ranging from 2s 6d to £1 if they put aside shoes for customers to collect when a new delivery arrived.[88] With tipping on the increase, tips in kind assumed greater significance, though cash tips continued to dominate. These trends alarmed the Bribery and Secret Commissions Prevention League, who had long held that a tip amounted to a secret commission or bribe.[89] That tipping was on the increase and tantamount to a bribe was well known by spring 1943. Backbenchers guf-fawed with laughter at the innocence of a fellow MP who, during a debate on ca-tering wages, told them: 'No one in a shop would ask me or expect me to give him a tip in order to get preferential service from behind the counter.' His fellow back-benchers admitted to tipping shop assistants in clothing shops, barbers, and por-ters, as well as waiters.[90] At around the same time the popular press, assuming its favoured role as people's tribune, exposed the abuse of tipping, prompting further parliamentary debate of the practice, while the Junior Minister of Food condemned the growing practice of tipping butchers and fishmongers.[91]

Paying for a meal in a club, hotel, or restaurant was another activity that lay on the boundary between grey and black markets. Not until 1942 did the government place any restrictions on eating out, which made it possible for the wealthy to

[85] See the Home Intel. weekly report in INF 1/292 at TNA: PRO.
[86] M-OA, FR 811, 'Ninth Weekly Report', 4 August 1941.
[87] M-OA, DR January 1948, DR 319.
[88] DR 201.
[89] Albert Crew, *The Law Relating to Secret Commissions and Bribes* (London, 1913), 103–7. See *News-Sheet of the Bribery and Secret Commissions Prevention League*, April 1939 and regularly through-out the war thereafter.
[90] HC deb, vol. 388, 31 March 1943, col. 222.
[91] HC deb, vol. 389, 13 May 1943, col. 824; HC deb, vol. 389, 27 May 1943, cols. 1729–30.

avoid the constraints of food rationing altogether. Due to widespread disapproval of this loophole, the MoF took steps to control the catering trade. Administrators decided not to ask caterers to collect coupons from diners, as calculating the coupon-value of the rationed ingredients per dish was too complex a task. Instead, the ministry decreed that a diner could buy no more than three courses, only one of which could be a main course, and that caterers could not charge more than 5*s* for the meal plus a cover charge of 6*d* in luxury establishments, and an extra half crown (2s 6*d*) if there was live music. Restrictions were also placed on the prices charged for drinks served with a meal.[92] The 'five-bob meal', which soon became the standard charge for a meal, continued until 1950.[93] In cahoots with restaurateurs and hoteliers, diners with deep pockets circumvented the new regulations easily. A meal might be cheap, but it became very expensive to check a hat or a coat, wine increased in price, and tips got bigger. Alternatively, the meal might be small, but diners would leave an establishment only to return to their table minutes later to order another meal.[94]

PULLING TOGETHER

Several things could restrict a person's ability to participate in grey markets—notably, time and money—but more important than these was that you had something which other people wanted. In a diary kept for M-O a middle-aged Glaswegian working in a shipping office noted proudly the continuation of a private arrangement to swap spare sugar for fruit. The terms of trade: eight eating apples for sugar left over from the weekly ration.[95] The importance of having something to exchange meant that allotment holders and gardeners with surplus produce were well placed to benefit from grey markets. Money, however, continued to matter. Wealthier rural residents—particularly those with friends and family in major urban areas—did very well out of this system.

The wartime letters of Virginia Potter, the young American wife of a Guards officer, documents the economy of gifting and bartering between the upper-middle-class residents of Datchet, Hampshire. Encouraged by the 'Dig for Victory' campaign and the romantic image of the cottager, Virginia saw it as her patriotic duty to turn the ornamental garden of the house she and her husband rented from Eton College into a kitchen garden. With the help of a cook, a land girl, and visiting friends, Virginia cultivated eighteen types of vegetable and five types of fruit, reared ducks, geese, hens, and rabbits, and participated in a pig club with her neighbours.

Virginia's household could not consume all the produce, so she would give away, barter, or sell any surplus. But this was not an *ad hoc* arrangement, as she

[92] British Library (BL), St Pancras, BBC Sound Archive, LP 44469 b02, Hugo Dunn-Meynell, 'The Five Bob Meal', 23 September 1982; Hammond, *Food*, i, 288–90; E. R. Chamberlain, *Life in Wartime Britain* (London, 1972), 82–3.

[93] *The Observer*, 2 May 1950.

[94] *The Times*, 27 June 1942; *Manchester Guardian*, 23 October 1942 and 20 July 1946.

[95] M-OA, War Diaries, Women, October 1941, D5390, 15 October 1941.

recorded her transactions in an account book and for a short time reared rabbits as collateral in barter exchange. With more leisure time and money than most in her community, Virginia was a major player in the local economy, her sales of produce bringing her £20 1s 0d during 1944, equivalent to £689.00 in 2010. Admittedly this was one of her best years; in 1943 she made £3 17s 3d. Her comparative advantage over others meant that she indulged in bartering to obtain luxuries, placing friends in her debt—which some had difficulty repaying. Few cottagers or crofters could have exchanged goose eggs for venison, as recorded in one of her letters from February 1944. She could also give away poultry, eggs, fruit, and vegetables in return for very scarce luxuries such as gin, port, tinned butter, and dates.[96]

Goods circulating in grey markets could, and did, change hands in several ways. The exchange circuit was not dictated by a good's symbolic value. Food, fuel, clothing, and the ration coupons that entitled someone to purchase some of them were not status goods. Contemporaries considered them necessaries, not luxuries, which was why there was widespread support for regulations restricting their price and distribution. Although a good's prestige did not determine how it circulated in a grey market, its physical characteristics might. Because of transport costs, bulky or perishable products were more likely to circulate locally. Naomi Mitchison attributed extensive grey marketing by her neighbours in Carradale to the fact that they were 'so far from a market', which meant that it was 'much simpler to sell to one another (for instance) than to a "recognized dealer"'.[97] Size and durability aside, the principal factor in determining how a good would circulate was the relationship between exchange partners and the recipient's ability to return the favour. A backyard poultry keeper might give his eggs to a friend or family member, barter them with neighbours who had a vegetable patch, or sell them at a reasonable price to neighbours with nothing to barter.

Within rural communities, pig-killing provides the clearest evidence of the social context to grey marketing. In nineteenth- and early twentieth-century England, killing the family pig was an annual social occasion and an opportunity to repay favours and debts incurred over the past year. Who deserved a portion of pork, which cut, and how much was the subject of much discussion before the arrival of the pig-sticker. Before 1940 the social significance of the pig had waned as pig-keeping declined,[98] but rationing reversed this trend. The number of families keeping a pig increased, pig clubs proliferated, and the pig regained some of its former social meaning. Having secured a MoF licence to slaughter a pig, the pig-keeper or pig club members decided how to apportion the meat. In this they were hindered by the terms of the licence, which specified whether some or all of the pig should be sold, and required that the remainder was consumed within the

[96] Brassley and Potter, 'A View from the Top', 223–42.

[97] M-OA, DR January 1948, DR 65.

[98] Robert Malcolmson and Stephanos Mastoris, *The English Pig: A History* (London, 1998), 116–20.

household or shared throughout the pig club. Giving away or selling any part of the carcass to people not named on the licence was an offence.[99]

Few pig-keepers stuck to the terms of a licence that prevented them from repaying their social obligations in bacon, pork, and offal. The pig-meat's renewed importance as an exchange good was reflected in the public outcry over the prosecution of a Lowestoft pig-keeper. The local Food Control Committee prosecuted the pig-keeper for giving small joints of pork to two relatives and a friend. The national press covered the case, the details of which incensed the Prime Minister, who thought it 'showed bureaucracy in its most pettifogging and tyrannical aspect, and could not see why a person licensed to kill a pig should not be allowed "to share it with friends"'.[100] The MoF bowed to critics of its policy towards self-suppliers of pigs, legalizing all gifts of bacon, pork, and offal while banning any sales.[101] Nevertheless, sales did take place—some receiving a joint at a preferential rate, while strangers paid a market price plus a black market premium.[102] Here lay the dividing line between the grey and black markets: the gift, the swap, and the paid favour on one side, and commodity exchange on the other.

Of these exchanges, the swap and the paid favour are the least studied. A short account of illegal dealing in the Essex village of Sheering brings out their unique features while illuminating the relationship between them. Sheering—on the east bank of the river Stort, 2½ miles to the north-east of Harlow—grew steadily in size throughout the austerity period, the population swelling from 973 in 1931 to 1,457 in 1961. Many of the new residents commuted to London by train, and it is thanks to one of these newcomers, a fifty-five-year-old university lecturer, that we have a detailed picture of the village's underground economy in 1948. The lecturer and his wife were pleasantly surprised to discover that their new home was 'remarkably free from "under the counter" selling', unlike their previous neighbourhood in Paddington, west London. As 'a country village where the majority of householders keep fowls or cultivate vegetable gardens' to augment their diets, there was limited demand for under-the-counter food. If he and his wife wanted extra potatoes or eggs, they could buy them from their neighbours.

These sales had the character of a paid favour. Vendors did not have to sell their garden produce and only chose to do so when local shopkeepers' stocks had run out, as they did not want to take custom from village shops. Local gardeners who sold fresh produce did not exploit their neighbours. Asking prices and selling prices were the same as, or usually lower than, those in the local shops. According to the lecturer, recipients of fruit and vegetables insisted that gardeners accept some payment, as they could not reciprocate.

> In some cases within my knowledge the practice began with gifts, out of pure kindness, to new comers; the new comers to the village, having nothing in the way of produce to give in return, refused to accept further gifts of this kind and [insisted] that

[99] Hammond, *Food*, iii, 727–36.   [100] Hammond, *Food*, iii, 732–3.

[101] *Manchester Guardian*, 12 June 1944.

[102] British Library (BL), National Sound Archive (NSA), cd ref. C900/01040 C1, 'Interview with Terry Huggins'.

the giver accept payment, the receivers in these cases being financially better off than the givers.

This brief account of the development of the paid favour in Sheering hints at a less worthy motive on the part of wealthy newcomers: their desire to avoid being in their poorer neighbours' debt—neighbours who they probably did not know well. To some extent motives were irrelevant as the effect of the transaction was the same: it created a weak tie between buyer and seller as the seller had not been paid in full. In Sheering at least the paid favour built and sustained community, bringing outsiders into local exchange networks. But, as the lecturer's account hints at, the social capital created in this way was not always desired by the individuals concerned.

The lecturer's experience of grey marketing appears to have been a typically rural one. Like him, a middle-aged housewife confessed to M-O that 'Living in the country I get certain things by barter and through kindness'.[103] Grey marketing followed a similar pattern in the West Country and East Anglia—both areas with a substantial number of kitchen gardens and smallholdings—and, in the case of the West Country, some of the most neighbourly of neighbours.[104] Villagers might suborn potential whistleblowers with a gift. By receiving gifts those with dubious loyalties compromised themselves. In one parish near Crediton, Devon, the locals ensured the complaisance of the village policeman with the occasional shoulder of pork.[105] This practice was not limited to the West Country. On Walney Island in Lancashire, when a farmer slaughtered a pig illicitly the local police absented themselves in return for a piece of pork.[106] Similar reasoning may have prompted the kindness that Sheering's established residents showed to newcomers.

Whatever the motivation, such acts inducted newcomers into local grey markets, which had grown out of older systems of exchange. Sociological studies of rural communities conducted during the late 1940s and 1950s recorded the importance of reciprocal exchange to upland farmers. Into the 1950s a hill farmer's success depended upon his neighbours' cooperation. Loaning agricultural equipment to a neighbouring farmer or helping him with sheep-clipping, threshing, and haymaking was commonplace.[107] Neighbourliness was less important in lowland and arable areas as farms were larger commercial enterprises with sufficient labour and machinery to work the land.[108] But arable farmers knew their neighbours were there if they needed them. Similar patterns of reciprocal exchange could be found within villages. As in Sheering, social distance shaped the practice of reciprocity. In

---

[103] M-OA, DR January 1948, DR 89.

[104] W. J. Turner, *Exmoor Village* (London, 1947), 64–6; First Report of the Departmental Committee of Inquiry into Statutory Smallholdings (PP 1965–6 Cmnd.2936 vii, 255); Geoffrey Gorer, *Exploring English Character* (London, 1955), 55.

[105] Sadie Ward, *War in the Countryside, 1939–45* (London, 1988), 78.

[106] Last diary, 25 January 1946, in Malcolmson and Malcolmson, *Nella Last's Peace*, 76.

[107] Alwyn D. Rees, *Life in a Welsh Countryside: A Social Study of Llanfihangel yng Ngwynfa* (1950; Cardiff, 1961), 91–100; T. Jones Hughes, 'Aberdaron: The Social Geography of a Small Region in the Llŷn Peninsula', in David Jenkins, Emrys Jones, T. Jones Hughes and Trefor M. Owen, *Welsh Rural Communities* (1960; 2nd edn., Cardiff, 1962), 159–63; Emmett, *North Wales Village*, 69–89.

[108] Alun Howkins, *The Death of Rural England: A Social History of the Countryside since 1900* (London, 2003), 171.

the Cumberland village of Gosforth, neighbourliness was more intense within the village where people lived closer together and saw more of one another than in the surrounding countryside where houses were more dispersed.[109]

Although contemporary studies gave no attention to paid favours within rural communities, monetary exchange was an important aspect of informal economic activity in upland and lowland areas before, during, and after the war. Farmers' wives earned 'pin money' by selling butter, chickens, and eggs. Like their employers' wives, rural labourers supplemented household income through pig-keeping, poultry-keeping, jam-making, and pickling. Of greater importance in the previous century, such enterprises flourished once more under austerity conditions.[110] The price that 'penny capitalists' charged for goods varied according to their relationship with their customers. Contemporary observers, who assumed that the profit motive drove all cash sales, missed the subtle difference between the paid favour and market exchange. When observing a paid favour, outsiders ascribed the low price to the vendor's lack of business acumen or education—a mistake replicated in studies of penny capitalism.[111]

The distinction, missed by outsiders, is readily apparent in participants' accounts of illegal dealing. When describing illegal cash purchases from neighbours, rural contributors to M-O emphasized the 'kindness' their neighbours had shown them and that their helpful neighbour was a 'friend'. A middle-aged wine merchant felt happy admitting that 'a farmer friend lets me have a few eggs', as did a municipal collector.[112] In stressing the occasional nature of these deals, the accounts underlined that such a sale was an act of courtesy—a favour.[113] Comparison made it clear that the profit motive was of limited importance compared to the paid favours that they received. Farmers making a profit from selling eggs and poultry to their neighbours or passing motorists were condemned. A farmer's wife felt that it was 'a great temptation' to herself and others like her 'to exploit the need of the townsman'—it went without saying that they did not exploit their rural neighbours.[114] A Berkshire poultry-farmer's wife who resisted this temptation did, however, make gifts of eggs and use them as tips locally.[115]

A similar relationship between non-monetary and monetary exchange in the countryside can be seen in towns and cities, despite differences between urban and rural grey markets. The neighbourliness, which underpinned the grey market, was not confined to the countryside, although people living in small communities were more likely to trust their neighbours to help them out in a crisis.[116] This was probably a reflection of the relative tightness of social networks in rural areas

---

[109] W. M. Williams, *The Sociology of an English Village: Gosforth* (1956; London, 1964), 140–54.

[110] Raphael Samuel, '"Quarry Roughs": Life and Labour in Headington Quarry, 1860–1920', in Raphael Samuel (ed.), *Miners, Quarrymen and Saltworkers* (London, 1977), 183–227; John Benson, *The Penny Capitalists: A Study of Nineteenth-Century Working-Class Entrepreneurs* (Dublin, 1983), 17–40; Malcolmson and Mastoris, *The English Pig*, 118–21; Nicola Verdon, '"...Subjects deserving of the Highest Praise": Farmers' Wives and the Farm Economy in England, c.1700–1850', *Agricultural History Review*, 51 (2003), 23–39; Joyce, 'The Black Economy', 245–54.

[111] M-OA, FR 2093, 'Report on a Somerset Village [Luccombe]', 11 May 1944.

[112] M-OA, DR January 1948: DRs 189 and 225.

[113] DR 202. [114] DR 20.

[115] DR 12. [116] Gallup, *Opinion Polls*, i, 177; Gorer, *Exploring English Character*, 55, on differences.

compared to those in urban ones. Nevertheless, dense and localized social networks similar to those in farming-centred communities could be found in working-class neighbourhoods. Members of these networks provided one another with practical help in times of financial hardship before the war.[117]

In working-class neighbourhoods, families adapted longstanding survival strategies to cope with the new problems that austerity threw up. The testimony of one south London family, the Moores, shows how the practice of mutuality expressed itself in grey marketing. Elizabeth Moore, who with her husband Stephen ran a small off-licence in Bell Green, exploited her social network to feed her family. When serving in the armed forces her sons sent food parcels home, as did her Canadian nephew. Another son worked at the local grocery, where one of the female assistants was keen on him. She tried to ingratiate herself with his mother by giving Elizabeth extra food. In addition to these gifts, Elizabeth exploited her access to scarce supplies of whisky to obtain extra food through barter. When a delivery of whisky arrived, she put some under the counter for the butcher in return for a joint. She also swapped whisky for tea with her youngest son's teacher. A friend of her eldest son who worked in a fishmonger's would also do the odd paid favour for Elizabeth, putting fresh fish aside for her when it came into the shop.[118]

Few working-class families had whisky to barter like the Moores. Some did have food from an allotment or pilfered goods to trade, but clothing coupons were the principal exchange good. Teaching unions criticized working-class mothers who used their children's clothing coupons in this way.[119] Women working as cleaners or taking in laundry found it easy to swap coupons with middle-class housewives, while factory workers could trade theirs with managers and co-workers.[120] Young women trading sex for goods from a PX (Post Exchange) or a quartermaster's depot was not unknown.[121] After the departure of the Americans, some took a keen interest in demobilized British servicemen, hoping to secure a few clothing coupons. The brazenness of such deals came as a shock for some servicemen.[122] In addition to having a ready supply of exchange goods, the Moores' position as shopkeepers meant they had large reserves of goodwill upon which to draw. Those with little or no local support appealed to others' charitable impulses to obtain a paid favour.[123]

---

[117] Joanna Bourke, *Working-Class Cultures in Britain 1890–1960: Gender, Class and Ethnicity* (London, 1994), 136–69; Avram Taylor, *Working Class Credit and Community since 1918* (Basingstoke, 2002), 13–45.

[118] Steale, *Working Class War*, 66.

[119] *The Times*, 16 September 1943 and 29 June 1944.

[120] Terrence Morris, *Crime and Criminal Justice since 1945* (Oxford, 1989), 18; Last diary, 20 April 1948, in Malcolmson and Malcolmson, *Nella Last's Peace*, 243.

[121] Norman Longmate, *The GIs: The Americans in Britain, 1942–1945* (London, 1975), 273; Juliet Gardiner, *Over Here: The GIs in Wartime Britain* (London, 1992), 113–15; David Reynolds, *Rich Relations: The American Occupation of Britain, 1942–1945* (London, 1995), 407–9; John Costello, *Love, Sex and War: Changing Values, 1939–45* (London, 1985), 311–22; Margaret Mead, *The American Troops and the British Community*.

[122] M-OA, DR January 1948, DR 170.

[123] IWM, Sound Archive, tape ref. 18295/3/1, Interview with Peter Lawrence, 'The Day War broke out', *West Country at War*, BBC Radio Bristol, 5 April 1999; Last diary, 9 January 1948, in Malcolmson and Malcolmson, *Nella Last's Peace*, 222. Harold Nicolson, 'Marginal Comment', *The Spectator*, 21 August 1942.

The ability of a working-class family to support itself through grey marketing was greatly helped by increased wartime mobility, which loosened working-class social networks, spreading them over larger distances.[124] Through their children, parents of evacuees forged links with people in reception areas, while adults 'trekking' to the countryside during the Blitz formed friendships with local people.[125] Young people working or stationed in distant parts extended the area that a family's social network covered and increased the number of people with which members of the network came into contact. This increased the chance of getting hold of goods in short supply. The result: a thriving traffic in eggs developed in the Scottish highlands and islands as the large numbers of servicemen stationed there sent eggs to their families in the south.[126] After the war, British conscripts serving in occupied Austria and Germany spread the net wider still. The cameras, watches, fountain pens, cutlery, and glassware that troops bought with cigarettes and shipped home to their families could be readily bartered, pawned, or sold. Some encouraged the traffic by sending cigarettes to friends and relatives stationed in Germany and Austria.[127]

Outside of the austerity period, mutual aid was less important in middle-class neighbourhoods as, with the exception of young parents, their more affluent residents did not need to rely upon each other for practical help. Here more diffuse social networks were the norm, and being a good neighbour meant taking in messages or parcels if there was nobody in next door.[128] Residents' families and friends were much less likely to live nearby—a tendency that became more marked the higher a person's income.[129] A post-war study of Banbury revealed that middle-class residents spent as much time, if not more, socializing with friends made at work or through membership of local churches, clubs, and societies than with their next-door neighbours—a pattern repeated elsewhere.[130] Austerity only changed these social networks temporarily as they found themselves drawn into grey marketing.

During austerity, mutual aid became a regular feature of middle-class social networks, strengthening ties between friends and neighbours. Higher taxation had eroded middle-class purchasing power, while rationing and price control placed

---

[124] E. C. Willatts and Marion G. C. Newson, 'The Geographical Pattern of Population Changes in England and Wales, 1921–1951', *Geographical Journal*, 119 (1953), 449–50.

[125] Dennis Briggs cited in Croall, *Don't You Know*, 53–4.

[126] Hammond, *Food*, ii, 93–4.

[127] See HC deb, vol. 423, 20 May 1946, cols. 33–4; and HC deb, vol. 433, 18 February 1947, cols. 1031–86; IWM, Sound Archive, tape ref. 20331/5/4, 'Interview with John Perkins', 22 May 2000 [Berlin]; IWM, Sound Archive, tape ref. 11035/6/6, 'Interview with John Brown', 14 November 1989 [Vienna]; IWM, Sound Archive, tape ref. 10166/30/29, 'Interview with Thomas Myers', 1988 [Berlin]; 'Loot Alley', *Picture Post*, 13 October 1945; Last diary, 13 September 1945, in Malcolmson and Malcolmson, *Nella Last's Peace*, 19.

[128] Gallup, *Opinion Polls*, i, 177; Gorer, *Exploring English Character*, 55.

[129] Gallup, *Opinion Polls*, i, 177; Elizabeth Bott, *Family and Social Network: Roles, Norms, and External Relationships in Ordinary Urban Families* (2nd edn., London, 1971), 52–96.

[130] Margaret Stacey, *Tradition and Change: A Study of Banbury* (Oxford, 1960), 101–15; Bott, *Family and Social Network*, 73–89; Peter Willmott and Michael Young, *Family and Class in a London Suburb* (1960; London, 1967), 96.

limits on what money could buy.[131] This prompted the members of the middle class to turn to friends and neighbours for help in obtaining a few home comforts and maintaining a semblance of their pre-war lifestyles. Outsiders—who felt excluded from these networks because of their social status or who chose not to exploit them because of religious or political beliefs—were highly critical of mutual aid, branding it 'black market'. Voluntary associations received most criticism from these outsiders—especially organizations that brought male professionals and businessmen together, such as Masonic lodges, Rotary clubs, churches, and Conservative clubs.[132] While these denunciations smack of jealousy and exaggeration, they had some justification. Members of such associations shared information and would help one another on occasion.[133] A secretary working in the London office of an American insurance firm provided a rare glimpse inside a city club, recording a lively debate between members about the rights and wrongs of black market dealing. Most admitted that they 'fiddled', while she maintained 'the rabidly unpopular position of stating [that I am] satisfied without having to fiddle'. As a consequence, work colleagues avoided discussing their fiddles in her presence, or talked in whispers.[134]

By focusing their attacks on formal sociability, especially between men, outside observers obscured the pivotal role that middle-class women played in grey markets. In her M-O diaries the middle-aged housewife Nella Last records how she and her friends struggled to maintain a middle-class lifestyle in Barrow throughout the 1940s. Her diaries show how they utilized personal connections to make their families' lives more comfortable. Christmas-card relations and members of the immediate family who had moved away from home came to their aid. Last bottled apples that her daughter-in-law posted from Northern Ireland, accepted pears from her aunt who lived in Barrow, obtained eggs from her friend Mrs Whittam, whom she had met through the Women's Voluntary Service (WVS), and got her unmarried son to post her his spare clothing coupons from London.[135] Whittam drew upon her network in a similar way: a daughter in America sent parcels of food and clothing.[136] Last gave as well as received gifts, saving food and tobacco which she put in a 'lucky bag' and took to her elderly aunt and uncle, who lived in a nearby village.[137]

Last was more circumspect in her dealings with her neighbours and acquaintances than with close friends and family. Although she did not borrow things from

[131] Penny Summerfield, 'The "Levelling of Class"', in H. L. Smith (ed.), *War and Social Change: British Society in the Second World War* (Manchester, 1986), 179–207; Roy Lewis and Angus Maude, *The English Middle Classes* (London, 1949), 203–17.

[132] M-OA, DR January 1948: DRs 175, 23, 169, and 308. Alan Bennett, son of a south Leeds butcher, satirizes such networks in the film *A Private Function*, directed by Malcolm Mowbray (HandMade Films, 1984).

[133] Mullins and Stockdale, *Talking Shop*, 65–6.

[134] M-OA, DR January 1948, DR 61.

[135] Last's diary, 4 October 1945, 3 November 1945, 19 February 1946, 5 November 1946, in Malcolmson and Malcolmson, *Nella Last's Peace*, 29, 39, 82, 131.

[136] *Nella Last's Peace*, 15 October 1947, 186.

[137] *Nella Last's Peace*, 3 November 1945, 39.

her neighbours, she felt obliged to lend things to them.[138] She did, however, swap bottled fruit for food points with the woman who cleaned the WVS canteen.[139] She also acted as an intermediary when her WVS friends swapped second-hand clothes for clothing coupons with her home help.[140] As a good customer with money to spare, a former Tory activist, and a charity worker, local traders offered her 'extras' on occasion. Although Last boycotted one greengrocer's shop because of the 'furtive passing of bags', she readily accepted the offer of an extra 3 lbs of oranges from her greengrocer at Christmas.[141] That Christmas, she also accepted two other offers of under-the-counter goods from the managers of a wine merchant's and a jeweller's. Last thought that gratitude for her work at the Red Cross charity shop lay behind these gestures.[142] Such paid favours were not, however, limited to the Christmas season, and she accepted under-the-counter goods whenever she was offered them. Last had no qualms about accepting free fish heads from the fishmonger, whom she considered a 'nasty wretch' and 'a bitch of a woman'.[143]

Whether townsman or countryman, working class or middle class, man or woman, grey marketing was rife. The categories in which individuals fell shaped the opportunities that they had for grey or black marketing. But the single most important factor in determining exchange relationships was social distance. Gifting was limited to family and friends, while barter and paid favours were limited to colleagues, neighbours, acquaintances, and regular customers. As social distance between exchange partners increased, the type of exchange became more impersonal and less reputable. Tipping, which many considered 'bribery', lay on the boundary between grey and black marketing. Like other grey market exchange types, tipping was socially embedded. Tips were rarely a one-off occurrence, as people shopped in the same stores and ate in the same restaurants. In the context of an ongoing relationship, a tip, which might be offered as an inducement or a reward, ensured that a shopper or a diner received special treatment. But the feeling that a tip was a thinly disguised payment was not the only reason for its uncertain status. While there was a popular perception that mutual regard inspired most gifts, swaps, and paid favours, the tip was seen by many as an expression of social inequality. People tipped their social inferiors. Together these concerns explain the moral ambiguity of the tip and underscore the importance of social relationships in determining what type of exchange would take place.

Can the 'economic way of thinking' explain this pattern of seemingly morally acceptable non-compliance? The centrality of gift-exchange to the 'Grey Market' suggests that it had more in common with a pre-modern gift economy founded on reciprocity than a modern market economy based on a price system. There seems little or no place for economic considerations. Such deals were about satisfying

---

[138] *Nella Last's Peace*, 6 January 1947, 143–4, and 28 October 1947, 194.
[139] *Nella Last's Peace*, 11 December 1945, 48.
[140] *Nella Last's Peace*, 20 April 1948, 243.
[141] *Nella Last's Peace*, 7 September 1945, 10, and 11 December 1945, 48.
[142] *Nella Last's Peace*, 15 December 1945, 54.
[143] *Nella Last's Peace*, 13 September 1945, 19.

needs, seeking comfort, or winning the regard of others, not securing material gain. Nevertheless, rational choice can explain, at least in part, the marked preference for grey market dealings that involved gifting, swapping, and mutual trading over black market dealings for profit.

The idea of the transaction cost is the key to such an explanation. Making a black market deal might be too costly. It took time for buyers and sellers to find one another and negotiate a price for unwanted or pilfered goods and coupons. Unable to conduct business openly for fear of being caught, it was hard to find information about the underground economy. By the time a deal had been struck, the goods might have perished or the coupons expired. Enforcing contract was a problem too. And then there was the cost of being caught. In the circumstances, grey market dealing with people known to you was less costly and more worthwhile than black market dealing—it was the rational thing to do. Grey marketing was a low-risk activity with a small but guaranteed reward, as you were unlikely to be caught and assured of getting something rather than nothing for your unmarketed surplus.

There was also a good business case for grey marketing by retailers. Contrary to contemporary belief, shortages of consumer goods did not see the straightforward replacement of pre-war buyers' markets by sellers' markets.[144] Thanks to government control schemes maintaining an element of choice in where you shopped, the consumer was not reduced to the role of supplicant. Offering a little extra from under the counter promoted customer loyalty and attracted new customers. It was also a good way to shift unwanted stock on which customers would be reluctant to spend money or points. Shopkeepers cherished customers who could afford the occasional price-controlled luxury. Fishmongers, greengrocers, and wine merchants pressed such extras on middle-class housewives such as Nella Last.[145] Even food retailers who received an allocation of rationed goods on the basis of the number of customers registered with them had to persuade their existing clientele to re-register every six months. They also had the opportunity to increase turnover through new registrations. A reputation for 'seeing your regulars right' helped to persuade customers to switch registration.

The fact that grey market exchange was morally acceptable made it possible for some traders to think about gifts, swaps, and paid favours in an instrumental fashion. This was not true of black market dealings that conflicted with social norms, which not only helps to explain why such dealings were less frequent but also suggests that rational calculation played a small but important role in what was otherwise a form of moral economy. Of course, would-be manipulators of the grey market had to behave consistently, acting as if they shared the values of other participants. Like those who accepted Pascal's wager, the would-be manipulators might even come to share the values that gave rise to the grey market. Whether or not they did so, identifying the fakers is nigh on impossible.

[144] Lewis and Maude, *Middle Classes*, 188–92, 197–8; J. B. Jefferys, *Retail Trading in Britain, 1850–1950* (Cambridge, 1954), 105–9.
[145] Last diary, 7 and 13 September, and 11 and 31 December 1945, in Malcolmson and Malcolmson, *Nella Last's Peace*, 11, 19, 48, 62.

Free of the moral stigma attached to black marketing, grey marketing involved a wide cross-section of Britons, all of whom participated in official markets too. When transferring goods or coupons, the participants in grey market deals might use monetary or non-monetary forms of exchange. Gifting and barter predominated, but credit and some types of monetary exchange such as the paid favour and the tip were also important. The gift and barter networks central to grey marketing did not run in parallel to official supply chains, as gifting and bartering were not part of the formal economy. Little was known about such networks, and no serious attempt was made to control them, as administrators suspected it would be more trouble than it was worth. More was known about grey market deals involving cash payments, as these 'paid favours' resembled the for-profit transactions of the formal economy and shadowed official distribution channels. And yet policymakers chose to exempt penny capitalists from detailed control and tolerated distributors' generous allowances. Their reasoning remained the same: strict control was not worth the effort.

3

Beating the ration: the 'Black Market'

'There are big men at the back of the Black Market; there is a big distributive organization; there is a big warehousing organization; there is a highly effective intelligence service.' At least that was what the leader writer for the country magazine
The Field thought in March 1941. The writer inferred that a British version of
America's Crime Inc must exist from the amount of food stolen as 'You cannot
store 40,000 eggs nor 5 tons of meat on the kitchen shelves. And these quantities
are not easy to distribute.'[1] This was the 'Black Market' of newspaper exposés, but
the profitable rackets run by criminal gangs represented a small part of a much
larger illegal underground economy. The 'Black Market' of large-scale organized
theft had little to do with the illicit retail markets that shadowed their legal counterparts and through which the bulk of black market goods flowed. As one Minister of Food put it, it was 'the traders and dealers in the black market who must be
watched because these are the people who deal in quantities of scarce foods large
enough to affect supplies to the public'.[2] His inspectors focused on rogue trading
and ration fraud, both systemic threats, while the police tackled the less serious but
higher-profile threat posed by criminal enterprises.

Enforcement generated vast quantities of information about black marketeering, much of which went uncollated and unanalysed. The official historian Richard
Hammond, who perused enforcement files before they were weeded and archived,
concluded that the record was 'so voluminous and so amorphous as to defy the
effort to extract a coherent story from it'.[3] Conceptual confusion made it even
harder for headquarters staff to make sense of the information contained in the
files. The term 'black market', which *The Field* and others associated with a criminal underworld, infected official discussion of evasion. Enforcement officers labelled evasion by suppliers as 'black market' in order to distinguish it from the
petty offences committed by consumers. In their hands, 'black market' had more
in common with the legal concept of a felony than it did with the economic idea
of an illegal market. Without this sense of a black market as an illegal arena embracing all offences that involved the exchange of a well-defined commodity between buyers and sellers, inspectors could not fully understand the information
they collected. Their black market was not a market in any meaningful sense, as it
consisted of isolated examples of rogue trading and criminal enterprise by suppliers.

[1] 'The Black Market', *The Field*, 14 March 1941.
[2] TNA: PRO, CAB 129/53, C (52) 215, Gwilym Lloyd-George, 'Enforcement of Food Controls',
26 June 1952.
[3] Hammond, *Food*, iii, xi.

Nevertheless, officials formed impressions about the black market, which they summarized in secret reports and internal histories.

Working from these files, Ina Zweiniger-Bargielowska describes a 'black market in foodstuffs centred on unlawful supply of food stolen in transit, illicit slaughter, and home production, as well as sale without coupons', while 'the actual trade in coupons, reuse of coupons, and forgery were prevalent with regard to clothes as well as petrol'.[4] Sixteen years earlier, Edward Smithies, who could not read what were then classified files, came to a similar view after studying court reports in the local press. Smithies concluded that theft, pilfering, and illicit production were the main sources of black market goods. Smuggling, a post-war phenomenon, was a minor source. His case studies of Birkenhead, Barnsley, Walsall, Brighton, and north London show that overcharging, imposing conditions of sale, and coupon-free sales were rife, while illicit manufacturing fed local markets in luxuries and home comforts such as cosmetics and toys.[5]

Like enforcement officers' accounts, these histories describe how people evaded the regulations, not how illegal markets functioned. They say little about the workings of illicit retail markets and supply networks, their relationship with one another, and with legitimate economic activity. Who did what, when, and why remains unclear. At the same time the image of local retail markets and regional or national supply networks under the control of a handful of a criminal business enterprises run by one man, a board, a ring, or a gang continues to distort discussion of the underground economy.[6] Although some black market operations involving stolen and counterfeit commodities and coupons came close to fitting this trope, local black markets were fragmented, not hierarchical. As a consequence, dealers, customers, and enforcement officers did not possess an overarching vision of black markets and their supply networks. Instead of detailing the weaknesses in individual control schemes, what follows describes the operation of local black markets and the networks that supplied them.

OFF THE BACK OF A LORRY

The 'Black Market' had little to do with the 'Grey Market' of gifting, swapping, and petty trading with which readers of *The Field* were most likely to have come into contact. The boundary between the two was not always clear, as the same things changed hands whatever an illicit deal's shade. The sources of supply were similar, including theft, and both markets involved monetary exchange. Despite these shared characteristics contemporaries felt there was a meaningful distinction. At issue was participants' motivation. Contemporaries thought greed drove black market deals, while considerations of material gain were of little or no importance in grey marketing. A cash deal was a paid favour if no profit was taken or the profit

---

[4] Zweiniger-Bargielowska, *Austerity*, 155.
[5] Smithies, *Crime in Wartime*; Smithies, *Black Economy*.
[6] Thomas, *Underworld at War*.

was reasonable, but paying a premium price signalled 'black market'. This is reflected in the way consumers differentiated between 'legal' and 'illegal' black market prices. In London during May 1947 'the "legal" Black Market price' for a dozen eggs stood at 6s. Anything above that was 'illegal', as it smacked of profiteering.[7] It was the market relationship between exchange partners and not the exchange of money that was the defining characteristic of a black market deal. This meant that there was considerable overlap between under-the-counter favouritism and under-the-counter trading, which helped dealers and customers disguise their motives from themselves and others. Need replaced greed and expenses replaced profits in personal accounts of black market deals, which turned a trade into a paid favour.

Unlike legitimate businesses for which under-the-counter trading was a profitable sideline, there was no difficulty in identifying the activities of criminal enterprises as black market. Criminal entrepreneurs made their living through selling illegal goods and services, diversifying into black markets during austerity, with legitimate businesses serving as a front for their activities. Ration fraudsters occupied a black market niche of equal significance to those taken by criminal diversifiers and business sideliners. Most, but not all, fraud was individual and unorganized. There were numerous ways in which ration fraudsters and others could evade the regulations as loopholes riddled the control schemes. The characteristics of the product, the person, and the place determined which loopholes a would-be black marketeer could exploit. These opportunity structures shaped the supply and distribution of black market goods.

Of the three types of supplier, criminal entrepreneurs attracted the most attention, while business sideliners had the greatest economic impact and ration fraudsters proved to be the most numerous. Judging by the available enforcement statistics, legitimate businesses—especially those involved in retailing—dominated the underground economy. Career criminals and ration fraudsters accounted for a minority of offences, though a single coup by a well-organized gang of thieves or forgers could pose a serious challenge to control.[8] Contrary to contemporary beliefs, Allied troops played little part in supplying black market goods. Stories of aerial and maritime smuggling, thefts of military stores, and canteen fiddles captured the public imagination but amounted to little. In stark contrast, Allied troops were a major source of black market goods in liberated Europe. Exchanging their illegal earnings into dollars or pounds blew apart official budgets for troops' foreign exchange dealings on both sides of the Atlantic. This was not a problem for commanders of American and Canadian forces in the UK, which confirms their troops' limited involvement in Britain's underground economy.[9] Troops' experiences of black marketeering overseas had little impact on their behaviour at home, with most demobbed servicemen observing the regulations on their return to the UK.

[7] M-OA, TC Food 6E, D. H., 'Black Market and Barter', 2 May 1947.
[8] Zweiniger-Bargielowska, *Austerity*, 165–6; Evasions of Petrol Rationing, 23.
[9] Walter Rundell Jr, *Black Market Money: The Collapse of US Military Currency Control in World War II* (Baton Rouge, LA, 1964), 10, 20.

Firms engaged in the under-the-counter trade—the type of suppliers who posed the biggest threat to control—were more likely to be small businesses than medium and large sized firms. For a small enterprise, illicit trade was a profitable sideline that could subsidize a struggling business. The policy of limiting civilian consumption meant suppliers and distributors of consumer goods saw turnover plummet. Unable to offset this decline through price increases, businesses faced falling profits if they could not cut costs or cross-subsidize controlled product lines. Small independent retailers were the most vulnerable. A department store could cut overheads by reducing floor space, while a chain store could cross-subsidize or close failing branches. These were not options for independents. Few stocked uncontrolled products that could cross-subsidize controlled lines. Restrictions on supplies meant diversification into substitutes or unrelated products was not possible either. Government controls also ruled out relocating to more affluent or more populous areas.

The plight of small shopkeepers aroused public sympathy. The government did little to ease the situation, although the BoT appointed a Retail Trade Committee to investigate the problems facing traders. The problems facing independent retailers were documented by the committee, according to which a fifth of shops in Glasgow and Leeds closed between January 1940 and December 1941 due to the harsh economic climate. Smaller shops were most severely affected. In Leeds, 25% of small single-unit shops had closed compared to 13% of medium single-unit shops and small and medium branches, and 11% of large shops. Non-food shops were more affected than were food shops. In Leeds, 24% of non-food shops had closed compared to 14% of food shops.[10]

Small garage owners were subject to similar pressures.[11] Through 1939 and 1940 civilian consumption of petrol fell by 23%, as did sales of lubricating oil and demand for repairs and servicing.[12] Garage owners had to contend with conscription too, and the MoL did not exempt mechanics and pump attendants from national service. In fact, the armed forces were keen to recruit trained mechanics to service growing fleets of vehicles and aircraft. Larger garages and dealerships coped with these problems by diversifying their businesses. Some assembled military vehicles imported from North America, while others won government contracts to repair and service military vehicles.[13] This was not an option for most garages. Many closed, with the number of filling stations falling from 35,200 in 1938 to 29,600 in 1946.[14]

Most retailers—garage owners included—clung onto their failing businesses as long as possible. Researchers working for M-O interviewed four hundred London shopkeepers between February and April 1941. Despite experiencing severe financial

---

[10] Charles Madge, 'War and the Small Retail Shop', *Bulletin of the Oxford Institute of Statistics*, 4 (1942), Supplement, 2, 1; Jefferys, *Retail Trading*, 101–9.

[11] Levy, *Shops of Britain*, 99–104.

[12] Calculated from figures in Gilbert Jenkins, *Oil Economists' Handbook*, 2 vols. (5th edn., London, 1989), Table 7.39, 196–7.

[13] Charles Graves, *Drive for Freedom* (London, 1945), 86–91.

[14] Ministry of Transport (MoT), *Petrol Stations: Report of the Technical Committee* (London, 1949), 10.

difficulties, the majority of retailers interviewed were not considering closing their shops. According to the author of the report:

> The effort involved in establishing and running the shop, and especially among elder people, the strong consequent feeling of possession and of inability to find any other place in a wartime economy, strains their patriotism. This patriotism still outweighs anxieties and resentments, but the balance is not heavy. It would take a great deal less to make retailers turn against the war than to make other people to do so.[15]

Garage-owners, like small independent shopkeepers, enjoyed being self-employed. They rated their independence highly and were reluctant to relinquish it.[16]

As a consequence, black market dealing was very tempting for independent traders such as local garage owners. The financial rewards of illicit dealing in petrol were substantial. In 1947 the dealer's margin on a gallon of petrol retailing at 2s 1d was 3½d—14%. This paled in comparison to the margin on black market petrol. In Eltham, south London, motorists paid a black market premium of between 1s and 4s per gallon. This was the price they paid for a one-unit coupon covering the sale. It meant that the dealer's margin on a gallon of black market petrol was between 1s 3½d—62%—and 4s 3½d—206%.[17] Forty miles outside London, motorists paid 4s for a gallon of black market petrol, a margin of 2s 2½d—106%.[18] This appears to have been the national standard at the end of 1947.[19] That year the average throughput of a petrol station on a minor road was 23,300 gallons. This meant that in 1947 the honest dealer had a turnover of £2,427 1s 8d and a gross profit of £339 15s 10d on petrol sales. Selling 1% of the annual throughput at the black market price of 4s a gallon increased gross profit by £22 6s 7d. Gross profit increased by £111 12s 11d—a third—if a dealer sold 5% of throughput at the black market price.[20]

Illicit profits of this magnitude could easily turn a struggling garage into a successful business, while the small amounts of petrol involved minimized the risk of being caught. In fact the 1% allowance for evaporation loss meant that the careful retailer could sell 1% of petrol on the black market risk free. As the extra money helped to maintain owners' pre-war lifestyles, there was no sudden change in behaviour to attract attention. Fiddling on the margins allowed garage owners and other small independent retailers to maintain a reasonable profit at low risk. Such satisficing behaviour was the norm in the pre-war motor trade and retailing more generally,[21] and petrol rationing did not alter this behaviour. The underdevelopment of the petrol black market bears this out. The most accurate estimate suggests that only 12.6% of civilian petrol passed through the black market.

[15] M-OA, FR 561, 'The Small Shopkeeper', 18 April 1941.
[16] Mullins and Stockdale, *Talking Shop*, 79.
[17] M-OA, DR January 1948, DR 236.
[18] DR 227.
[19] See DR 296 and DR 319.
[20] MoT, *Petrol Stations*, 14.
[21] Simon Phillips and Andrew Alexander, 'An Efficient Pursuit? Independent Shopkeeping in 1930s Britain', *Enterprise and Society*, 6 (2005), 278–304.

While public discussion focused on the plight of the independent retailer, wholesalers and producers faced similar economic challenges that increased the appeal of illicit trading. Reports and rumours about conditional sales and speculative dealings at wholesale fruit and vegetable markets fed the initial moral panic about evasion in spring 1941. Journalists and cartoonists likened wholesalers to the 'wicked, quaint fruit-merchant men' in Christina Rossetti's poem 'The Goblin Market', while Richmal Crompton wrote a *Just William* story about William's attempt to corner the local market in firewood.[22] Retailers encouraged disgruntled customers to blame wholesalers for overcharging and conditional sales, arguing that they had to recoup the black market premiums paid to wholesalers in order to remain solvent.[23]

Once control ended, government admitted that evasion by wholesalers had proved troublesome. In 1957, three years after food rationing ended, an official report into marketing of horticultural produce dismissed public concerns about speculators cornering wholesale markets, but it did admit that sharp practice had been a problem since at least the 1920s. Salesmen did not always pass growers the full amount received from the sale of their produce, or inflated their costs. Cash sales and low accounting standards had made it easy for wholesalers to disguise such tricks. Despite legislation that gave growers the right to inspect their wholesalers' books, the smaller producers dare not exercise this right for fear of being blacklisted by all the wholesalers in their local market.[24] Wartime and post-war shortages shifted the balance of power slightly as wholesalers took care not to offend growers by keeping their fiddles within reasonable bounds.

Primary wholesalers made no attempt to keep their customers happy, squeezing secondary wholesalers and retailers hard. The conviction of United Kosher Poulterers Ltd, its directors, and its secretary for overcharging customers in spring 1941 revealed the problems facing firms that sold price-controlled goods. Formed by a merger of all but one of London's wholesale kosher poulterers in 1934, the firm scoured the provinces for poultry, paying whatever price poultry farmers demanded for their birds at country sales. They processed all such purchases at their depot in Stepney before selling them to Jews and non-Jews at the maximum price plus 4d per pound if shechita and a further 1d per pound for delivery. According to a senior enforcement officer 'this was most extortionate, for this 1d per pound was charged even when the birds were fetched from the premises of the wholesalers, and was charged even to regular retailers who had dealt with the wholesalers for years and who collected the purchases they had made'. 'A further practice of the wholesalers was to sell boiling fowls as roasters—a transaction which meant they were selling a cheaper commodity for the price of a dearer one.'[25]

---

[22] Charles Esam-Carter, 'Goblin Market', *New Statesman and Nation*, 21 (31 May 1941); 'Goblin Market', *Punch*; Richmal Crompton, 'William makes a Corner', in Crompton, *William does His Bit* (1941; London, 1988), 111–12.

[23] TNA: PRO INF 1/292 Pt. 1, 'Home Intel. weekly report no. 38', 18–25 June 1941.

[24] Report of the Committee on Horticultural Marketing (PP 1956–7 Cmnd.61 xiv, 241), 115–20.

[25] London Metropolitan Archives (LMA), Clerkenwell, ACC/3121/E3/27/2, 'Interview with divisional food officer', 21 March 1941.

Giving short weight, adulteration, and imposing conditions of sale were wheezes as common as overcharging, disguised or otherwise, or selling poor-quality goods at high-end prices. Conditional sales were the most common. As early as January, intelligence reports from London noted: 'There are complaints of an imposition which wholesalers are said to be forcing on retailers, "who can only buy onions by arranging to take supplies of other goods which he cannot sell".'[26] Two years later the government continued to receive secret reports of retailers imposing conditions of sale. Housewives complained that they were obliged to buy lettuces and peas to obtain fruit or tomatoes. Retailers defended this practice, saying that they were forced to make conditional sales to maintain their margins, as wholesalers only sold them the produce conditional on buying other produce.[27] In some cases this was a 'good' reason rather than a 'real' reason for dishonesty. Nevertheless, retail trade associations felt they had reasonable grounds for complaint, lobbying government to tackle the issue on several occasions.

Like the legitimate enterprises of the formal economy, the illegitimate businesses of the underground economy mobilized for war. Criminal entrepreneurs became the principal suppliers of stolen or counterfeit goods and coupons. In response to excess demand for controlled goods, thieves targeted shops, factories, warehouses, freight yards, and lorry parks where they might find cloth, clothing, food, petrol, or tobacco. In rural areas poachers and rustlers stole livestock, poultry, fish, and game. Increased security made little difference. Due to the labour shortage, businesses could not be too discriminating about who they employed. This made it easier for career criminals to obtain work as drivers or a night watchmen, or find an insider willing to help them. Unsurprisingly, there was an increase in shop breaking, warehouse breaking, and thefts of goods in transit. The Commissioner of the Metropolitan Police Sir Philip Game drew attention to the problem in his annual report for 1944, noting that 'Experience shows how quickly the contents of a stolen lorry can be disposed of and the lorry abandoned empty in a side street'.[28] His successor Sir Harold Scott returned to the subject of theft and receiving of stolen goods regularly throughout the 1940s. Indeed, this was the decade in which the phrase 'Did it drop off a lorry?' entered the vernacular—'a graceful, delicate way of asking "Was it stolen?"' according to the lexicographer Eric Partridge.[29]

Lorry hijacking and thefts from unattended lorries caused great concern to ministry inspectors, as it involved well-organized gangs targeting road transport. Working closely with the authorities, firms increased security. In London and the Home Counties the police increased mobile patrols and implemented a convoy system for valuable loads. Employers forbade drivers from travelling alone. Lorries and vans were not to be left unattended and unlocked. When parked, drivers had to immobilize their vehicles by removing the rotor contact from the distributor or locking the steering wheel. Vehicles could stop only at designated lorry parks en route to

[26] TNA: PRO, INF 1/292 Pt. 1, 'Home Intel. weekly report No. 14', 1–8 January 1941.
[27] TNA: PRO, INF 1/292 Pt. 3, Home Intel. weekly report No. 144, 29 June–6 July 1943.
[28] Report of the Commissioner of Police of the Metropolis for the Year 1944, 6.
[29] Partridge and Beale, *Dictionary of Catch Phrases*, 93.

their destination. Yet these precautions could be overcome with ease if thieves colluded with drivers and their mates.[30] Pubs, greasy spoons, transport cafés, truck stops, and lorry parks were excellent meeting places—something the reporter Arthur Helliwell made much of in his newspaper column detailing the habits and exploits of London's spivs. In north London the Black Bess Café on East Finchley's High Road, and the truck stop at Bignell's Corner—the first service area on the A1 after leaving London—came to be known as places to buy and sell black market goods.[31] In Westmorland the Jungle Café just off the A6 garnered a similar reputation.[32]

In 1949 the Road Haulage Executive investigated the problem. As part of their investigation, officials compiled figures for thefts from vehicles owned by the newly nationalized haulage firm Carter Paterson that operated from its London depots. The value of the insurance claims ranged from £1 8s 7d for a parcel of bedding to £704 7s 10d for 7 tons of tobacco. The biggest thefts involved tobacco, with cigarettes and clothing a distant second and third respectively. Most of the thefts took place in central London, close to the depots, or on the main arteries leading to the western side of the city. Although an occasional load disappeared on Shooter's Hill, these latter-day highwaymen were more likely to be found in the inner London boroughs of Shoreditch, Southwark, and Stepney, close to freight yards, warehouses, depots, wharves, and docks, and the outer London boroughs straddling the main roads heading westwards out of the capital (see Fig. 3.1). A second national study, which the executive conducted during the first three months of 1952, revealed that forty-one of the sixty-one lorries stolen that quarter were recovered minus all or part of their load. In fourteen cases management suspected that the thieves received inside help. More than half of thefts took place within Greater London, with thieves preferring to strike vehicles left unattended overnight in the street.[33]

It was often harder to dispose of stolen goods than it was to take them. The nature of most controlled goods exacerbated the thief's dilemma. Most goods were bulky or perishable, which made them difficult to conceal and dispose of gradually. The larger a haul the more serious a problem the thief faced. Controlled items did have some advantages over smaller, higher-value stolen goods such as jewellery: they were easier to steal and hard to trace once consumed. Petty thieves with limited experience and few criminal contacts hawked the goods they stole around their neighbourhood, visiting shops, pubs, clubs, cafés, and people's homes. If they were fortunate they might stumble across a professional fence willing to buy the goods from them. Luckier still were those thieves who already knew a fence.[34]

---

[30] TNA: PRO, AN 13/1224, 'Report on stolen lorries', n.d. [1952].

[31] Sidney Day, *London Born: A Memoir of a Forgotten City* (London, 2006), 138–41.

[32] BL, NSA, Millennium Memory Bank, C900/02617 C1, 'Interview with Lenore Knowles', interviewed by John Watson.

[33] TNA: PRO, AN 13/1224, 'Report on stolen lorries', n.d. [1952].

[34] Dick Hobbs, *Doing the Business: Entrepreneurship, the Working Class and Detectives in the East End of London* (Oxford, 1988); Janet Foster, *Villains: Crime and Community in the Inner City* (London, 1990); Stuart Henry, *Hidden Economy: The Context and Control of Borderline Crime* (London, 1978); Gerald Mars, *Cheats at Work: An Anthropology of Workplace Crime* (London, 1982); Jacqueline L. Schneider, 'Stolen-Goods Markets: Methods of Disposal', *British Journal of Criminology*, 45 (2005), 129–40.

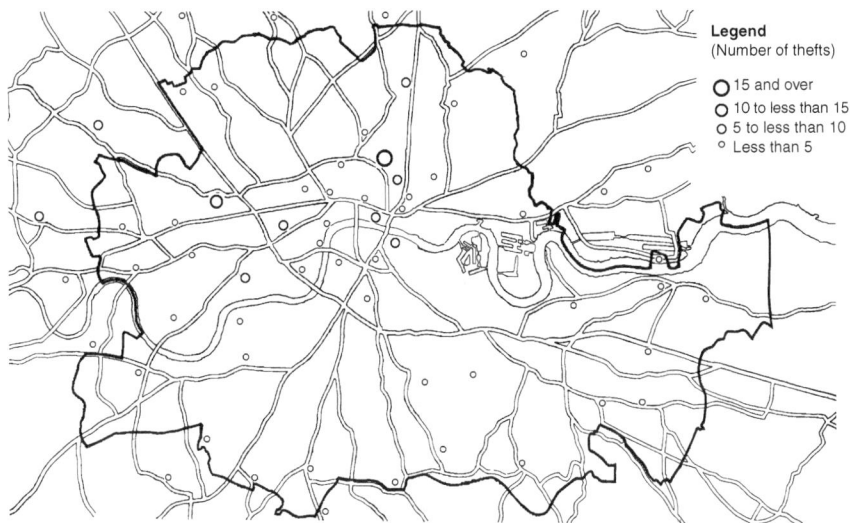

Fig. 3.1. Thefts from Carter Paterson vehicles within Greater London, 1 January to 31 December 1949.

Sources: Bartholomew's Reference Atlas of Greater London (8th edn., Edinburgh, 1948) and TNA: PRO, AN 13/1224, 'Losses by pilferage from vehicles owned by Carter Paterson & Co Ltd in the London area', 1949.

Professional receivers of stolen goods conducted their operations from both residential and commercial addresses. The residential fence sold stolen goods through local social networks, which was how thieves might learn of their existence. Commercial fences ran legitimate businesses that served as fronts for their operations. Pawnbroking, secondhand dealing, and scrap dealing provided the best cover for a general fence prior to the war.[35] Of these trades, pawnbroking had the worst reputation. A pawnbroker fencing stolen goods featured in the MoI film *Partners in Crime*—the only propaganda short about black markets made during austerity. Although the Pawnbrokers Association considered it an unjustified slur, the government did not.[36] Some of the most successful commercial fences, such as the East End wardrobe dealer Arthur Harding, welcomed a reputation for receiving and selling stolen goods. It brought to their door suppliers and customers from whom they could obtain information that they could sell to detectives in return for immunity from prosecution.[37]

Experienced thieves preferred to work with fences who could dispose of large quantities of controlled commodities through legitimate channels. Such receivers tended to be legitimate businessmen. This was the case in Leeds. In 1945 a

[35] The terms are Mike Sutton's. See Mike Sutton with Katie Johnston and Heather Lockwood, 'Handling Stolen Goods and Theft: A Market Reduction Approach', *Home Office Research Study*, 178 (1998).

[36] HC deb, vol. 381, 8 July 1942, cols. 778–9, w.a.

[37] Klockars, *Professional Fence*; Raphael Samuel, *East End Underworld: Chapters in the Life of Arthur Harding* (London, Routledge, 1981), 259–60.

convicted thief serving time in Armley gaol told detectives investigating black marketeering that a taxi driver and a fence dominated the local market in stolen cloth. When large quantities of cloth were stolen from vans, warehouses or shops, thieves would often approach the same taxi driver to help them transport the cloth to one of four receivers. The most important of these receivers lived in a terraced house in the Drighlington area of the city. He bought cloth from thieves directly, and paid them with cash advanced by his sister. The fence would then sell the cloth to other fences and legitimate businessmen. Should the fence's offer not be to their liking, local thieves could turn to one of three other professional re-ceivers. The best of these lived in a terraced house in Beeston. Thieves considered him a 'good "fence"' because he could distribute sizeable quantities of cloth through his wife's secondhand clothing business. Another prisoner told detectives about a fifth receiver—a firm of rag merchants in Mabgate Mills near the city centre, with a London connection that made their operations of national signifi-cance.[38] Investigations involving police in Leeds and London bore out both in-formants' accounts.[39]

The privileged position of these specialist fences meant that their willingness to receive stolen goods might prompt crime. This was a perilous business for the thief. The magistrate Leo Page uncovered such a case when interviewing young adult prisoners for his book *The Young Lag*. In 1944 a group of five young men stole a car, broke into a warehouse, and stole several bales of cloth, which they drove away and hid in an empty shed. They took the risk because one of the gang had a West End 'contact' who would dispose of the cloth. After stealing the cloth the gang contacted the fence, who offered them £200 for the bales. Having arranged to buy the bales, the fence betrayed the gang to the police to earn immunity from prosecution.[40]

Some fences initiated thefts, finding a buyer before placing an order with a thief. This was a more business-like arrangement, which minimized the risk of being caught in possession of stolen goods. Such an arrangement lay behind London's black market in meat. On occasion, subcontractors operating 'tramping vehicles', or new drivers working for large haulage firms, stole their loads and sold them fences in the East End.[41] A Catalan bookseller working undercover for the MoF penetrated one of these operations in wartime Whitechapel. Posing as a struggling businessman interested in developing a profitable black market sideline, the book-seller befriended a local factory owner who bought containers of frozen and chilled meat from drivers transporting loads of meat from the docks to depots across London.[42] Drivers would drop the meat at the factory en route to meat depots,

[38] TNA: PRO, HO 45/23812 863,760/7, 'Alleged black market at Leeds', 13 February 1945.
[39] Leeds Local History Library, *Annual Report of the Chief Constable of Leeds City Police for 1944* (Leeds, 1945), 7; *The Times*, 31 July 1945; Leeds Local History Library, *Annual Report of the Chief Constable of Leeds City Police for 1945* (Leeds, 1946), 8.
[40] Leo Page, *The Young Lag: A Study of Crime* (London, 1950), 67–8.
[41] London, Museum of London, Museum of Docklands Oral History Project, 'Interview with Paul North', 72.
[42] IWM, Dept. of Doc., 62/25/1, 'Statement of William Biswell', n.d.

markets, or cold stores, which the factory owner would later sell wholesale to friends and local butchers.[43]

Like chilled and frozen meat stolen from the docks, the animals taken by gangs of poachers and rustlers needed to be disposed of quickly. Although not averse to trapping rabbits, these urban gangs concentrated their efforts on luxury foods such as salmon, trout, and venison that could be sold to high-class restaurants and hotels. This trade increased after the war.[44] For similar reasons rustlers targeted turkeys prior to Christmas after taking orders from poulterers and consumers willing to pay high prices, no questions asked.[45] The seasonal boom in turkey rustling was a frequent topic for newspaper cartoonists such as Joseph Lee and Carl Giles.[46] Rustlers did not ignore their traditional victims—moorland sheep—but they found turkeys simpler to handle as they were easier to conceal, slaughter, and sell.[47]

The difficulty of disposing of stolen goods made dealing in stolen coupons more attractive to thieves and receivers. In most cases it was more profitable and less risky for criminals to steal ration coupons than rationed commodities, as coupons were easier to conceal and transport. They did not perish either, remaining valid for up to a year. Opportunistic thieves and solitary professionals such as pickpockets, housebreakers, and shopbreakers stole both coupons and ration books from consumers and retailers. When a Bath store detective searched the handbag of 'an extremely clever pickpocket' with eight previous convictions for theft, she found nine food books and thirty-five clothing books, some of the spoils of forty-five thefts.[48] With a street value of £5 for a complete clothing book in 1944 and £6 a year later, a skilled thief could make a good living this way.[49] But the number of books stolen in this way did not pose a threat to control. Far more worrying for the authorities were the activities of teams of professional thieves.[50]

From the middle of the war onwards, criminals involved in project crime began to target regional government offices a few days before they would release a new issue of coupons or ration books. The clerk at the Romford Food Office with responsibility for the ration book issue considered the books well protected, as he kept them in a cellar which could be entered only via a single door that was alarmed and padlocked. At night, two watchmen patrolled the building. The precautions followed ministry procedures to the letter, but they did not prevent thieves breaking into the cellar and stealing almost 12,000 clothing books with a street value of

[43] IWM, Dept. of Doc., 62/25/1, 'Notes', 11 October [1943].

[44] Report of the Committee on Poaching and Illegal Fishing of Salmon and Trout in Scotland (PP 1950 Cmd.7917 xi, 219); Report of the Committee on Cruelty to Wild Animals (PP 1950–1 Cmd.8266 viii, 425).

[45] *Manchester Guardian*, 11 December 1945.

[46] Joseph Lee, 'London Laughs', *Evening News*, 14 December 1946, 28 November 1947, 14 December 1948 and 23 December 1953; Carl Giles, *Sunday Express*, 13 December 1953 and 19 December 1954.

[47] *News Chronicle*, 1 September 1943; *Manchester Guardian*, 24 December 1945; *The Times*, 2 January 1951.

[48] *Manchester Guardian*, 6 February 1945.

[49] Hargreaves and Gowing, *Civil Industry*, 328; *Manchester Guardian*, 30 October 1945.

[50] Peter Beveridge, *Inside the CID* (London, 1957), 101.

£5 each in 1945. The gang broke into the cellar through an outside lavatory, pulling up the floorboards before knocking through the adjacent cellar wall.[51] Such lax security precautions, by comparison to jewellers, banks, or payroll offices, enticed professional thieves.

Night watchmen—the first line of defence—were easily overcome, their silence bought with cash. Stumbling across a break-in, night watchmen and beat policemen were well advised to avoid confronting thieves who often carried guns. A Gateshead policeman was lucky not to be wounded when he chased two men making off with 103,000 clothing coupons stolen from the local food office. One of the men fired three pistol shots at the policeman from close range.[52] Breaking into a deserted town hall or church hall at night—the would-be thieves' next task—posed few problems for experienced criminals such as 'Mad' Frankie Fraser or Robert Allerton, as on most occasions a 'jemmy', the short steel crowbar beloved of thieves, sufficed to spring locked doors, cupboards, and boxes.[53] Teams of thieves had no difficulty cracking the out-dated safes used in more security-conscious government offices, and once inside they could reasonably expect a haul similar in value to that stolen from the Romford office. The single biggest raid involved the theft of five million clothing coupons from a War Office depot in south-west London in autumn 1943. In an extraordinary move the BoT cancelled the entire issue of five-coupon vouchers while reassuring the public that the number stolen represented less than 1% of all coupons in circulation.[54]

Less frequently thieves stole used coupons destined for destruction. Security precautions were usually tighter, as the ministries employed firms with considerable experience in destroying confidential waste for banks, financial services, and government. There were also fewer disposal facilities than there were regional offices. Moreover, the flow of coupons was less predictable as batches arrived irregularly throughout a rationing period. Inside information was vital to success. At the end of 1942 the Metropolitan Police caught a gang stealing cancelled coupons from the London Waste Paper Company after tests revealed that eighteen coupons that a beat officer found in a gutter had been chemically 'washed' to remove cancellation marks and expiry dates. From the cancellation marks the police traced the coupons to the Battersea depot. Detectives discovered that several of the company's young female employees feeding the coupons into shredding machines had been pocketing large bundles of coupons, which they passed to criminal contacts.[55]

As with stolen goods, it was far more challenging to market coupons than it was to steal them. Small numbers of coupons could be hawked to legitimate businesses

[51] *The Times*, 18 June 1945; IWM, Sound Archive, tape ref. 11852/2, 'Interview with Fred Barnes', 1986; Fred Barnes, 'The Great Romford Ration Book Robbery', in Peter Watt, *Hitler v Havering: 1939–1945* (Aveley, 1994), 82.

[52] *Manchester Guardian*, 20 August 1946.

[53] Frankie Fraser as told to James Morton, *Mad Frank: Memoirs of a Life of Crime* (London, 1994), 31; Tony Parker and Robert Allerton, *The Courage of His Convictions* (London, 1962), 77.

[54] *Manchester Guardian*, 18 September 1943.

[55] TNA: PRO, MEPO 3/2004, 'Police report', 13 December 1942; BL, BBC Sound Archive, tape ref. H7889/5, *Coupons and Nylons: The Underside of VE Day*, Radio 4, 11 October 1996, 'Interview with "John"'.

to cover coupon-free sales or to consumers themselves. Describing stolen coupons as spare coupons disguised their true origin, and doing so assuaged a potential customer's suspicions and allowed them to sidestep any qualms about a 'black market' purchase, increasing a thief's potential market. General fences like Arthur Harding would also handle small numbers of coupons and ration books. The teams involved in raids on government offices needed an experienced distributor if they were to put hundreds of thousands of coupons into circulation before officials could cancel an issue or publicize the stolen coupons' serial numbers. Once again, there were few criminals with the resources to distribute such a large number of coupons quickly and safely. This gave the distributor the upper hand in the relationship. Such distributors had a background in the relevant trade or had experience of distributing commodities similar to coupons such as counterfeit currency. It was here, at the wholesale level, that the trade in stolen and counterfeit goods and coupons converged, centring on specialist distributors who handled both commodities.[56] In fact, the traffic in coupons, whether forged or stolen, came to resemble a single retail market. There were, however, significant differences between the sources of supply.

Unlike theft, forgery was a craft that required specialist knowledge and expertise which could not be acquired through trial and error or learning from old lags when serving time in gaol. Most counterfeiters had a background in printing, as a small printing firm provided an excellent front for counterfeiting. Printers possessed the necessary materials, equipment, and workspace to produce forged ration documents. There was also no need to disguise the sound of printing. The ease with which jobbing printers could forge ration documents, and the obvious temptation to do so when there was little business, meant that they received a great deal of police attention when forged coupons flooded the market. To minimize the risk of being caught, some printers kept their counterfeiting operation at arm's length, setting up print shops in offices and residential homes. This created a new problem: explaining the resultant noise to residents and neighbouring businesses. It was also a risk for the owner of the property. A Notting Hill accountant who sublet a room in his office to a forger received a sentence of seven years' penal servitude for his part in a conspiracy to produce more than a thousand clothing books.[57]

Wherever the workshop was located, the biggest challenge facing the would-be counterfeiter was obtaining a supply of paper. The problem facing rogue printers was not in finding high-quality paper—the paper used in official documents was of poor quality—but in finding any paper at all. In some cases it was the search for paper for legitimate jobs that brought printers into contact with criminals.[58] Only central government and the armed forces had seemingly limitless supplies of paper and ink. Some of this was put at the disposal of professional forgers working for

---

[56] Samuel, *East End Underworld*, 259–60; Thomas, *Underworld at War*, 173–5; Hill, *Boss of Britain's Underworld*, 142–3.

[57] *Scotsman*, 21 February 1948.

[58] Steve Holland, *The Mushroom Jungle: A History of Postwar Paperback Publishing* (Westbury, 1993), 31–2.

the intelligence services, but there is no evidence that these conscripts continued their criminal activities as a profitable sideline.[59]

After the Bank of England and HMSO, the air force ran the best in-house printing operation in the public sector out of RAF Medmenham, Buckinghamshire. This was the base of the Allied Photographic Interpretation Unit, whose work was of vital importance to the Allied strategic bombing offensive. At least one member of the unit misused equipment and materials to produce counterfeit coupons. The man, who had no previous convictions for forgery, photographed petrol coupons and used the resultant images to produce printing plates. With access to the best printing technology and good-quality paper, the forgeries were some of the best that petrol inspectors encountered.[60]

In the private sector, publishing firms and newspapers had equipment and materials that their employees could misappropriate. The most brazen operation involved the *Glasgow Herald* print shop. In 1946—a boom year for forged coupons—detectives and clothes inspectors traced counterfeits circulating in Glasgow and Edinburgh back to two etchers working at the newspaper. On Saturday afternoons the two men used the print shop to produce printing plates for clothing coupons and £5 Clydesdale Bank bank-notes. According to a member of the ring that distributed the counterfeits, the etchers contacted a local criminal through a mutual friend. After viewing the plates and a sample of forged coupons at a city hotel, the criminal agreed to fund the operation. He secured a £150 loan, which the etchers used to buy a printing press, paper, and ink, and found a house in which the press could be set up. He also found buyers for the coupons in Glasgow and Edinburgh.[61]

Unlike the rogue RAF serviceman and the *Glasgow Herald* print workers, most convicted coupon forgers had a history of counterfeiting dating back to the inter-war years. Recognizing the demand for coupons and the ease with which ration documents could be forged compared to currency, established forgers switched their operations from counterfeiting banknotes and national insurance stamps to forging ration documents. Accomplished forgers kept production separate from distribution. They would pass the forged coupons to a distributor who specialized in 'placing' or 'dropping' counterfeits. Each was responsible for running their end of the operation and ensuring its security. To tighten security still further, the two parties might work through intermediaries. By compartmentalizing their operations, forgers made it much harder for police to detect them.[62]

As with the market in stolen goods, the knowledge that there was a person capable of distributing large numbers of coupons might inspire a forger. The

[59] M. R. D. Foot, *SOE* (London, 1990), 154; David Garnett, *The Secret History of the PWE: Political Warfare Executive 1939–1945* (London, 2002), 112, 174, 223.

[60] *Cambridge Daily News*, 10 January 1946; TNA: PRO, POWE 33/1480, 'Forged petrol coupons', 15 October 1945, and 'Forged petrol coupons: additional information', 18 October 1945.

[61] *Scotsman*, 1 and 2 November 1946; Robert Colquhoun, *Life begins at Midnight* (London, 1962), 71–4; George Yandell, 'The "Harry Limes" of Britain', *Sunday Dispatch*, 14 May 1950.

[62] Henry T. F. Rhodes, *The Craft of Forgery* (London, 1934), 82; Smithies, *Black Economy*, 50; Colquhoun, *Life begins*, 71–4.

distributor might even initiate an operation, bankrolling and organizing the entire thing. If possible, distributors preferred to employ 'droppers' to 'place' forged coupons. Distancing themselves from selling coupons was a basic security precaution. They also preferred it if their droppers sold coupons wholesale. Such operations could be vertically integrated or non-integrated. Non-integrated operations were more secure, but the financial arrangements more complex. A distributor might buy coupons from a forger at a fixed price per coupon, charge commission, or demand a percentage of the profits. The same was true of the droppers.

Criminals with a background in distributing counterfeit notes and national insurance stamps were well placed to dominate the market for stolen coupons as well as the market for forged coupons. The source of supply might be different but the customers were the same, as were the methods of distribution. There was significant overlap between the commercial fence and the distributor of forged coupons. Alternatively, less experienced thieves dealing in small quantities of stolen coupons might fence the coupons themselves. Others might rely on residential fences who exploited local social networks to sell stolen coupons. To shift a large volume of stolen coupons before the authorities could cancel the issue, thieves needed the expertise of a commercial fence.

The supply and distribution of counterfeit goods differed greatly from that of forged coupons. Illicit manufacturing operations tended to be small-scale cottage industries, due to the difficulty of obtaining raw materials, containers, and labels. Whisky was a favourite of the counterfeiters who found a large and undiscriminating clientele amongst American service personnel. Wherever there was a large concentration of American troops, small-scale whisky counterfeiting flourished. Watering down whisky or filling empty bottles with cold tea were the most popular tricks. A more sophisticated method was to fill an empty whisky bottle with tea to the neck then pour a layer of molten wax over the tea before filling the bottle's neck with watered-down whisky.[63]

Glasgow became the centre for the trade in counterfeit whisky. It had a comparative advantage over other cities, as it was the centre of the Scottish whisky industry with a thriving underworld and a large local retail market swollen by Allied troops passing through the city. Glasgow's Central Station was one of the best places to sell counterfeit whisky. Locals hawked £5 bottles of whisky that bore famous labels around the concourse to rail travellers. The bottles contained cold tea, but customers were usually miles away from the station before they discovered the trick.[64] Glaswegians were less likely to fall for this con. Instead, counterfeiters sold them watered-down whisky or whisky mixed with methylated spirits. Publicans proved enthusiastic buyers of concoctions of whisky and meths, as a reputation for a regular and copious supply of whisky boosted custom. It was a lucrative trade for counterfeiters who obtained meths at £5 per gallon. After adding colouring and flavouring, the 'whisky' could be sold at £22 per gallon.[65]

---

[63] Longmate, *GIs*, 210; Gardiner, *'Over Here'*, 80.   [64] Longmate, *GIs*, 210.
[65] Colquhoun, *Life begins*, 68–71.

Whisky aside, counterfeiters focused their efforts on producing gin, perfumes, make-up, nylon stockings, and toys. Like whisky, there were no effective substitutes for such price-controlled luxuries. The backyard industry producing counterfeit goods marketed its products through informal retail outlets. Supply chains linking illicit manufacturer to consumer were short, and it was not uncommon for market traders and street traders to produce the goods themselves. Donald Hume, who later achieved notoriety as a double murderer, made his living by hawking bottles of 'Finlinson's Old English Gin', made from surgical spirits, around West End nightclubs.[66] But it was the market in fake cosmetics that caused the authorities greatest concern. Prior to the war, many retailers sold their own toilet preparations alongside branded goods, so had the know-how needed to produce counterfeit goods. This made enforcement difficult and prompted the authorities to emphasize the health risks associated with black market cosmetics in a vain attempt to dampen demand amongst young women.[67] Ultimately, the high level of consumer demand for cosmetics and other luxury goods ended the trade in counterfeit goods. Once illicit manufacturers realized that their customers would buy their products, branded or not, they ceased producing counterfeits.

The practice of mixing cosmetics at the back of a chemist's shop, watering down whisky in a pub, or covering coupon-free sales in a tailor's shop with forged or stolen coupons highlight the connections between criminal enterprises supplying black market goods and legitimate businesses. That criminals marketed stolen goods via informal outlets was well known before the war began. The shady reputation of secondhand dealers, pawnbrokers, market traders, street traders, hawkers, and peddlers owed something to the links that some of them had with criminals.[68] It was also one of the reasons for the equivocal attitude to small advertisements and mail order. Although they continued to be important outlets for illegal goods during austerity, more formal enterprises assumed a larger role in the underground economy. Wholesalers and retailers formed a ready market for coupons that they could use to cover coupon-free sales to customers, while restaurateurs and hoteliers—especially those looking for rare ingredients—were not averse to buying stolen food. Indeed, this was how several well-known Soho restaurants specializing in foreign cuisines were drawn into black market dealing.[69] Routine theft from larger kitchens before the war helped the black market trade in stolen food develop rapidly.[70] Although control reversed the pre-war flow of goods out of the kitchen, the people involved remained the same. Professional thieves and counterfeiters preferred dealing with legitimate businesses, as they could sell large quantities of illegal goods quickly to a small number of people. This minimized the risk of being caught. Hawking and peddling was small-time. 'Mad' Frankie Fraser—a 'proper'

[66] John Williams, *Hume: Portrait of a Double Murderer* (London, 1960), 25.

[67] Zweiniger-Bargielowska, *Austerity*, 185–91; ITN Source, BGX408160095, 'War on Black Market Cosmetics', *British Paramount News*, 3 November 1941.

[68] Jerry White, *The Worst Street in North London: Campbell Bunk, Islington between the Wars* (London, 1986), 176–87; Day, *London Born*, 106, 140–1.

[69] *Manchester Guardian*, 4 March 1941; *The Observer*, 25 October 1942; Hugo Meynell, *Five Bob Meal*.

[70] Mars, *Cheats at Work*, 187–8.

thief—considered the 'spivs' involved in the retail end of the trade amateurish mugs.[71]

Although professional criminals and the shady businessmen in league with them dominated the counterfeiting and theft of goods and coupons, most black market-eering was in the hands of the men and women with whom people had always done business. After all, these were the business people who had the goods to sell and clipped the coupons. For many of them, black marketeering continued pre-war business practices, both normal and criminal. Conditional sales, favouritism, upgrading, and side payments were normal practice in many distributive trades, while criminal acts such as giving short weight, adulteration, and mislabelling were so common as to be considered customary in others.[72] Each trade had dodges and fiddles peculiar to it. In the pre-war meat trade a minority of butchers substituted horse-meat for pork in 'pork' sausages or put it in pies. Disguising and selling con-demned meat was another con practiced by a minority in the meat trade.[73] Owners of garages and petrol stations colluded with lorry drivers in fiddling their expenses. Knowledge of such practices was widespread amongst traders, who acquired it by word of mouth or from reading trade journals. Austerity conditions encouraged sharp practices, all of which were illegal under consumption controls. Although the black market can be represented as a continuation of pre-war practices, this was not how business people understood it. By criminalizing normal practice and un-derlining the antisocial character of criminal practices, the new regulations made it harder for entrepreneurs who followed these practices to continue to behave in this way. If traders found ways to justify their behaviour that allowed them to maintain a non-deviant self-image, these acts of self-justification distinguished pre-war from wartime and post-war practices. For them the black market represented a business sideline that had much in common with pre-war practice whilst remaining morally distinct from it.

Unlike the trade in stolen and counterfeit goods and coupons, the under-the-counter trade flowed through the same channels as the official one in controlled goods. On occasion the traffic in black market goods short-circuited official chan-nels, bypassing several steps in the supply chain. Buyers from restaurants and hotels in central London scoured the Home Counties and East Anglia, looking for small producers willing to make illegal farm-gate sales, bypassing middlemen.[74] It could even distort official channels as retailers scrabbled to register with wholesalers who could supply them with black market extras. From the consumer perspective the black market origins of goods obtained under-the-counter were not always clear.

---

[71] BL, BBC Sound Archive, Ref. No. H 7889/5, *Coupons and Nylons*, Radio 4, 11 October 1996.

[72] Jim Phillips and Michael French, *Cheated Not Poisoned? Food Regulation in the United Kingdom, 1875–1938* (Manchester, 2000); Bee Wilson, *Swindled: The Dark History of Food Fraud from Poisoned Coffee to Counterfeit Candy* (Princeton, NJ, 2008).

[73] R. Perren, *The Meat Trade in Britain, 1840–1914* (London, 1978); and R. Perren, 'The Retail and Wholesale Meat Trade 1880–1939', in Derek J. Oddy and Derek S. Miller (eds.), *Diet and Health in Modern Britain* (London, 1985), 66–80.

[74] BL, NSA, Millennium Memory Bank, C900/01040 C1, 'Interview with Terry (Terence) Roy Huggins', interviewed by Eva Simmons.

They could be 'overs' finagled by minimizing losses or items from an officially sanctioned stock clearance. It might be a coupon-free sale covered by other customers' unused coupons. In fact, a premium price was the only reliable indicator of a good's black market origins.

The most interesting aspect of the under-the-counter trade was the traffic in ration coupons which made it possible to obtain extra supplies for sale on the black market. The methods for evading price control were a continuation of pre-war practices, but the trade in coupons was new. Retailers, not wholesalers or producers, took the lead role in organizing it. By allowing consumers to 'bank' their coupons with retailers, the authorities helped the trade to develop. Officials intended this concession to make life easier for civilians. Depositing a ration-book page with a retailer freed customers from the fiddly business of calculating coupon values and tearing them out. In doing so, customers trusted retailers not to exploit them. Shopkeepers were quick to realize the possibilities for grey and black market dealing that coupon banking afforded them. Acting like a retail banker, a shopkeeper could pool the coupons that customers deposited. This allowed them to maximize turnover, as they could balance under-consumption by one customer against under-consumption by another.

Unlike the grey marketeer guilty of under-the-counter favouritism, the black marketeer charged customers extra for this service. The retailers best placed to exploit the opportunities that coupon banking presented for black marketeering were those with a socially mixed clientele who had a wide range of household incomes. It also helped to have experience of check trading and savings clubs, as the skills required to operate a coupon bank were similar. It also meant that customers approached ration coupons as they would shop tokens and vouchers. Working-class housewives and commercial drivers, who tended to be the customers with healthy coupon balances, might receive payment for their unused coupons in cash or kind. The more astute demanded it, creating a true market in coupons. When retailers failed to provide this service, petty criminals who bought and sold coupons stepped in. One such dealer was John Basnett, a self-proclaimed 'spiv' who later achieved fame as jazz trumpeter 'Spanish Fred'. Basnett bought spare clothing coupons from working-class women and sold them to middle-class women. At lunchtime on market-days, Basnett frequented pubs in the centre of Ormskirk, Lancashire, buying coupons from working-class housewives having a break from shopping. He sold the coupons door-to-door in middle-class areas, charging 3s or 3s 6d for a coupon that he had bought for 6d or 1s.[75]

Distinct from theft and forgery—at least in traders' minds—the under-the-counter trade conducted to preserve a reasonable profit margin brought some entrepreneurs into contact with criminals, augmenting the ranks of disreputable businessmen engaged in smuggling, long-firm fraud, or fencing stolen goods.[76] Having a reputation for black market dealing increased the number of offers of

---

[75] Paul Addison, *Now the War is Over: A Social History of Britain 1945–51* (London, 1985), 47–8.
[76] Michael Levi, *The Phantom Capitalists: The Organisation and Control of Long-firm Fraud* (London, 1981); H. G. A. Cross, John Adam and J. Collyer Adam, *Criminal Investigation: A Practical Textbook for Magistrates, Police Officers and Lawyers* (4th edn., London, 1949), 314.

stolen, counterfeit, or smuggled goods that businesses received, as criminals assumed that white-collar criminals were more likely to accept dubious invitations than were law-abiding traders. The source of supply might be different, but the trade in coupons, whether counterfeit, stolen or unwanted, was the same at retail level. Failing that, they might succeed in blackmailing a business into handling illegally obtained goods. In major urban areas a reputation for under-the-counter trading attracted the attention of predatory criminals such as the London gangster Jack 'Spot' Comer. First in Leeds and then in London, Spot pressured evaders into paying him protection money. For Spot and other racketeers, wholesalers and retailers were a new and easy form of prey compared to their usual victims, illegal street bookies and prostitutes, who would call upon police or locals for support in order to resist extortion attempts.[77]

The legal barriers to entering a legitimate trade were high, which left much illegal traffic in the hands of business sideliners. Not only was it impossible to open a new business without a licence, but few outsiders possessed the knowledge and expertise required to run a farm, a factory, a wholesaler's, or a shop. This kept criminal entrepreneurs out of these trades. Unlike the businesses of their existing clients involved in gambling and prostitution, racketeers selling protection chose not to take over their new clients' businesses, as their criminal connections and willingness to use violence were of little use to the *legitimate* trader. The only aspect of black market activity in which there was direct competition was the trade in coupons. Street bookmakers and their runners had the skills and contacts to diversify into the coupon traffic. They knew how to run an illegal business by avoiding unwanted police attention, and their predominantly working-class clientele had spare coupons to trade. The opportunity to increase their earnings through the traffic appealed to runners, as taking bets from work colleagues was often only one of several illegal services that runners provided.[78]

The trade in coupons highlights the connections between business sideliners and criminal diversifiers, but neither had much to do with the third source of supply: ration fraud. Consumers perpetrated most ration fraud due to the difficulty of performing detailed checks of numerous applications for supplementary rations and replacement coupons. Although traders could, and did, pad envelopes of coupons with paper and inflate sales, coupon checkers swiftly detected such blatant fraud. The authorities appreciated the ease with which fraudsters could exploit arrangements for issuing supplementary rations and replacement coupons. Additional petrol rations and lost clothing books posed the biggest problems. Under the petrol control scheme, certain classes of private motorist, such as people living in rural districts with poor public transport links, were eligible for supplementary rations. Ineligible motorists made fraudulent statements of needs, while

[77] Hank Janson, *Jack Spot, Man of a Thousand Cuts* (London, 1959); James Morton, *Gangland Bosses: The Lives of Jack Spot and Billy Hill* (London, 2004); Wensley Clarkson, *Hit 'Em Hard: Jack Spot, King of the Underworld* (London, 2003).

[78] Carl Chinn, *Better Betting with a Decent Feller: A Social History of Bookmaking* (2nd edn., London, 2004), 109–12; M-OA, DR January 1948, DR 129.

the eligible overstated their needs or used the petrol for purposes other than ministry officials intended. Commercial and government users also misused their supplies. After the trade in unwanted commercial coupons,[79] the abuse of supplementary and commercial rations was the biggest threat to petrol rationing.

The exploitation of the system for replacing lost clothing books posed a threat of similar magnitude to the clothes rationing scheme. During the scheme's first year the BoT received 781,900 applications for replacement coupons, issuing 26,944,400 coupons. Suspecting a ramp, the Board ceased to replace coupons in full. Inspectors monitored applications, interviewing applicants who made dubious or frequent claims.[80] A variant on the lost or stolen clothing book scam was to pretend that your coupons had been destroyed after the bombing of your house; but this was harder to fake, with the result that it was less popular than the lost-book con.

Despite the possibilities for organized ration fraud, there is no evidence to suggest that professional fraudsters targeted the rationing schemes. Clothes inspectors noticed that the majority of claims came from 'the little streets of big cities, and there seemed an odd connection between the various claims'.

> Thus, Mrs Brown of Number Nine would claim on Monday; on Wednesday Mrs Jones at Number Eleven would stake her claim; and, lo!—on Friday Mrs Smith at Number Thirteen and Mrs Robinson at Number Fifteen would 'lose' their books and obtain new ones. And while Mrs Brown modestly claimed one book, by the time Mrs Robinson appeared on the scene that lady would calmly put in a bid for nine books, one for each of her large family. The word went round and soon the people in the next road joined in…and the next…and the next until a whole community found it an easy and profitable pastime.[81]

Closer to a contagion than an organized attempt to defraud, such epidemics occurred due to the existence of a thriving local traffic in unused coupons.

BLACK MARKET-PLACES

Although black market supply chains spanned the country, linking remote rural settlements to major conurbations, the illicit retail markets that they fed, like their licit counterparts, focused on Britain's towns and cities, where most potential customers lived. Given that most black market goods reached customers through formal and informal retail outlets, illegal retail markets reflected official retail markets with one difference: small independent retailers with precarious finances handled a higher proportion of the illegal than the legal trade. Located in places of varying size, there was a clear shopping hierarchy between settlements and within the larger population centres, shaped by the same forces as its legal counterpart, which geographers and planners were only just beginning to

[79] Payton-Smith, *Oil*, 217–20, 292–3.
[80] TNA: PRO, BT 64/1519, 'The history of the lost ration document', August 1948.
[81] George Yandell, 'The "Harry Limes" of Britain', *Sunday Dispatch*, 14 May 1950.

understand.[82] One of the most important of these forces was consumer demand as reflected in civilians' shopping habits. As a rule, consumers preferred to shop locally for items bought on a regular basis, such as food, travelling further afield for items bought occasionally, such as shoes, clothing and furniture.[83]

Shortages of consumer goods prompted shoppers to change their habits only slightly, though their experiences altered more dramatically.[84] Women, who did most everyday household shopping, began to cast their nets wider when buying unrationed everyday foods, trawling several shops and market stalls instead of relying on one retailer. The consumer–retailer tie prevented this from happening in the case of rationed foods but not in the case of other non-food items. Under austerity conditions shoppers would also travel further for convenience and speciality goods. Shortages meant that trips to buy durable goods came to be about hunting for an item rather than shopping around for the best deal. By 1948 it was common for middle-class housewives to scour shops in working-class neighbourhoods for points-rationed goods that were too expensive for locals. Another change was that shopping was no longer limited to discrete trips or times. Shortages taught civilians to be always on the lookout for goods in short supply, buying them whenever and wherever they could, and adopting a hunter-gatherer strategy. Of course, such developments placed working women with limited time and rural residents with limited mobility at a disadvantage.[85]

What held true for legally obtained goods also held for black market goods, with the result that the illegal shopping hierarchy ran in parallel to the legal one. This can be seen in the surviving minutes of local food control committees. Informal and formal retailers in hamlets and villages were more likely to be involved in grey market dealing with locals than black market dealing. But in rural districts close to urban areas, retailers had the opportunity to sell black market food to people from outside the district. This was particularly marked in areas that attracted large numbers of day-trippers and holidaymakers before the war. Strangers stopping to ask farmers and growers if they would sell them food alerted producers to the potential for direct sales to outsiders. South Westmorland is a case in point.

Although South Westmorland Rural District was one of the most sparsely populated rural areas in the country, with a population density of 0.12 persons per acre, it was well connected to the north and south by the A6 trunk road and the west coast main line, which passed through the area. The South Westmorland economy, which stretched from the eastern edge of the Lakeland fells in the west to the Yorkshire dales in the east, rested on upland farming and tourism. At the district's heart

[82] A. E. Smailes, 'Urban Hierarchy in England and Wales', *Geography*, 29 (1944), 41–51; F. H. W. Green, 'Town and Country in Northern Ireland', *Geography*, 34 (1949), 89–96; F. H. W. Green, 'Urban Hinterlands in England and Wales: An Analysis of Bus Services', *Geographical Journal*, 116 (1950), 64–81.

[83] John K. Walton, 'Towns and Consumerism', in Martin Daunton (ed.), *The Cambridge Urban History of Britain, iii: 1840–1950* (Cambridge, 2000), 720–1.

[84] See Zweiniger-Bargielowska, *Austerity*, 117–23 on 'this frustrating, time-consuming, and dispiriting' experience.

[85] M-O, *People in Production: An Enquiry into British War Production Part 1* (London, 1942), 226–33; see M-OA, FR 3055, 'A report on shopping', November 1948.

lay the market town of Kendal, through which visitors to Windermere and the Lakes passed, and Barrow-in-Furness and Lancaster were the nearest towns of equal importance. Judging by contemporary bus services, the town's hinterland took in the 'urban' districts of Shap and Windermere, as well as South Westmorland.[86] Day-trips and holidays to Lakeland remained popular throughout the 1940s. Like other middle-class families living in towns near the Lakes, the diarist Nella Last and her husband Cliff would drive from Barrow-in-Furness to the southern Lakes at the weekend. This procession of 'pleasure motorists' irritated locals such as Arthur Ransome, who resented the fact that these outsiders could save petrol for a day-trip while locals had just enough to go shopping once a week in Kendal.[87] Tourism continued despite the withdrawal of the basic petrol ration for private motorists in 1942–45 and 1947–48 as holidaymakers took to trains and buses. The wealthy preferred taxis or hire cars to the buses.[88] Any fall in visitor numbers failed to have a dramatic impact on local economy, as evacuees, service personnel, and latterly prisoners of war replaced tourists.

The large number of strangers staying in south Westmorland or passing through it affected the shape of the local underground economy. Not surprisingly, illegal farm-gate sales of home-made and home-grown produce to outsiders, as well as neighbours unwilling or unable to catch the bus or drive to Kendal, were common. One full-time food inspector assisted by four sanitary inspectors struggled to police such transactions.[89] Drawing upon their experience of enforcing the sanitary acts, the local inspectors took a persuasive rather than a coercive approach to enforcement, visiting farmers at short notice to check up on them and offering them advice or issuing warnings if they discovered any infringements. The inspectors undertook periodic campaigns such as the milk and ice cream enforcement drive towards the end of the 1943 tourist season, but these proved a temporary irritant that was easily borne.[90]

Recognizing the voracious appetite for locally produced butter, eggs, milk, and meat—something visitors felt deprived of in towns and expected an abundance of in the countryside—some local hoteliers and caterers obtained extra supplies illegally. This might involve an arrangement with a local farmer or a deal with a catering supplier from as far afield as Blackpool.[91] It was easier to collect evidence of such arrangements than it was for the numerous but occasional sales of farm produce to

[86] Arthur E. Smailes, 'The Urban Mesh of England and Wales', *Transactions and Papers of the Institute of British Geographers*, 11 (1946), 87–101; F. H. W. Green, 'Urban Hinterlands in England and Wales: An Analysis of Bus Services', *Geographical Journal*, 116 (1950), 64–81.

[87] Chris Sladen, 'Wartime Holidays and the "Myth of the Blitz"', *Cultural and Social History*, 2 (2005), 215–46.

[88] For example, the classicist A. F. S. Gow booked a car to drive him from Cambridge to Llandrindrod Wells—a round trip of 360 miles—for his summer holiday in 1941. A. S. F. Gow, *Letters from Cambridge, 1939–1944* (London, 1945), 52.

[89] TNA: PRO, MAF 67/166, 'Kendal Metropolitan Borough and South Westmorland Rural District Joint Food Control Enforcement Subcommittee (FCES) minutes', 2 October 1940.

[90] TNA: PRO, MAF 67/166, 'Kendal and South Westmorland FCES minutes', 4 August, 2 October, and 3 November 1943.

[91] TNA: PRO, MAF 67/166, 20 May and 3 June 1942.

private individuals. Yet there was rarely enough evidence to merit a prosecution for anything other than failure to keep proper records.[92] Far more significant were illegal farm-gate sales to buyers, from Kendal and elsewhere. These buyers, like the four Kendal traders who were prosecuted for offences in Manchester in 1942, operated at a regional level.[93]

Illegal dealing began to take on a more formal aspect in larger villages and small towns with parades of convenience stores that served residents and people from the surrounding countryside. Judging by the minutes of Featherstone Urban District Food Control Committee, however, such black market operations were unsophisticated. The mining town of Featherstone ('Ashton'), 2½ miles south-west of Pontefract in the West Riding of Yorkshire, was the subject of the classic community study *Coal is Our Life*. With a population of 13,935 in 1951 and a population density of 3.15 persons per acre, Featherstone was a small town rather than a pit village. The enforcement subcommittee did little during its fourteen-year existence, dealing with a small number of suspected offences that the public brought to its attention.

What black marketeering there was involved high-street stores and corner shops overcharging for basic foods such as eggs, tomatoes, pork dripping, milk, and cocoa.[94] This pattern reflected local demand. With miners' wives following 'the tradition of good plain food and plenty of it', there was little call for unusual ingredients and no money to buy them.[95] When miners' wages improved after the war, the extra money went on 'slight luxuries' such as sweet cake, tinned fruit, and cooked meat.[96] One local store catered to the increased demand for everyday treats by obtaining chocolates and sweets illegally and selling them to customers coupon-free at inflated prices.[97] Shopkeeper favouritism was another problem, but its legal status was unclear. With the exception of registered customers receiving their ration, shopkeepers and shop assistants could refuse to serve a customer—a legal right that provided useful cover for both grey market and black market dealing. A miner who complained to the Food Control Committee described one such exchange circuit in exceptional detail. He resented the fact that Mrs B refused to sell him sweets while exchanging them for fruit from Mrs C, who also swapped fruit for cake from Mrs D.[98]

Under-reporting, which was a problem for Featherstone's Food Control Committee and others like it, makes it hard to gauge the extent of overcharging or shopkeeper favouritism. Food shopping was a woman's task that entailed shopping in local stores on a daily or weekly basis, with a fortnightly visit by bus to Castleford

[92] TNA: PRO, MAF 67/166, 21 May 1941 and 8 April 1942.
[93] TNA: PRO, MAF 67/166, 4 November 1942.
[94] TNA: PRO, MAF 67/171, 'Featherstone Urban District Food Control Committee (FCC) minutes', 19 September and 21 November 1940, and 3 July 1941; TNA: PRO, MAF 67/171, 'Featherstone FCES minutes', 12 March 1941.
[95] Norman Dennis, Fernando Henriques, and Clifford Slaughter, *Coal is our Life: An Analysis of a Yorkshire Mining Community* (2nd edn., London, 1969), 198.
[96] *Coal is our Life*, 199.
[97] TNA: PRO, MAF 67/171, 'Featherstone FCES minutes', 13 March 1950.
[98] TNA: PRO, MAF 67/171, 4 November 1943; see 23 November 1942.

market fifteen minutes away or Pontefract market five minutes away, and a trip to Leeds every two or three months. Most of the weekly housekeeping money that miners gave their wives went on food bought 'on tick' locally with the account settled once a week.[99] In this context, registering with food retailers formalized long-standing credit relations that left housewives beholden to shopkeepers. The scarcity of supplies tipped the balance of power in this asymmetric relationship further in the shopkeeper's favour. This goes some way towards explaining the small number of consumer complaints that the Food Control Committee received. But shopkeepers had to be careful not to charge too much. In this tight-knit community people stuck to the rule that 'you didn't steal from people that you lived and worked with'.[100] If retailers asked for too much too often, they could not count on their customers' silence. Profiteers 'stealing' from miners' families deserved no protection.

As settlements increased in size and complexity, so too did illegal retail markets in food. Romford in Essex was considerably larger than Featherstone, and boasted a black market in fresh fruit and vegetables centred on the market-place and a black market in rationed meat. Civilians could also obtain extra food and drink from black market sources by eating out at a small number of cafés and clubs. In 1939 Romford was an important market for agricultural and consumer goods. With 88,002 residents it was a large town—one of 157 urban areas with a population of more than 50,000 in 1951. With a well-established market, sizeable population, an advantageous location twelve miles east of London, and in the midst of mixed farms and market gardens that could supply black market food, Romford had reputation as a centre for black marketeering.[101] The food enforcement sub-committee struggled to control stallholders selling fresh fruit and vegetables in the market-place. Failure to display official price lists, imposing conditions of sale, overcharging, and giving of short weight were the most frequent offences. The same offences caused the Kendal authorities a headache.[102] Most of Romford's stallholders committed these offences at one time or another, with the Best, Curies, Emmett, Gradinsky, and Harris families guilty of repeated offences. Test purchases and surveillance operations revealed that Palmer's (Wholesale) Butchers and Cater Brothers, each with several stores around town, overcharged customers and illicitly slaughtered livestock on their farms. Integrated businesses like these two firms, who reared, slaughtered and processed livestock before the war, were well placed to obtain black market supplies that they could sell to customers. Retailers with a sideline in other black market goods could be found across the town. The increased willingness of shoppers to trawl shopping parades and corner shops outside their immediate area meant that black marketeers need not occupy premises in the town centre to gain custom. They provided a special service for which people were willing to travel further. There were also positive advantages to a suburban location.

[99] Dennis et al., *Coal is our Life*, 17, 196–201.

[100] Royce Turner, *Coal was our Life: an Essay on Life in a Yorkshire Pit Town* (Sheffield, 2000), 222.

[101] W. R. Powell (ed.), *A History of the County of Essex, vii* (London, 1978), 56–64; Smithies, *Crime in Wartime*, 59–61; Thomas, *Underworld at War*, 150.

[102] TNA: PRO, MAF 67/166, 'Kendal and South Westmorland FCES minutes', 3 June, 1 July, 5 August, 2 September, and 2 October 1942.

Not only was it cheaper but it also drew less attention from the authorities, who concentrated on policing the market and town centre. The fact that most neighbourhood and corner shops were small independents under severe financial strain increased the temptation to make illegal deals, reinforcing these centrifugal forces.

Street traders experienced similar financial pressures to owners of small local shops, but market stalls and barrows aside, informal food retail outlets are absent from the Romford records and those of other local Food Control Committees. This has less to do with the difficulty of policing informal retailing than the limited involvement of hawkers and peddlers in food retailing. Hawkers and peddlers selling goods and coupons in entertainment venues, workplaces, and from door to door in residential areas were important black market retailers. This was especially true of the trade in clothing and household goods, much of which remained in the hands of door-to-door salesmen. The North East Region Price Regulation Committee based at Leeds, whose minutes are the only ones to survive, spent nearly as much time tackling street traders as it did shopkeepers.[103] Indian peddlers were a particular obsession.[104] Network sales, usually but not always associated with grey marketing, also escaped the attention of food inspectors who focused on licensed retailers. Such private sales to friends, relatives, neighbours, and colleagues were the most important channel for illegal goods before and after austerity.

The pattern of illegal food retailing in market-places, town-centre shops, neighbourhood shopping parades, and corner shops that was found in Romford and Kendal was similar to that found in cities and conurbations. Even under austerity, civilians would not travel beyond a certain distance for convenience or speciality goods. Although illicit retail markets in cities resembled those found in large towns, differing in scale only, the supply chains that fed them were longer and more complex. Some of these black market operations were of national as well as regional significance. With a population of 512,850 in 1951, Sheffield was the country's sixth largest city and a provincial hub. As a major urban centre, the city's underground economy was larger and more complex than that found in large towns such as Romford or market towns such as Kendal. The city also had a reputation for organized crime dating back to the 1920s.[105] Between September 1939 and September 1953 the Sheffield County Borough Food Control Committee handled 1,079 cases.[106] It was ten years before the Featherstone enforcement subcommittee dealt with its seventy-eighth case; and the Sheffield subcommittee considered its seventy-eighth case in April 1941, just as black markets entered the public consciousness.[107]

[103] Minutes of the North East Region Price Regulation Committee can be found in BT 94/539–549 at TNA.

[104] For example TNA: PRO, BT 94/549, 'Minutes of the local price regulation committee (North Eastern region)', 20 June 1951.

[105] See J. P. Bean, *The Sheffield Gang Wars* (Sheffield, 1981).

[106] TNA: PRO, MAF 67/175, 'Sheffield County Borough FCC minutes', 21 September 1953.

[107] TNA: PRO, MAF 67/173, 'Sheffield FCES minutes', 7 April 1941.

As in other urban areas, illegal dealing in meat posed a serious problem for the Sheffield County Borough Food Control Committee. Black market meat could be bought from butchers on The Moor, one of the main shopping streets, or in Castle Folds Market. The retail end of illegal supply chains that reached into the city's rural hinterland, similar to those linking Kendal to Manchester or Romford to London, could be found also in working-class neighbourhoods outside the city centre. Beasts slaughtered in Stubley and Dronfield on the edge of the Peak District to the south of Sheffield, and animals killed in the villages of Woodsetts and Lindrick between Worksop and Dinnington to the east of the city, found their way into butchers' shops in Attercliffe and Hillsborough.[108] As in Romford, small and medium-sized butchers' firms with wholesale, catering, and retail businesses dominated the illicit trade in meat. Unlike retail butchers working for chains such as Dewhurst, these local butchers had the expertise, equipment, and contacts to slaughter livestock, dress the meat, and sell it quickly.[109] Local family firms that struggled to see off the pre-war challenge posed by the multiples recognized and exploited their comparative advantage.

One black market peculiar to large urban areas involved the sale of horse-flesh. Sheffield was one of the principal centres for the slaughter of horses for human consumption before the war. Although much of the meat was exported, horse-flesh formed an important part of the local working-class diet. The same was true of Leeds, London, and Newcastle,[110] and between 1942 and 1946 a thriving black market developed in Sheffield.[111] Despite horse-flesh dealers' increasing costs, the official price of horse-flesh stood at 1s per pound from 1941 onwards. In these circumstances the only way for a dealer to break even, let alone make a profit, was to overcharge customers. The Horses and Ponies Protection Association also alleged that pressure to turn a profit had led to inhumane slaughter.[112] Faced with rapidly increasing demand for this unrationed meat, there was a great temptation for unscrupulous dealers to pass off condemned meat as horse-flesh. And this was made easy, as many dealers combined a slaughterhouse with a knacker's yard.[113] Meat from sick, injured, or fallen animals killed and removed from farms, and old cows and horses brought into the yards for slaughter, appeared in the shops as 'horse-flesh' or was sold under the counter coupon-free.[114] The MoF recognized the problem but did nothing to tighten control until 1949, when officials considered that the costs of tackling the problem no longer outweighed its benefits.

Black market dealing in fresh fruit and vegetables was also more sophisticated in cities than in towns, operating at a national as well as regional level. Like their

[108] TNA: PRO, MAF 67/174, Sheffield FCC, 'Revocation procedure', 2 September 1946.

[109] TNA: PRO, MAF 67/175, Sheffield FCC, 'Revocation procedure', 7 February 1949.

[110] Report of the Departmental Committee on Export and Slaughter of Horses (PP 1950 Cmd.7888 xii, 9), 4–5.

[111] TNA: PRO, MAF 67/175, Sheffield FCC, 'Revocation procedure', 3 May, 4 September, and 6 September 1948.

[112] The Times, 24 June 1952, 3.

[113] Export and Slaughter of Horses, 9.

[114] TNA: PRO, MAF 83/3157, 'Addendum to the Report on Meat and Livestock: Knackers yards and the Marking of Meat', 2 February 1948.

legitimate counterparts, dishonest Sheffield wholesalers travelled long distances to obtain fresh produce. They procured supplies by offering to pay growers a substantial black market premium. Buyers judged untrustworthy by growers or a commercial threat by rival wholesalers risked being informed on—which is what happened to one Sheffield trader when he tried to buy soft fruit in and around Wisbech in Cambridgeshire, one of the chief market gardening areas in England.[115] Some local farmers and growers dealt with black marketeers from Leicester and London as well as Sheffield.[116] As in Kendal and Romford, there was a ready market for black market foodstuffs amongst Sheffield's caterers.[117] Selling to caterers was a sensible strategy, as it limited producers' and wholesalers' exposure to the risks associated with operating in local illicit retail markets. Inspectors found it harder to police deals that took place on private premises than those that took place in shops or markets open to the public.

While the surviving records of Food Control Committees, such as those for Sheffield, Romford, and Kendal and South Westmorland, reveal much about the organization of illicit retail and wholesale food markets, there are no comparable records relating to the illicit trade in other non-food convenience goods and specialist goods. What does survive supports the picture of illicit markets dominated by struggling small and medium-sized family businesses for which black market dealing was a sideline. Street traders posed a particular problem. The results of government investigations and fragmentary information from other sources suggest that the black market trade in petrol took place around the country. Although it shadowed the white market in petrol, the black market centred on garages in rural areas where demand for extra petrol was highest, and secondhand car dealers—Warren Street, the centre of London's used car trade, was legendary in this regard—and truck stops where hauliers could exchange spare commercial petrol coupons with garage owners and private motorists.[118] With long-distance lorry drivers passing through rural south Westmorland on the A6, there was great scope for petrol black marketing and pilfering of road freight at local transport cafés, truck stops, and petrol stations. The Jungle Café on the A6 a few miles south of Shap Summit, and some distance from a major settlement, was the most notorious.[119]

DOING THE BUSINESS

From wherever would-be black marketeers operated, they needed to attract the attention of shoppers looking for a 'little extra', while running the risk of being

---

[115] TNA: PRO, MAF 67/174, Sheffield FCC, 'Revocation procedure', 6 January 1947.

[116] BL, Millennium Memory Bank, C900/01040 C1, 'Interview with Terence Roy Huggins', interviewed by Eva Simmons.

[117] TNA: PRO, MAF 67/175, Sheffield FCC, 'Revocation procedure', 2 February 1948.

[118] Evasions of Petrol Rationing; David Hughes, 'The Spivs', in Michael Sissons and Philip French (eds.), *Age of Austerity: 1945–1951* (1963; Harmondsworth, 1964), 86.

[119] BL, Millennium Memory Bank, C900/02617, 'Interview with Lenore Knowles', interviewed by John Watson.

caught by law enforcement or having their money or goods stolen by other criminals. There were three business strategies open to traders seeking to limit these risks. The first was the 'closed' market strategy in which buyers and sellers knew each other. Retailers would sell only to people they knew or people introduced to them by existing customers. This minimized the risk to sellers, but it limited turnover. This was a familiar strategy to the fences, illegal bookmakers, and petty criminals who diversified into black market dealing. The consumer–retailer tie imposed by the MoF pushed grocers and butchers towards the 'closed' black market. Adopting the strategy imposed an additional cost on otherwise legitimate retailers. Not only did they turn away strangers, but the furtive nature of the deal could scare away existing customers who were accustomed to dealing openly with their retailer and were now worried about being ripped off or disliked feeling like a criminal. Others enjoyed the risk, and got a thrill from beating the system.

The alternative 'open' market strategy in which buyers and sellers did not know one another was much riskier for sellers, though it boosted sales. This strategy was a good option for sellers of price-controlled goods and those rationed goods that did not require customers to register with a retailer. Their openness to passing trade made this an attractive strategy for the owners of garages and petrol stations, as well as market traders and street traders. Hawkers and peddlers plying their trade around pubs, clubs, and cafés also adopted it.

A seller's success in implementing the open-market strategy rested upon his ability to judge a buyer's intentions from verbal and physical cues. In Romford market, stallholders came before the food enforcement subcommittee several times, with the surname Gradinsky appearing more often than any other. This family dominated the illegal trade in seasonal produce during and immediately after the war. Highly competitive and easy to observe, it was difficult for the family business to grow in Romford's open market without attracting unwanted attention from commercial rivals and law enforcement. Having cornered the local market for early tomatoes in 1946, other Romford stallholders reported the family to the enforcement subcommittee for overcharging. The investigation revealed that the family bought the tomatoes before the new season's retail prices came into effect, and were legally entitled to set their own price.[120] As a result of this and other incidents, food inspectors knew the stall. This attention threatened the business, as inspectors found it easier to make a test purchase from a market stall than from a shop. Surrounded by crowds of impatient customers on busy market-days, stallholders and their assistants did not always recognize an inspector. Yet the family proved adept at handling this hazard, securing trader's licences for several family members so that there was always someone who could run the stall should one of the family receive a trading ban or attract too much attention from the authorities.[121] By selling their produce from a barrow elsewhere in the town centre, they spread the risks of being caught still further.[122]

[120] TNA: PRO, MAF 67/52, 'Romford FCES minutes', 17 June 1946.
[121] TNA: PRO, MAF 67/52, 12 July 1943.
[122] TNA: PRO, MAF 67/52, 3 November 1942.

Most shopkeepers adopted a third 'semi-open' strategy, conducting illicit deals with trusted customers and, on occasion, plausible strangers. The accessibility of their premises and the fact that most retailers sold a mixture of controlled goods, only some of which required customers to register for rations, made this a sensible strategy for most shopkeepers. The same was true for established traders with a known pitch or route and a sizeable number of regular customers. When the family of Romford costermongers had the opportunity to open a greengrocer's shop, they took it. It was far easier for the family member who ran the shop to avoid prosecution than it was for those running the stall and barrow. On two occasions the subcommittee received complaints from the shop's customers about overcharging but took no further action for lack of evidence.[123] With only one entrance it was easier to spot one of the local inspectors, whom the family knew by sight, entering the shop. This made test purchases difficult, leaving inspectors with uncorroborated testimony from aggrieved customers. With inspectors unable to catch the greengrocer overcharging, the enforcement subcommittee could only issue him with warnings.

It is far easier to discern the retail location, business strategies, and supply chains of black marketeers than it is to discover the prices they charged for their goods. Neither government economic advisers nor their academic peers studied black market pricing, as economists were a scarce commodity not to be wasted on surveying the underground economy.[124] Until 1947 it was widely assumed by economic commentators that black markets must be seller's markets in which prices matched free market prices. Poorly versed in supply and demand theory, informed opinion considered that neither price control nor rationing affected demand for a product. They also assumed that the system of direct and indirect controls on consumption did not reduce purchasing power. This led them to conclude that the black market price represented the 'free' price.[125] Even the President of the BoT Harold Wilson, a former economics lecturer who should have known better, subscribed to this simplistic view of black market prices. North American economists quickly dismissed this view when they began to pay serious attention to the issue in the late 1940s.

Arguing from theory, the North Amercians showed how controlling one good increased demand for its substitutes. This reduced demand for the controlled good. Increased taxation and forced savings reduced demand further by mopping up excess purchasing power. Factoring in the economic costs associated with black marketing and any moral inhibitions cut effective demand still further. In reality, excess demand for a controlled good was not the difference between the quantity that would be demanded at the same price in the pre-war market and the quantity supplied under price control or rationing. In these circumstances the black market price could be lower than the 'free' price. When taking the behaviour of suppliers into account, the

---

[123] TNA: PRO, MAF 67/52, 4 February and 17 June 1946.
[124] Charles Reid, 'The Crooked Smell', *The Observer*, 14 December 1947.
[125] Michael Michaely, 'A Geometrical Analysis of Black-Market Behaviour', *American Economic Review*, 44 (1954), 635.

picture became increasingly complex. With lower aggregate demand for a controlled good, the quantity supplied via official and black markets was lower than it would be in a free market. If black market demand increased, then black market supplies expanded at the expense of official supplies. If the new black market price was high enough then it might also increase overall supply as firms increased production to meet demand, perhaps at the expense of markets in substitutes or other products.

Theorists of black market prices could not test their ideas, as the enforcement agencies did not collect price data systematically. On occasion, ministry inspectors and police announced the street value of the goods and coupons they seized, but this was more about publicizing official victories in the campaign against black marketeers and proving the investigating officers' effectiveness than it was about monitoring black market demand. It was also a way for investigating officers to prove their worth, as the value of the property that an officer recovered was almost as important as the number of arrests he made and his clear-up rate in securing promotion. Such facts featured prominently in detectives' memoirs.

Price data taken from court reports are equally patchy. From 1942 onwards the higher courts had to determine the black market value of goods and coupons before sentencing convicted black marketeers, as new regulations required them to impose fines that would remove the proceeds of crime. Although judges received expert advice from enforcement agencies, their calculations varied in a way that could not be explained in terms of supply and demand. Hearing a compensation case in June 1946, a Birmingham County Court judge put the value of a single valid clothing coupon at £1, which put the value of a partially used 1945/46 civilian clothing book at a minimum of £30.[126] The city's coupon dealers would have been delighted to realize such a price when the black market price was widely believed to range between 2s and 2s 6d per coupon.[127] As inaccurate as such valuations could be, judges, unlike magistrates, attempted to obtain price data to produce monetary estimates. Given that magistrates dealt with the bulk of offences, this represents a significant gap in the available data.

Only Richard Fry, Financial Editor of the *Manchester Guardian*, made a detailed inquiry into black market prices towards the end of 1946. He wanted to see whether the Labour government's cheap money policy was feeding inflation. If it was, black market prices would be rising as increasing amounts of money chased a strictly limited supply of controlled goods. After consulting 'official and highly unofficial sources', Fry and his staff concluded that black market retail prices became increasingly volatile during the second half of 1946, reflecting shifting patterns of effective demand. His sources led him to believe that the average price of a clothing coupon, which ranged from 2s to 2s 6d in May—not much higher than the 2s per coupon that the BoT thought standard in 1944—stood at 1s 6d six months later. With the exception of nylon stockings, which fetched up to £4 per pair on the black market compared to a legal price of 10–15s, demand for black

---

126 *Manchester Guardian*, 4 June 1946.
127 Richard Fry, 'The Black Market', *Manchester Guardian*, 13 May 1946.

market clothing and textiles was falling as supplies increased. During the first half of the year black market food prices stood at twice or three times the official price, but were now much higher.

Fry's investigation confirmed the obvious point that prices varied according to location. In rural districts the black market premium for eggs was half the fixed price, but those same eggs could sell for up to four times their official price in central London. Country dwellers paid a little more than the official price for a gallon of black market petrol, while Londoners might pay as much as 7s 6d.[128] These price differences reflected local demand, availability of supplies, and transport costs. In the countryside the black market price of fresh produce was low due to backyard production and the ease with which extras could be secured locally through the grey market. With limited scope for backyard production there was much greater demand for black market food in towns, which was also costly to transport there, driving prices higher. The price of black market petrol tended to be lower in the countryside too, as rural motorists could obtain petrol or spare commercial coupons, whether directly from farmers and lorry drivers or indirectly through a garage, with comparative ease.

Fry's investigation did, however, miss one of the peculiarities of black market pricing: expiry dates. The longer a coupon's expiry date, the more valuable it was; and as the expiry date came closer the coupon declined in value. Valid coupons fetched much higher prices on the black market towards the beginning of a rationing period than they did towards the end. This suggests that unwanted coupons flooded the market towards the end of a rationing period, driving the price down. In 1947, M-O noted that coupons went for '1/6 each until the recent issue became valid then the price jumped to 2/6 and 3/-'.[129] These price movements were best seen in the markets for petrol coupons and clothing coupons, the development of which was not hampered by the retailer-tie, unlike that in food coupons. Fry continued to monitor movements in black market prices into the late 1940s. Returning to the topic in September 1947, before the financial crisis forced the government to tighten consumer controls, he noted no changes in prices.[130] The black market price of a clothing coupon remained stable for another year before expanding supplies saw it tumble again in late 1949. This sharp price decline persuaded Harold Wilson that the time was right to end clothes rationing.[131]

Black market demand turned the market for stolen goods upside down. Prior to the war a thief could expect a fence to pay them a third of the new or secondhand retail price for unused or used goods. Experienced thieves asked for half the wholesale price, or based their asking prices on the fence's retail prices.[132] Typically, stolen goods retailed for considerably less than the legitimate retail price. Commercial

[128] Richard Fry, 'The Dangers of Spending', *Manchester Guardian*, 18 November 1946.
[129] M-OA, TC Food 6E, 'Black market and barter', 12 May 1947.
[130] Richard Fry, 'Where the Money Goes', *Manchester Guardian*, 29 September 1947.
[131] Wilson, *Memoirs*, 103–4.
[132] Sutton et al., 'Handling Stolen Goods', 57–8; Peter Quennell (ed.), *London's Underworld: being Selections from 'Those that will not work' the fourth volume of 'London Labour and the London Poor' by Henry Mayhew* (London, 1950), 305–10.

fences could sell stolen goods at new or secondhand prices, but the hawkers and residential fences who sold most stolen goods could not disguise their origin with the result that they sold stolen goods at a considerable discount. Half the retail price was the most common price for fast-moving stolen goods due to the rational and emotional attractiveness of the half price offer to most consumers. With burgeoning demand for controlled goods, black market prices for stolen goods matched, and sometimes exceeded, new or nearly new retail prices.[133] As there was no discernible difference between stolen goods and goods from official channels, criminals—particularly commercial fences—could ask for the same black market premium as did business sideliners. High demand and large profits help explain the increases in both the number of receivers and the amount of stolen property which they handled. The austerity boom in the stolen goods market perturbed successive Metropolitan Police Commissioners, whose annual reports charted its rapid growth between 1938 and 1948 and gradual decline into the 1950s.

Without legitimate wholesale and retail prices to which to refer, thieves and forgers found it much harder to determine a fair price for coupons. During 1942 commercial fences in East End London, such as the wardrobe dealer Arthur Harding, paid 1s each for forged clothing coupons, and bought unwanted coupons at the same rate, exchanging £3-worth of secondhand clothing for a complete clothing book containing sixty unused coupons. Harding bought stolen coupons for half that price or less, paying between 4d and 6d per coupon. He used the coupons to cover his wealthier customers' black market purchases, and made £20 for every £3 he spent on clothing books, which represented a tax-free return of 5s 8d per coupon. He made more on stolen coupons, however, clearing between 6s 2d and 6s 4d per coupon.[134] The gangs stealing and distributing coupons that Harding bought made much less. The same year, a London distributor negotiating the purchase of half a million coupons from a Glaswegian gang agreed to pay the gang 2½d per coupon. Selling to Harding, the distributor would have made only 3½d per coupon, despite most of the risk falling on himself and his placers.[135]

Price stability points to the fact that black markets were far from perfect. Sellers approached black market pricing in the same way as they did all pricing. Amongst retailers, few of whom had the skills to determine market prices, it was standard practice to add a customary mark-up. In some cases suppliers specified what this should be, which is why black market prices tracked official prices. The Petroleum Board's zoning of prices according to distance from a refinery continued to influence black market petrol prices, leading to marked variations in price between rural areas if not between rural and urban areas. The relationship between legal and illegal markets in fresh fruit and vegetables provides another example of price stickiness. Although these markets came closest to the economic ideal of a perfect market containing many buyers and many sellers, black market prices were expressed in terms of the official price. These customary prices reduced the transaction costs associated with black market dealing. The remarkably stable price of

[133] Klockars, *Professional Fence*, 57–8 n. 4.   [134] Samuel, *East End Underworld*, 259–60.
[135] *The Times*, 17 February 1942.

coupons shows the psychological and practical limitations that the coinage placed on illegal prices. The prices quoted by Fry and others stuck closely to coin denominations: 'one bob' (1s), 'two bob' (2s), and 'half a crown' (2s 6d) could be paid easily using a variety of small-denomination coins. Their stability bears comparison with the remarkably consistent rules of thumb applied in stolen goods markets.

Imperfect as they were, the fact that Fry and others could identify a generally prevailing price confirms that illegal markets did exist. A black market deal was not a one-off transaction that took place in an informational vacuum, as at least one contemporary economist thought it was.[136] Press exposés and court reports filled the vacuum, as articles such as Fry's supplied newspaper readers with price information that allowed them to distinguish a good deal from a bad one. Civilians used this information to 'wangle' more than their fair share of controlled goods. A slang term of First World War vintage, 'wangling', came into its own during the Second World War when consumers 'wangled' and sometimes 'fiddled a bit extra'.

To wangle additional supplies successfully, consumers not only needed opportunities to use illicit markets, but also had to have the means to recognize, assess, and exploit those opportunities. Means, motive, and opportunity are the key to understanding whether consumers used illicit markets and how they used them. Many civilians had an economic motive for illegal dealing, either need or greed. They also had the financial means to act on their desires when given the chance. Although residence, occupation, and income limited such opportunities, few people had no chance of evading the regulations. Their ability to take their chances depended upon their knowledge of illegal markets. Consumers had to know how to buy illegal goods. They needed to know a supplier and how to reach a deal. This did not pose a problem for those involved in grey markets, as they were the latest manifestation of social institutions for non-market exchange. The same was not true of black market transactions.

Some buyers and sellers knew how to buy and sell illegal goods thanks to pre-war experience, but most had to acquire contacts and expertise. This was not as hard as it might at first appear. Although information about black markets was scarce, maldistributed, and inefficiently communicated by comparison to information about official markets, it circulated widely through word of mouth and the media. Search costs might be higher in black markets, but not prohibitively so. A contemporary American study suggested that most women would find a back-street abortionist after asking five other women.[137] There was far more information about black market dealing in the public and private realms than there was about abortion. People were also happier to talk about illegal dealing because it was less stigmatized and more people were involved. Presumably, you must have needed to ask fewer people to get a reliable tip.

Others took a more direct approach, asking retailers whether they would sell goods off-ration or above ceiling prices. Soliciting black market goods was not an

---

[136] A. K. DasGupta, 'The Theory of Black Market Prices', *Economic Weekly*, 2 (1950), 97–101.
[137] Nancy Howell Lee, *The Search for an Abortionist* (Chicago, 1969).

offence. To save face if the answer was 'no', customers asked for black market goods in a roundabout fashion. A common approach was to give a hard-luck story followed by the question 'Do you know where I might get some coupons?' Pump attendants at filling stations were sensitive to these conversational gambits. When a librarian made an off-hand remark to an attendant, the attendant offered to supply him with coupon-free petrol.

> I pulled up at a large Bristol garage—one of the largest in fact. I asked for three gallons of petrol. When I paid the person, I said, jokingly, as I tendered the units: 'I suppose you want these.' He replied, 'I'm afraid I do, sir. If you're stuck at any time I expect I could help you out—at a price.'[138]

It was common to approach a retailer directly whether a person wanted black market petrol or a 'little bit extra' of some other controlled good.[139] In fact, retailers tired of special pleading complained about wheedling customers.[140]

Black marketeers pursuing open and semi-open business strategies made the task of finding a dealer even easier for potential customers. Sometimes petrol pump attendants, car mechanics, and garage owners offered to supply a motorist with coupon-free petrol or petrol coupons without being asked. An unsolicited approach was more likely if the motorist was an acquaintance or a regular customer.[141] Occasionally, hawkers and peddlers approached people in pubs, clubs, workplaces, transport cafés, and service stations. Hawkers selling matches, food, cigarettes, and newspapers were a common feature of pubs and clubs in working-class districts and town centres during the 1930s and 1940s, as were prostitutes and bookmakers.[142] Not surprisingly, they were also centres for the trade in stolen goods.[143] Many of the petty thieves and hawkers who plied their trade in pubs diversified during the 1940s, trading in the new lines of forged, stolen, and surplus coupons.[144] Advertising their presence by sporting a double-breasted full 'American Look' suit—contemporary gangster chic— they were easy to spot. The clothes signalled that the wearer was likely to be a 'general dealer', or at the very least knew where you could find 'one of the boys'.[145]

By 1947 these flashily dressed street traders, now labelled 'spivs' rather than 'wide boys', had come to represent the retail end of regional or national criminal networks supplying black market goods. Public understanding of how illicit retail markets and their supply networks operated had not advanced since *The Field* presented the black market as a structured hierarchy under the control of professional criminals in 1941. This image, which owed more to the crime octopus of

---

[138] M-OA, DR January 1948, DR 229.   [139] DR 183 and 196.

[140] DR 12; Addison, *Now the War is over*, 32.

[141] Mitchison diary, 14 May 1941, in Sheridan, *Among You taking Notes*, 142–3.

[142] M-O, *The Pub and the People: a Worktown Study* (2nd edn., London, 1987), 208–9, 268–9; and B. D. Nicholson, 'Drink', in London School of Economic and Political Sciences, *The New Survey of London Life and Labour*, 9 vols. (London, 1930–35), ix, 257.

[143] White, *Worst Street*, 184–5; Hobbs, *Doing the Business*, 142–3.

[144] M-OA, DR January 1948: DRs 2 and 291.

[145] Mark Roodhouse, 'In Racket Town: Gangster Chic in Austerity Britain, 1939–1953', *Historical Journal of Film, Radio and Television*, 31 (2011), 541–59.

popular fictions than lived experience, distorted contemporary views and continues to shape historical writing.[146] The reports of two departmental committees—a secret one into the meat black market and a published one into the petrol black market—did little to alter this perception.[147] The fact that most black marketing involved unscrupulous businesses and took place within authorized channels went unrecognized. Legitimate businesses were by far the biggest suppliers of black market goods, and dominated the market in ration coupons. They were also an important channel through which stolen and counterfeit goods and coupons could flow. Although dishonest business people were central to the operation of illicit retail markets, the under-the-counter trade was a minor part of their business that kept struggling businesses afloat. As a result, for most people their black market dealings took place in a familiar retail setting.

Official definitions of what constituted the black market obscured the centrality of these business sideliners. For government, as for the media, the black market involved 'large-scale and organized illegal dealing', which excluded petty and technical offences. Officials did, however, add one further qualification: at no point should black market goods flow through official channels. Lecturing the would-be Allied military administrators of liberated Europe on food enforcement in June 1944, the head of the MoF Enforcement Division Monro repeated the standard definition that 'a black market offence is an offence involving illegal transactions in food obtained otherwise than through the authorized channels'. This, he explained, included the sale of meat from illicitly slaughtered animals, but excluded overcharging and conditional sales by wholesalers and retailers who obtained their supplies legally.[148] It is also unclear whether Monro classified the traffic in unused coupons, smuggling, theft, fraud, and forgery as black market. Excluding these popular illegal transactions from the definition impoverished official understanding of the underground economy.

***

Britain's underground economy experienced a long mid-century boom due to the economic controls introduced during the first two years of the Second World War. The longstanding practices of gifting, bartering, and doing paid favours flourished. Britons lumped together these disparate types of monetary and non-monetary exchange under the label 'grey market'. Seemingly arbitrary to officials who classified evasion by offence, the repertoire of exchanges dubbed 'grey market' shared some but not all characteristics. But there was one property that all the exchanges in this polythetic category had in common: most people saw nothing wrong in them. People considered grey marketing to be socially and morally acceptable, as such

---

[146] Mary E. Murphy, *The British War Economy* (New York, 1943), 260–3; Dexter M. Keezer, 'Observations on Rationing and Price Control in Great Britain', *American Economic Review*, 33 (1943), 281; Maude, *Black Market*; Smithies, *Crime in Wartime*; Smithies, *Black Economy*; Thomas, *Underworld at War*; Donald Thomas, *Villain's Paradise: Britain's Underworld from the Spivs to the Krays* (London, 2005).

[147] See the unpublished Boddinnar committee reports in MAF 83/46 at the National Archives, and the Parliamentary Papers for the Russell–Vick committee report on Evasions of Petrol Rationing Control.

[148] Monro, 'Enforcement', 266–7.

exchanges caused no obvious harm while having obvious benefits, strengthening social bonds and increasing individual welfare. The absence or irrelevance of the profit motive confirmed that grey marketing was illegal but socially acceptable. It also highlights the link with the sector of the underground economy, which has been described as an 'economy of regard' or an 'economy of favours'. This continuity with the inter-war period explains the mushrooming of the grey market.

Black markets appeared overnight for similar reasons, and illicit markets in coupons and goods grew out of pre-existing markets. The markets in stolen and counterfeit goods mobilized for war as criminals switched their attention to controlled goods and ration documents. Legitimate businesses evaded the new regulations, using customary fiddles and cheats practised by a minority of traders before the war. The illegal transfer of unwanted coupons and rations was central to both types of market. This could work to the advantage of black marketeers, as it allowed them to deceive themselves and others about any profit motive.

Although the grey market was far larger than the black market, neither market realized its full potential. Their underdevelopment and size relative to one another is a puzzle that challenges a purely economic explanation of evasion. Traders and consumers had the means, motive, and opportunity to evade the regulations. Even the best-designed control scheme could not accommodate individual preferences. Some people would always want more controlled goods than they could get hold of, while others would always under-consume. Despite shifts in consumer demand from tightly controlled goods to loosely or non-controlled goods, forced savings, and higher taxes, there was plenty of cash sloshing around the economy that could be used to pay for black market goods. Information was not a problem either; and although scarce, it was readily available. Clearly, some people chose not to participate in grey or black market deals. The solution to this explanatory puzzle might lie in the history of enforcement and punishment. Was it the risk of being caught and punished that held people back? If it was, they behaved rationally. This would obviate the need to consider alternative reasons for limited non-compliance such as patriotism or the law-abiding character of the British—two explanations favoured by contemporaries. This is the question addressed in Part II.

PART II

'A STIFF ROD IN PICKLE': ATTACKING BLACK MARKETS

Introduction

Having intoned 'Here is the News' the BBC newsreader Frank Phillips worked his way through the nine o'clock evening news headlines for Wednesday, 11 March 1942. He led with the story of an unsuccessful attack on the German battleship *Tirpitz* off the coast of Norway two days earlier. The undamaged *Tirpitz* downed two torpedo bombers before retiring under a heavy smoke-screen. Next was the announcement of Sir Stafford Cripps' 'Mission to India'. Cripps hoped to persuade Indian politicians to accept British plans for Indian self-government. With no news to report from Burma and other theatres, Phillips turned to home news. Earlier, the Minister of Food had told the House of Lords that the white loaf would disappear from shop shelves and only brown National Wheatmeal Bread would be sold. The white loaf was not to return to the shops until October 1956. The next item was the Home Secretary's announcement that the government would introduce tougher penalties for black market offences. Phillips alerted his listeners to the fact that 'Mr Morrison will be speaking about this at the end of the News'.[1]

After the news bulletin, in the five-minute 'Postscript to the News' slot, Herbert Morrison reassured the six million listeners who had not switched off their sets that the government was doing all it could to crack down on black marketeers. Morrison, the son of a London policeman, had 'a stiff rod in pickle' with which to beat anyone convicted of a serious black market offence. The stick, hardening in vinegar until needed, was a maximum sentence of fourteen years' penal servitude plus a heavy fine.[2]

Although his politics differed greatly from those of his father, a working-class Tory, Morrison shared his dad's view of criminals as a class apart for which crime was a choice—a rational choice. If the costs of a crime outweighed its benefits, then people would not commit crime. Vigorous policing and harsh penalties would make non-compliance risky and expensive, deterring offenders from reoffending

[1] BBC Written Archive Centre (WAC), Caversham, News Scripts, *Home News Bulletin*, BBC Home Service, 11 March 1942, 21:00 hrs.

[2] BBC WAC, Talk Scripts, Herbert Morrison, 'Black Market', *Postscript to the News*, BBC Home Service, 11 March 1942, 21:30 hrs.; BBC WAC, R9/11/6, 'General Listening Barometer Week 11', 11 March 1942.

and others from evading the regulations in the first place. Those who miscalculated the risk or who looked for it would be punished severely. This view of crime informed the government's response to black markets.

Whatever former policymakers and administrators wrote in their published memoirs, they did not place their trust in the patriotism and law-abiding character of the British alone when determining enforcement policy.[3] They remained pessimistic about the power of altruism to control individual self-interest when tested. In public they celebrated the underdevelopment of Britain's black markets, heralding this as proof of Whitehall's administrative genius and testament to the strength of British character. When distilling ten years' experience of rationing into a series of lessons for future administrators, the economist Brian Reddaway downplayed the importance of 'test shopping, flying squads and the like' in favour of designing a scheme that enforced itself, the year he spent working on a scheme to stop the black market trade in red petrol forgotten.[4] In private, Reddaway and others recognized the need to enforce the law rigorously. Lord Woolton hinted at both in his memoirs, praising the British for their forbearance before detailing the steps he took to enforce the law, creating an undercover unit to target black marketeers and imposing 'literally ruinous' penalties for offences.[5]

The economic understanding of crime that Morrison shared with Woolton and others bears close resemblance to the model developed by the economist Gary S. Becker. Morrison might not have understood Becker's formulae, but he would have understood and agreed with the economist's statement that 'a person commits an offence if the expected utility to him exceeds the utility he could get by using his time and other resources at other activities'.[6] This could explain what the supply and demand for black market goods and the availability of criminal opportunities cannot: namely, the underdevelopment of the grey and black markets. If the public considered the chance of being caught high, and the likely punishment harsh, then few would choose to commit a crime. But public perception of the risks involved in non-compliance rested on personal experience, hearsay, and media representations. These were themselves a function of the volume of resources pumped into enforcement activity and the ability of government publicists to project an image of vigorous and fair enforcement in the media.

The importance of enforcement to our story of black marketeering has been hinted at by other historians who stuffed it into a portmanteau of explanatory variables.[7] While it is true that more bureaucrats controlled fewer people in the UK than in the USA, it is not the number of officials administering and enforcing the regulations that matters. What matters is their effectiveness, which raises several questions. Did the government departments responsible for control develop coherent enforcement policies? And could they implement them uniformly and in full? The first question, addressed in Chapter 4, is the easiest to answer, as it focuses on

---

[3] Zweiniger-Bargielowska, *Austerity*, 153–4.   [4] Reddaway, 'Rationing', 192.
[5] Woolton, *Memoirs*, 230–1.   [6] Becker, 'Crime and Punishment', 176.
[7] Mills and Rockoff, 'Compliance', 209–12.

the formulation of enforcement policy in Whitehall. Answering the second question requires us to examine both enforcement and punishment across the country, tackled in Chapters 5 and 6 respectively. Taken together these chapters chart new territory by providing a detailed study of regulatory enforcement involving multiple ministries and agencies, not just the familiar axis of the Home Office and the police. From these chapters it becomes clear that while the various ministries drew up compliance regimes that would pass muster with today's advocates of 'responsive regulation', recognizing as they did that crime was a choice and the people who made that choice were selectively rational, the attitude and behaviour of the enforcement agencies and the courts turned enforcement into a lottery.[8] This made rational calculation of the risks and rewards of evasion impossible.

[8] See Ian Ayres and John Braithwaite, *Responsive Regulation: Transcending the Deregulation Debate* (New York, 1992) for more on 'responsive regulation'.

4

War and order: securing compliance

In August 1939 officials at the BoT Food (Defence Plans) Department, who would form the nucleus of the second MoF, outlined the four points that would inform food enforcement policy until the ministry's demise in 1955. These were: '(a) Wide publication. (b) A System of inspection to spread knowledge and to assist the Trade and Public in obeying it. (c) Investigation of contraventions; and finally (d) Prosecution if necessary.' More fundamental was the requirement that 'An order to be effective must be acceptable to the Trade and Public'.[1] This advice, like the four points that preceded it, reminded administrators that policing and prosecution were part of a broader approach to securing compliance that embraced efforts to gain public support for control and close loopholes in the regulations. Officials hoped that together these measures would reduce non-compliance to a level at which food inspectors and their auxiliaries, the police, could cope. Thanks to resource constraints, the BoT and the MoFP had arrived at similar compliance strategies by 1943.

Dependent upon 'bluff and goodwill'[2] for its success, this approach to regulatory enforcement was inherently unstable. Careful design might minimize leakages from control schemes, but it could not prevent evasion, while coercion was impossible, as inspectors, like the goods whose distribution they policed, were in short supply. Reviewing staffing figures in spring 1947, a Treasury official looking for cuts found it 'remarkable' that the MoF and the BoT could police elaborate regulations 'in these days of shortage and black-market tendencies' with so few inspectors.[3] What the cost-cutting bureaucrat failed to appreciate was that the inspection regime was a public relations exercise focused on reassuring a law-abiding majority while deterring a criminal minority. In doing so controllers accepted the risk of a sudden breakdown in compliance if goodwill evaporated or their bluff was called.

DESIGNING OUT CRIME

For the economist Brian Reddaway, who helped devise several rationing schemes, good design was the basis of any compliance strategy. Reflecting on his experiences at the BoT, Reddaway advised future controllers that 'The successful enforcement

[1] TNA: PRO, MAF 72/562, 'Enforcement', n.d. (August 1939).
[2] Hargreaves and Gowing, *Civil Industry*, 329.
[3] TNA: PRO, T 161/1303/55816, W. H. J. to Sir Herbert Brittain, 24 April 1947.

of a rationing system and the avoidance of a black market is not primarily a matter of test shopping, flying squads and the like, but rather of devising a rationing system which will be relatively easy to enforce, and which will, indeed, to a large extent "enforce itself".[4] For Reddaway, passing coupons back along the distribution chain in exchange for rationed goods was the key to 'automatic' enforcement. Observing this and other maxims has been seen as the key to higher levels of compliance with British price control than with its American counterpart.[5]

The civil servants who drew up pre-war plans for food and petrol control had a limited appreciation of such design principles, while Reddaway's colleagues at the wartime BoT had to learn them afresh. By respecting such principles, controllers minimized but did not eliminate evasion. Rediscovering, adding to, and acting on these maxims took until 1943. In the interim, controllers, propelled by trade interests and public opinion, made elementary mistakes that increased opportunities for evasion. Much to their annoyance, political and resource constraints prevented administrators and economists from remedying some of these early errors, which had important consequences for the effectiveness of the ministries' compliance strategies.

When it came to price fixing, controllers aimed to stabilize the cost-of-living index by setting the prices of basic goods from source to sales point at a level that consumers could afford while securing a reasonable profit for producers and suppliers.[6] Experience during the First World War had taught that fixing retail prices alone encouraged honest suppliers to market goods immediately and sell them close to their point of origin. While this allowed them to maximize profits by minimizing transport and storage costs, it created localized shortages. Leaving wholesale and producer prices 'free' also forced retailers to absorb price rises, which drove the honest out of business and encouraged the dishonest to evade the regulations.

If price control was to avoid such problems, the regulations had to be horizontally integrated as well as vertically integrated. This involved regulating secondary markets in used goods as well as markets in substitutes and related products. Leaving such markets uncontrolled frustrated official attempts to fix prices as traders sold new goods as used goods. It also encouraged suppliers to switch from producing and dealing in a controlled commodity to supplying uncontrolled substitutes or related products. Like vertical integration, horizontal integration did not eliminate abuses of price control, but it did reduce incentives to evade.[7]

Regulators opted to fix maximum prices and profit margins at every stage from producer to consumer. They preferred to specify maximum prices that were readily understood and easy to police. This was possible only when a commodity arrived in the hands of consumers in much the same form as it had been when it left the producer. When processed foods or manufactured goods were involved, regulators

[4] Reddaway, 'Rationing', 192.
[5] Mills and Rockoff, 'Compliance'.
[6] Price Stabilization and Industrial Policy (PP 1940–1 Cmd.6294 viii, 311).
[7] This was the settled view of contemporary economists. See A. C. Pigou, *The Economics of Welfare* (1920; 4th edn., London, 1938), 229–41 and Jules Backman, *Government Price-Fixing* (New York, 1938).

preferred to specify maximum profit margins expressed in cash terms ideally but more usually as a percentage. Often controllers laid down a maximum profit margin subject to an overriding ceiling price for manufacturers in order to limit their ability to maintain margins by inflating costs.[8]

To make their task easier, price fixers sought to standardize products and grades—another lesson taken from the previous conflict. Controllers regulated the quality and quantity of raw materials in manufactured goods by fixing raw material quotas and setting minimum product standards.[9] When it came to elaborate finished articles, regulators standardized designs as well. Simplifying these standard designs had the added benefit of economizing on raw materials. This was the origin of utility schemes in clothing, furniture, and other products. The drive towards standardization was accompanied by a push towards industrial rationalization.[10]

Wherever possible, regulators encouraged mergers, cartels, trade associations, and other forms of industrial combination, as this made supervision easier and price negotiations simpler.[11] The resultant deals were closer to the ideal of the self-enforcing agreement, as most, if not all, traders had been involved in talks. This ensured that deals reflected customary pricing practices, which lent legitimacy to official price schedules. The smaller number of traders involved, which made it easier to reach agreement, also made supervising their behaviour simpler. Finally, taxation and forced savings schemes bolstered price control by reducing excess demand.[12]

While accurate, this summary of the elements and principles of price control, recorded in contemporary studies of the wartime system,[13] belies the time it took for regulators to realize this vision. Despite agreement on the need to control prices in 1939, planners did not envisage the imposition of general price control once war broke out, though basic foods and fuel would be subject to price control and rationing immediately.[14] Public concern about a repeat of First World War profiteering forced Neville Chamberlain's National Government to cobble together a scheme for general price control to prevent profiteering by traders in non-food goods, which was hurried through parliament to enter the statute books in November 1939. Within four months, the War Cabinet agreed on the inadequacy of the act.[15]

---

[8] Political and Economic Planning, *Government and Industry: A Survey of Relations between the Government and privately-owned Industry* (London, 1952), 78; Hargreaves and Gowing, *Civil Industry*, 610–12; E. F. Nash, 'Wartime Control of Food and Agricultural Prices', in Chester, *War Economy*, 200–38.

[9] G. C. Allen, 'The Concentration of Production Policy', in Chester, *War Economy*, 167–81.

[10] Hargreaves and Gowing, *Civil Industry*, 507–9.

[11] *Civil Industry*, 556–7; Hammond, *Food*, i, 78; and TNA: PRO, POWE 33/21, 'History of the Petroleum Board', n.d. (1950).

[12] Monica Felton, *Civilian Supplies in Wartime Britain* (London, 1945), 16–17.

[13] See Jules Backman, *Rationing and Price Control in Great Britain* (Washington, DC, 1943); and James S. Earley, L. Margaret Hall, and Marjorie S. Berger, *British Wartime Price Administration, 1939–1943* (Washington, DC, 1944).

[14] Neil Rollings, 'Whitehall and the Control of Prices and Profits in a Major War, 1919–1939', *Historical Journal*, 44 (2001), 517–40.

[15] Hargreaves and Gowing, *Civil Industry*, 77–8.

Initially, government envisaged this as a permanent form of control, giving officials the authority to raise standstill prices in order to take account of rising costs. It soon became apparent that the system was unenforceable due to the difficulty of establishing a product's price on a given date—usually 21 August 1939—the wide variation in prices charged for it by suppliers, and the act's failure to provide for an inspectorate to enforce the regulations. If price control was to be successful in the medium to long term, a simpler and more effective method of fixing prices was needed.[16] Despite its patent inadequacies, the BoT did not remedy the situation until 1941 when Oliver Lyttleton piloted the Goods and Services (Price Control) Act, 1941 through parliament.[17] Finally, schedules specifying maximum prices and profit margins replaced standstill orders, which were now seen as a way to buy time to devise more permanent regulations. The new act was part of a broader policy of control that aimed to stabilize the working-class cost-of-living index, not just the prices of specific commodities. Until this point evasion flourished—something official historians conceded.[18]

The early years of food and fuel control were equally unedifying. The controllers had a weak grasp on the basic principles of price fixing at the war's outset.[19] Hard-pressed civil servants rushing to complete plans for control immediately before the war lifted maxims from internal war histories.[20] The wisdom contained in them was not always understood, while experts who might have helped them to do so were ignored. The ideas of Arthur Pigou, author of *The Political Economy of War* and *Economics of Welfare*, had no discernible influence on planning, while the relevant volumes in the British series of the Carnegie *Economic and Social History of the World War* went unread.[21] Unsolicited advice from former controllers also went unheeded.[22]

This limited appreciation of the reasoning behind their predecessors' maxims helps explain some of the initial mistakes that the MoF made. Criticized for allowing 'profiteering' in British onions, Lord Woolton fixed their retail price without taking steps to control supplies or their distribution. Onions promptly disappeared from shop shelves in distant markets, and the same thing had already happened to home-produced eggs. This pattern of public criticism leading to retail price control followed by shortage repeated itself several times over the ensuing months.[23] Much to civilians' annoyance, first rabbits, then groceries, and finally turkeys disappeared from shop shelves. The problem worsened in spring 1941 when city dwellers complained about the price and availability of the new season's produce.[24]

---

[16] *Civil Industry*, 78–80.

[17] *Civil Industry*, 555–62; *Price of Goods Act, 1939*, 2 & 3 Geo. 6, ch. 118.

[18] *Civil Industry*, 75–91.

[19] BoT, *Report of the Food (Defence Plans) Department* (London, 1938), 9–10, 14.

[20] Woolton, *Memoirs*, 179.

[21] British Library of Political and Economic Science, London, Bev ii/B/39/2, Lennox-Boyd to Beveridge, October 1939, and Beveridge to Lennox-Boyd, 24 October 1939.

[22] Kevin Manton, 'Sir William Beveridge, the British Government and Plans for Food Control in Time of War, c.1916–1941', *Contemporary British History*, 23 (2009), 363–85.

[23] Hammond, *Food*, i, 185–6.

[24] TNA: PRO, INF 1/292 pt. 1, 'Home Intel. weekly report no. 23', 5–12 March 1941; 'Home Intel. weekly report no. 33', 14–21 May 1941; and 'Home Intel. weekly report no. 38', 18–25 June 1941.

Regulating the price of these foods was an irredeemable mistake. Seeking to re-assure the public, Woolton had committed his ministry to fixing the price of sea-sonal, perishable foods for which there was wide variation in individual demand. Price control worked best if uncontrolled prices were resistant to change.[25] Unfor-tunately, prices of these foods were not sticky, which meant official prices dated quickly. Worse still, these foods were neither essential nor in the basket of goods used to construct the cost-of-living index. Deregulation was not an option, as fail-ure would have undermined general confidence in food control. Half-heartedly pursued, these unenforceable schemes absorbed resources that could have been better deployed elsewhere and brought control into disrepute.

By mid-1941 controllers had relearned the fundamentals of effective price con-trol and remedied mistakes wherever possible. Nevertheless, the best-designed schemes remained easy to evade. As well as overcharging customers or giving them short weight—the most obvious offences—traders might impose a condition of sale that required customers to buy an uncontrolled good at an extortionate price when purchasing a controlled good at the fixed price. They might also levy unnecessary delivery fees and sales charges, or use them to disguise bribes, commission pay-ments, or tips from customers. Another wheeze was to indulge in quality deteriora-tion to maximize profits by adulterating or mislabelling a product. If there was an uncontrolled secondary market, traders could also sell 'used' goods for more than the official retail price. Similarly, traders might buy eggs for hatching or livestock for breeding or store at auction for an uncontrolled price, which they sold illegally to consumers at above ceiling prices. The regulations outlawed these and other of-fences, but inspectors and forensic accountants found them hard to detect.[26]

When it came to devising effective and enforceable rationing schemes—a but-tress to price control—officials had a better understanding of the elements of good design. Contemporaries recognized three forms of rationing: quasi-rationing, permit rationing, and coupon rationing. Quasi-rationing determined whose needs should be met first from available supplies. As such, it replaced informal rationing by queuing or by shopkeepers keeping goods 'under the counter' for favoured cus-tomers with a state-sanctioned system of over-the-counter favouritism. Quasi-rationing—known officially as 'priority rationing'—was a very loose form of control in stark contrast to permit rationing. Under permit rationing, consumers applied for buying permits that allowed them to purchase specific items. If they met the eligibility criteria, the authorities granted them a buying permit or a sup-plementary ration. Coupon rationing was more egalitarian than this. All consum-ers received a fixed number of coupons that entitled them to buy up to a guaranteed amount. Economists further distinguished between three forms of coupon ration-ing: a specific ration of a single commodity, a group ration of related products, and a general expenditure ration.[27] Specific rations could be expressed in terms of either

---

[25] J. K. Galbraith, 'Reflections on Price Control', *Quarterly Journal of Economics*, 60 (1946), 475–89 at 481–3.
[26] Hugh Rockoff (ed.), *Price Controls* (Aldershot, 1992), x–xi; Monro, 'Enforcement'.
[27] M. Kalecki, 'General Rationing', *Bulletin of the Oxford Institute of Statistics*, 3 (1941), 1–6.

value or quantity, while group rations and expenditure rations could be expressed only in terms of monetary value or point value. Generally, buying permits and quasi-rations related to quantity, not value.

Most British rationing schemes developed between 1940 and 1943 were either specific or group rationing schemes of various hues. By 1943, flat-rate specific rations were seen as the best way to control consumption of essential commodities in scarce supply for which there was no substitute and whose demand was predictable, regular, and universal. Group rationing was reserved for goods consumed irregularly and in widely varying quantities. The MoF, which was responsible for most wartime rationing schemes, introduced specific rationing of bacon and ham, sugar, tea, butter and margarine, and cooking fats during 1940, as well as a group ration for meat based on value, all of which required registration with a retailer. The ministry introduced a group ration for preserves in March 1941, and in December 1941 it introduced points rationing for tinned meat, tinned fish, and tinned vegetables, with a separate personal points scheme covering chocolate and sweets from July 1942. The ministry made limited use of quasi-rationing, setting up special distribution schemes for a small number of 'protective' foods such as milk, oranges, eggs, and vitamins, giving priority to the needs of expectant mothers, nursing mothers and their infants, children, and the ill.[28] After the war, the ministry rationed bread for two years from July 1946, and quasi-rationed potatoes for six months from November 1947.[29]

Specific rationing was the basis for petrol rationing, which was the first rationing scheme to be introduced in the UK. The scheme combined a straight ration for all private motorists, with supplementary rations for those in specific groups who applied for them. With smaller and smaller supplies available for civilians due to the U-boat blockade and the increasing demands of the armed forces, the MoFP withdrew the 'basic' ration for all motorists in July 1942. From then until the restoration of a basic ration in June 1945, petrol was the only major commodity to be subject to a form of permit rationing.[30] The ministry also allocated coal supplies to coal merchants and their registered consumers as a percentage of those customers' pre-war consumption. Unlike food rationing, no coupons were involved.[31]

Clothes rationing, introduced in June 1941, was the most important scheme operated by the BoT. It was the first group ration in the UK to use points as the basis for rationing.[32] The board also issued buying permits for furniture and industrial clothing, and operated a series of priority schemes for odd items such as imported alarm clocks for workers and strainers for invalids and infants. The distribution schemes employed by the board and its fellow rationing departments

[28] MoF, *How Britain was Fed in War Time: Food Control, 1939–1945* (London, 1946); and Impresario (Sir Martin Roseveare), *The Market Square: The Story of the Food Ration Book 1940–1944* (London, 1944).

[29] Zweiniger-Bargielowska, *Austerity*, 24.

[30] Evasions of Petrol Rationing, 7–8.

[31] Court, *Coal*, 154–7.

[32] Alan Booth, 'Economists and Points Rationing in the Second World War', *Journal of European Economic History*, 14 (1985), 297–317.

changed little from 1942 until the end of the war, when the economic purpose of control changed.[33]

Enforcing most of these rationing schemes depended upon passing ration documents back along the supply chain. If retailers sold rationed goods without taking coupons from their customers, they could not replace their stocks legally. The same was true of the wholesaler contemplating supplying the dishonest retailer coupon-free, and so on back to the start of the supply chain where the ministry or its agents counted, checked, and then destroyed the coupons. It would not have worked without rating coupons on the basis of an unchanging characteristic of a good. For example, clothes coupons reflected the amount of cloth in a garment.[34]

If passing back coupons was to work for commodities with long, convoluted supply chains, coupon banking was essential. To reduce counting, checking, and mailing of coupons to manageable proportions, thus reducing costs and human errors, all traders opened coupon accounts with their bank. Bank staff counted and checked retailers' coupons once, issuing coupon cheques to cover their purchases against the number of coupons paid into the account. The BoT introduced such a scheme as an adjunct to clothes rationing in 1942.[35] The MoF introduced coupon banking in 1943, requiring traders to open points accounts at their local food office.[36]

The picture was quite different if consumers registered with retailers to obtain their ration. The MoF and the MoFP—the only departments to require it—issued retailers with buying permits covering their registered customers' rations. Registration suited the distribution of inexpensive perishable foods such as bacon and ham, sugar, meat, cheese, fat, and preserves, which civilians purchased frequently from local stores. Knowing the exact quantity that each shop required made for orderly distribution. It also worked for coal. Although food retailers collected coupons, which they passed to their local food office, officials checked them rarely. Given the volume of food and the number of purchases involved, regular checks, let alone passing back coupons, was too costly and too slow. Instead, officials relied upon customers complaining about retailers' abuses.[37]

All British rationing schemes contained a design flaw, which neither passing back coupons nor registration could remedy. When determining ration levels the authorities could not take individual preferences, needs, and incomes into account, which ensured that there were always some consumers with more coupons than they needed and some with fewer. Under registration this left food retailers with a surplus.[38] Although issuing supplementary rations, allowing people to eat out coupon-free, and encouraging self-supply allowed some to obtain more than their fair share legally, an under-the-counter trade was inevitable without effective coupon checks. The practice of depositing pages of coupons with food retailers made this easy to disguise. When shortage of manpower forced the ministry to abandon coupon checking in December 1941, retailers were free to reallocate coupons

---

[33] Hargreaves and Gowing, *Civil Industry*, 303–42.   [34] Reddaway, 'Rationing', 195.
[35] *Manchester Guardian*, 5 June 1942.   [36] Hammond, *Food*, i, 294–307.
[37] Reddaway, 'Rationing', 190–3.   [38] Hammond, *Food*, ii, 754–5.

between their customers, thus turning rationing into a pay-as-you-go system. Equally, consumers could gift, barter, or sell unwanted rations.[39]

The allocation problem manifested itself differently when it came to the passing-back system. Here there was potential for an illicit market in spare coupons to develop, in addition to pay-as-you-go systems organized by retailers or illicit exchange networks involving consumers.[40] The only solution was to make rations convertible, but officials rejected proposals to buy back unwanted coupons or legalize a secondary market in spare coupons, as they felt that such plans ran counter to their aim of orderly and equitable distribution. Instead, they introduced unenforceable bans on consumers transferring ration documents and retailers accepting loose coupons. As was the case with unwanted rations under the registration system, this resulted in illegal transfers of spare coupons.[41]

While registration avoided the problem of coupon trafficking, it had a further, unique flaw: the reliance on customer complaints for its enforcement. By lodging a formal complaint, consumers alienated local shopkeepers and their favoured customers, and lost any chance of receiving 'extras' themselves. The passing-back system also had a problem of its own. While retailers could increase turnover, they could not expand stocks unless the authorities gave them extra coupons.[42] This limit on business growth incentivized retailers to buy coupons illegally, as the authorities were loathe to issue extra coupons.

Contemporary economists and former administrators had long appreciated the intractability of these fundamental problems with price control and rationing. Although there was always a way around the regulations, a well-designed scheme need not add to these weaknesses. Rediscovering and applying the principles of good design learned during the First World War took longer than it need have done. In the meantime, mistakes were made that could not be remedied. As a result, opportunities for evasion multiplied unnecessarily, making enforcement harder. Keen to retain the public's confidence, which was central to their compliance strategies, ministers promised, and led the public to expect, more than their officials could deliver.

PERSUADING THE PEOPLE

'An order to be effective must be acceptable to the Trade and Public', concluded a food official on the eve of war. William Beveridge, permanent secretary of the first Ministry of Food, made much the same point in October 1939. Writing to a newly appointed junior minister, Beveridge stressed that 'in food control publicity is of great importance'. His former boss Lord Rhondda had understood this, taking pains 'to secure a "good press" for his measures'.[43] Their successors as permanent

---

[39] *Food*, ii, 544–7.   [40] Hargreaves and Gowing, *Civil Industry*, 327–8.
[41] Zweiniger-Bargielowska, *Austerity*, 183–4.
[42] Hargreaves and Gowing, *Civil Industry*, 327.
[43] Cited in Manton, 'Beveridge', 373.

secretary and minister, Henry French and W. S. Morrison, failed to appreciate this. Beveridge had to wait until April 1940 for the appearance of a latter-day Rhondda in the figure of Lord Woolton.

Explaining his approach to enforcement, which would shape other departments' compliance strategies, Woolton stressed the need to persuade people that control was necessary, efficient, and fair. Before agreeing to any new regulation, he asked his civil servants, 'Will the general mass of the public accept this as a necessary and a sensible provision?' If the measure lacked public support, Woolton rejected the regulation 'because we should never have been able to afford the police force to make it effective'. If food control was to be a success, it was necessary to persuade the public of its 'justice and impartiality'. It was equally important to secure 'general public acceptance of the correctness of its purpose and the fairness of its administration'.[44] His determination to take the public with him prompted Woolton to speak regularly to reporters, talk on radio programmes, and appear in newsreels. Leaving administration to his permanent secretary, Woolton established a 'benevolent and faintly folksy' image for the ministry.[45]

Selling food control to people was easy, but retaining public support for it was far harder. Politicians had little trouble in persuading people of the need to impose or extend control before 1943. Due to recent historical precedent, the public understood the consequences of uncontrolled wartime inflation. Rising prices, shortages, queues, and strikes loomed large in memory of life on the Home Front during the First World War, and above it all floated the figure of the profiteer, whom the public blamed for these problems.[46] Food control, introduced in 1917, proved an effective solution to these difficulties, damping down prices and sharing supplies around. With decontrol in 1921, food profiteering returned, which burnished the reputation of this imperfect and *ad hoc* system. As a result, there was no need to make the economic case for control. With a second 'great' war imminent, the press, echoing public opinion, demanded that government control prices and ration essential goods as soon as hostilities began.[47] Rather than selling control to a sceptical public, Woolton and others found themselves resisting, and sometimes succumbing, to popular pressure to fix prices and ration goods.

To retain popular support, Woolton strove to convince the public that price fixing and rationing were fair, which became a key theme of all the rationing ministries' publicity. His predecessor, Morrison, was the first government minister to invoke popular notions of distributive justice in defence of rationing. In a broadcast talk, Morrison said that food rationing, based on the principle of 'share

[44] Woolton, *Memoirs*, 230.

[45] Richard J. Hammond, 'British Wartime Food Control: Some Addenda to an Official History', *Food Research Institute Studies*, 3 (1962), 183–94 at 189.

[46] Jean-Louis Robert, 'The Image of the Profiteer', in Jay Winter and Jean-Louis Robert (eds.), *Capital Cities at War: Paris, London, Berlin, 1914–1919* (Cambridge, 1997), 104–32; Christine Grandy, ' "Avarice" and "Evil Doers": Profiteers, Politicians, and Popular Fiction in the 1920s', *Journal of British Studies*, 50 (2011), 667–89.

[47] Gallup, *Opinion Polls*, i, 25 and 27.

and share alike', would ensure 'perfect fairness in distribution'.[48] Woolton developed the rhetoric of fairness further, promising that rationing would ensure 'fair do's all round' and asking civilians to 'play fair by one another' and observe the regulations.[49] By doing so he moved the ministry away from the principle of strict equality in rationing, implied by Morrison's use of the expression 'share and share alike', to the vaguer notions of 'fair do's' and 'fair play' which could embrace equity and need as well as equality—three popular criteria used to determine a just distribution of resources. Under Woolton, the ministry made a conscious effort to bolster support for rationing by incorporating such popular notions in a 'national food code'. Throughout summer 1941 Woolton retailed the concept of a public and personal food code, informed by the principle of 'fair shares' and 'fair play'.[50]

Like the MoF, publicity was central to the compliance strategies of the BoT and its Petroleum Department. In fact, the BoT coined the iconic slogan 'fair shares for all' in its clothes-rationing publicity. Although the slogan became inextricably linked with rationing, it was not uncontroversial. On reading the slogan in the copy for the advertisements announcing the introduction of rationing, the junior minister Captain Waterhouse 'questioned whether this had not a tinge of Socialism about it'.[51] Despite Waterhouse's doubts, the Publicity Committee approved the slogan. Interestingly, the President of the Board Oliver Lyttelton, a Conservative MP, avoided using the phrase in his broadcast talk about the new scheme.[52]

Lyttelton was perhaps aware that he and his fellow ministers ran the risk of undermining support for control by promoting its fairness. Invoking norms of fairness raised expectations about distributive justice that controllers found hard to meet. Dissatisfaction with Whitehall's ever-changing definitions of what constituted a fair price, a fair profit, or a fair share, and suspicion of the calculations used to arrive at them, could prompt evasion. As the man responsible for clothes-rationing publicity from December 1941, the journalist Nicholas Davenport was more aware of this problem than most. Despite ministerial misgivings, the theme of fairness captured in the slogan 'Fair Shares For All' had, until this point, been central to clothes-rationing publicity.[53] Davenport—a social radical—objected to its continued use, as 'The same number of coupons which a poor woman required to buy a cloth coat would enable a rich woman to buy a mink coat'. Much to his annoyance his superiors 'insisted on propagating this outrageous social lie'.[54]

[48] *The Times*, 8 January 1940; BBC WAC, Talk Scripts, W. S. Morrison, 'The Rationing Scheme', *From the Front Bench*, BBC Home Service, 6 January 1940, 21:20 hrs.

[49] *The Times*, 28 August 1943; BBC WAC, Talk Scripts, *Food Forum*, BBC Home Service, 19 September 1941, 21:20 hrs.

[50] HL deb, vol. 119, 29 May 1941, cols. 327–34; BBC WAC, Talk Scripts, Lord Woolton, 'Food', *From the Front Bench*, BBC Home Service, 13 June 1941, 21:15 hrs.

[51] Francis Meynell, *My Lives* (London, 1971), 269.

[52] BBC WAC, Talk Scripts, Oliver Lyttelton, 'Announcement on Clothes Rationing', *Home News Bulletin*, BBC Home Service, 1 June 1941, 09:00 hrs.

[53] Meynell, *My Lives*, 269.

[54] Nicholas Davenport, *The Memoirs of a City Radical* (London, 1974), 132.

As Davenport's colleague Brian Reddaway admitted, clothes rationing delivered 'terribly weak fair shares'.[55] Although the point of rationing was 'orderly distribution and a certain degree of equity', administrators had limited aspirations when it came to fair shares. Reddaway judged rationing schemes 'reasonably' or 'sufficiently' equitable if the public preferred them to 'the alternative "system" of queues, favoured customers, shop-crawling, and the like'.[56] As a proof of fairness, Reddaway's test was politically inadequate from early in the war. Consumers soon forgot the scramble for supplies before rationing began. In some instances there had been no scramble, as rationing started before shortages emerged, and in the circumstances, comparing rationing with its alternatives was a counterfactual exercise that convinced few. Having promised fairness, the authorities came under increasing pressure to define fair shares.

Although official publicity asserted the fairness of control, it did not explain the criteria used to fix prices and draw up ration scales. There is little difficulty in identifying the ideas informing fair shares policies, as the notion of 'equality of sacrifice' invariably cropped up when politicians discussed them. The origins of the idea lay in mid-nineteenth-century discussions of Adam Smith's view that taxes should be proportional to income. Equal sacrifice theory—especially the principle of equal proportional sacrifice—was of critical importance in securing popular support for the Gladstonian fiscal tradition and establishing the British state's reputation for class neutrality.[57] During the First World War, policymakers applied the concept to the question of taxation of wartime profits. Responding to popular demand for a curb on profiteering, politicians began to apply the idea of equality of sacrifice to price regulation too. Given the sacrifices that ordinary consumers were making for the war effort, the principle required producers and distributors to forgo the extra profit created by wartime shortages. Government used the principle to justify price controls and an excess profits tax. The concept, balanced against a perceived need to maintain incentives for entrepreneurs, remained central to inter-war plans for price control in any future 'great' war.[58] All agreed that in the event of another war consumers should pay a just price that secured reasonable profits for producers and distributors.

Deciding what a 'reasonable' profit or a 'just' price amounted to in pounds, shillings, and pence was already a contentious issue before talk of fair shares made it worse. None of the rationing ministries fixed prices at levels which ensured that either the poorest or the average consumer could buy the same quantity of goods in wartime as they had consumed in peacetime. The ministries did not possess the information or expertise to calculate affordability. Ensuring equal sacrifice, whether

---

[55] Keith Tribe, 'Interview with Brian Reddaway', in Keith Tribe (ed.), *Economic Careers: Economics and Economists in Britain 1930–1970* (London, 1997), 71–85 at 82.

[56] Reddaway, 'Rationing', 183.

[57] Adam Smith, *The Wealth of Nations*, v, 2.25; Martin Daunton, *Trusting Leviathan: The Politics of Taxation in Britain, 1799–1914* (Cambridge, 2001), 136–79 and Daunton, *Just Taxes: The Politics of Taxation in Britain, 1914–1979* (Cambridge, 2002), 13, 106–7; Ross McKibbin, 'Why was there no Marxism in Great Britain?', *English Historical Review*, 99 (1984), 297–331.

[58] Rollings, 'Whitehall and the Control of Prices', 520–6.

defined in absolute, proportional, or marginal terms, was beyond them. Instead, they opted to stabilize the working-class cost-of-living index, knowing that it bore little relation to the actual cost of living due to the outdated pre-war basket of goods on which it was based. In the absence of powerful consumer interest groups, it fell to organized labour to press the government on this issue. But the Trades Union Congress did not object to the use of an index with which it was familiar, whatever its failings, as it had long formed the basis of wage negotiations with employers. As a result, genuine grumbles about high prices did not receive a public airing, with important consequences for evasion.

Caught between the trade associations demanding a fair profit and a public haunted by the spectre of the profiteer, ministry officials could not use such a crude method to determine what constituted a fair profit. Initially, government price-fixers issued standstill orders pegging prices to those charged for the same items in August 1939, though this was a temporary measure while ministry cost-accountants drew up price schedules on the basis of cost plus a 'reasonable' margin of profit. The issue here was of whose costs should form the basis of the calculations. Should it be the high-cost, average-cost, or low-cost supplier? While the percentage or cash margin differed from product to product, what suppliers considered a 'fair' profit held steady. They read 'fair' margin as synonymous with a 'reasonable' or an 'ordinary' profit—concepts central to inter-war debates about resale price maintenance. In 1931 producers and small independent retailers, united in their attempt to hinder the growth of price-cutting chain stores, defined a reasonable profit as that of the 'ordinary business of average efficiency'. Rarely were such figures based on costings; the reasonable profit was the customary mark-up applied by the trade.[59]

The MoF adopted this definition of a fair profit with an important addition: maximum retail prices had to 'incorporate margins providing for the remuneration of all the links in the chain of distribution at its longest'.[60] This preserved the pre-war distribution network, ensuring that consumers continued to shop where they always had done. Although smaller retailers complained about 'double margins' to the multiples who were entitled to a wholesale and a retail margin, the ministry's approach to price fixing lessened any antagonism by keeping the least efficient producers, wholesalers, and retailers in profit. The manufacturing and distributive trades under the control of the BoT fared less well.

The BoT, which did not need to worry about maintaining production or distribution as the shopping and speciality goods they controlled were not purchased on a daily basis, determined that 'retail margins should be no more than was required to secure distribution of consumer goods in the simplest and most efficient way, irrespective of pre-war profits and of the expenses of the particular business'.[61] The less efficient businesses had to adapt their operations to fit official margins or cease

[59] BoT, *Restraint of Trade* (London, 1931) cited in Hermann Levy, *Retail Trade Associations: A New Form of Monopolist Organisation in Britain* (London, 1942), 101–9.
[60] Hammond, *Food*, i, 105.
[61] Hargreaves and Gowing, *Civil Industry*, 596.

trading. Unable to increase their turnover by attracting customers with lower prices, these firms had to cut costs in order to survive. Falling turnover, poor accounting skills, and high fixed costs meant that a significant minority of small traders teetered on the brink of bankruptcy.[62] For this minority of struggling traders the black market gave them the opportunity to restore their businesses to profitability. The same was true of a much smaller number of food trades, such as the ice cream industry, that were treated with equal ruthlessness by the MoF. The BoT was aware of this problem, launching a series of official inquiries to placate trade associations and their allies on the Liberal and Conservative backbenches, but they did not change their policy, although they took a few steps to ameliorate conditions for the worst affected.[63]

When it came to price fixing, the MoFP and its agent the Petroleum Board found themselves in a worse position than either the MoF or the BoT. They needed to maintain the network of garages and petrol stations so that commercial and private motorists could obtain petrol whenever and wherever they needed to. But the number of motorists was small and falling, leading to precipitous declines in garages' turnover. Sales of spare parts, tyres, and other accessories, as well as servicing and repairs, made these businesses profitable. With fewer vehicles on the road, turnover fell and the petrol price could not increase to make up the difference. Amongst owners of garages and petrol stations, particularly those on minor roads, dissatisfaction with official prices was high and thus the temptation to dabble in the black market was strong.[64]

Regulators applied the principle of equal sacrifice, which guided their price policies, to rationing as well. Officials sought to distribute rationed goods to consumers equitably, balancing the needs of different groups of consumers against one another while avoiding conflict between them. The architects of rationing distinguished between essential, semi-essential, and non-essential consumption. Officials used this typology to classify individual goods. Balancing the need to streamline the rationing bureaucracy and the desire to avoid social conflict with the principles of equity, the authorities began by rationing essential goods. Drawing on traditions inherited from the First World War, the MoF preferred to divide available supplies of essential foods equally between all civilian consumers rather than base rations on an individual's nutritional requirements. In the administrators' eyes these essential rations were equivalent to the untaxed personal allowance. While administrative capacity pushed the ministry in this direction, a well-stocked national larder made this egalitarian approach possible. If supplies had been much lower, the authorities would have had to ration essential foods according to nutritional needs. In such circumstances, official ration scales would

---

[62] J. B. Jefferys, *Retail Trading in Britain, 1850–1950* (Cambridge, 1954), 105–9; Hermann Levy, *The Shops of Britain: A Study of Retail Distribution* (London, 1947), 119–33.

[63] BoT, *Third Report of the Retail Trade Committee* (London, 1942), 5–6.

[64] Mark Roodhouse, 'Black Market Activity in Britain, 1939–1955' (Ph.D. thesis, University of Cambridge, 2003), 61–2.

have represented an unacceptable cut in consumption and change in diet for many civilians, providing a fillip for black marketeers.

While flat rations might accord with a political philosopher's notion of fair shares, the MoF acknowledged that most Britons would consider strict equality unfair. As an internal memorandum noted, 'Rationing is essentially inequitable; it provides the same quantity of an article for each person without any consideration of their needs or habits or of their capacity to secure alternatives.'[65] Allocating food according to individual need was too costly to contemplate. Instead the government developed 'welfare schemes' to augment flat rations, fortifying flour and margarine with vitamins, expanding communal feeding, giving priority to the needs of children under sixteen, and expectant and nursing mothers in the distribution of 'protective' foods, and introducing supplementary rations for some manual workers.[66]

As well as the theme of fairness, common to all the rationing ministries' publicity campaigns, the MoF and the Petroleum Department developed a second theme about sailors' sacrifices to bolster support for control. This was an easy link to establish in the public mind due to extraordinary stories such as that of the oil tanker MV *San Demetrio*, abandoned in the mid-Atlantic after being set ablaze by a German battleship, reboarded, and sailed home. Although this and similar stories did not persuade the public of the need for rationing, official propaganda and news coverage stressed that civilians should be grateful for rations imported at such high cost and avoid wasting them. The Petroleum Secretary Geoffrey Lloyd made this point in a broadcast talk about the *San Demetrio* in January 1941. After paying tribute to the bravery of the crew and all other the sailors bringing petrol to Britain, Lloyd asked motorists to consider the human cost of petrol and reduce the amount they consumed.[67] The MoI exploited the story's propaganda potential throughout the war, publishing an account of the voyage by the author F. Tennyson Jesse in 1942, and helping Ealing Studios to produce the film *San Demetrio– London* the following year.[68]

Propaganda calling to mind the blood sacrifice represented by imported consumer goods was not an option for BoT publicists, who envied the ability of their colleagues in the Petroleum Department and the MoF to indulge in emotional blackmail. While the 'food people' could 'put a black market steak in the balance against a sailors' life', the BoT press officer found it harder to persuade the public of the dangers of black market clothing. The consequences of the 'shell that isn't made against the silk stocking that is' were not as readily apparent.[69] For the Battle

[65] Hammond, *Food*, i, 125.

[66] Zweiniger-Bargielowska, *Austerity*, 32–2; James Vernon, *Hunger: A Modern History* (Cambridge, MA, and London, 2007), 193–5.

[67] IWM, Dept. of Doc., 85/46/27, Geoffrey Lloyd, *Postscript to the News*, BBC Home Service, 22 January 1941, 21:25 hrs.

[68] F. Tennyson Jesse, *The Saga of the San Demetrio* (London, 1942); Charles Barr, *Ealing Studios* (2nd edn., London, 1993), 22, 35–8.

[69] TNA: PRO, BT 64/3032, C. C. J. Simonds, 'Note of my meeting with Yandell this afternoon', 3 September 1942.

of the Atlantic's duration, this was a major difference between BoT propaganda and that of the MoF and MoFP. No group risked their lives to clothe the people.

In addition to general publicity campaigns, the MoF launched anti-black market campaigns to reassure the public that it had evasion under control. When black marketeering became a cause of concern in 1941, the ministry responded directly to public anxiety through press briefings, newsreel addresses, and parliamentary speeches. In so doing, Woolton and his deputy Gwilym Lloyd George confirmed the existence of black markets in controlled foods whilst reassuring the public that inspectors would find offenders, and that an array of administrative and criminal sanctions would be used to punish malefactors severely. Later that summer, MoF advertisements tackled the issue directly, making the point that black marketeers would not thrive without a ready supply of willing customers.[70] Howard Marshall, the director of public relations, continued the campaign into the autumn. His office lobbied the BBC to produce a feature about black marketeering, supplying the Features Department with a script for a radio play and a moralizing epilogue by Lord Woolton. Pressured to fill the airwaves, the Features Department accepted the script readily, making few changes.[71] According to the producer, the moral of the play was that 'the apparently innocent, well-meaning housewife who wangles an extra couple of eggs is unconsciously part of a chain tied at the other end to criminal gangsterism'.[72] In his afterword Woolton rammed home this point, which was the nub of Marshall's publicity campaign.[73]

MoF anti-black market publicity was unique. The BoT, its Petroleum Department, and the Central Price Regulation Committee did not respond to press-fuelled panics about profiteers, racketeers, and black marketers with well-orchestrated publicity campaigns. The Petroleum Department chose not to launch campaigns against non-compliance, issuing figures for prosecutions and convictions instead. The BoT, its parent department, took a similar line, encouraging crime reporters to cover major cases while choosing not to launch anti-black market campaigns or make an effort to mobilize traditional moral authorities such as the Anglican Church to condemn black markets.[74] The Chairman of the Central Price Regulation Committee Raymond Evershed used a radio talk to brand evaders of price controls as 'unpatriotic and selfish'—the flipside of fair shares rhetoric—but this was his only anti-black market salvo.[75]

Officials working for these bodies feared that a publicity campaign would give the impression that evasion was widespread, believing that law-abiding civilians

---

[70] 'Food Facts No. 46: It Isn't Clever', *The Times*, 18 June 1941; 'Food Facts No. 53: Black Sheep—Black Markets', *The Times*, 14 August 1941; 'Food Facts No. 59: Not With The Blind Eye, Please', *The Times*, 17 September 1941.

[71] BBC WAC, R19/92 C63, S. Potter to P. Creswell, 1 October 1941.

[72] BBC WAC, R19/92 C63, S. Potter to R. Westerby, 30 September 1941.

[73] BBC WAC, R19/92 C63, *Black Market*, BBC Home Service, 7 October 1941, 20:00 hrs.

[74] Payton-Smith, *Oil*, 217; TNA: PRO, BT 64/871, 'Publicity Committee minutes', 2 January 1942; TNA: PRO, BT 64/793, G. W. Yandell, 'Board of Trade response to Swiss questionnaire about the black market', n.d. (December 1945).

[75] BBC WAC, Talk Scripts, Sir Raymond Evershed, 'Black Market', BBC Home Service, 7 May 1942, 18:00 hrs.

would think that they were missing out while others broke the regulations with impunity. This, they worried, could bring about a tipping point at which the level of non-compliance was too high for the departments' enforcement arms to tackle, and precipitate the breakdown of control. The MoI, which ran all government publicity campaigns except for MoF ones, encouraged controllers in this view. In 1941, senior MoI officials rejected calls from Howard Marshall at the MoF for a series of propaganda shorts about black markets, arguing that such films would mislead the public as to the nature and extent of evasion, and breed suspicion and resentment while not tackling a problem best dealt with through administrative action.[76]

THE WITHERED ARM OF THE LAW

Well-designed control schemes and publicity exhorting the public to obey the regulations were not enough to secure high levels of compliance alone. Given the irredeemable design flaws in control and the risks inherent in fair shares rhetoric, the regulators' compliance strategies depended upon levelling a credible threat of coercion. The MoF, and latterly the other departmental controllers, recognized this, forming inspectorates to police the regulations. With limited resources these inspectorates developed regulatory styles that combined coercive and persuasive tactics to secure compliance from people whom they imagined were rational self-interested actors. The larger the inspectorate, the more emphasis it placed on deterrence, and the greater the likelihood that it would use criminal sanctions rather than administrative penalties. Played out in front of the public, this game of cops and robbers was as much about reassuring the honest as it was about persuading the dishonest to obey the regulations.

The experience of food control during the First World War left officials in the Food (Defence Plans) Department in no doubt about the importance of enforcement. Consequently, the second MoF began its life with an Enforcement Division. With less experience to draw upon, the Mines Department and Petroleum Departments, semi-autonomous BoT departments that merged to form the MoFP in 1942, reached the opposite conclusion, eschewing the need for independent inspectorates to police fuel and petrol rationing. The departments' pre-war plans had made no provision for fuel and petrol inspectors. Their parent department, the BoT, repeated this mistake when circumstances forced officials to contrive a system of price control in late autumn 1939. The result of their hard work, the Prices of Goods Act, left enforcement to local Price Regulation Committees who would deal with complaints from the public. There were, however, no inspectors to investigate complaints about overcharging.[77]

---

[76] TNA: PRO, INF 1/73, Pt. 1 (or INF 1/284), 'Executive Board minutes', 13 August 1941; INF 1/251, Pt. 5, 'Films Division proposals', 2 October 1941; INF 1/249, 'Home Planning Committee minutes', 18 December 1941.

[77] Prices of Goods Act (1939), 2 & 3 Geo. 6, ch. 118; Hargreaves and Gowing, *Civil Industry*, 79.

The Petroleum Department recognized its mistake within eight months of the beginning of petrol rationing, appointing the first petrol inspectors in May 1940. The BoT took somewhat longer to acknowledge the problem, repeating the mistake once more when it introduced clothes rationing in June 1941. Within days the Coordination Committee overseeing the imposition of control appealed to the police and local authorities to help them to enforce the regulations. Now painfully aware of the issue, senior officials gave the task of enforcing clothes rationing to the Investigation Section—a forensic accountancy staff that had been enforcing limitation of supplies orders since December 1940. This was a curious blunder, as the BoT President Oliver Lyttelton had already taken steps to remedy the obvious problems with enforcing price control. Early in 1941 Lyttelton persuaded the Lord President's Committee—the key Cabinet committee for Home Front policies—to authorize the creation of a price inspectorate with the argument that 'the shorter supplies become, the less willing members of the public will be to report offences, if only they can get what they want'.[78] The Goods and Services (Price Control) Bill, introduced to parliament eleven days after clothes rationing came into effect, provided for a price inspectorate answerable to the Central Price Regulation Committee. Within three months of the Bill becoming law in late July, the first full-time price inspectors began work.[79]

The appointment of price inspectors and the restructuring of the Investigation Section were the first signs of the rationing ministries' compliance strategies converging. Against a backdrop of tightening supplies and mounting concern about illegal dealing, the departments devoted yet more resources to enforcement. In 1942 the BoT expanded the number of clothes inspectors working with the accountants of the Investigation Section. George Yandell, a retired detective superintendent recruited from Scotland Yard, took control of the enlarged inspectorate. A further reorganization in summer 1942 left Yandell in charge of a new Investigation Branch which incorporated both the forensic accountants and the clothes inspectors.

Developments at the Petroleum Department mirrored those at its parent department. In September 1941 the Petroleum Inspectorate doubled in size, expanding from twenty-four to forty-eight inspectors, and was placed under the control of a chief inspector, William Collins, another detective superintendent on loan from the Yard. A new Enforcement Section of the Rationing Division, directed by the former Manchester solicitor George Ryan, provided legal advice to the inspectorate and helped them to prepare cases for the BoT Solicitor's Department. Under the direction of a barrister, the Prosecutions Branch of the Solicitor's Department handled petrol rationing cases as well as all clothes rationing cases. In 1948 the branch employed ten barristers and seven solicitors to prepare and conduct these cases, subcontracting a third of them to local solicitors.[80] On merging with the

---

[78] TNA: PRO, CAB 71/3, LP (41) 10, 5 February 1941.
[79] Goods and Services (Price Control) Act (1941) 4 & 5 Geo. 6, ch. 31; TNA: PRO, BT 64/74, 'Draft Instructions for Inspectors appointed under the Goods and Services (Price Control) Act', n.d. (October 1941).
[80] HC deb, vol. 448, 4 March 1948, col. 504.

Mines Department to form the MoFP in summer 1942, the Petroleum Inspectorate, now Investigations Branch, assumed responsibility for enforcing fuel and lighting Orders as well as motor fuel Orders.

While the Petroleum Department, the BoT, and the Central Price Regulation Committee busied themselves with creating inspectorates, the MoF Enforcement Division reorganized and expanded its headquarters staff, creating a Central Enforcement Intelligence Bureau (CEIB) under Calcutta's retired police commissioner Sir Charles Tegart. In creating the CEIB and appointing Tegart, the permanent secretary Sir Henry French placated Woolton, who was determined to create a unit to tackle large-scale evasion of food control, which he believed was an emergent threat. Peter Cheyney, author of numerous hard-boiled detective novels, appears to have given the minister the idea, offering Woolton the services of his detective agency Cheyney Research and Investigations for a fee. Enforcement officials resisted the suggestion, as Cheyney and his agents intended to act as *agents provocateurs* to gather intelligence and secure evidence.[81] Despite his officials' concerns, which led him to drop Cheyney, Woolton pursued the idea further, asking the lawyer Sir William Crocker to conduct an independent investigation into London's meat black market.[82] Unable to persuade Woolton of the folly of this approach, French aimed to bring these *ad hoc* investigations under his control. By creating the CEIB, French appeased Woolton, who appreciated Tegart's work, and stopped the minister from building up a private intelligence agency.[83]

Despite the expansion in the number of enforcement officers, the men in charge of the inspectorates were under no illusions about their ability to police control orders effectively. In 1942 an opportunity to force the police to help their inspectorates presented itself to the rationing ministries. Encouraged by press reports, the public thought evasion widespread and demanded that the government take action early that year. This was one of the more serious criticisms of Churchill's ministry after Singapore fell to the Japanese.[84] Somewhat reluctantly the Prime Minister agreed to tighten some controls and enforce all of them more rigorously. Having overhauled their enforcement arms, the regulators persuaded the Home Office to issue a circular urging chief police officers to cooperate with their local inspectors.[85]

Tegart led on the issue of police cooperation, while Yandell and his counterparts at the Petroleum Department, Collins and Ryan, spent the summer reorganizing their departments' enforcement operations. Meeting with the permanent secretary

---

[81] TNA: PRO, MAF 100/15, Sir Henry L. French to W. H. Kirby, 27 June 1941; L. F. C. Maclean to French, 3 July 1941; Woolton to French, 6 July 1941; and French to Peter S. Cheyney, 7 July 1941.

[82] Sir William Crocker, *Far from Humdrum* (London, 1967), 219–20.

[83] Woolton, *Memoirs*, 230.

[84] M-OA, FR 1149, Tom Harrisson, 'Some Thoughts on Greyhounds and National Unity', March 1942.

[85] Churchill Archives Centre (CAC), Cambridge, CHAR 20/67: M.60/2, Churchill to Woolton, 28 February 1942; S.3/2, Churchill to Lord Cherwell, 10 March 1942; and M.79/2, Churchill to Sir John Anderson, 11 March 1942; TNA: PRO, HO 45/25135, 870415/11, Home Office circular 863,760/4, 18 August 1942.

to the Home Office, the head of the Home Office Police Department, and HM Inspectors of Constabulary, Tegart and his boss Sir Henry French persuaded them to allow food inspectors to attend the recently revived regional detective conferences, which had been scrapped earlier in the war. Police also invited local price inspectors, fuel inspectors, and clothing inspectors to attend, with the results that ministry inspectorates and police began to share intelligence. Since September 1941 the Criminal Records Office at New Scotland Yard had compiled a Black Market Index containing the particulars of known black marketers, and the MoF kept a similar index. Now it was possible for investigating officers to consult both indices.[86]

The same political pressures that prompted the police to cooperate more closely with ministry inspectorates in 1942 saw them stress the need to deter offenders. In March, after a sustained press campaign calling for harsher prison sentences and tougher fines that Lord Woolton secretly encouraged, the Home Secretary Herbert Morrison increased penalties for black market offences. The penalties on summary conviction went from a maximum of three months' imprisonment and a fine of £500, or treble the value of the black market goods, whichever was the greater, to a new maximum of twelve months' imprisonment and the existing maximum fine *plus* a new minimum fine, which was an amount equal to the profit made by the offender. The minimum penalty was a new departure that magistrates resented, as it removed their discretion in sentencing and implied that the sentences they had been imposing were unduly lenient. The penalties on indictment were much greater, the maximum being fourteen years' penal servitude, increased from two years, and a fine of £5,000, increased from £500, or treble the value of the goods, whichever was the greater, *plus* the court's estimate of the illicit profit.[87] This was Morrison's 'stiff rod in pickle'. The new penalties for black marketeering were severe by comparison to the typical sentence of three to four years' penal servitude for robbery with violence.[88] It was the second time in three months that the Home Office had increased maxima for black market offences. Under pressure from the MoF, backbenchers, and the press to prevent magistrates being lenient, Morrison had already raised the maximum fine from £100 to £500, or three times the illicit price of the goods, the fine being the larger of the two amounts.[89]

This episode affords a unique insight into official understanding of black marketeering. The focus on deterrence in internal discussions points to a view of serious offenders as rational and self-interested. For them, evasion was an economic crime that needed to be analysed in economic terms. Harsher punishment, ministers argued, would remove the financial incentives to evasion. Black marketeers—the ostensible target of the new penalties—were, however, few in number.

[86] See TNA: PRO, MEPO 3/1956 for information about the CRO's Black Market Index. This index is currently closed to researchers.

[87] Order in Council amending Regulations 55 and 90 of the Defence (General) Regulations, 1939 (S. R. & O. 1942 No. 501).

[88] Robert Murphy, *Smash and Grab: Gangsters in the London Underworld* (London, 1993), 44.

[89] Order amending Regulations 55 and 62C of the Defence (General) Regulations, 1939 (S. R. & O. 1941 No. 1981).

According to Morrison, the main reason for introducing tougher penalties was to reassure a law-abiding majority, as 'The prevalence of such offences has a bad effect on public morale and it is important that drastic measures be taken to check them'.[90] With little statistical evidence of widespread evasion, ministers thought of non-compliance as a problem of perception that left unchecked might become a self-fulfilling prophecy.

One of several problems that regulators encountered with the new penalties demonstrates their expressive function. The Home Office became increasingly concerned about the vague definition of black market offences as 'breaches of control'. In 1943 the Parliamentary Counsel and the Home Office considered amending Regulation 55 to clarify what constituted a 'breach of control'.[91] Several ministers made orders under Defence Regulation 55(1A) that did not involve controlled articles whose breach was not serious enough to merit the heavier penalties.[92] The regulation did not differentiate between black market and technical offences, and the maximum penalties appeared to apply to both types of offence. Officials were concerned that excessive penalties might be imposed for minor offences, angering the public and undermining respect for the law. The BoT, MoF, and MoFP opposed amending the regulation because it would embarrass the government and send out the wrong message to the public. The implications of amending the regulations for public relations convinced the Home Office to drop the idea.[93]

That ministers were conscious of the fragility of public support for the administration and enforcement of control can also be seen in the response to the press accusation that the BoT and MoF used *agents provocateurs*. In late August 1942 the London evening papers reported the allegation, made by a defence lawyer during the hearing of a clothes rationing case at Old Street Police Court, that a female BoT official persuaded a stallholder in Hoxton market to break the law.[94] This followed swiftly on the publication of a column in *The Spectator* attacking the Board's clothes rationing inspectors. In his column, Harold Nicolson recounted a well-polished tale about a man, soaked after being caught in a rainstorm, entering a shop in a Devon village and asking the shopkeeper if he could buy a pair of socks, as the pair on his feet were sodden. The man explained that he had no clothing coupons but promised to post some to the shopkeeper once he got home. After purchasing the socks the man revealed that he was an inspector, and later prosecuted the shopkeeper, whom the court convicted and fined. Nicolson admitted that the story was only hearsay, but recounted a similar case that he knew of personally. He deplored the use of test purchases, which he believed undermined public support for control. The public, Nicolson felt, disliked the use of an unfair

---

[90] TNA: PRO, CAB 71/8, LP (42) 52, 6 March 1942.

[91] TNA: PRO, HO 45/25135, 870,415/25, Sir John Stainton to Sir Oscar Dowson, 21 June 1943.

[92] TNA: PRO, HO 45/25135, 870,415/25, Stainton to Dowson, 25 January 1943.

[93] TNA: PRO, HO 45/25135, 870,415/25, Sir Alexander Maxwell to French, 12 July 1943.

[94] TNA: PRO, BT 64/3022, Yandell to Sir Stephen Low, 2 September 1942.

and 'un-English' method to enforce control that led them to empathize with law-breakers, besmirching the government's reputation for fairness.[95]

Press reports of the Nygate case and *The Spectator* column prompted public criticism of enforcement officers' test purchases. A day after *The Spectator* column appeared, the *Manchester Guardian* published a leader entitled 'An Odious Revival' criticizing test purchases.[96] Columnists and leader writers continued to criticize the use of test purchases during September,[97] and several MPs asked questions about the Board's use of them, expressing outrage at the practice.[98] Articles in the trade journals of the police and the lay magistracy, such as *Justice of the Peace and Local Government Review*, criticized their use too.[99] In response C. C. J. Simmonds, BoT Director of Public Relations, wrote to editors of newspapers and journals justifying the Board's reliance on test purchases. George Yandell drew up instructions for his inspectors on their use, extracts from which Hugh Dalton read in response to a parliamentary question about the use of test purchases. Simmonds also sent copies of the instructions to the press.[100]

The junior minister Captain Charles Waterhouse responded to Nicolson's allegations directly, writing a letter to *The Spectator* rebutting the allegations. According to Waterhouse, the Devon story had no basis in fact. Turning to the second incident, he pointed out that while the story was true in detail it did not cover all the facts: the shopkeeper concerned had consistently evaded the regulations, and it was only after four successive inspectors had made illegal purchases that the Board undertook a prosecution. Waterhouse pointed out that there was a shortage of experienced enforcement staff. 'It is therefore inevitable that on occasions the stringent rules laid down to prevent enticement are not strictly observed. But the cry of "*agent provocateur*" is apt to become popular as the latest thriller.'[101]

The scandal about test purchases spilled over, forcing Lord Woolton to rebut allegations about his ministry's use of *agents provocateurs* at a press conference. Off the record, Woolton appealed to the reporters to restrain themselves.

> It does not do any good to this country, which after all is completely upset in its social life: we are leading a new sort of life with all this Government control of what used to be a free country, and it does not do any good if we are going to give the impression that there is something in Government that is going round spying on people.[102]

Woolton, Dalton, and Waterhouse succeeded in quelling public fears. However, public concern about *agents provocateurs* resurfaced periodically throughout the 1940s; and each time the ministries responded forcefully to such allegations,

---

[95] Harold Nicolson, 'Marginal Comment', *The Spectator*, 21 August 1942.

[96] *Manchester Guardian*, 22 August 1942.

[97] *News Chronicle*, 12 September 1942.

[98] HC deb, vol. 383, 8 September 1942, cols. 20–1; 9 September 1942, cols. 147–8; and 11 September 1942, cols. 503–4.

[99] 'Agent Provocateurs', *Justice of the Peace and Local Government Review*, 3 October 1942.

[100] HC deb, vol. 383, 8 September 1942, cols. 20–1; *John Bull*, 10 October 1942.

[101] *Spectator*, 25 September 1942.

[102] TNA: PRO, MAF 102/126, 'Notes of press conference', 1 September 1942.

rebutting them in detail.[103] The importance of maintaining a public reputation for procedural justice did not escape officials and ministers.

Despite general agreement on the elements of an effective compliance strategy, the rationing ministries' policies continued to exhibit a greater degree of variety than either control schemes or ministerial publicity did. Under Lord Woolton, the MoF laid a greater emphasis on deterrence than the BoT and MoFP did, both of whom placed more weight on working with traders and consumers. Inspections, warnings, and administrative penalties were part of each enforcement agency's armoury, but the clothing inspectors, price inspectors, and fuel inspectors made more use of them than did their MoF colleagues. In private, the departments disagreed about the place of persuasion in enforcement—a clash of ideas which was not resolved until Colonel J. J. Llewellin replaced Lord Woolton as Minister of Food at the end of 1943.

Llewellin brought MoF prosecution policy into line with the other rationing ministries in 1944. His predecessor Lord Woolton was adamant that all offenders should be prosecuted, and had been since his appointment in 1940. Asserting his will had not been easy, as Enforcement Division did not exercise complete control over prosecutions for food crimes. In England and Wales, local Food Control Committees and Divisional Food Offices could, and did, prosecute minor offences, instructing a local solicitor to do so without reference to headquarters. Enforcement Division possessed a monopoly over major cases. In England and Wales it passed these cases to the Treasury Solicitor's Department, who prepared and prosecuted them. Prosecution arrangements differed in Scotland and Northern Ireland, where the Scottish Procurator Fiscal's Office and two solicitors employed by the Northern Ireland Food Division handled all cases.[104]

Reviewing the enforcement statistics at the end of the first year of control, Lord Woolton suspected that English and Welsh Food Control Committees allowed part-time local inspectors to issue warnings to traders and consumers at their discretion. The minister felt 'bound to express the view that a practice which was perfectly proper in the case of the Acts in question [the Food and Drugs Act and the Weights and Measures Acts] and under peacetime conditions is not appropriate to the enforcement of measures of food control under war time conditions, and should be discontinued except in cases of an obviously trivial character'.[105] As a consequence of this review, officials tightened central control over prosecutions—a reversal of previous policy.[106] In addition, Food Control Committees needed their Divisional Food Officer's sanction if they wished to pay a solicitor a fee in excess of a fixed sum. Neither could they brief counsel without his approval. Divisional Food Officers needed headquarters' approval if they wished to employ a solicitor or counsel for a large fee.[107]

---

[103] 'The Police and the Law', *Police Journal*, 17 (1944), 87–90.

[104] TNA: PRO, MAF 75/40, 'Record of Enforcement Division', n.d. (1950).

[105] TNA: PRO, MAF 150/632, 'Enforcement: Review of Procedure', n.d. (September 1940).

[106] TNA: PRO, MAF 102/123, 'Notes of press conference', 15 April 1940; and MAF 100/5, Woolton to Lord Reid, 27 February 1942.

[107] Monro, 'Enforcement', 265.

By 1943 the practice of prosecuting all first-time offenders—even those consumers and traders who had made inadvertent mistakes or were guilty of technical or petty offences—was undermining the ministry's reputation for procedural justice and antagonizing magistrates and judges. As with public concern about the employment of *agents provocateurs* and the use of powers of search and seizure in 1942, Llewellin moved swiftly to allay public fears and preserve his ministry's reputation for fair dealing. The new minister ended Woolton's prosecution policy in summer 1944. As a direct result of Llewellin's decision, the number of successful prosecutions fell from 25,667 in 1944 to 17,256 a year later.[108] Ben Smith, the first Minister of Food in the post-war Labour government, continued this policy while intensifying investigation and prosecution of serious cases such as theft of controlled foods, illicit slaughter of livestock, and black market dealing in poultry and eggs.

The MoF focus on deterrence was in stark contrast to the other ministries' enforcement styles. Given the extent of price controls, the number of prosecutions for overcharging and related offences was derisory. In 1946, price controls covered 48% of consumer expenditure, and yet price regulation committees prosecuted a mere 973 cases[109] (see Table 1.2). This is not surprising, as the price inspectorate pursued a policy of flexible enforcement based on visiting traders and manufacturers, and investigating occasional complaints from the public. According to the instructions issued to inspectors, they should ensure that the owners of a business, visited for the first time, understood the regulations if they discovered any irregularities in the books. A talk, a leaflet, and a verbal warning sufficed. The purpose of subsequent visits was to check that 'the advice given has been followed'. If it had not, 'a serious view' would normally be taken of the case.[110]

The BoT and the MoFP were more robust in their responses to evasion than the Central Price Regulation Committee, but their compliance strategies could still be characterized as flexible and accommodating. The BoT made frequent use of verbal and written warnings to clothes rationing offenders. Responding to a request for information from the Swiss government in late 1945, Yandell estimated that the Investigation Branch cautioned 4,000 people per year.[111] The MoFP made frequent use of oral and written warnings too. Its Enforcement Branch allowed inspectors to issue a verbal warning for petty contraventions by first-time offenders. If a second breach of control came to an inspector's attention, the inspector collected evidence and wrote a report for headquarters. On the basis of the report, headquarters staff decided whether to pass the case to the Prosecutions Branch or

[108] Data are from 'Summary of prosecutions and penalties imposed' tables in MAF 100/5 and MAF 156/289 at TNA: PRO.

[109] Dow, *Management*, 176 for extent of price control; Hargreaves and Gowing, *Civil Industry*, 91 for prosecution data.

[110] TNA: PRO, BT 64/74, 'Instructions for Inspectors appointed under the Goods and Services (Price Control) Act', n.d. (October 1941).

[111] TNA: PRO, BT 64/793, Yandell, 'Board of Trade response to Swiss questionnaire about the black market', n.d. (December 1945).

issue a written warning, depending on the seriousness of the offence and the likelihood of securing a conviction.[112]

Like the MoF, the MoFP and the BoT could suspend or cut a traders' supply of controlled goods without taking legal action. They could also remove a traders' licence, putting them out of business. Both types of sanction saved the cost of going to court and proved a very effective way of punishing recidivistic traders. Officials were more likely to reduce or withhold supplies than they were to remove a trader's licence. Rationing officials could automatically adjust supplies if standard checks revealed discrepancies between supplies delivered and coupons surrendered. Enforcement officials had little or no involvement in this process. Removing a trader's licence was a much more serious step, as it took away someone's livelihood, inconvenienced customers who need to shop elsewhere, and required ministerial authorization.

The clothes rationing, petrol rationing, and price inspectorates' reliance upon visits, warnings, and administrative sanctions bolstered by the occasional criminal prosecution reflected BoT experience of regulatory enforcement—the department from which the inspectorates all sprang. The similarities in their policies also reflected their smaller size. A crime control approach was not an option if there were only twenty-eight price inspectors to police the entire country.[113] The fact that the Board of Trade Solicitor, and later the Treasury Solicitor, handled all prosecutions in English and Welsh courts for the Board, the Central Price Regulation Committee, and the MoFP was another factor that ensured a consistency of approach.[114]

By the end of the war, all four ministry inspectorates would have agreed with the MoFP that:

> Inspectors are the eyes and ears of the Ministry. Prosecution is only a means to an end. The nature of the Inspectors' duties puts them in direct contact with the Public and they should be in a position to supply information on the general application of the various Orders issued by the Ministry from time to time. In addition to their work of investigating suspected infringements they should be on the alert to detect any sign of 'black market' activities and to be able to supply any information on local conditions. Preventive work is most important and the Inspectors' knowledge of the Regulations enable them to give advice and on occasions verbal warnings to the Public with whom they come in contact. It therefore follows that Inspectors should direct their efforts 'in the field' and spend as little time as possible on office work.[115]

The vagaries of the supply situation for individual commodities, as well as the resources available to each inspectorate, created differences in the emphasis each placed on preventing, detecting, and prosecuting particular types of offences, but

---

[112] TNA: PRO, POWE 10/351: 'Report on discussion on matters relating to the establishment of the Enforcement Branch and the Fuel Inspection Branch', 3 September 1942; and J. Milborrow and R. Thatcher, 'Report of Staff Inspection on Enforcement Branch', 25 May 1948.

[113] HC deb, vol. 376, 26 November 1941, col. 765.

[114] TNA: PRO, BT 103/1403, E. M Parsey, 'Prosecutions Branch, Board of Trade, 1945 to 1953', June 1953.

[115] TNA: PRO, POWE 10/351, G. Ryder to Wright, 10 October 1942.

the principles informing each ministry's compliance strategy bore a strong resemblance to one another.

The discussions chaired by Morrison in spring 1942 marked the first step towards this weak cross-departmental consensus. Given the impossibility of establishing watertight control and the shortage of inspectors to fix leaks, these strategies were a calculated bluff. All recognized the importance of persuading traders and consumers of the necessity for control so that they would comply with the regulations willingly. Ministers and their officials highlighted the fairness and transparency with which they administered and enforced control schemes. Publicity emphasized the fairness of official ration scales and price lists, casting evaders as selfish, and, in the context of war, unpatriotic. Controllers also underlined that evaders would be found out and dealt with according to due process of law. Any penalties would be tough, but proportionate to the offence. While publicizing the measures in place to tackle black marketing, government departments stressed that evasion was a minor irritant, which their enforcement arms were tackling firmly and effectively. As a package of measures, it was as much about reassuring the law-abiding that they were not mugs to obey the regulations as it was about deterring would-be criminals from evading control.

Official strategies and tactics for securing compliance remained broadly similar, despite shifts in emphasis after 1943. In preparation for the transition from war to peace, all rationing departments closed loopholes and tightened enforcement as they anticipated increased evasion from summer 1944 onwards. While the majority of civilians deemed control necessary, their continued support for austerity policies was contingent upon the perceived fairness and effectiveness of control. From this perspective it was inevitable that consent and its corollary compliance would weaken once the public doubted the need for control. Controllers anticipated that this process would begin when victory seemed inevitable. These changes were well publicized, with the MoF taking the lead in stressing the toughness of its approach, as was by now usual for this most prosecution-minded of ministries. This was not accompanied by publicity campaigns explaining the need for post-war control. Enforcement tightened again in the wake of Britain's post-war 'Financial Dunkirk'. The Labour government also ramped up the fair-shares rhetoric to limited effect[116] as growing numbers of people questioned the need for control. The renewed emphasis on enforcement began to ease in 1949 as the financial situation improved.

Once decontrol was a realistic prospect, policy shifted again, with compliance strategy becoming synonymous with enforcement policy. Beginning with Harold Wilson's 'bonfire of controls' in autumn 1948, ministers stressed the need to abolish crime rather than design it out. Their civil servants jettisoned unnecessary and unenforceable regulations instead of closing loopholes in existing schemes. Poorly designed schemes that dated back to the early years of control were some of the first to go. After 1951, little effort was made to sell 'fair shares' policies to the

---

[116] William Crofts, *Coercion or Persuasion? Propaganda in Britain after 1945* (London, 1989), 45–7.

public. Conservatives preferred to make the case for decontrol, emphasizing the moves that they had already made towards deregulation. They assumed that support for control had or soon would evaporate. This undercut compliance strategies based upon securing willing cooperation backed by the threat of coercion. Without public goodwill, compliance strategies came to rest upon enforcement alone. In 1952 its aim, according to the Minister of Food, was 'to prevent open scandal in the form of widespread and flagrant evasions' by 'checking abuses which represent a real threat to supplies of rationed food and the rationing system itself'.[117] Bluffing—which was what this pared-down strategy amounted to—was risky. As the next chapters show, enforcement had never been a convincing bluff.

[117] TNA: PRO, CAB 129/53, C (52) 215, Gwilym Lloyd-George, 'Enforcement of Food Controls', 26 June 1952.

5

On the street: enforcing the law

In June 1950, at the insistence of his permanent secretary, the Minister of Fuel and Power Philip Noel-Baker sent a disingenuous letter to his colleague the Home Secretary 'paying tribute to the way in which the Police Forces have discharged the burden of enforcement which the rationing of petrol has laid upon them for more than ten years'. Noel-Baker's letter went on to note that it could not have been easy for Chief Constables 'to divert the energies of their sorely strained Forces to the pursuit of petrol offences' especially as the public did not understand their seriousness.[1] Although the letter did not hint at it, the manner in which the police 'discharged the burden of enforcement' had been a source of considerable frustration to Noel-Baker and his predecessors.

Like other rationing ministries, Noel-Baker's department saw policing as a vital part of a broader compliance strategy that placed as much emphasis on persuading the public of the need for control and its fairness as it did on enforcing the regulations. To some extent, enforcement activity was itself a public relations exercise as small ministry inspectorates could not hope to enforce the regulations rigorously or uniformly across the country. Yet, if the inspectorates were to succeed in deterring would-be offenders and reassuring the law abiding, they had to give the impression that control was enforced firmly and fairly. In this, they needed the help of the police. But, as the small petrol inspectorate learned to its cost, it could not reply upon police assistance. Less than a year before Noel-Baker wrote his letter praising the police, ministry enforcement staff had been busily preparing a blacklist of police forces that refused to cooperate with them. Periodically, the Home Office would encourage the police to work closely with ministry inspectors, but to little effect. In June 1948, with the petrol black market in the headlines, detectives attending the south-eastern regional conference spent more time discussing two instances of bestiality in Weybridge and Littlehampton than they did black marketeering.[2]

The troubled relationship between petrol inspectors and police brings into relief the issue that undermined the rationing ministries' ability to play the bluff on which their compliance strategies were based. Whitehall officials had to contend with the 'principal–agent' problem of aligning the interests of inspectors and police officers with their own. As ministry agents who possessed extensive discretionary powers, inspectors could veto enforcement policies by deciding when to report an

---

[1] PRO: POWE 33/1511, 'P. Noel-Baker to J. Chuter Ede', 8 June 1950.
[2] Minutes of Detectives' Conference No. 6 District, 29 June 1948, PRO, MEPO 3/1868.

offence to their superiors, or determining how much effort to put into an investigation. The same was true of the police, who could sometimes rely upon their superiors for support against central government. For a range of reasons, individual, institutional, and structural, and in a variety of ways, inspectors and police exercised their veto. The resultant pattern of enforcement was local and particular. This had important consequences for the level of compliance, as it made enforcement appear arbitrary and even hypocritical, frustrating rational calculation of costs and benefits, and undermining respect for the law.

A HOUSE DIVIDED

An enforcement apparatus, hastily designed and built in the first two years of the war, compounded the localism and particularism of enforcement activity. Apart from asking the police to cooperate with ministry inspectors, policymakers gave little thought to the enforcement structure. The result of the controllers' lackadaisical approach was a system that divided the responsibility for policing regulations between four inspectorates: the Central Price Regulation Committee's inspectorate, the BoT Investigation and Enforcement Section, the MoF Enforcement Division, and the MoFP Enforcement Branch. With limited resources, these inspectorates relied upon the police for assistance—which was rarely forthcoming.

The division of responsibilities between four enforcement agencies was of lasting benefit to black marketeers. Multiple, but not overlapping, jurisdictions brought with them the problems of duplication of effort and coordination without building into the system the checks and balances on abuses of power that overlapping jurisdictions could have brought. Other countries assigned responsibility for policing economic control to one agency. In Japan the economic police (*keizai keisatsu*) enforced such regulations, while in the USA the Office of Price Administration (OPA) had sole responsibility for policing black markets. As a consequence, the *keizai keisatsu* and the OPA did not rely upon other agencies for information or expertise, thus avoiding spending time on inter-agency cooperation and wasting it on repeating work done by others. Corruption posed a problem to both the *keizai keisatsu* and the OPA, but it did not cripple them.[3]

The British system of four ministry inspectorates with national jurisdictions covering the supply chains for controlled commodities and 209 police forces with territorial jurisdictions for all crimes committed in their area, whether or not they involved black market dealing, meant that coordination was a recurrent problem for government enforcement policy. This absorbed a lot of inspectors' time. For example, price inspectors had to liaise with BoT accountants, distribution officers,

[3] See Christopher Aldous, *The Police in Occupation Japan: Control, Corruption and Resistance to Reform* (London, 1997), and Owen Griffiths, 'Need, Greed, and Protest in Japan's Black Market, 1938–1949', *Journal of Social History*, 35 (2002), 825–58 on the *keizai keisatsu*; and Clinard, *Black Market*, 51–88, on the US OPA.

and other enforcement officers working in their area 'to avoid the danger of dupli-
cating work and of giving to the public an impression of lack of coordination'.[4]
Whether the British system avoided the problem of corruption remains an open
question. Although corrupt officials working in local and divisional offices were a
sporadic problem—most notably in post-war Brighton—there were no prosecutions of crooked inspectors. Nevertheless, defence lawyers and backbench MPs accused inspectors of corruption on occasion.[5]

Beginning in summer 1942, the MoF Enforcement Division—the largest of the
four inspectorates—made several unsuccessful attempts to improve coordination
between law enforcement agencies with an interest in black market dealing. As
head of Enforcement Division's intelligence bureau, Sir Charles Tegart attempted to
build relationships with his counterparts in other agencies. Tegart recognized the need to develop links with other ministry inspectorates, the police, the
railway police, the GPO Investigations Branch, HM Customs and Excise, the
Military Police, the RAF Police, the NAAFI investigation staff, the American
Military Police, MI5, and MI6. It did not occur to him or his superiors that tax
inspectors or the Bank of England might possess useful information about black
marketeers. Of these agencies, the police were the most important potential allies.
With the support of the Home Office, Tegart and his staff attended the eight English and Welsh Police District Chief Constables' Conferences and their Detectives'
Conferences.[6]

The police may have been the inspectorates' most important partners, but
they had little time for the enforcement officers' work. The minutes of the Detectives' Conference for Number Six Police District, which covered much of south-
east England, reveal initial suspicion and then active dislike of 'economic
policing'. From August 1942, food, clothing, and fuel inspectors attended the
bimonthly meetings of the conference.[7] Over the coming months various ministry headquarters staff attended the conference, lecturing those present on changes
in the regulations and the enforcement apparatus. The rationing ministries' concerns came to dominate the agenda, to the annoyance of senior detectives and
their superiors. In July 1944 the Chief Constables reasserted their control over
the conference, making meetings quarterly and limiting membership to police
detectives. Ministry inspectors would be invited to attend a meeting if matters
relating to their work were to be discussed—but they never were. The chief police
officers created a separate conference on security matters to which they invited
MI5 representatives, but no similar provision was made for ministry inspectors—a clear signal of the importance that chief police officers in the Home

---

[4] TNA: PRO, BT 64/74, 'Instructions for Inspectors appointed under the Goods and Services
(Price Control) Act', n.d. (October 1941).

[5] George Yandell, 'Ministry Clerks In Coupon Frauds', *Sunday Dispatch*, 18 June 1950; TNA:
PRO, MAF 150/661, 'Report of enquiry into allegations of inefficiency, mal-practice, bribery and
corruption among officials', 1948.

[6] TNA: PRO, MAF 100/30, 'Note of a conference at the Home Office', 26 June 1942.

[7] TNA: PRO, MEPO 3/1868, 'No. 6 district detectives' conference minutes', 13 August 1942.

Table 5.1. Prosecutions for petrol rationing offences in Great Britain during 1947

Description of offence	Police	Inspectors
Stealing, receiving, and unlawful possession of petrol	501	
Misuse of petrol	635	
Supply and acquisition of petrol without coupons or otherwise than against valid coupons	148	95
Unlawful transfer of coupons	85	162
Forgery	33	31
Miscellaneous offences	253	29
Total	1,655	317

Source: Evasions of Petrol Rationing, 23–4.

Counties attached to economic policing.[8] A post-war initiative to improve inter-agency coordination was equally short-lived. Concerned by an increase in the theft and pilferage of rationed foods moving off the docks, the MoF established Food Security Committees for each of Britain's major ports.[9] Less than a year after the establishment of a committee for the Port of London, the Metropolitan Police ceased to attend meetings, and the London committee, like many others, foundered soon after.[10]

The lack of police enthusiasm for enforcing control made the inspectorates' jobs harder. Not only did the ministries need the police to act as auxiliaries, augmenting the number of enforcement officers, but they also needed their help to mount operations. Although inspectors possessed extensive powers of entry and search and seizure, they did not have the police powers of stop and search, nor arrest. Like intelligence officers, ministry inspectors needed uniformed police officers to accompany them on raids, to set up roadblocks, and to cordon off an area. Without the work of police traffic patrols, the ministry could not have tackled the problems of petrol misuse and theft (see Table 5.1). Inspectors also wanted to tap into police detectives' sources of information about black market dealing. The collusive nature of evasion meant that detectives with established relationships with local criminals were more likely to know about black marketeering. As a result, ministry inspectors needed to forge alliances with detectives, but prosecution policy and the culture of the CID made this difficult.

Senior officers judged a detective's effectiveness by his record for 'clearing up' crimes. The emphasis on clear-up rates, or the percentage of his cases that a detective solved, created an individualistic and entrepreneurial culture within plain clothes branches. Due to ministry prosecution policies, working with the inspectorates to enforce economic regulations would not improve a detective's clear-up

[8] TNA: PRO, MEPO 3/1868, 'No. 6 district detectives' conference minutes', 27 July 1944.
[9] TNA: PRO, MEPO 3/3046, A. F. Perrott to Sir Harold Scott, 10 October 1948.
[10] TNA: PRO, MEPO 3/3046, Supt. H. W. Hawkyard to (A.C.C. (Crime)), 31 May 1949.

rate. Detectives—who frequently 'pinched' the best cases from uniformed officers to boost their clear-up rates—had to hand over most black market cases to ministry enforcement staffs for processing, particularly the larger and hence more appealing ones for an ambitious detective.[11] Ministry enforcement officials drew up the policy because they felt police prosecutions for trivial offences brought the regulations into disrepute, turning the public and the courts against control. Also, an inspector's familiarity with the regulations meant that the inspector was more likely to secure a conviction than a beat policeman or a detective. In the circumstances it was not surprising that detectives preferred to investigate those black market offences that bore a close resemblance to 'traditional' crimes such as fraud, forgery, robbery, and theft. Often these involved known criminals and could be prosecuted under the criminal law without reference to the rationing ministries. Given police expertise in these areas, the inspectorates pinched such cases rarely.

Taking away the responsibility for investigating and prosecuting most black market offences from the police would not have had such devastating consequences if it were not for the absence of other incentives. In a circular urging Chief Constables to cooperate with the ministry inspectorates, the Home Office suggested that inspectors possessed useful intelligence about thieves and fences for stolen goods, and hinted that an inspector might find it easier to secure a conviction against a known criminal for a black market offence than the police would for a 'traditional' crime.[12] Experience showed both claims to be unfounded. Due to their exclusively economic jurisdictions and the large area covered by each inspector, the inspectorates did not have information that they could trade with detectives in return for assistance. Also, detectives do not appear to have experienced any difficulty in securing convictions against known criminals, fabricating evidence if needs be.[13]

A few inspectors managed to form alliances with detectives, but they had had illustrious careers in the CID. Their reputation combined with their knowledge and experience of the 'job', and their personal contacts within the police service and with its most regular customers, smoothed relations. The aura that surrounded former Scotland Yard detectives was of great help to ex-Superintendent George Yandell at the BoT, and his MoF colleagues, ex-Detective Superintendent 'Big Jack' Sands, ex-Chief Detective Superintendent Arthur Askew, and ex-Chief Detective Inspector Bill Barker.[14] Tegart's reputation as a counter-terrorist expert, built up during his 25-year career in the Indian police, enabled him to forge links with senior figures in the Metropolitan Police and the security services. But few inspectors could trade on such a reputation. Solicitors, retired army officers, and former council officials had no pull with the police, while former policemen with

---

[11] Barbara Weinberger, *The Best Police in the World: An Oral History of English Policing from the 1930s to the 1960s* (Aldershot, 1995), 82–5; TNA: PRO, HO 45/25135, 870415/11, 'Home Office circular 863,760/4', 18 August 1942.

[12] 'Home Office circular 863,760/4'.

[13] Weinberger, *Best Police in the World*, 83.

[14] Jack Henry, *What Price Crime?* (London, 1945), 67; *Daily Mirror*, 16 April 1942.

less illustrious careers were treated little better than retired officers working as shop detectives or security guards.

At the most senior level the rationing ministries had no resources to share with an overstretched police service, which meant that Chief Constables who harboured ambivalent or hostile attitudes towards economic regulation had no reason to force their officers to cooperate with ministry inspectors. Although the number of full-time police officers in England and Wales increased from 61,610 in 1939 to a peak of 93,646 in 1941, so too did their workload.[15] As well as crime control and traffic duties, police assumed new responsibilities relating to national security, civil defence, and economic regulation.[16] Petrol rationing reduced the number of motor vehicles on the roads, but wartime police duties more than made up for the declining importance of traffic duties. The regulatory burden on police increased as police strength dwindled from its peak in 1941 to a trough of 54,897 in 1946, returning to pre-war levels in 1950.[17]

Given the demands on police resources, the service could not hope to enforce price and rationing regulations effectively. Reflecting on enforcement policy in 1946, Detective Inspector Symes of the Metropolitan Police admitted that every one of the 14,230 officers in the force would have to put aside all other duties, including the detection and prevention of crime, if the Metropolitan Police undertook to detect and prosecute black market offenders.[18] Ensuring that they were up to date with the defence regulations already absorbed a large amount of police officers' time. Keeping abreast of legal developments had not posed a problem for police during the inter-war years as officers did not have to cope with a torrent of new laws and regulations. Reading Police Orders to keep themselves informed of recent legislative developments was not onerous. However, this system could not cope with the flood of regulations passed under the 1939 Emergency (Defence) Powers Act. Experienced police officers found themselves studying the law for the first time since their training. Reservists and Special Constables faced a tougher struggle, as they needed to master the defence regulations as well as the criminal law. Recognizing a gap in the market, legal publishers produced guides through the regulatory jungle for perplexed police officers. In 1940 Butterworth and Company published *Emergency Police Law* by Cecil Moriarty and James Whiteside, and Butterworth began to include notes on emergency legislation in new editions of *Police Law*, the standard work of reference for police.[19] Others produced handy-sized

---

[15] Calculated from figures in the *Annual Abstract of Statistics*.

[16] Frank Elmes, 'The Organisation, Functions and Duties of Police Forces under Conditions of Modern War', *Police Journal*, 25 (1952), 237–45.

[17] See T. A. Critchley, *A History of Police in England and Wales* (2nd edn., London, 1978), 232–6; David Ascoli, *The Queen's Peace: The Origins and Development of the Metropolitan Police 1829–1979* (London, 1979), 245–50; Roy Ingleton, *The Gentlemen at War: Policing Britain 1939–1945* (Maidstone, 1994); Weinberger, *Best Police in the World*, ch. 7; and Clive Emsley, *The English Police: A Political and Social History* (2nd edn., London, 1996), 166–9, for a survey of policing during the 1940s.

[18] TNA: PRO, MEPO 2/7677, 'The Police and Food Offences', 2 July 1946. Figure for police strength from the Report of the Commissioner of Police for the Metropolis for 1946.

[19] Weinberger, *Best Police*, 28, n. 3.

guides to the law that beat constables could slip into a tunic pocket, while police journals included columns explaining emergency legislation.[20]

Resource constraints served to conceal a more fundamental reason for police reluctance to cooperate with ministry inspectorates: officers of all ranks did not consider that enforcing economic regulations was police work, despite amassing considerable experience of regulatory enforcement prior to the war. Prior to the war, local authorities had preferred to task the police with enforcing economic regulations, such as those governing weights and measures, rather than appoint inspectors at considerable additional cost to rate-payers. Local borough councils had the most success in this regard, exploiting their control of watch committees to foist these responsibilities onto the police. As a result, police officers acted as inspectors of explosives, food and drugs, petroleum, shops, and weights and measures in many parts of the country. In rural areas these duties and other regulatory tasks took up a great deal of police time.[21] The police referred to these tasks as 'extraneous duties', which reflected their disdain for regulatory enforcement. Such duties are not discussed in Charles Reith's influential wartime meditation on *British Police and the Democratic Idea*. Reith restated the longstanding view that the primary duty of the police was to maintain order and to prevent, detect, and prosecute crime.[22]

The police loathed regulatory enforcement, resisting the imposition of their largest extraneous duty—the regulation of traffic—during the inter-war period. As far as the 1929 Royal Commission on Police Powers and Procedures was concerned, traffic duty was an extraneous duty; it was not police work, diverted scarce resources from police work, and most importantly it alienated the public. According to the Royal Commission:

> ...the creation and growth of new offences has led to a large number of law-abiding citizens being, for the first time in their lives, brought into conflict with the law. The result is a feeling of hostility or state of friction, which is foreign to the normal relations between the police and the bulk of the public, and a disposition to withhold that assistance and cooperation in the suppression of other offences which the public has generally been ready to afford.[23]

Such was the background to relations between the police and the ministry inspectorates.

Chief police officers expressed similar views about price and rationing regulations at meetings of the Central Conference of Chief Constables almost twenty

---

[20] For example the first and subsequent four editions of *An ABC for Special Constables and Police War Reserves* (London, 1939) by C. R. Hewitt. For examples of columns see C. H. Rolph cited in Clive Emsley, 'The Second World War and the Police in England and Wales', in, Cyrille Fijnaut (ed.), *The Impact of World War II on Policing in North-west Europe* (Leuven, 2004), 151–72; and 'Criminal Law and Practice in Scotland' and 'Recent Judicial Decisions' in the *Police Journal*.

[21] E. J. T. Collins, 'Food Adulteration and Food Safety in Britain in the 19th and Early 20th Centuries', *Food Policy*, 18 (1993), 95–109.

[22] Charles Reith, *British Police and the Democratic Idea* (London, 1943), 3–4.

[23] Report of the Royal Commission on Police Powers and Procedure (PP 1928–9 Cmd.3297 ix, 127), 81.

years later. The enforcement of the red-petrol scheme—introduced in summer 1948 by the MoFP as a way of preventing private motorists using commercial petrol by adding a trace chemical to commercial petrol and dyeing it red—brought the Chief Constables' views into the open. When Chief Constables discussed the proposed scheme privately, several of those present voiced the opinion that 'The measure is very unpopular with a section of the public, and the Police are very much concerned about its enforcement as it is outside the province of crime. The Police fear reactions on the good relationship between the public and themselves as a result of steps that will have to be taken.'[24] At a meeting with ministry officials, the Chief Constables gave practical reasons for their opposition to the scheme. Several officers argued that the testing equipment—consisting of a piece of coat-hanger wire, a paper clip, chromatographic paper, and three sample bottles—was 'cumbersome' and that dipping the tank was too 'complicated' for its traffic patrols, many of whom were accomplished car mechanics. The Chief Constables accepted that the scheme would be implemented as it had prime-ministerial backing, but made it clear that the MoFP could not expect the overworked police to rigorously enforce the scheme.[25]

Officials—prompted by ministerial enthusiasm for a scheme that promised to reduce consumption of commercial petrol and make it possible to restore a basic ration for private motoring without increasing oil imports—did not accept the usual police caveats about resource constraints, and continued to push for effective police enforcement. This forced the Home Office to break cover and side with the police. Meeting with the MoFP committee investigating ways to combat the petrol black market, the permanent secretary told him that 'The police were being brought into conflict with a public opinion which does not feel people are really committing an offence in evading the petrol rationing scheme'. This attitude was a 'menace to the state'. As the committee prepared to leave, the permanent secretary sounded a conciliatory note, stating that 'If the Government make up their minds that this is a social mischief that must be stopped, then the police will cooperate in this most invidious and distasteful task'. The reference to 'this most invidious and distasteful task' made it clear that police cooperation would be unenthusiastic.[26]

The permanent secretary's reference to 'public opinion' echoed the Chief Constables' concerns about relations with 'a section of the public'—a disguised reference to the middle class. Overworked police officers of all ranks resented enforcing price and rationing regulations, which brought them into conflict with a significant number of middle-class people for the first time. Despite inter-war concerns about traffic regulation bringing large numbers of 'respectable' people into conflict with the law, the proportion of the upper working class and middle class prosecuted for motoring offences remained small until the post-war boom in car ownership. Defence

---

[24] TNA: PRO, HO 358/7, 'Central Conference of Chief Constables prelim. meeting minutes', 15 October 1947.
[25] TNA: PRO, HO 358/7, 'Central Conference of Chief Constables minutes', 26 February 1948.
[26] TNA: PRO, MEPO 2/8793, 'Note of meeting', 26 February 1948.

regulations, on the other hand, affected every civilian, rough and respectable alike. The responsibilities for national security and civil defence which the regulations imposed on the police service did not bring police into conflict with the bulk of the population. Although civil defence measures were irksome, the public appreciated the necessity of fire precautions and lighting regulations. In fact, the role played by the police during air raids strengthened public respect for them.[27]

The same was not true of enforcement of price and rationing regulations—a fact that did not go unnoticed by the police. Reflecting on the effects of war on crime in 1949, the Association of Chief Constables in Scotland noted with unease that 'many persons who are otherwise honest and respectable have no compunction about offending against the law in relation to rationing and controls'.[28] At regional and national conferences of Chief Constables, chief police officers expressed concern that rigorously enforcing economic regulations, whose breach civilians did not think of as a crime, threatened to undermine their public legitimacy.

The Home Office, mindful of the strains emergency legislation placed on police resources and relations with the public, did not want to add to the service's burden. This was one of the few areas in which the Home Office did not assert itself during the 1940s.[29] When enforcement officials from the rationing ministries urged the central conference to do more, the Chief Constables present made it plain that to do more than they were already doing to enforce the regulations would place their national security, civil defence, and crime fighting duties at risk, and in some cases refused to do anything, as regulations were unenforceable.[30] At these meetings Home Office officials posed as disinterested brokers while fending off requests that the police undertake additional duties, securing the Chief Constables' gratitude and preserving their power and influence for more important battles about the reform of the police service. The result, from the perspective of the ministry inspectorates, was an unsatisfactory compromise.

The police did not ignore their duty to enforce economic control, but they did not go out of their way to enforce it. With Home Office backing, the rationing ministries secured the cooperation of the larger and more modern forces in periodic enforcement drives. This was what happened in the case of the red-petrol scheme. The Home Office persuaded ten police forces in England and Wales to participate in 'Operation Dip' (see Fig. 5.1). Over an August bank holiday weekend, police checked the tanks of 1,590 private vehicles for the presence of red petrol, of which eighteen tested positive. The operation was a propaganda success, receiving extensive coverage in the local and national press that gave the impression that this was a national operation—a ruse employed regularly by the ministry inspectorates.[31]

[27] Report of HM Inspectors of Constabulary for the year ended 29th September 1945 (PP 1945–46 (168) xii, 193).

[28] TNA: PRO, HO 45/25079, 'Chief Constables' (Scotland) Association reply to IPPC questionnaire', n.d. (1949).

[39] Emsley, English Police, 166–9.

[30] TNA: PRO, HO 358/4, 'Central Conference of Chief Constables minutes', 6 May 1943.

[31] TNA: PRO, POWE 33/1511, 'Publicity for Enforcement Measures', 26 July 1948; TNA: PRO, POWE 33/1511, H. Haddow to G. Watkinson, 3 August 1948.

Fig. 5.1. Location of testing sites for Operation Dip, 31 July 1948.
Source: TNA: PRO, POWE 33/1511, 'List of places and times of tests', 30 July 1948.

Chief constables ensured that all of their officers knew of the defence regulations, regularly issuing Police Orders summarizing recent developments, but they did not encourage their officers to enforce the regulations. Police passivity irritated ministry enforcement staff, but without Home Office support they were powerless to influence the police. Occasional enforcement drives such as Operation Dip did not satisfy them. In late 1948 the MoFP took the unusual step of monitoring police enforcement of the red-petrol scheme. Officials used statistical returns from the police, reluctantly agreed to by the Home Office, to identify forces enforcing the scheme laxly.[32]

---

[32] TNA: PRO, POWE 33/1511, 'Home Office circular 86/1948', 26 April 1948 and 'Home Office circular 166/1949', 11 August 1949.

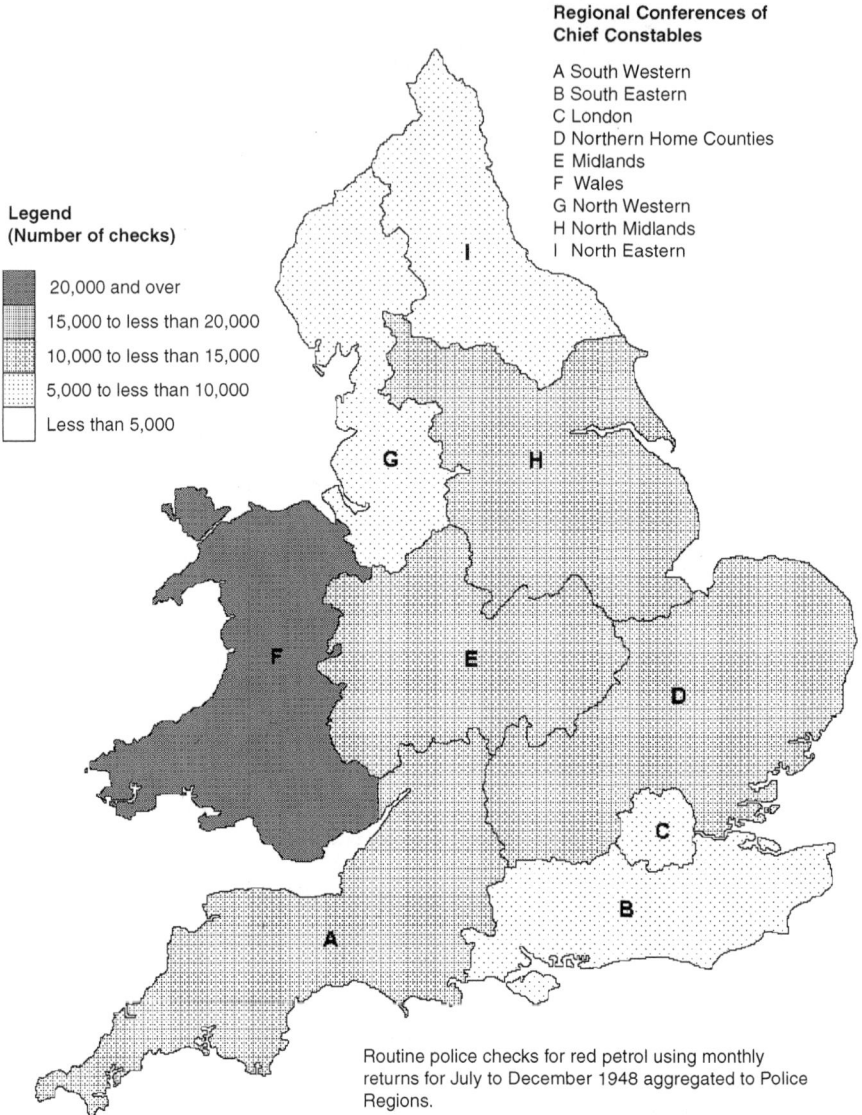

Regional Conferences of Chief Constables

A South Western
B South Eastern
C London
D Northern Home Counties
E Midlands
F Wales
G North Western
H North Midlands
I North Eastern

Legend (Number of checks)

20,000 and over
15,000 to less than 20,000
10,000 to less than 15,000
5,000 to less than 10,000
Less than 5,000

Routine police checks for red petrol using monthly returns for July to December 1948 aggregated to Police Regions.

Fig. 5.2. Routine police checks of private vehicles for red petrol, 1 July to 31 December 1949.

Sources: Calculated from monthly returns for the number of tests for red petrol performed by Police Forces in England and Wales in POWE 33/1511 at TNA.

Inspectors visited the blacklisted forces to stress the importance of enforcing the scheme, and mapping these figures by police region reveals startling variations in enforcement (see Fig. 5.2). Not surprisingly, motorized police forces whose patrols cars carried the testing equipment carried out the highest number of checks. But even these forces enforced the scheme selectively, carrying out only a small number of checks.

Close analysis of the police returns demonstrates that the average motorist was unlikely to have his vehicle's petrol tank dipped. Police traffic patrols and ministry inspectors in England and Wales checked a total of 29,920 vehicles during August 1949. Combining these data with figures from the 1950 Road Traffic Census, it is possible to gauge the likelihood of a vehicle being checked. Motorists made almost three million journeys in August 1950. If the volume of traffic were similar in August 1949, then every hundredth motorist would be stopped. Of those stopped, one in five was checked, and English motorists were less likely to be stopped than were Welsh motorists. Roughly one in every 200 motorists would be stopped in England, whereas one in every twenty-five motorists would be stopped in Wales. Naturally, the more journeys a motorist made, the more likely he was to be stopped.

As enforcement of the red-petrol scheme demonstrates, the lack of police interest in 'economic policing' and their consequent reluctance to cooperate with ministry inspectorates meant that enforcement of control varied across the country. If a Chief Constable considered that a breach of a control order was a serious offence, the police worked closely with local and regional inspectors to enforce the regulations. If he did not, black marketeers operated with impunity.

Given the reluctance of the police to enforce the regulations, the ministry inspectorates appeared a more reliable tool for implementing Whitehall's compliance strategies. Headquarters staff controlled the work of ministry inspectors, using centrally determined procedures and guidelines to limit the inspectors' ability to exercise their discretion; but this did not prevent enforcement differing between regions. Although the BoT and MoFP enforcement arms were the size of small borough police forces with 89 and 103 staff respectively in 1947, the staff at headquarters found it difficult to control enforcement at regional level, let alone local level. Regional enforcement staffs were responsible to their regional controllers as well as the headquarters enforcement staff. This system worked well if a regional controller and the director of enforcement held similar views, but this was rarely the case. Writing in 1943, Chief Enforcement Officer Ryder reported that

> the majority of RPOs [Regional Petroleum Officers] have indicated to me at one time or another that they and their officers regard enforcement questions as a troublesome excrescence on their proper duties, and were only anxious to be rid of them: others, among whom are two still in the service, indicated that they were entirely opposed to any attempts at enforcement, which they regarded as 'not cricket' and 'un-English'.

According to Ryder, 'uninstructed zeal' was far more trouble than indifference and hostility. He disliked the zealots 'who have or believe themselves to have legal knowledge acquired in the administration of Borrioboola-Gha. Some of their past efforts at applying this knowledge in England made my hair curl'.[33]

The larger an inspectorate, the greater the difficulties that headquarters staff faced in controlling it. The MoF, with the largest enforcement arm of the three rationing ministries, faced the biggest problems when it came to ensuring consistent

---

[33] TNA: PRO, POWE 10/390, G. Ryder to Hemming, 21 June 1944.

enforcement and creating a common organizational culture. With a staff of 1,069 in 1946, the MoF Enforcement Division was larger than 197 of the UK's 209 police forces. In size it ranked alongside the City of London police force, whose average daily strength stood at 1,079.[34] Members of the Enforcement Division could be found working at local food offices, divisional food offices, and headquarters, with offices at Colwyn Bay in North Wales and St James' Street in central London. This tripartite structure created tensions between part-time local staff on the one hand and full-time divisional and headquarters staffs on the other, as the local staff felt that their superiors had little appreciation of the nature of the work they did. The merger of local and regional inspectorates in 1946 and the creation of a central training school in 1947 did little to improve the situation.

The tensions inherent in the structure of food enforcement manifested themselves immediately. Following ministry guidance, local food control committees employed a food inspector to investigate suspected cases of evasion. The local weights-and-measures inspectors were the natural choice for the job due to their experience of consumer regulation. When the weights-and-measures authority and the food control committee covered the same geographical area, weights-and-measures inspectors were often involved in the enforcement of food control in addition to their normal duties, as was the case in Leeds, Scarborough, and Rotherham. Food inspection work had little impact upon the weights-and-measures inspectors' professional identity. Members of the Incorporated Society of Inspectors of Weights criticized the amateurism of food inspectors who did not share their background throughout the period of control.[35] The MoF's emphasis on detection and prosecution of food offences rankled with weights-and-measures inspectors, who gave a higher priority to prevention and saw prosecution as a last resort. Headquarters staff disliked the inspectors' regulatory approach to enforcement, deeming verbal and written warnings to be an inappropriately lenient way of dealing with offences against emergency legislation.[36]

Differences of opinion about how best to implement enforcement policy also affected divisional staffs and headquarters staff. Retired policemen and servicemen dominated at divisional and national level with a leavening of lawyers and accountants. Although police officers and servicemen had starkly different backgrounds, this was not the fault line running through divisional offices and headquarters. During the 1930s a significant number of Chief Constables were retired army officers, so the former detectives had experience of working with military men.[37]

---

[34] Report of HM Inspectors of Constabulary for the Year ended 29th September 1946 (PP 1946–47 (134) xiii, 541); Eighty-fourth Report of HM Inspector of Constabulary for Scotland for the Year ended 31st December 1946 (PP 1947–48 Cmd.7247 xii, 311).

[35] J. W. Hopkinson, 'Combining Weights and Measures Duties with Food Control', *Monthly Review of the Incorporated Society of Inspectors of Weights and Measures*, 49 (1941), 115–16; Leslie M. Griffiths, 'Good-bye to All That', *Monthly Review of the Institute of Weights and Measures Administration*, 62 (1954), 122.

[36] J. A. White, 'Price Control Orders and the Society', *Monthly Review of the Incorporated Society of Inspectors of Weights and Measures*, 49 (1941), 51, 56.

[37] D. S. Wall, 'The Ideology of Internal Recruitment: the Selection of Chief Constables within the Tripartite Arrangement', *British Journal of Criminology*, 34 (1994), 330.

Rather, enforcement staffs split between enforcement officers with experience of the British criminal justice system and those without. Old India hands with decidedly authoritarian attitudes held several of the most senior posts in the Enforcement Division throughout the period of food control.

The first Director of Enforcement, Alex Monro, joined the ministry on his retirement from the Indian Civil Service in 1939. During his directorship he appointed former members of the Indian police and court services to important posts in the Enforcement Division. The most prominent of these was Sir Charles Tegart, who headed the CEIB from its creation in 1942 until his death in 1945. Tegart formed the CEIB in his own image, appointing his successor as chief of police in Calcutta, Lionel Colson, as his deputy, and several others with experience of tackling Indian terrorists. Monro and Tegart pushed for a more robust approach to crime control, criticizing the timidity of the local inspectors and police with whom they had to work. Although most officers' and inspectors' work was excellent, too many 'did not realise the urgency of the task for which they were engaged and were content with masterly inactivity'.[38] For their part the detectives from the Metropolitan Police disapproved of the Indian police officers' cavalier approach to investigation and prosecution, which they felt jeopardized the probability of securing a prosecution.

Monro's preference for men with a similar background to himself defined the character of the Enforcement Division into the post-war years. In 1949, five of the eighteen divisional enforcement officers were Companions of the Indian Empire (CIE), while half of the enforcement staff in the divisional offices for south-east England in Tunbridge Wells and south-east Scotland in Edinburgh were CIEs.[39] The appointments made by Monro's successor Captain Henry Murphy bolstered the position of the 'old sweats'. Murphy—a retired naval officer—had a preference for retired senior army officers, many of whom had served in South East Asia Command. The appointment of Major-General Henry 'Taffy' Davies—a brigadier on the general staff of first the Burma Army and then the Burma Corps—as Assistant Director in charge of Investigation Sub-Division set the tone. Lawyers, accountants, and British police officers working for the Enforcement Division had little influence.

Overstretched, lacking in experience, and divided amongst themselves, the attitude of the police towards the ministry inspectorates and their work assumed great significance. Without police assistance, which was not forthcoming, a flexible enforcement style was the only sensible approach for the inspectorates to take, as they were too few in number to police the economy on their own. The position faced by MoFP Enforcement Branch is a case in point. In 1948 the ministry employed eighty-five fuel inspectors to enforce its petrol and fuel rationing schemes. They had to police 3,734,000 motor vehicles on 45,442 miles of road and 28,600

---

[38] Kathleen F. Tegart, 'Charles Tegart: Memoir of an Indian Policeman' (unpublished memoir, Cambridge, South Asian Studies Library, 1976), 304.

[39] TNA: PRO, MAF 286/30, 'Ministry of Food Enforcement Headquarters Division directory', February 1949.

petrol stations.[40] This could not be done without the help of police traffic patrols, which meant that the chief enforcement officer and other senior civil servants invested a lot of time in maintaining good relations with the Home Office and chief police officers. The history of the MoFP red-petrol scheme well illustrates the political and practical problems that ministry inspectorates encountered if they eschewed regulatory enforcement in favour of the criminal-justice approach favoured by ministers.

A LAW UNTO THEMSELVES

The importation of aspects of the police service's organizational culture into the newly formed ministry inspectorates had other important consequences for enforcement, decreasing the probability of some people being caught while increasing others' chances of being collared. The large number of retired police officers who became inspectors brought their informal working rules with them, introducing them to their new colleagues with no policing experience. These rules informed both police officers' and inspectors' suspicions, and the exercise of their discretionary powers. Initially, the beliefs about the nature of crime and its causes, which underpinned these heuristics, reflected police perception of crime and the prejudices of wider society. As the ministry's enforcement arms gained more experience of black market dealing, they began to form their own working rules that differed slightly from those of the police. Well-dressed young working-class men were the objects of police suspicion, as were street traders and general dealers, many of whom were youthful penny capitalists in sharp suits. Inspectors had less contact with such people than did beat policeman and detectives, but they harboured similar suspicions. As a rule, ministry enforcement officers distrusted Jewish traders and Indian pedlars, and the police had much the same attitude. Given the paucity of information about the causal beliefs that gave rise to police suspicions, it is almost impossible to assess the influence of society's prejudices on individual decision-making compared to that of enforcement experience. That they both had some sway at street level is easy to demonstrate.

The media image of the 'Black Market' as an interlocking network of highly organized criminal gangs influenced officials' perception of evasion and shaped the formulation of enforcement policy. Frequently occurring images of Jewish black marketeers and spivs in the press and other news media conditioned inspectors' and police officers' beliefs about the character of offences and offenders, as well as the prevalence of evasion. The police viewed Jewish traders, and working-class youths in spivvy American Look suits with suspicion. Unlike ministry inspectors, police possessed powers to stop and search people that enabled them to act on their suspicions immediately. The defence regulations gave police the additional power

[40] See *Annual Abstract of Statistics*; MoT, *Petrol Stations*, 14; MoT, *Road Traffic Census, 1950* (London, 1952).

to stop anyone, whether or not they suspected them of committing a crime, and demand that they produce their identity cards.[41]

Although the police did not record the occasions on which they used these powers, there is some evidence that the image of the Jewish black marketeer and the spiv guided police behaviour on the street. A Jewish railwayman complained to the Board of Deputies after being stopped and searched by two police officers on his way home from work in July 1942. The police did not believe the railwayman when he explained that he had just bought the two bottles of whisky he was carrying from a distiller in Aldgate. On reading the surname Shumkovsky on the man's identity card, one of the officers twice asked him whether he was Jewish and if his employers were Jewish. The officer went on to say that 'although the Jews form approximately only 0.0001 of the population, the majority of Black Market cases are committed by Jews'. He also alleged that the Jews convicted of storing black market goods in a local synagogue would have been severely punished if it had not been for the pro-Semitic attitude of the judge. When the distiller confirmed the man's story, the officers apologized for any inconvenience they had caused him and allowed him to go.[42] The incident could be dismissed as the result of individual prejudice, but it was symptomatic of the troubled relationship between police and East End Jews that dated back to the 1880s.

The police were not the only agency to be affected by popular anti-Semitic prejudice. Due to the concentration of Jewish traders in the food and rag trades, Jewish-sounding names cropped up regularly in prosecutions. Interpreted through the prism of popular anti-Semitism, these cases encouraged racial profiling—a deeply controversial policy, publicly disavowed by politicians. When the press reported that Brigadier Ford, the divisional food officer for the East Midlands, had told a group of German journalists visiting Nottingham in 1947 that Jews committed the bulk of black market offences, the Minister of Food John Strachey faced hostile questions from his fellow Labour MP Tom Driberg. Strachey informed the Commons that he had asked for Ford's resignation as an internal inquiry 'established that Brigadier Ford made certain statements which could be construed as casting reflections on the Jewish race'. Strachey accepted Ford's assurances that this was not his intention, but demanded his resignation, adhering to the principle that public officials should be above suspicion of impartiality.[43]

Like the stereotype of the Jewish black marketeer, the popular image of the spiv influenced police behaviour and amplified deviance. Although it is difficult to study the exercise of police discretion in the past, there are illuminating passages in police memoirs. In his memoirs, John Gosling, a Metropolitan Police detective involved in undercover operations against black marketeers, opined:

---

[41] C. C. Moriarty and J. Whiteside, *Emergency Police Law* (London, 1940); and Neil Stammers, *Civil Liberties in Britain during the Second World War* (Beckenham, 1983).
[42] Board of Deputies of British Jews, London, C6/10/29, 'Statement of Harry Shumkovsky', 17 July 1942.
[43] HC deb, vol. 440, 21 July 1947, col. 835.

Few thieves can wear a hat properly or choose a good suit. A crook may, when he is in the money, pay ten guineas for a hat—but he will always put it on his head at the wrong angle: either crammed on his crown regardless or tilted at a cocky angle. He may buy his suits from Savile Row and pay a hundred guineas for them: but they will always have a zoot-suit style about the lapels and drapes, and the coat collar will sit on the back of the shoulders.[44]

Detectives and uniformed officers alike treated working-class youths sporting an American Look suit with suspicion, assuming they were 'spivs' or 'cosh boys'— juvenile delinquents aping spiv style.[45]

Ministry inspectors were more likely to come into contact with market stall-holders and general dealers who conformed to the spiv stereotype of a sharp-suited, fast-talking Londoner than with illegal street traders. Well schooled by regular tangles with beat policemen, unlicensed 'fly' traders selling combs and elastic on Oxford Street frustrated price inspectors' attempts to prosecute them for over-charging by helping one another and refusing to give their particulars.[46] This was a common experience for enforcement officers, who preferred to leave the control of street trading to police who knew the traders and the places they frequented. MoF enforcement officers, who paid close attention to major poultry and livestock markets, particularly those within reach of London, had the most contact with the 'spivs'. The presence of London buyers at a sale, particularly unknown buyers, immediately raised food inspectors' suspicions that spivs had descended on the market. Such fears prompted the ministry to ask senior detectives from across the Home Counties to look for illegal dealing in hatching eggs at sales in Bishops Stortford, Braintree, Chelmsford, Dartford, Maidstone, and Woking.[47]

Inspectors encouraged farmers, auctioneers, and police to distrust the well-heeled and well-dressed London dealer, citing cases at detectives' conferences such as that of the dealer who arrived at Stowmarket auction mart in a chauffeur-driven car at closing time. The man spoke to the head drover, asking where he might buy some store cattle, and was introduced to an important cattle-farmer. The dealer bought some cattle, paying by cheque which later bounced, and neither the buyer nor the cattle, which were sent by rail to Chertsey, Surrey, could be traced.[48] Petrol inspectors came into contact with spivs too, referring to them as the 'dealer' or the 'general dealer type'—an allusion to the occupation which most illegal traders gave to the courts, and historically an occupation associated with gypsies, costers, hucksters, and fences. Such code found its way into the descriptions of men wanted for black market offences printed in the *Police Gazette*.[49]

[44] John Gosling cited in Steve Chibnall, 'Whistle and Zoot: The Changing Meaning of a Suit of Clothes', *History Workshop Journal*, 20 (1985), 72.

[45] Robert Fabian cited in Steve Chibnall, 'Whistle and Zoot', 73.

[46] TNA: PRO, MEPO 2/10416, 'Divisional area commanders' conference minutes', 9 April 1946.

[47] Smithies, *Crime in Wartime*, 59–64; TNA: PRO, MEPO 3/1868, 'No. 6 district detective conference minutes', 28 March 1944.

[48] TNA: PRO, MEPO 3/3090, 'No. 5 district detective conference minutes', 5 August 1949.

[49] TNA: PRO, POWE 33/1480, Col. T. R. P. Warren, 'External circular: forged petrol coupons, additional information', 18 October 1945.

The 'dealer type', based on a mixture of shrewd observation and prejudice, highlights the importance of the interaction between enforcement agencies' experience of policing black markets and pre-existing social attitudes. This is most clearly seen in clothing inspectors' attitudes towards Indian pedlars, who received much less attention in the press than Jewish black marketeers. Commercial travellers—of whom Indian pedlars were a conspicuous minority—proved difficult to regulate and played an important role in illegal dealing. Between the wars, single men from the Punjab, both Sikhs and Muslims, came to Britain to work as pedlars and hawkers of cloth and clothing, amongst other things.[50] During the war these pedlars found it increasingly difficult to sell drapery, as they could not obtain regular supplies from wholesalers. Many quit the trade, taking jobs in war factories. Nevertheless, some pedlars continued to sell drapery when they could get hold of goods and coupons, which soon brought them to official attention.[51] In autumn 1942 the clothing inspector attending the detectives' conference for southern England reported the problem posed by Indian pedlars and other aliens, highlighting the activities of nine Indian pedlars living at a house in Portswood Road, Southampton, whom police suspected of coupon-free trading in the surrounding countryside.[52]

A rash of similar cases over the next eighteen months led the Investigation Section to presume that all Indian pedlars dabbled in the black market. Reporting the conviction of a twenty-six-year-old Indian pedlar for giving a Glasgow warehouse fake clothing vouchers in spring 1944, *The Scotsman* noted the remarks made by the Assistant Procurator-Fiscal. According to him, 'the Board of Trade were exercised by the trading of Indian pedlars', who typically made a 200% profit on a coupon-free sale.[53] The linkage of Indian pedlars with black markets became a cause of concern for the India Office, who worried that it might arouse hostility towards Indians in Britain and India more generally, unconsciously echoing the fears of the Board of Deputies of British Jews about the image of the Jewish black marketeer.[54]

The working rule that all Indian pedlars were black marketers persisted into the post-war period. In 1946 the *Daily Mirror* reported that BoT inspectors were targeting Birmingham's 'floating population' of Indians who they believed to be behind two rackets: the selling of lacquer as nail varnish, and scenting RAF lubricating oil and selling it as brilliantine.[55] Only months before the abolition of clothes rationing, senior officials instructed the Board's coupon checking offices to check all clothing vouchers from traders with recognizably 'Indian' names such as Singh, Ali, and Mohammed.[56] Disentangling the relationship between cause and effect is very difficult. Reading the minutes of the Leeds Price Regulation Commit-

---

[50] Rozina Visram, *Asians in Britain: 400 Years of History* (London, 2002), 255, 260–2, 266–7.

[51] Bashir Mann, *The New Scots: The Story of Asians in Scotland* (Edinburgh, 1992), 150.

[52] TNA: PRO, MEPO 3/1868, No. 6 district detectives' conference minutes, 8 October 1942.

[53] *The Scotsman*, 3 March 1944.

[54] Visram, *Asians in Britain*, 268.

[55] *Daily Mirror*, 4 December 1946.

[56] TNA: PRO, BT 64/465, 'Coupon Banking: Procedure for Dealing with Coupons and Transfer Vouchers received from Banks', 11 October 1948.

tee's 635th meeting, of June 1951, complaints made about A. Rashid and Jalal Deen Baroo of Sheffield for overcharging customers for utility clothing stand out to contemporary readers more than similar complaints about Sheffield's Linda Lee and Harry Armitage. Such unfamiliar names were probably more salient to enforcement staff too, which may have given rise to the impression that Indian pedlars played a larger part in black market dealing than they did distorting enforcement activity.[57]

The law enforcement agencies' working rules that prompted them to focus on the activities of Indian pedlars and other marginal groups, the division of responsibilities between four ministry inspectorates, and the unwillingness of the police to cooperate fully with the inspectorates, undermined the ministries' enforcement policies and skewed the pattern of enforcement activity. An equally important factor distorting policing of black market dealing was the character of the offences themselves: not only were they collusive and hence victimless, but also economic and technical, which made it hard for anyone unversed in the regulations to recognize a breach of control when it took place.

The complexity of the regulations was both an excuse for police recalcitrance, masking deep dislike for regulatory enforcement, and the reason for rationing ministries taking the responsibility for prosecution out of the hands of the police, which was a further disincentive for police. Detectives did assist the inspectorates to investigate breaches of control orders resembling the 'traditional' crimes of forgery and theft. Such offences, unlike overcharging for goods, failure to keep accurate business records, or supplying false information, did not clash with police ideas of what police work should entail. Police officers did not consider evasion of control to be criminal, nor did they want to enforce regulations that might alienate 'respectable' opinion. For these reasons the police concentrated on attempts by professional criminals to forge ration coupons and steal ration coupons or rationed goods. They also enforced a small number of new regulations that served police purposes. After stealing, receiving and unlawful possession of petrol, the second-largest category of petrol rationing offence prosecuted by police during 1945, 1946, and 1947 was misuse of petrol.[58] This was an offence that was easy to prove, which made it appealing to uniformed officers looking to boost their arrest and clear-up rates. Bringing a lesser charge avoided the hassles associated with processing a case, and ensured that the credit remained with the beat officer or patrol car driver. It was also a way for senior officers to disguise the lack of meaningful cooperation with enforcement inspectors.

The economic and technical character of breaches of the control orders was not the only feature of black market offences to mould enforcement. As controlled goods flowed downstream from producers to consumers, normally passing through the hands of manufacturers, wholesalers, and retailers, the number of people engaged in illegal transactions and the frequency of an individual's transactions

---

[57] TNA: PRO, BT 94/549, 'North Eastern Local Price Regulation Committee minutes', 20 June 1951.

[58] Evasions of Petrol Rationing, 23.

increased, while the volume and value of the goods involved in each transaction decreased. In short, most offenders committed petty offences. Collusion between buyers and sellers of black market goods meant that inspectors and police could not rely on members of the public denouncing one another, though these played an important part in enforcement work. The techniques needed to police black markets were those of the investigative accountant and the undercover detective, as law enforcement officials seldom stumbled across illegal dealing.

Beat policemen, such as Sergeant Brecon of the Birmingham City Police, chanced on black market activity rarely, as most illegal dealing took place on private premises. In his pocket book, Brecon recorded seventy-eight incidents throughout March 1941 to April 1942. Only five of these incidents concerned theft—three of money from gas meters, and two of petty theft from work.[59] During a six-week period in the autumn of 1942, PC Atkin of Sheffield City Police dealt with approximately one minor case of theft every day, most of these cases involving children. The only case connected to breaches of control that Atkin investigated was the theft of a small number of clothing coupons.[60] Detectives had little more experience of illicit trading than their uniformed colleagues had. Detectives and uniformed officers in rural areas probably had even less contact with black market activity. Given the rarity of stumbling across an illegal deal, police and inspectors depended upon well-publicized drives against individual offences, combining police stop-checks with unannounced inspections, and undercover operations, based on intelligence from informers and intercepted communications, to tackle black markets.

Despite regular appeals for information, the law enforcement agencies received few complaints from the public—particularly members of the trades and industries that the ministries sought to control. Public reluctance to inform the authorities about evasion undermined enforcement of price regulations during the first two years of control. Before the creation of an inspectorate, the price regulation committees relied upon members of the public to inform them of breaches of the price control orders. Reviewing this period, the official historians of price control noted that 'Complaints from members of the public related for the most part to the grosser forms of profiteering by small shopkeepers in such things as electric torches; traders themselves were unlikely to complain in view of their unwillingness to incur the hostility of their suppliers'.[61] The number of prosecutions for price offences jumped from 153 in 1941 to 448 in 1942 after the establishment of a price inspectorate that looked for offences.[62]

The minutes of Featherstone Urban District Food Control Committee's enforcement subcommittee support the view that most complaints involved retail sales. During the fourteen years of its existence the subcommittee investigated a

[59] Cited in Weinberger, *Best Police*, 140.
[60] IWM, Dept. of Doc., Misc. 62 (956), 'Notebook of PC Walter Atkin', 13 October–29 November 1942.
[61] Hargreaves and Gowing, *Civil Industry*, 79.
[62] *Civil Industry*, 91.

small number of black market cases, almost all of which local people had brought to its attention. Under-the-counter favouritism, giving of short weight, and over-charging irritated the people of 'Ashton'—the pseudonym used for the town in the community study *Coal is Our Life*—prompting them to complain to the authorities.[63]

Few people who knew of black market dealings informed police or inspectors about them, because the dealings did not injure their interests. Bartering or trading of unwanted coupons and rations benefited vendor and vendee without harming anyone else. The same was true of transactions involving the resale of price-con-trolled goods by private individuals. Occasionally, people complained to the authorities out of jealousy or spite because the same opportunities were not afforded to them. Scores could be settled this way too. Other civilians considered it their public duty to inform police or inspectors about breaches of control. Moral outrage at the actions they deemed to be immoral, selfish, and unpatriotic prompted these public-spirited individuals. But such informers were few in number, as most people did not denounce others, fearing the consequences that informing might have on their social relationships. There were numerous stories of traders refusing to serve customers who had informed on other traders, and people persecuting neighbours who had informed on their neighbours. Dread of being 'sent to Coventry' stopped most people from telling the authorities about evasion.[64]

Disgust for tale-bearers was as important, if not more important, than anxiety about the social consequences of informing as a factor inhibiting the potential tell-tale. As the threat to national survival dwindled and austerity dragged on, public disapproval of delators and informers balanced dislike for black marketeers. In early 1946 the panel on the BBC radio programme *The Brains Trust* prompted a public debate about the issue. The national press fulminated against Professor Cyril Joad and his fellow members of the panel when they gave morally equivocal answers to a question about black market activity. A London listener calling himself 'John Citizen' wrote to *The Brains Trust*, saying 'I know that my neighbour buys in the black market. To inform the police openly would cause friction for a lifetime. To inform them secretly would be almost as dirty a trick as this. What should I do?' Malcolm Sargent, conductor, felt that citizens should not act as informers, and advised the questioner to do nothing. Sir Arthur Salter, former civil servant and Conservative politician, felt that every citizen was duty-bound to assist the police, but did not think the questioner should inform the police about his neighbour's activities. Salter suggested the questioner gather information about his neighbour's source of supply and pass this onto the police. Following the principle of 'do unto your neighbour as you would that your neighbour would do unto you', Professor Cyril Joad, Professor of Philosophy at Birkbeck College, recommended doing nothing.[65]

---

[63] TNA: PRO, MAF 67/171, 'Featherstone FCC minutes', September 1939–October 1953.

[64] See Melanie Tebbutt, *Women's Talk: A Social History of Gossip in Working-Class Neighbourhoods, 1880–1960* (Aldershot, 1995) for importance of social sanctions.

[65] BBC WAC, Talk Scripts, *Brains Trust*, BBC Home Service, 29 January 1946.

The authorities handled spontaneous communications from the public about illegal dealing with great care. Public-spirited individuals who reported suspect activity to police were often more of a hindrance than a help, as their motives were unclear and they lacked a sense of proportion. Information from anonymous letters and telephone calls was handled with even more care. It was difficult to respond to communications such as this one sent to a London fuel inspector from 'A friend who is against forgery':

> Dear Sir, If you would like to know where forged petrol coupons are being sold watch 100 Great Portland Street car dealer, the person in question is a young man, short and fair hair, grey overcoat, sorry cannot tell his name as I only have the information. [Signed] A friend who is against forgery.[66]

The text of the letter does not explain the author's motives, nor does it identify the source of the author's information. The fuel inspector could not question the anonymous letter writer, and the only way he could test the reliability of the information was to identify the car dealer and question him or put him under surveillance—which meant spending a considerable amount of time checking a vague tip-off that might lead nowhere. The fuel inspector chose to do nothing, and filed the letter for future reference.

Acting on anonymous information could, and did, involve the authorities in conflicts between rival black market operators. Following the tip-off from 'A friend against forgery' might have dragged the fuel inspector into a conflict between rivals in London's used car trade. A private investigator working for the Minister of Food recorded such an incident.

> There are other restaurants in Cambridge who also get illegal supplies of meat, one especially is the A who is also owned by a Greek, of late some of the customers from the O have gone there, this has upset the O and he wanted to put the A on the spot, so Mr O sent a note to the Food Office (The Food Office is over the O Restaurant) exposing the activities of Restaurant A and told them that Mr A was getting supplies from the Black Market, Mr O from a top window watched Mr A arrive with a leg and told the Food Officer that now was the time to call. The Food Inspector went to A Restaurant and asked if he could look around.[67]

The inspector discovered the restaurateur's rival preparing sausages from horse-flesh, and the rival was penalized with a fine of £5 plus costs. The butcher, who had supplied both restaurants with black market meat, pleased 'Mr A' had not given him away, gave 'Mr A' all the meat he wanted. By his silence, 'Mr A' had saved the butcher from damaging publicity and a possible £500 fine.

Far more useful to the authorities were participating informants, paid in cash or kind, whose motives were clear and whose actions could be controlled. The practice of paying informers had official backing, reaffirmed by the Labour Cabinet in 1949.[68] With the exception of the fuel inspectorate, the police and ministry inspec-

---

[66] TNA: PRO, POWE 33/1480, 'Anon. Letter', 10 March 1946.
[67] IWM, Dept. of Doc., 62/25/1, 'Note', n.d.
[68] TNA: PRO, CAB 128/16, CM (49) 68, 24 November 1949.

torates made frequent payments to informers. Of all the agencies policing black markets, the Metropolitan Police made the heaviest use of informers. During the financial year beginning on 1 April 1949 they paid £8,786 2s 9d in rewards and gratuities to informers, and in the same period MoF informants received £95 0s 0d.[69] The Metropolitan Police's figure represented a considerable drop on spending during the previous financial year, when they paid informers a total of £10,156 5s 0d. Comparable BoT figures do not exist, but a Prime Ministerial response to a parliamentary question in November 1949 is revealing. Asked about the employment of informers, Prime Minister Clement Attlee listed those government agencies that paid informers, distinguishing between standard MoF practice and occasional BoT payments.[70]

The Metropolitan Police were experts in undercover policing—a fact acknowledged by other forces and agencies. Under direct orders from the assistant commissioner Sir Ronald Howe to put a stop to coupon forgery and organized theft of rationed goods, the wartime head of the Flying Squad, Detective Chief Inspector Peter Beveridge, encouraged his officers to cultivate participating informants.[71] With Beveridge's backing, Detective Inspector Jack Capstick and the six Flying Squad officers under his command recruited informers from club owners, hostesses, and prostitutes working in the West End. The tips received from these informers proved invaluable. The Squad's biggest success in Beveridge's drive against black marketers—the arrest of 'Flash Izzy' and his accomplices—rested on a tip-off from an informer. A soldier on leave, whom Capstick had arrested a few months earlier for warehouse breaking on the basis of another tip-off—told the detective about 'Flash Izzy', a black marketeer operating in Kentish Town and Camden, and suggested he track down Army deserters stealing lorries for him. A Soho club hostess—another of Capstick's sources—put him onto the girlfriend of a deserter. Capstick followed the woman, who led him to the deserter. Fearful of being returned to the Army, the deserter agreed to cooperate with the police, and took Capstick to the run-in where drivers brought their stolen loads. Forensic evidence from the run-in and the deserter's evidence tied Isaac Bernfield ('Flash Izzy') to the theft of a lorry-load of silk, and led to his conviction, the deserter's conviction, and the conviction of three others.[72]

The names of the soldier and the club hostess who supplied Capstick with the tips that prompted the investigation did not feature in court, and press coverage of the case made no mention of the two informers or the deserter's cooperation with the police.[73] Banned by the police commissioner from using paid informers since

---

[69] Metropolitan Police Archives, London, Metropolitan Police Fund Annual Financial Statement and Estimate (1950). MoF figures compiled from W. A. Brock to W. H. Fisher, 24 August 1949, Brock to E. V. Francis, 10 March 1950, and Brock to Francis, 28 June 1950 in T 223/81 at TNA: PRO.

[70] HC deb, vol. 470, 24 November 1949, cols. 522–4.

[71] Peter Beveridge, Inside the CID (London, 1957), 101.

[72] John Capstick and Jack Thomas, Given in Evidence (London, 1960), 56–67.

[73] Daily Express, 31 March 1942.

1935, and wanting to protect their sources identities, London detectives did not discuss informants publicly.

Convinced of the value of paid informers in wartime, the head of Scotland Yard, Chief Constable Percy Worth, suggested to the police commissioner that the Metropolitan Police create a specialist unit to collect criminal intelligence. The new commissioner Sir Harold Scott agreed with Worth and put the idea to the Home Secretary. Prompted by official and public concern about a post-war crime wave, the Home Secretary approved the police commissioner's request to create the four-man unit at the end of December 1945. Under Jack Capstick's direction, the Special Duty Squad collected intelligence on persistent and dangerous criminals, which they fed to the Flying Squad. By creating a specialist unit, senior officers made it easier to monitor the handling of paid informants, assuaging their fears about detectives developing corrupt trading relationships with active criminals. Reassured by the new structure and happy with the personnel assigned to the unit, the Commissioner's Office poured money into the squad. The amount paid to informants increased dramatically, leaping from £927 18s 6d during the financial year ending 31 March 1945 to a peak of £10,156 5s 0d during the financial year ending 31 March 1949—the unit's last full year of operation.[74]

The Special Duty Squad dealt with four types of informant: those who gave information to police in the expectation of financial reward or other benefit; participating informers who provided information about others with whom he or she was actively engaged in the planning and commission of offences; tasked informers who were actively managed by police to gather specific information on suspected criminals for an extended time period (which sometimes involved participation in the planning and commission of offences); and grasses who agreed to testify in court on the activities of their former criminal associates in the expectation of some form of advantage—normally a substantial sentence discount.

During the Squad's first six months, acting on intelligence from their informants, Squad members seized 50,000 forged clothing coupons and arrested seven members of the gang responsible for forging the coupons. Between January 1946 and September 1949 detectives arrested 789 people, cleared up 1,566 cases, and recovered property worth £256,896 on the basis of intelligence from the Special Duty Squad—an effect out of all proportion to its size. The Squad was a success, prompting Leeds City Police and other forces to establish similar units; but its effectiveness diminished once career criminals and crime reporters learned of its existence, and in 1949 it was disbanded. With the Squad's demise, the police and the ministry inspectorates ceased to employ informants on a regular basis.

Paid informers were important in efforts to enforce price and rationing regulations, but so was the interception of communications. The MoF intercepted communications regularly between 1940 and 1955, obtaining warrants to tap 431 telephone lines and five warrants to intercept letters, parcels, and telegrams sent to

---

[74] Mark Roodhouse, 'The "Ghost Squad": Undercover Policing in London, 1945–49', in Gerard Oram (ed.), *Conflict and Legality: Policing mid-Twentieth Century Europe* (London, 2003), 171–91.

suspected black marketeers. The police also obtained Home Office warrants for mail intercepts and telephone taps when investigating black marketeers. Black marketeers did not expect such techniques to be used against them, but they could counter them with ease. On learning from a corrupt officer that their telephones were being tapped, a gang trading in stolen meat took the obvious precautions of discussing business face-to-face whenever possible, and of using code if a telephone call was unavoidable.[75] Although the MoFP and the BoT did not obtain any warrants, illustrating once again the difference between their approach to enforcement and that of the MoF, all the inspectorates made occasional use of information from Postal and Telegraphic Censorship.[76] If a censor read a letter or telegram soliciting gifts of controlled goods, they passed on the information to the relevant ministry. Information from Postal Censorship alerted the clothing inspectors to the activities of enterprising Canadian servicemen stationed in Britain who were illegally importing Canadian clothes to sell, disguised as gifts, to British civilians within weeks of the introduction of clothes rationing.[77] From summer 1941 the rationing ministries ceased to use evidence from Postal Censorship in court after the Scottish Lord Advocate brought the matter to the Cabinet's Home Policy Committee. The committee did not want the legal basis of censorship challenged in the courts. The ministries did, however, continue to act on intelligence from Postal Censorship until it ended in 1945.[78]

Detectives and inspectors used the information from opened mail, telephone taps, and informers to direct their covert operations and criminal investigations. Often, investigating officers would mount a surveillance operation to check intelligence before launching an undercover operation or a criminal inquiry. Both the police and the inspectorates made regular use of surveillance techniques. On one job, food inspectors observed the entrance to a café in Hastings from an upper window in a garage opposite the café. After fourteen hours of counting the number of customers who entered and left the café, the inspectors visited the café and compared their figures to the owner's record of the number of meals served. The records did not tally with the inspectors' head count, so the ministry prosecuted the owner.[79]

If surveillance confirmed that intelligence was reliable, and could not secure the evidence necessary for a prosecution, the agencies might consider infiltrating an officer or an informant into a gang, organizing a sting, or an officer befriending a criminal. For the most part the inspectorates did not involve themselves in infiltrating gangs or befriending black marketeers, concentrating their efforts on the simplest type of sting operation: the test purchase. The Flying Squad during the war, and the Special Duty Squad after the war, made occasional use of infiltration

---

[75] IWM, Dept. of Doc., 62/25/1, 'Note', n.d.

[76] Report of the Committee of Privy Counsellors appointed to inquire into the Interception of Communications (PP 1956–7 Cmd.283 xi, 125), 43.

[77] TNA: PRO, BT 64/869, 'Coordination Paper 50: Canadian Soldiers' Racket', (8) July 1941.

[78] TNA: PRO, MAF 100/17, French to A. Taylor, 22 May 1941.

[79] Victoria Seymour, *Court in the Act: Crime and Policing in WWII Hastings* (St Leonards on Sea, 2004), 104–5.

and befriending operations. But like the inspectorates, most of the squads' undercover jobs were buy-and-bust operations. The inspectors adhered closely to departmental guidelines for test purchases after the accusation that such purchases amounted to the adoption of *agent provocateur* tactics. According to the BoT, 'Test Purchases should only be made at establishments in respect of which complaints have been recently received, and the question of coupons should not be raised by the office, but rather left to the person contacted, who, if possible, should not be a young and inexperienced assistant.'[80]

The inspectorates preferred test purchases to more complex operations because they were cheap and easy to mount. They were also less likely to go wrong, and easier to defend in court. Like the reliance on participating informers, this skewed enforcement. A test purchase from a retailer was much easier to carry out than one from a wholesaler. Without going to the trouble of creating a false identity and establishing a relationship of trust with a wholesaler, the inspector could walk into a store posing as a member of the public and seek to buy controlled goods. Despite the official message that buyers of black market goods were as much a part of the problem as the dealers, resource constraints meant that it was more cost effective for the law enforcement agencies to focus on suppliers. Once again resource constraints combined with public antipathy to undercover policing, and the difficulty of gaining access to private premises without showing a warrant meant that the focus on suppliers narrowed to retailers and caterers. For similar reasons street traders received a disproportionate amount of attention from the authorities.

This pattern of enforcement activity had a marked influence on the characteristics of the typical black market offender. The bulk of prosecutions for food crimes concerned retailers. MoF Enforcement Division data reveal that on average 74.0% of the 4,487 persons prosecuted for food offences every December between 1945 and 1951 were traders. Retailers accounted for 54.7%, caterers for 7.4%, wholesalers for 2.8%, and producers for 9.1%.[81] This was both a function of the number of traders at the end of the distribution chain and the focus on low-level dealers. In the main, the more serious offenders were middle-aged businessmen with a leavening of female shop assistants, female shoppers, and working-class penny capitalists. Between 1939 and 1945 only 8.5% of persons convicted for price and rationing offences in the higher courts were women. Standing at 8.2%, the proportion of women convicted in lower courts was similar. Almost 90% of those convicted for price and rationing offences were 21 or older.[82] The figures support, but do not confirm, the contemporary view, which they undoubtedly shaped, that evasion involved 'not only the kinds of people, who would, in the ordinary course of events, be involved in shady dealings on the margins of the law, but large numbers of middle-class people who would never have considered themselves criminals in the commonly understood sense of the term'.[83] The preponderance of social groups

[80] TNA: PRO, BT 64/3022, Yandell, 'Board of Trade enforcement circular', n.d. (September 1942).
[81] Calculated from Zweiniger-Bargielowska, *Austerity*, 166, Table 4.6.
[82] Criminal Statistics: England and Wales, 1939–1945.
[83] Morris, *Crime and Criminal Justice*, 18.

such as Jews in London's retail clothing and grocery trades meant that inspectors netted an apparently disproportionate number of Jews that confirmed enforcement officers' suspicions of Jewish traders.[84] Whitehall officials tended to read these enforcement data positively, viewing them as a reliable guide to evasion rather than a reflection of enforcement activity.

The likelihood of evasion coming to the attention of ministry inspectors was low due to the collusive nature of such offences and the resource limitations faced by the enforcement agencies. This also affected the quality of the information on which officials at headquarters based their policies. Enforcement and prosecution policies took account of these resource constraints, emphasizing the need to secure compliance with the regulations through publicity campaigns and well-designed control schemes, and asking the police to act as auxiliaries to the much smaller ministry inspectorates. But the lack of victims to report illegal dealings and the shortage of manpower, combined with the economic character of the offences and each agency's organizational culture, had a much greater impact on street-level enforcement, determining the tactics and methods that the agencies employed to deal with evasion. In their turn, the chosen tactics and methods defined who was and who was not subject to the regulations, turning enforcement into a raffle, whilst also skewing official perception of black markets, which fed back into the policymaking process.

   Although compliance strategies demonstrated that ministers and officials appreciated some of the limitations that resource constraints placed on enforcement activity, they showed little or no understanding of the impact that enforcement structure, organizational culture, and the collusive nature of the offences had on policing. With the notable exception of the MoFP, the rationing ministries did not treat enforcement data as performance indicators. As a consequence, manufacturers had little reason to fear law enforcement agencies that rarely mounted undercover operations and almost always announced their intention to visit a factory. The factors that led inspectors and police to focus their efforts on hoteliers, restaurateurs, market traders, shopkeepers, and shop assistants also went unnoticed. Naturally, government rhetoric did not acknowledge the reality of haphazard enforcement, but it did not escape some people's attention. Well publicized 'enforcement drives' might boost the number of eggs received at packing stations, but numbers fell quickly once a drive came to an end. Selective enforcement of price and rationing regulations made it hard for people to gauge their chances of being caught and prosecuted. As we shall see in the next chapter, whether they would be convicted of an offence and what sentence they could expect to receive was even less predictable.

---

[84] LMA, ACC/3121/C13/03/007/37, 'Interim Report of the Statistical Committee of the Trades Advisory Council', May 1944.

6

Sitting on the bench: the legal lottery

The contradictory attitudes of the courts towards economic regulation compounded the difficulties that the rationing ministries encountered when implementing their compliance strategies. Although the law enforcement agencies tackling illegal dealing determined which cases came to court, they exerted little influence over the outcome of court hearings. In the majority of cases the responsibility for the verdict and the sentence rested with the magistracy. As Lord Woolton and others found to their cost, they guarded their independence fiercely and did not take kindly to politicians' attempts to influence sentencing practices. The political nature of most appointments to the magistracy combined with the magistracy's dogged resistance to political interference made it hard to predict how summary justice would be administered. This was also true of the judiciary who heard the most serious black market cases and passed sentence after hearing a jury's verdict.

JUSTICES OF WAR AND PEACE

Magistrates handled the bulk of prosecutions for black market offences with only the most serious black market cases tried at Quarter Sessions or Assizes. During the years 1940–45, higher courts in England and Wales convicted a total of 998 people of black market offences. Over the same period summary courts convicted 103,544 people of black market offences, of whom 1,185 were sentenced to terms of imprisonment and 101,729 fined.[1] It is clear that magistrates preferred to fine black market offenders. A study of black market cases heard at Old Street Magistrates' Court during 1943 conducted by the Jewish Trades Advisory Council provides a more detailed insight into sentencing practices (see Fig. 6.1). Between April and December 1943 the two stipendiary magistrates at Old Street Magistrates' Court heard 155 black market cases, of which twenty-eight involved Jewish defendants. Only ten defendants were discharged, and another twenty-two defendants had the case against them dismissed under the Probation of Offender's Act. The magistrates convicted 113 of the defendants and committed ten defendants for trial.

Although a fine was the most probable sentence for a black market offence, this cannot be interpreted as indicating undue leniency on the part of justices. The preference for fining black market offenders reflected a general wartime trend to make

---

[1] Criminal Statistics: England and Wales, 1939–1945, 13.

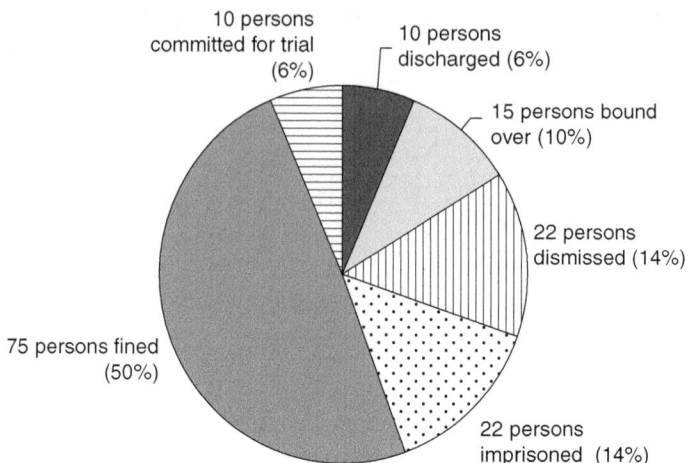

Fig. 6.1. Outcomes of black market cases at Old Street Magistrates' Court, April–December 1943.

Note: Researchers classified prosecutions for offences committed against the criminal law as well as defence regulations 55 and 56 as 'black market cases'.

Source: LMA, ACC/3121/C13/03/007/37, 'Interim Report of the Statistical Committee of the Trades Advisory Council', May 1944.

less use of custodial sentences. The Home Office Advisory Council on the Treatment of Offenders attributed this trend to 'the desire of the courts to free all they could for essential work and for service in the armed forces'.[2] Due to changes in the criminal law dating back to 1914, which forced justices to give people time to pay a fine and hold a second hearing before imprisoning them for non-payment, and wartime increases in working-class incomes, the number of people imprisoned in default of fines declined.[3] Of the 32,225 people received in English and Welsh prisons during 1938, the last full year of peace, 7,936 or 24.6% of the total had been committed for non-payment of fines. In 1944—the last full year of the war—3,737 or 12.2% of prisoners received had been imprisoned for defaulting on fines.[4] The Scottish Prisons Department recorded a similar trend, the proportion of people imprisoned for non-payment falling from 49.6% in 1938 to 20.7% in 1944.[5]

---

[2] Home Office Advisory Council on the Treatment of Offenders, 'The War and Criminality in England and Wales', in International Penal and Penitentiary Commission (IPPC), *The Effects of War on Criminality* (Berne, 1951), 114, 119.

[3] A. H. Manchester, *A Modern Legal History of England and Wales, 1750–1950* (London, 1980), 258–9.

[4] Report of the Commissioners of Prisons and the Directors of Convict Prisons for the Year 1938 (PP 1939–40 Cmd.6137, v, 261); and Report of the Commissioners of Prisons and the Directors of Convict Prisons for the Year 1945 (PP 1946–7 Cmd.7146, xiv, 155).

[5] Annual Report of the Prisons Department for Scotland for the Year 1938 (PP 1938–9 Cmd.5967, xiv, 467); and Report on Prisons in Scotland for the Years 1939–1948 (PP 1948–9 Cmd.7747, xx, 635).

The number of fines imposed on black market offenders conceals more than it reveals, masking local variations in sentencing practices. A Home Office funded study of sentencing in twelve English magistrates' courts during the years 1951–54 revealed that some courts could be shown to be using imprisonment more frequently than the national average even when the nature of the offences and the offenders were taken into consideration.[6] Surveying the administration of English justice from his office in the House of Lords, Sir Claud Schuster, permanent secretary to the Lord Chancellor from 1915 to 1944, noticed a clear pattern in lay magistrates' sentencing practices: borough magistrates tended to be more lenient than county magistrates. When the Minehead Chamber of Trade and the local MP protested at the severity of the penalties imposed in two cases of overcharging by the Dunster Bench, Schuster dismissed the protest out of hand. Writing to his opposite number at the Home Office, Schuster noted:

> The moral to be drawn is that it is an excellent thing that Dunster is in a Petty Sessional Division of the county of Somerset and has not a Borough Bench of its own, and that therefore the sympathies felt by one small tradesman for another have not been allowed to deflect the course of justice. During the last war we had constant trouble with small Borough Benches which absolutely refused to convict on flagrant breaches of Regulations concerning retail trade, or, when they did convict, imposed nugatory penalties.[7]

Schuster believed a leavening of Tory landowners from the countryside around Dunster was a good thing, as it prevented the local shopocracy from controlling the Bench. The problem was made worse by those magistrates who sat on borough Food Control Committees or Enforcement Subcommittees declining to hear food cases they had helped to initiate.[8] Such conflicts of interest prevented those most likely to hand down exemplary sentences from hearing the case.

There was more to Schuster's comments than personal prejudice. A higher proportion of the justices sitting on borough benches owned or managed a business than justices sitting on county benches. There were also more salaried and waged magistrates on borough benches.[9] As a consequence, borough magistrates were more likely to know the traders brought before them than their rural counterparts. They were also more likely to understand the difficulties traders faced. Schuster worried that traders pleading ignorance of the regulations received a sympathetic hearing from borough magistrates who chafed under the same regulations. It was not unknown for the magistrates hearing a case to have broken the law themselves. In 1943 the Lord Chancellor removed a Yorkshire draper and a Welsh butcher

---

[6] Roger Hood, *Sentencing in Magistrates' Courts: A Study in Variations of Policy* (London, 1962), 121.

[7] TNA: PRO, HO 45/25135, 870415/22, Sir Claud Schuster to Sir Alexander Maxwell, 6 January 1943.

[8] 'Practical Points', *Justice of the Peace and Local Government Review*, 106 (1942), 190; 'Practical Points', *Justice of the Peace and Local Government Review*, 106 (1942), 419.

[9] Royal Commission on Justices of the Peace 1946–1948: Report (PP 1947–48 Cmd.7463, xii, 733), 7–8.

from the Commission of the Peace after their fellow justices convicted them of price and rationing offences.[10] Neither case made national news, but three years later that of Alderman Arthur Reeve did. Convicted of obtaining meat for the Stratford Justices' mess without a licence in November 1946, Lord Jowitt had Reeve, who chaired the Stratford Bench, removed from the Commission of the Peace.[11]

There were also marked differences in sentencing practices between individual magistrates, particularly stipendiary magistrates who sat alone, which reflected their philosophies of punishment. Sybil Campbell, Stipendiary Magistrate at Tower Bridge Magistrates' Court from 1945 to 1961 and former Divisional Food Officer (Enforcement) for London from 1939 to 1944, gained a reputation for handing down harsh sentences for pilfering of foodstuffs and other goods in short supply.[12] Her colleague Frederick Langley at Old Street Magistrates' Court from 1932 to 1947 took a similar stance, announcing his intention to hand down exemplary sentences for black market dealing in cucumbers and rhubarb in open court.[13] Yet Claud Mullins at South Western Magistrates' Court in Balham from 1931 to 1947 questioned the need for food rationing and disliked strict enforcement of the regulations. Each magistrate's position reflected her or his approach to punishment. Mullins placed greater emphasis on rehabilitation than did Langley and Campbell. Deterrence and prevention weighed more heavily with them than they did with Mullins.

Lay magistrates with the same political views about control who agreed on the seriousness of black market offences imposed very different penalties for similar offences. Like the stipendiaries Langley and Campbell, Sir Waldron Smithers, Conservative MP for Bromley and chairman of the local bench, believed black market offences to be serious crimes that merited harsh sentences to prevent offenders from reoffending and to deter others. In 1942 Smithers wrote to the Home Secretary Herbert Morrison demanding tougher punishments for black market offenders. In Smithers' considered opinion, everyone convicted of Black Market activities should be liable to:

(1) The death penalty.
(2) Flogging.
(3) A minimum of 14 years' penal servitude.
(4) A deprivation of all property.
(5) Deprivation of the rights of a citizen.

Morrison, not known for his liberal instincts, noted wryly next to Smithers' list of punishments, 'Surely in reverse order!' Smithers went on:

---

[10] TNA: PRO, LCO 33/65, L. Page to Vt. Simon, 16 February 1943; TNA: PRO, LCO 33/67, L. Page to Vt. Simon, 10 November 1943.
[11] *Daily Mirror*, 24 December 1946.
[12] Patrick Polden, 'The Lady of Tower Bridge: Sybil Campbell, England's first Woman Judge', *Women's History Review*, 8 (1999), 506–26; Sybil Oldfield, 'Campbell, Sybil (1899–1977)', in *Oxford DNB*, ix, 861–2.
[13] *The Times*, 8 August 1945.

Black marketeers are cowards, and a few drastic examples of shooting or flogging would soon end this scandal, which is not diminished by the pious utterances of Ministers. The recent example in America of the electrocution of six spies might well be copied in this country, both in spy and Black Market activities.[14]

Like Smithers, Sir C. K. Allen, Oxford don and local Justice of the Peace, was a Conservative. Both men disliked bureaucracy and red tape, but accepted rationing and price control as a wartime necessity to be removed as soon as post-war economic conditions allowed. Allen—a harsh critic of delegated legislation—went so far as to praise the Defence Regulations as 'a great and bold achievement of national defence', but he was far less enthusiastic than Smithers about punishing wrongdoers, noting that 'It was exceedingly distasteful to Englishmen to have to imitate totalitarian methods in order to vindicate democracy.'[15]

Not only did the differences between borough and county benches, stipendiary and non-stipendiary magistrates, and individual justices' views of punishment make it hard for law enforcement agencies to predict the outcome of a court case, there was also increasing resentment amongst magistrates at the amount of work created by price control and rationing. Although the number of people dealt with summarily for non-indictable offences, such as Sunday trading and vagrancy, fell during the war, this was more than offset by the new category of offences against Defence Regulations and an increase in the number of indictable cases. Blackout offences aside, a significant proportion of the new offences related to black market dealings as did many of the cases of theft that drove the increase in the number of indictable offences dealt with summarily.[16]

The additional load of black market offences weighed heavily upon the magistracy. The Magistrates' Association noted in their annual report for 1941:

> The large number of regulations which have been made to deal with conditions brought about by the war has resulted in a great increase in the work of the courts of summary jurisdiction, particularly in relation to the Lighting Restrictions and Food Control, and in many cases the magistrates' clerks and their assistants have had to cope with this additional work with staffs reduced by the call to war service.[17]

Local studies of the magistrates' courts in Clerkenwell, Hampstead, Hastings, and Mansfield bear this out.[18] The burden of hearing the vast number of black market cases fell unevenly on the 19,000 English and Welsh lay magistrates. Nearly half of county magistrates sat for less than eleven days a year, while just under a third of borough magistrates sat for less than eleven days a year. Older magistrates were more likely not to attend than younger magistrates, but the older magistrates

---

[14] TNA: PRO, HO 45/25135, 870415/10, Sir W. Smithers to H. Morrison, 12 August 1942.

[15] Sir C. K. Allen, *Law and Orders: An Inquiry into the Nature and Scope of Delegated Legislation and Executive Powers in English Law* (2nd edn., London, 1956), 54.

[16] Criminal Statistics: England and Wales 1939–1945, 24–5, 30–7.

[17] *The Magistrates' Association Annual Report, 1941*, 5.

[18] Gillian Tindall, *Two Hundred Years of London Justice: The Story of Hampstead and Clerkenwell Magistrates' Courts* (London, 2001), 100–1; Tom Gamble, *Court in Time: Magistrates in Mansfield 1891–1978* (Mansfield, 1999), 74–6; Seymour, *Court in the Act*, 30–1.

who did attend court did so more often. Given that most magistrates were middle-aged when they were appointed to the Bench and that 28% of male magistrates were aged seventy or older (65% were over the age of sixty) in 1948, the label 'younger magistrate' infantilized the middle-aged.[19] During the war, elderly magistrates had handled an even higher proportion of black market cases. The lay magistracy became a gerontocracy early in the war. As the 'younger' magistrates joined the armed forces or took up civil defence posts, summary justice came to be administered by an ageing and ailing magistracy who were unfamiliar with the new regulations; and the same was true of police courts with stipendiary magistrates.[20] In police courts the older stipendiary magistrates were left to cope with the growth in cases as the younger stipendiary magistrates joined the forces or involved themselves in the civilian war effort.[21]

Keeping abreast of the defence regulations, of which rationing and price regulations were part, proved difficult for magistrates. Between 1939 and 1955 the Treasury published twenty-one editions of the *Defence Regulations*. One year into the war, Edward Samson of the Magistrates' Association felt that 'The vast volume of emergency legislation and orders has been beyond what the lay magistrate can reasonably be expected to familiarize himself or herself with.'[22] For much of the war, transport difficulties prevented the association from holding meetings outside London to brief magistrates about the new regulations. As a result, the lay magistracy relied upon their clerks to keep them informed about these regulations. In their turn, Justices' Clerks relied upon the latest edition of *Defence Regulations*, *Stone's Justices' Manual*, published annually and often out of date before going to print, and official circulars from the Lord Chancellor's Office and the Home Office for information about changes to defence regulations.

When deprived of legal advice from their clerk, lay magistrates could make embarrassing mistakes. When the case of a Justices' Clerk, prosecuted for filling out an application form incorrectly, came before his bench, the defence solicitor bamboozled the seven lay magistrates who heard the case with a spurious legal argument that convinced them to dismiss the charges. Reviewing the case for the Lord Chancellor, Lord Justice Tucker concluded that the magistrates had made a 'bad decision'; there was a case to answer, but this could not be attributed to 'dishonesty or conscious bias'. In the absence of their usual clerk, Lord Tucker felt that the magistrates had been

> in the position of Jury retiring to consider their verdict without having heard any summing up...They obviously needed some guidance as to what were the real issues to which they should address their minds. Such guidance was not forthcoming from their Chairman, who is well advanced in years and was, I think, lost without the assistance which he was accustomed to receive from his Clerk.[23]

---

[19] Royal Commission on Justices of the Peace.

[20] Sir Thomas Skyrme, *History of the Justices of the Peace*, 3 vols. (Chichester, 1991), ii, 267; Tindall, *Two Hundred Years of London Justice*, 101.

[21] Tindall, *Two Hundred Years of London Justice*, 101.

[22] *The Magistrates' Association Annual Report, 1940*, 2.

[23] Report of an Enquiry upon the Proceedings at the Hearing of Two Informations before Justices of the Aberayron Division of the County of Cardigan on 24th April 1946 (PP 1946–7 Cmd.7061, xiii, 51).

Even stipendiary magistrates, who worked full time and possessed legal training, found the regulations difficult to understand. Under pressure to administer justice swiftly, stipendiaries could misinterpret government Orders. Sitting at Clerkenwell Police Court in 1940, Herbert Metcalfe, a stipendiary magistrate and former barrister, fined a cosmetics firm £1,250 and 50 guineas costs for selling cosmetics intended for export on the domestic market. Having found the firm guilty of evading the regulations, Metcalfe spent a few minutes calculating the fine using pencil and paper. The maximum penalty that he could impose for the offence was £1,000 or three times the profit made as a result of the offence, whichever was the higher. During the court hearing it had been determined that the company made a profit of £5,000, making the maximum fine Metcalfe could have imposed £15,000 plus costs. According to his clerk F. T. Giles, the circumstances of the case merited a fine of £12,500, but Metcalfe did not ask Giles to check his calculations before announcing the fine. Having announced the fine, it was too late to alter it.[24]

During the first two years of the war, magistrates undertook this additional work 'in a very unselfish spirit'.[25] For many magistrates the administration of justice was their contribution to the war effort, and they viewed offences against the defence regulations with great seriousness, imposing harsh sentences for minor offences. In fact the Magistrates' Association worried that patriotic enthusiasm threatened to undermine the due process of law. The editor of the Association's bulletin *The Magistrate* warned that

> A lively sense of the dangers to which the state is now subject must not be allowed to run away with us... It is fatally easy to fall into the error of thinking that the worse the offence the less is to be the evidence required for conviction, or, what is more subtly dangerous, acting on this notion without clearly thinking it out.[26]

Enthusiasm for administering justice waned during the third year of the war as economic regulations multiplied and caseloads increased. The petty nature of most offences irritated stipendiary and non-stipendiary magistrates alike. Claud Mullins, a Metropolitan Stipendiary Magistrate sitting at South Western Magistrates' Court, deplored the Borough of Wandsworth Food Control Committee's heavy-handed enforcement of the food regulations. The Wandsworth Food Committee 'issued summonses freely'.

> From Wandsworth I had many summonses against most of the main grocery firms, in all of which they were only technically liable, the offences having been committed by their staff. These firms were working under immense difficulties. I well remember the solicitor for one of these firms explaining to me that the young lady who charged the wrongful penny entered the company's service four days before the offence and left two days later. The low spot came when I had to decide whether a costermonger had broken the conditions of his licence to sell vegetables when he sold rhubarb, which, I was solemnly told, is a fruit.[27]

[24] F. T. Giles, *Open Court: Pages from the Notebook of a London Magistrates' Clerk* (London, 1964), 127–30.
[25] *The Magistrates' Association Annual Report, 1941*, 5.
[26] 'Emergency Law and the Bench', *The Magistrate*, 5 (1940), 298.
[27] Claud Mullins, *Fifteen Years' Hard Labour* (London, 1948), 72.

The Lord Chief Justice shared Mullins' concerns about heavy-handed enforcement of food control clogging up the courts with petty cases. Hearing an appeal against a decision by the Bridport justices to throw out a MoF case, Lord Goddard expressed exasperation at the petty nature of the offence, asking 'Can a Divisional Enforcement Officer of a Ministry never turn a blind eye to anything?'[28]

The police and ministry inspectors alienated magistrates further by presenting their cases poorly. Senior MoF officials acknowledged that the ministry had gained a reputation amongst magistrates for presenting badly prepared cases.[29] Three months earlier the ministry persuaded the Home Office to issue a circular to chief police officers asking them to hand over black market cases to their local Divisional Enforcement Officer. Ministry enforcement officials felt that most police prosecutions were ill-advised and poorly prepared, and brought the law into disrepute with magistrates and the public.[30]

Magistrates' dissatisfaction with heavier workloads, annoyance at byzantine regulations, and irritation with petty prosecutions made it more and more difficult for prosecutors to predict the outcome of black market cases. Weighing up the chances of obtaining a successful conviction became even harder when the impact of local feeling on magistrates was taken into account. Once the invasion threat receded and an Allied victory appeared inevitable, the public became increasingly concerned that the authorities treated minor black market offences as crimes rather than misdemeanours. In these changed circumstances, enforcing rationing and price regulations did not improve the popularity of the magistracy. A conviction or a sentence for a black market offence that was perceived to be unfair could make magistrates unpopular locally and undermine respect for the courts and the law more generally.[31] The Magistrates' Association recognized the problem facing their members and urged justices to enforce the controls sensitively.

> Some will say that the law must be vindicated, and until regulations are formally revoked they must be obeyed. Others will say that such proceedings would bring the law into contempt, which is precisely not the way to vindicate it...Public opinion always tends to run ahead of law. There is always a time lag. We content ourselves with merely expressing the hope that magistrates will not be put into the position of feeling themselves bound by law to act contrary to common sense.[32]

Of course, individual magistrates' definitions of what constituted common sense was shaped by the views of their peers as much as by those of their local communities.

Due to the politics of the magistracy, 'common sense' would often mean imposing nominal sentences for offences against temporary regulations that criminalized economic transactions that were perfectly legal before the war. The political nature

---

[28] 'Cox v. Greenham', *The Times*, 25 October 1944.
[29] TNA: PRO, MAF 150/632, 'Notes of meeting', 27 November 1942.
[30] TNA: PRO, HO 45/25135, 870415/11, 'Home Office circular 863,760/4', 18 August 1942.
[31] Skyrme, *Justices of the Peace*, ii, 267–8.
[32] 'When Control Ends', *The Magistrate*, 7 (1944), 4–5.

of the appointment process ensured that many lay magistrates were Conservative or Liberal party members who opposed unnecessary controls and bureaucracy. The effects of this became very apparent in February 1949 when the Chairman of the Carmarthen Justices Colonel Delmé Davies-Evans imposed a nugatory fine of one shilling without costs on a haulage contractor found guilty of using red petrol in his car. Davies-Evans, a Conservative local councillor, should have also given the contractor an automatic twelve-month driving ban, but he disapproved of this penalty. Two days later the Lord Chancellor had Davies-Evans name removed from the Commission of the Peace.[33]

Davies-Evans accused the government of removing him on account of his political views, and received vociferous support from the National Society for the Restoration of Basic Petrol and Welsh Young Farmers.[34] The local MP and several other MPs and Peers wrote to the Lord Chancellor criticizing Lord Jowitt's decision; but more worrying was the criticism in the *Justice of the Peace and the Local Government Review*, which many magistrates read. By his actions Jowitt appeared to punish Davies-Evans for criticizing the government and exercising discretion in sentencing. All justices had the right to criticize legislation and exercise their discretion in sentencing.[35] But these criticisms were misplaced, as Davies-Evans did not have the power to waive the statutory penalty of a twelve-month driving ban. The Lord Chancellor could have done nothing if Davies-Evans had used his discretionary powers correctly: imposing the statutory ban and no other punishment.[36] Praised by popular dailies on the right of British politics and vilified by those on the left, Davies-Evans gained national notoriety for a short time—an achievement that later merited a brief obituary in *The Times*.[37]

Few magistrates followed Davies-Evans' example and resisted the regulations publicly or made statements criticizing the methods used to enforce the law in open court, preferring to subvert the regulations by imposing nominal sentences or doggedly sticking to the letter of the law. A City of London magistrate sitting at Guildhall dismissed a police prosecution of a motorist accused of making an unnecessary journey by car to attend a funeral when the police failed to produce a timetable or a representative of London Transport to prove that the driver could have caught a Number 11 bus to get there on time instead of driving there himself. Unfortunately for the motorist the Court of Appeal overturned the magistrate's decision.[38] The motives for such actions were various—hostility towards economic control, unwillingness to antagonize local opinion, a dislike of undercover policing —but the exercise of discretionary powers convinced policymakers, administrators, and law enforcement officials that the magistracy looked unfavourably on ministry prosecutions.

[33] *Daily Mirror*, 23 February 1949.   [34] *Western Mail*, 24 February 1949.
[35] *Justice of the Peace and Local Government Review*, 5 March 1949.
[36] TNA: PRO, LCO 33/76, Lord Jowitt to Quintin Hogg, 22 March 1949.
[37] *Daily Mirror*, 23 February 1949; *The Times*, 1 December 1953.
[38] C. H. Rolph, *Living Twice: An Autobiography* (London, 1974), 134–6.

JUDGE AND JURY

The behaviour of the judiciary was less wayward than the magistracy, but the outcomes of black market cases in the higher courts were just as unpredictable. The judiciary did not attempt to control the government's exercise of discretionary powers during the war, and when personal rights came into conflict with national security, the courts ruled in the government's favour.[39] When it came to black market offences, judges fell in line with the government. Handing down a sentence for black market offences at the Old Bailey, Lord Chief Justice Viscount Caldecote likened the offender to a 'saboteur'.[40] Judges looked askance at magistrates who did not punish black market offenders severely. Speaking before passing sentence in a black market case, Circuit Judge Mr Justice Charles criticized sentencing practices in magistrates' courts: 'There have been too many foolish fines which do not punish anybody at all.'[41] Judicial support for the regulations had a lasting effect on the criminal law relating to corporations too. In 1944 four separate court judgments in black market cases established that companies could be convicted of deception and conspiracy. This was a quiet legal revolution establishing that a company could be convicted of a crime when proof of *mens rea*, or a guilty mind, was a requirement of the offence. These judgments identified the company with the acts of senior officers, as opposed to being held accountable for the actions of its employees.[42]

Judicial attitudes towards illegal dealing changed after the war. The Labour government found that the patriotism of English and Scottish judges, who saw themselves as the guardians of national legal traditions, was now an obstacle to the effective enforcement of the regulations. Hesitantly at first, but with increasing confidence, judges on both sides of the border denounced the regulations and the methods used by ministry inspectors as alien to English and Scottish law. Within six months of the Japanese surrender, Mr Justice Charles, who had lambasted magistrates for lenient sentencing in black market cases during the war, criticized the BoT for issuing warrants to investigative accountants that gave them extensive powers of search and seizure.[43] The intrusive character of the regulations did not sit comfortably with serviceable fictions about the English legal tradition. According to the law lord Viscount Simonds, what made the English law unique was its focus on the individual in a community and the stress it placed on order, justice, and liberty.[44] It was hard for Simonds and his colleagues to reconcile this deeply held belief with the realities of post-war economic control. Judicial patriotism, so useful

---

[39] J. A. G. Griffith, *The Politics of the Judiciary* (4th edn., London, 1991), 115–16.

[40] *The Times*, 11 July 1942.

[41] *The Times*, 14 February 1942.

[42] *DPP v. Kent and Sussex Contractors* [1944] KB 146 and [1944] 1 AER 119; *R. v. ICR Haulage, Ltd* [1944] KB 551 and [1944] 1 AER 691; *Moore v. Bresler* [1944] 2 AER 515 and *The Times*, 11 May 1944; *R. v. Sorsky* [1944] 2 AER 333.

[43] *The Times*, 11 February 1946.

[44] Lord Simonds, 'Law', in Sir Ernest Barker (ed.), *The Character of England* (Oxford, 1947), 112–35.

in wartime, combined with the judiciary's aesthetic dislike of hastily drafted regulations, its fear that the regulations undermined public respect for the law, and its conservative politics to frustrate the Labour government's attempt to tighten enforcement policy.

Rayner Goddard, who dominated the criminal-justice system as Lord Chief Justice from 1946 to 1958, did much to shape these attitudes. Like the police, Goddard felt more comfortable handling 'traditional' crimes associated with illegal dealing such as stealing and receiving of controlled goods. Speaking at the Annual Judges' Dinner in 1948, Goddard encouraged his fellow judges to punish thieves and receivers of controlled goods. He felt that long custodial sentences would prevent such criminals from offending and maintain public respect for the law.[45] According to Goddard's chief clerk, judges at the Old Bailey, in the Court of Criminal Appeal and out on Circuit, rarely if ever deviated from this stern policy of deterrence.[46]

Lord Goddard's attitude towards offences against the defence regulations was more equivocal. He disliked the defence regulations and the methods used to enforce them. In a judgment relating to trafficking in eggs, Lord Goddard criticized the obscure wording of the regulations, which made them hard to understand. In Goddard's opinion it was 'surely desirable that orders creating criminal offences should be stated in language which the persons who may commit the offences—in this case, quite humble people, like cottagers—can understand'.

> I am certainly not prepared to support such orders and to find persons guilty of criminal offences when the orders which they are charged with violating are couched in language which is open to all sorts of meanings and causes all sorts of difficulties, so that the persons to whom they apply cannot know whether they are acting legally or not, unless possibly they get counsel's opinion, or at any rate a solicitor's advice.[47]

Goddard believed that a criminal offence should be easy for the police, the courts, and the public to understand, and that the punishment for the offence should be clear and strictly imposed. By 1951 Goddard was publicly questioning the need for the continuation of convoluted emergency laws, the contravention of which many people had ceased to consider criminal. In the case of Willcock v. Muckle, Goddard expressed the view that 'To use Acts of Parliament passed for particular purposes in wartime when the war is a thing of the past—except for the technicality that a state of war exists—tends to turn law-abiding subjects into lawbreakers, which is a most undesirable state of affairs.' He was also concerned that enforcing unpopular emergency laws threatened to undermine public support for the police.[48] Goddard's position on the defence regulations was consistent with his authoritarian position on criminal law. In his maiden speech in the House of Lords, Goddard expressed his belief that the effectiveness of the criminal-justice system depended upon public support.[49] If the enforcement of temporary defence regulations threat-

---

[45] *The Times*, 7 July 1948.
[46] Arthur Smith, *Lord Goddard: My Years with the Lord Chief Justice* (London, 1959), 124.
[47] *Brierley v. Phillips and Brierley v. Brear* [1947] 1 KB 541.
[48] *Willcock v. Muckle* [1951] 2 KB 845.   [49] HL deb, vol. 155, 28 April 1948, col. 491.

ened to undermine respect for the criminal law, then the defence regulations should be removed as soon as possible.

Many judges shared Goddard's uneasiness at post-war controls. Fining a furnishing company one shilling on each of six counts of overcharging and failing to keep proper records, the Northern Circuit judge Mr Justice Stable criticized the BoT for issuing unintelligible control orders.

> These controls we all recognize have been effective in this country because the vast majority of citizens are decent, law-abiding people who want to play the game and want other people to play the game. If the law is in such a condition that nobody can understand it, the position will be that people will give it up in disgust, and it would be no surprise if juries refused to convict. I hope this matter will be put right soon.[50]

'Owlie' Stable was not known for his leniency and could be outspoken in his condemnation of the 'thieves' kitchen' that was the black market, but this was balanced by his dislike of legalism and bureaucracy.[51] Scottish judges held very similar views. Reflecting on effects of the war on crime for the International Penal and Penitentiary Commission, a Scottish Sheriff noted that 'some of my personal friends, who have not come before the Court, and who, in bygone times, would have scrupulously observed statutory laws and regulations, no longer feel morally bound by them, and rather than observe such of them, as they do not approve—or at least regard as harsh—would break them, and risk detection and punishment'.[52]

The judiciary's dislike of control orders went deeper still. The terms in which Mr Justice Stable attacked BoT regulations suggest exasperation at the 'jumble of orders which are quite unintelligible' to the layman and took considerable time for him to comprehend. Poor drafting and commercial jargon offended the aesthetic sensibilities of those with legal training. It also increased judicial workloads. By the autumn of 1942 prosecutions for offences against the defence regulations were 'adding considerably' to the work of the Central Criminal Court. Sir Gerald Dodson, who heard many such cases as Recorder of London, found some of the regulations 'so obscurely worded that it was almost impossible to interpret them without much argument and loss of time. Cross-references infested the whole scope of this form of legislation, causing great annoyance and infinite delay.'[53]

Amongst judges, jurists, and lawyers Order No. 1216 of 1943 came to symbolize the worst aspects of the regulations. The euphony of its full title made it something of a classic.

> The Control of Tins, Cans, Kegs, Drums and Packaging Pails (No. 5) Order, 1942 (*a*), as varied by the Control of Tins, Cans, Kegs, Drums and Packaging Pails (No. 6) Order, 1942 (*b*), the Control of Tins, Cans, Kegs, Drums and Packaging Pails (No. 7) Order, 1942 (*c*), the Control of Tins, Cans, Kegs, Drums and Packaging Pails (No. 8) Order,

---

[50] *The Times*, 24 July 1946.
[51] *Manchester Guardian*, 11 March 1941 and 10 March 1942; Frederick Lawton, 'Stable, Sir Wintringham Norton (1888–1977)', *Oxford DNB*, lii, 25–6.
[52] TNA: PRO, HO 45/25079, 'Sheriffs-Substitute's reply to IPPC questionnaire', 26 May 1949.
[53] Gerald Dodson, *Consider Your Verdict: The Memoirs of Sir Gerald Dodson Recorder of London, 1937–1959* (London, 1967), 107.

1942 (*d*), and the Control of Tins, Cans. Kegs, Drums and Packaging Pails (No. 9) Order, 1942 (*e*), is hereby further varied in the Third Schedule thereto… by substituting for the reference 2A therein the reference 'A (1)' and by deleting therefrom the reference 2B.

This Order shall come into force on the 25th day of August 1943, and may be cited as the 'Control of Tins, Cans, Kegs, Drums and Packaging Pails (No. 10) Order, 1943,' and this Order and the Control of Tins, Cans, Kegs, Drums and Packaging Pails (Nos. 5–9) Orders, 1942, may be cited together as the 'Control of Tins, Cans, Kegs, Drums and Packaging Pails (Nos. 5–10) Orders, 1942–3.'

'According to an explanatory note, for which legal professionals were grateful, this Order of 169 words 'enables tin plate to be used for tobacco and snuff tins other than cutter lid tobacco tin'.[54] Judges had sympathy for the plight of manufacturers and traders who BoT officials expected to understand and observe such orders.

Defence barristers attempted to exploit such concerns with some success. Sir Neville Faulks, who prosecuted BoT and MoF cases from 1946 onwards, had to counter this and similar arguments regularly. 'In those days the accused would say that the Board of Trade regulations were incomprehensible bureaucracy, while the restaurants who were caught red-handed in breach of Food regulations would cry "*agent provocateur*", at my witness, but of course there was no other way of proving your case than by planting a witness there.'[55] Accusing law enforcement agencies of entrapment pandered to another judicial worry about control orders which magistrates had been expressing concerns about since the middle part of the war.

Like the magistracy, the judiciary disliked the use of covert operations to enforce the regulations, but judges, with the notable exception of Lord Goddard, were reluctant to say so publicly.[56] The judiciary were uneasy about the law enforcement agencies using such methods, even though the 1929 Royal Commission on Police Powers and Procedure accepted that undercover officers might have to participate in an offence to gather evidence. There were several reasons for judicial unease: Lord Goddard and Travers Humphreys disapproved of entrapping individuals in any circumstances as it was un-English, while the former Lord Chancellor Lord Maugham disliked undercover operations being used to investigate minor rationing and price offences involving otherwise respectable people, as such operations were to be used in serious cases involving hardened criminals.[57] Senior Scottish judges and lawyers disapproved of the policing methods used to detect black market offences for similar reasons. Test purchases, postal intercepts, and wire taps were deemed to be alien to the spirit of the Scottish legal system. In April 1941, Lord Advocate Thomas Cooper instructed the procurators fiscal not to launch prosecutions for food offences based on evidence from censoring inland mails. Cooper wished to avoid a Scottish court ruling that the government censorship of inland mails was illegal—an outcome he feared likely.[58] Cooper's cautiousness

[54] Cited in Allen, *Law and Orders*, 204.
[55] Sir Neville Faulks, *No Mitigating Circumstances* (London, 1977), 118.
[56] *Brannan v. Peek* [1948] 1 KB 68.
[57] HL deb, vol. 124, 6 October 1942, cols. 539–42.
[58] TNA: PRO, MAF 100/17, T. M. Cooper to Woolton, 28 April 1941.

showed that the Crown Office appreciated the courts' dislike of ministry inspectors and their methods; it also precipitated a serious row with Lord Woolton, who thought that Cooper's reluctance to admit postal intercepts as evidence undermined enforcement of the regulations.

Although judges like Cooper could control trials by deciding what to admit as evidence, their dominance of the courtroom was not complete, as the responsibility for the verdict lay with the twelve people sitting in the jury box. The presence of a jury added another element of uncertainty to court proceedings, albeit one that lawyers were used to and to whose whims ministers were reluctantly reconciled. The criminal jury at mid-century was famously described by the judge Sir Patrick Devlin as 'predominantly male, middle-aged, middle-minded, and middle-class'.[59] Although younger than the average Justice of the Peace, the typical juror had much in common with the magistrate, as property qualifications excluded non-householders, most of whom were women, from jury service, while the lack of financial compensation before 1949 prevented the working class from sitting on a jury.[60] A contemporary study of the politics of the jury, cross-referencing jury lists with canvassing records, revealed that these exclusions ensured that the jury, like the magistracy, was more favourably inclined towards the Conservative and Liberal parties than the Labour party.[61] Despite criticisms of its composition, cost, and competence—usually from the left—the criminal jury was seen as an essential safeguard of liberty and a repository of contemporary common sense.[62]

The concern for government was that a common-sense decision when it came to black market offences could often be at odds with the law, because jurors, like magistrates and judges, deemed the regulations themselves or the methods used to enforce them as repugnant. The prosecution could do little about this. In court districts with a sizeable working-class population, prosecutors had long exercised their right to 'stand by' a juror without showing cause in order to exclude jurors whose sex, age, occupation, or residence suggested that they might give the defendant a favourable hearing. In dockyard pilfering cases London prosecutors would always ask dockers and any juror with a criminal record to 'stand by'.[63] Outside the London docklands challenges tended to be rare, as the defence, who could challenge a juror too, might retaliate by lodging challenges of their own.[64] Attempts to rig juries in favour of the prosecution were also hampered by the high level of residential mobility during and immediately after the war. Jurors, like lay magistrates, were in scarce supply due to conscription and evacuation. Even if these obstacles could be overcome, hand-picking a jury was futile, as Devlin's 'male, middle-aged, middle-minded, middle-class' jury was unlikely to support control unquestioningly.

[59] Sir Patrick Devlin, *Trial by Jury* (2nd edn., London, 1966), 20.
[60] Anon., *Justice in England* (London, 1938), 48–55.
[61] R. M. Jackson, *The Machinery of Justice in England* (3rd edn., London, 1960), 250.
[62] Simonds, 'Law'.
[63] Museum of London, Barbican, Museum of Docklands Oral History Project, 'Interview with Glyn Hardwicke', 20.
[64] Devlin, *Trial by Jury*, 29.

In fact the very groups excluded from jury service—the working class and women—were those most likely to support control.

'FOOLISH FINES' AND 'NUGATORY SENTENCES'

During the war, complaining about inadequate sentences was a common refrain amongst ministry inspectors and detectives, who felt that the regulations and the courts placed too much emphasis on due process of law and not enough on crime control. The system of maximum fines imposed on convicted black market operators was a particular source of irritation. The fines related to the offences that could be proved in court, which were often a small fraction of the number of offences committed before being caught. Senior police officers advocated the ability to pay being the only limit on the size of a fine. H. M. Howgrave-Graham, Secretary to the Metropolitan Police from 1927 to 1946, used a dialogue with an anonymous senior officer to put the case for such harsh fines. Defaulters would be imprisoned. The anonymous officer—a foil for H. M. Howgrave-Graham—supported the idea of sequestrating property in 'really bad cases'. In peacetime the officer felt that only 'the big swindlers' merited such punishment.

> But in wartime or whilst controls and rationing are still on, there are plenty. The man who tries to make big money illegally out of such conditions surely deserves to be outlawed in the sense of being deprived of the protection of the law which enables him to possess what he has got.[65]

Sir Charles Tegart, head of the MoF enforcement intelligence bureau, shared similar views to Howgrave-Graham's anonymous policeman. He applauded those magistrates and judges who 'gave sentences sufficiently severe to be really effective and sometimes accompanied their pronouncing of them with a verbal rap over the knuckles calculated to make anyone but the most conscienceless feel ashamed of his behaviour'.[66] Tegart felt, like many policemen and ministry inspectors, that the fines imposed by most magistrates were too low to act as an effective deterrent to black market offenders.

Lenient sentences for black market offenders undermined morale amongst law enforcement officers. Tegart found it 'disheartening, after months of research, observation and the painstaking collection of evidence, to see a man who has been robbing the public of tons of butter and sugar or gallons of oil fined a sum which probably means no more to him than a week's pocket-money'.[67] As a result, Tegart and other enforcement inspectors put less energy into investigations. Given the 'light' sentences imposed on offenders, police officers chose to concentrate their efforts on those cases where they felt they had a higher chance of securing a conviction and a sentence reflecting the seriousness of the offence and the investigative effort. In their sentencing practices magistrates confirmed the belief that the

---

[65] H. M. Howgrave-Graham, *Light and Shade at Scotland Yard* (London, 1947), 139.
[66] Tegart, 'Charles Tegart', 304–5.   [67] 'Charles Tegart', 304.

majority of black market offences were not of a serious nature and were therefore unworthy of police attention.

The perceived leniency of the courts infuriated law enforcement officials and politicians. Concerned about the effects of sentencing practices on their staffs' morale and the public's willingness to comply with the regulations, government ministers tried to influence the courts. Talking to food reporters in February 1942, Lord Woolton praised the magistrates and judges who had handed down heavy sentences for black market offences. He went on to say: 'I am obliged to rely on the determination of the Courts to stamp out these black markets by making them unprofitable, and, where the offence justifies it, removing the operators from the field of their operations'.[68] Woolton appeared to be responding to public pressure for tougher sentences for black market offences, but he had in fact connived with allies in the press to generate public indignation at lenient sentences. Responding to British military reverses, the press had been calling for greater sacrifices on the Home Front since autumn 1941 and berating magistrates for handing down inadequate fines for black market offences. Typical examples of 'lenient' sentences were a fine of 5s with £3 costs for selling milk 62% deficient in milk fat, and a fine of £50 for selling goods above the maximum price, which left the offender with a profit of £1,051.[69] To give some sense of proportion, defaulting on the payment of these fines would have resulted in prison sentences of seven days and three months respectively.[70]

At a press conference three weeks earlier, Woolton had gone off record to criticize the courts.

> I am rather worried about this black market business because we have given the Judiciary very great powers and, as you know, it is a part of the rules of the game that Ministers do not criticise the Bench. That is why I have gone off the record. Some of the fines that are being imposed are ridiculous, and unless the Bench are prepared to take the profit out of crime, and having taken the profit out to inflict a punishment as well, it is not any use my giving them the power to do it; and, as the Minister, I cannot do any more than bring people up before the Court.

Still off the record, Woolton asked reporters to 'help it along a bit, because I have noticed that when you feel you have an opinion you are able in your papers to give expression to it without restraint'.[71]

The resultant campaigns in the *Daily Mirror* and *News Chronicle* made it easier for Woolton to persuade his ministerial colleagues to toughen black market penalties. The Home Secretary sent a circular to Justices of the Peace encouraging them to use the provisions of the new Order in Council and punish black market offenders more severely.[72] In April, Osbert Peake exhorted magistrates to impose the new maximum sentences for black market offences in a speech to a conference of Midlands magistrates in Birmingham.[73] George Yandell, BoT Chief Investigation

---

[68] *The Times*, 18 February 1942.   [69] 'Inadequate Fines', *The Magistrate*, 6 (1942), 79–80.
[70] James Whiteside, *Hayward and Wright's Office of Magistrate* (8th edn., London, 1950).
[71] TNA: PRO, MAF 102/125, 'Notes of press conference', 27 January 1942.
[72] *The Times*, 23 March 1942.
[73] Osbert Peake, 'The Administration of Justice in Time of War', *The Magistrate*, 6 (1942), 99.

Officer, addressed the annual general meeting of the Magistrates' Association shortly after journalists and politicians criticized his Investigation Branch for using *agent provocateur* tactics. After describing 'the three Cs' of the black market—clothing, cosmetics, and coupons—Yandell told those present that he had not come across a genuine case in which his inspectors acted as *agents provocateurs*, and reassured them that the Board of Trade solicitor would refuse to prosecute a case with the slightest hint of *agent provocateur* methods. He believed that press publicity prompted the guilty to accuse the board of underhand methods as a 'red herring', and finished by asking magistrates to impose 'exemplary sentences'.[74]

But central government's ability to effect the administration of justice was limited. The Home Secretary did not appoint magistrates or judges—the Lord Chancellor did. The Lord Chancellor could remove magistrates on the grounds of undue leniency, but this was difficult to prove.[75] Attempts by other ministers to use the press to influence sentencing had a limited impact, and could backfire. Senior MoF officials felt that press reports criticizing the courts helped to secure stiffer penalties for theft of controlled foods and cases of overcharging, but this effect was short-lived.[76] Responding to what he felt was unjustified criticism of magistrates, the editor of *The Magistrate* published a trenchant defence of a magistrate's right to criticize shoddy legislation.[77] No senior government minister repeated Woolton's attempt to influence the courts. In April 1944, J. J. Llewellin changed MoF prosecutions policy. Unlike his predecessor Lord Woolton, Llewellin realized that the policy of prosecuting every minor offence alienated the public, which made the courts less likely to look favourably on ministry prosecutions.[78]

Disillusioned by their dealings with the criminal-justice system, the rationing ministries placed increasing emphasis on the use of administrative penalties to tackle serious and repeat offenders. Speaking to an audience of military officers preparing to impose civil military administration on liberated Europe in 1944, the deputy secretary of the MoF Supply Department spoke for many of his colleagues when he advised:

> In fighting the 'black market' there is no better weapon than this. Fines rarely do more than remove part of the illicit profit—prison sentences leave the offender's family to carry on the business for him and he will one day emerge to enjoy his gains, but to revoke his licence is to put a stop to his activities during the rest of control.[79]

Such advice pays tribute to the courts' ability to frustrate the rationing ministries' carefully devised compliance strategies. Verdicts and sentences for similar offences varied widely once the courts' initial patriotism wore thin. Lay magistrates were less likely to convict, and more lenient in their sentencing if they did, than were

---

[74] Yandell, 'Black Market', viii–x.
[75] R. M. Jackson, *The Machinery of Justice in England* (Cambridge, 1940).
[76] TNA: PRO, MAF 102/125, 'Notes of press conference', 17 February 1942.
[77] 'Some Aspects of Control', *The Magistrate*, 6 (1942), 132–5.
[78] TNA: PRO, MAF 100/32, P. J. Wheeldon to Divisional Food Officers, 6 April 1944.
[79] P. G. R. Whalley, 'Introduction to Commodity Control', in MoF, *Administration of Food Control*, 129.

stipendiary magistrates. The fact that lay magistrates came from a similar social stratum to offenders goes a long way towards explaining this tendency, which was particularly marked in small boroughs. With less legal training than stipendaries, lay magistrates were more likely to see themselves as enforcing the will of the local community than impartial representatives of the law. Personality and politics mattered too. Some magistrates had a reputation for leniency and others for severity, but there was only a weak correlation between such attitudes and a justice's politics. Party politics came to the fore once the war ended, as the magistracy—the majority of whom were Liberal and Conservative appointees—found themselves out of sympathy with the Labour government's economic policies.

Similar attitudes could be found in the higher courts. Like lay magistrates, juries viewed their role as bringing common sense to bear. As representatives of their local communities, they meted out communal justice. Naturally, this varied according to the nature of the communities from which they came. The notorious reluctance of working-class juries in east London to convict pilferers is a good example of this.[80] Judges did not see their role in quite the same light. For them, upholding the majesty of the law mattered. If judges believed that pettifogging regulations and overweening police powers threatened to bring the law into disrepute, the ministries could not count on the judiciary's support. In this regard the use of test purchases—a key tactic for inspectors and police alike—was a frequent source of conflict.

When it came to sentencing, ministers had difficulty appreciating the value of judicial discretion, which they thought ran counter to their belief in the deterrent effect of tough penalties. In theory, penalties for black market offences were severe, but even the harshest of judges felt that a sentence of fourteen years' penal servitude and confiscation of property unduly tough by comparison to existing penalties for serious property crime. Less than a month after the introduction of these penalties, the Lord Chief Justice, sitting in the court of criminal appeal, stated that sentences of ten years' penal servitude, which had been common a decade earlier, should be passed rarely.[81] Equally, ministers despaired at what they considered unduly harsh sentences that made the government look vindictive. Punitive sentences could evoke public sympathy for the most unlikely of people. When an Essex magistrate fined the secretary of the local waterworks company £145 plus 10 guineas costs for making three unnecessary journeys, the longest of which involved a 90-mile round trip, there was a public outcry.[82] If frustration got the better of ministers and they tried to influence the courts, their efforts usually backfired. Rather than do the government's bidding, judges and magistrates reasserted their constitutional independence by judging each case on its merits and taking the opportunity to criticize ministerial interference in court. When combined with selective enforcement, this judicial independence, which might or might not work in a defendant's favour, made it exceedingly difficult for people to accurately assess the risks and the rewards of evasion.

---

[80] 'Interview with Glyn Hardwicke', 19.   [81] *The Times*, 21 April 1942.
[82] Smithies, *Crime in Wartime*, 96.

***

Comparisons drawn between compliance with price controls in austerity Britain and affluent America that emphasize the relative tightness of British control, point to enforcement as central to any explanation of the high level of compliance with UK regulations. In addition to its comprehensive and well-designed control schemes, the British government devoted more resources to administering and enforcing them than did the US Federal government.[83] There were many more enforcement officials per person in the UK than in the USA, and when police numbers are included the discrepancy in resourcing increases further. The criminologist Marshall Clinard and his colleagues at the US OPA envied the resources available to their cousins across the Atlantic. In 1946 the OPA had 3,600 investigators to ensure that a population of 141,936,000 obeyed the price and rationing regulations—a ratio of one investigator for every 39,427 people.[84] By comparison, the MoF employed 1,585 inspectors on 30 June 1947, while the BoT and the MoFP paid 392 and 97 inspectors respectively.[85] With an estimated total population of 49,571,000 that month, this worked out as one inspector for every 23,901 people.

Yet this comparison flatters to deceive by ignoring the realities of enforcement and punishment on British streets. By 1942 the rationing ministries had adopted broadly similar compliance strategies that placed greater emphasis on deterrence and prosecution than cooperation and inspection. Having done their utmost to design schemes that minimized opportunities for evasion and secured public support for them, they took a firm stand against black markets. Ministers assumed that would-be offenders were greedy and selfish individuals who were unmoved by appeals to their altruism or enlightened self-interest. As a result, officials set out to deter potential evaders and reassure the law-abiding that free-riding was limited in scope. Because inspectors were few in number by comparison to the police, official publicity tried to give the impression that the chances of being caught and punished were higher than they really were. Tough administrative and criminal penalties were intended to serve as a further deterrent.

The bluff on which the ministries' compliance strategies rested was unconvincing. Unable to align their interests with those of inspectors and police officers, ministry staff failed to implement enforcement policies uniformly. At times, press coverage that drew attention to variations in policing or criticized the reliance on undercover methods made enforcement appear capricious and unfair, and also made calculating the risk of detection very difficult. It was even harder to assess the probability of punishment, as trial verdicts and sentences varied greatly. The government's attempts to influence the courts backfired, as magistrates and judges felt it more important than ever to exercise judicial discretion in order to assert their independence from government. Such interventions also had the unintended consequence of giving the impression that offenders could expect lenient treatment by the courts.

[83] Mills and Rockoff, 'Compliance', 209–12.   [84] Clinard, *Black Market*, 64.
[85] HC deb. Vol. 441, 4 August 1947, cols. 124–5 w.a.

The implication of this analysis of enforcement for the explanation of non-compliance is profound. Regardless of whether we share the view of criminals as rational actors, the way ministry inspectors, police, and courts enforced the regulations made rational calculation impossible. An offender's chances of being caught, prosecuted, convicted, and punished varied dramatically according to what their offence was, when they committed it, and where it took place. The likely punishment for an offence was also hard to assess, but the uncertainty of punishment was probably less important than the uncertainty of detection—at least, that is what an influential tradition of penal theory maintained.[86] But the legal lottery and the mixed messages emanating from the courts cannot have helped. Reversing the economist Gary Becker's notorious dismissal of the value of social theory in explaining criminal behaviour, these findings demand that we take social mechanisms other than rational choice into account when seeking to explain evasion. A plausible account requires us to make use of *'ad hoc* concepts of differential association, anomie, and the like'.[87]

The most interesting of these *'ad hoc'* mechanisms are social norms. In recent years, law and economics—an interdisciplinary endeavour that Becker's economic analysis of crime helped spawn—has focused its attention on those norms that place limits on the expression of individual self-interest, especially norms of fairness that give rise to legal bans on usury, profiteering, and ticket touting.[88] Beginning with a close reading of more than 300 responses to a contemporary survey of black markets, Part III considers how social norms—particularly those relating to fairness in the exchange, distribution, and use of controlled goods— both encouraged compliance and limited non-compliance with price and rationing regulations.

[86] Leon Radzinowicz, *A History of Criminal Law and its Administration from 1750, Vol. 1: The Movement for Reform,* 1750–1833 (London, 1948), 282.

[87] Becker, 'Crime and Punishment'.

[88] For example Christine Jolls, Cass R. Sunstein, and Richard Thaler, 'A Behavioral Approach to Law and Economics', *Stanford Law Review,* 50 (1998), 1471–550, and Robert C. Ellickson, 'Law and Economics discovers Social Norms', *Journal of Legal Studies,* 27 (1998), 537–52.

PART III

'BLACK SHEEP—BLACK MARKETS': MAKING MORAL CHOICES

Introduction

In August 1941 the MoF announced that it had taken new powers to 'put the crooked dealer out of business by revoking his licence'. The newspaper advertisements publicizing this measure to tackle black market supply reminded readers that they needed to look to their behaviour as 'black markets exist for black sheep'. 'There wouldn't be a black market if there weren't customers for it.'[1] This underlined a point made by the junior food minister a few days earlier in a radio broadcast.[2] From then on the moral complicity of civilians who bought black market goods became a recurring theme in government propaganda. *Partners in Crime*, a MoI film released a year later, ended with an Old Bailey judge facing the camera and addressing a 'Mrs Wilson' sitting in the audience waiting to see the main feature. Moments earlier the film showed Mrs Wilson, a middle-class housewife, pressing her butcher for 'a little bit extra'. In pompous and stentorian tones the judge, played by Robert Morley, compares her and others like her to 'common criminals, parasites preying on the body of a community at War', dismissing the 'illogical pleas' that 'if I don't somebody else will' and 'I only took a little' before she can make them.[3]

If the buyer was no better than a common criminal, the seller was akin to a Nazi saboteur. Backbenchers made the link in their parliamentary speeches, as did newspaper cartoonists such as Sidney Strube. Above the caption 'Brothers under the skin', the *Daily Express* cartoonist pictured a German U-boat captain shaking hands with a food racketeer.[4] His rival Zec made the same point with a cartoon of a medal with the legend 'For profitable service in the black market' encircling a swastika with a rat at its centre.[5] The representation of the black marketeer as society's enemy continued in peacetime. Now, the antisocial 'spiv'—the preferred label for the post-war black marketeer—sabotaged the reconstruction effort. The image of antisocial black marketeers and their thoughtless female customers, which the government and its allies at the BBC did much to encourage, stigmatized illegal transactions. Only the unpatriotic, greedy, and selfish individual evaded economic control.

---

[1] *Daily Express*, 11 August 1941. [2] *Manchester Guardian*, 7 August 1941.
[3] TNA: PRO, INF 6/460, *Partners in Crime* script, 1942; *Partners in Crime*, directed by Frank Launder and Sidney Gilliat (Gainsborough Pictures, 1942).
[4] *Daily Express*, 12 May 1941. [5] *Daily Mirror*, 7 March 1942.

This rhetoric, which was central to the rationing ministries' compliance strategies, succeeded in framing the issue of non-compliance as a moral as well as an economic problem, setting the terms of public debate and restraining individual action. This worked well because politicians had long appreciated Barbara Wootton's much later observation that 'the public is always better at ethics, which are warm and real, than economics, which are cold and abstract'.[6] As Chapter 7 demonstrates, government placed an important obstacle in the way of rational choice by foregrounding the ethical dimension to economic life. This turned people into casuists who employed familiar justifications for breaking the law. But, as the remaining chapters of Part III go on to argue, there were limits to the framing effects generated by invoking the norms of conventional society.

The negative image of evasion was challenged after the war. Believers in free markets blamed unnatural economic controls instead of immoral individuals for black markets. In some sections of the media the spiv became a working-class anti-hero thumbing his nose at authority, or a figure of fun providing light relief in austere times. Contesting the representation of non-compliance lessened the stigma attached to evasion in conventional culture. This made it easier for people subscribing to conventional norms to overcome their moral inhibitions to illegal dealing. The need to justify one's behaviour to oneself or others using familiar neutralization techniques lessened. Mixed messages about the rights and wrongs of evasion after the war weakened further the loose grip that conventional norms had on the behaviour of some social and occupational groups. Villains, who participated in a criminal subculture that rejected conventional norms of behaviour, needed to be bilingual, mastering two vocabularies of motivation—one for justifying themselves to fellow criminals, and one for excusing their actions if caught.

---

[6] Barbara Wootton, cited in Jim Tomlinson, 'Re-inventing the "Moral Economy" in Post-war Britain', *Historical Research*, 84 (2011), 356.

7

'We all fiddle': legitimating evasion

One of the most startling findings of Geoffrey Gorer's 1951 survey of English social behaviour and attitudes was the frequency with which the English broke the law. The anthropologist chose to devote one article in a series reporting his findings to readers of *The People* to the issue. Under the headline 'Nearly all the English admit they keep breaking the law!' Gorer reported that only one in fifty respondents to his survey agreed with the statement 'None of my family has ever got anything off the ration' when asked to select a statement that best represented their attitudes towards 'fiddling'.[1] This was news. The law-abiding character of the English, and the British more generally, was a cherished national myth, burnished by indigenous and foreign observers, as was their reputation for fair dealing and respect for their police and court systems.[2] Official reassurances that evasion was a minor irritant that the authorities had in hand reinforced this idea, as did pointed comparisons with the black market free-for-all on the Continent. Focusing on black marketeers, not their more numerous customers, and the Jewish traders amongst them also helped Britons to distance themselves from this problem—an unintended consequence of the wartime discourse of Britishness.

But Gorer's findings were not really news to his readers, most of whom knew of black market dealings in their area and categorized their own offences as 'grey market'. Comparing British experience with what was known of black marketing elsewhere in Europe in a 1948 essay for the Bureau of Current Affairs, Angus Maude warned 'that we should do well to think very carefully before boasting about our superiority to foreigners in the matter of morality and discipline', as 'It could be true that the British are a more moral and disciplined race than others; but they have not been so severely tested.'[3] In an article accompanying Maude's essay, the bureau director advised schoolteachers and others intending to base a discussion on the essay that this would be a tricky topic to handle. He attributed this to the 'natural human tendency to think of the black market as what the other fellow does, and to class our own transactions among the lighter shades of grey'.[4] Self-deception about the legal and moral status of one's fiddles and wangles was

---

[1] *The People*, 23 September 1951; see Gorer, *Exploring English Character*, 229–36.

[2] Arthur Bryant, *The National Character* (London, 1935), 104–5; D. W. Brogan, *The English People: Impressions and Observations* (London, 1943), 94–5; Reith, *British Police and the Democratic Ideal*, 1–10; Pierre Maillaud, *The English Way* (London, 1945), 35, 37, 43, 236, 240–1; Simonds, 'Law', in Barker, *Character of England*, 112–35.

[3] Maude, 'Black Market', 6.

[4] Boris Ford, ' "No Questions asked"?', in Maude, *Black Market*, 14.

widespread, highlighting both the success that ministers and officials had in shaping public opinion, and its limits.

AVOIDING EVASION

Stigmatizing evasion had the greatest impact on those individuals who subscribed to conventional middle-class norms. The framing effect that official publicity, mediated by the press and radio, had on the behaviour of 'respectable' people is seen clearly in 325 responses to a question about black market dealing in the M-O monthly directive for January 1948. In this postal survey, M-O asked members of its 'national panel' of volunteer writers: 'How would you define "Black Market dealings"? Do you know of any such dealings in your area? If so, please describe them.' These questions were part of a much longer 'directive', which included questions on New Year resolutions and capital punishment. Like them, black marketing was a topical subject of social and political interest. Public concern about rising crime, and black market offences in particular, had risen sharply during the third quarter of 1947 after the government resumed publishing crime figures.

Including a question about crime was a first for M-O. It is also one of the earliest self-report studies of crime conducted in Britain. The weaknesses of such studies are well known. Often participants refuse to talk about their criminal behaviour, or downplay their involvement in crime for fear of incriminating themselves, creating a bias towards reporting petty dealings. On the other hand, the bravado of some participants leads them to exaggerate their crimes. Finally, some criminal behaviour goes unreported because the respondents are unaware that they are committing a crime.[5] Although some of the replies exhibit these weaknesses, the majority do not. Few panellists refused to discuss black market dealings for fear of incriminating themselves or others. Only nine people chose not to answer the questions on black market dealings. Several admitted to black market dealings, whilst many more implied that they evaded the regulations. Under-reporting of black market offences may not have been a serious problem, due to the volunteers' commitment to M-O's ideals and their positive experiences of the way M-O handled their replies, keeping them confidential and using them responsibly. At the end of a long and detailed reply to the questions about black market dealings a young panellist wrote: 'I know I can rely on you not to let this sort of information get round. I do not wish to be mixed up either in a libel action or a police prosecution.'[6]

The panel was not, and did not attempt to be, a representative sample of the population. In 1947 *The New Statesman* published a letter from M-O appealing for volunteer writers to join their panel, and by 10 April a total of 987 people had replied to the advertisement. M-O assessed 500 of the replies they had received.

---

[5] See Clive Coleman and Jenny Moynihan, *Understanding Crime Data: Haunted by the Dark Figure* (Buckingham, 1996), ch. 3.
[6] M-OA, DR January 1948, DR 131.

72% of respondents were men, and the majority of respondents were under forty years of age. There was an approximate 50/50 split between those who were single and those who were married. The majority of female respondents were housewives, whilst the men tended to be white-collar workers with clerical, medical, research, or industrial jobs. Most of the respondents held progressive or left-wing views, volunteering because they believed that M-O was doing socially useful work.[7]

Those panellists who replied to the January 1948 directive share these characteristics. The majority of writers who responded to the directive were male: 53% were male, 39% were female, and the sex of the remaining respondents was unknown. The average age of male respondents was 36 years and 6 months, whilst the average age of female respondents was approximately 42 years and 7 months. Most women were in their thirties or forties, while the bulk of the men were in their twenties or early thirties. Approximately two-thirds of the men were married, compared to three-fifths of the women. Less than one-tenth of the women were widowed. Of the 325 respondents, 284 supplied information about their occupations. The vast majority of men and women in gainful employment had professional, technical, commercial, or clerical jobs. 34% of the respondents who gave an occupation were not gainfully employed, being students, housewives or retired. Of the 174 people whose occupation could be classified using the Registrar General's Social Class schema from the 1951 Census, 70% of the men and 67% of the women had occupations that placed them in Classes I and II—the upper and middle classes.[8]

Although the directive respondents were not representative of the population at large, they cast light on the mentality of the upper and middle classes—the groups whose participation in black markets occasioned most comment and greatly alarmed the law-and-order bureaucracy. As in the case of traffic laws, otherwise law-abiding people found themselves contravening the price and rationing regulations.[9] Doing so meant breaking the law and contravening conventional values, creating a conflict between an individual's behaviour, either actual or desired, and that person's image of themselves as a respectable law-abiding citizen, whether they aspired to respectability or thought they ought to be respectable. Through campaigns such as 'Black Sheep—Black Markets' the authorities forced people to acknowledge the discrepancy between their behaviour and their attitudes. Being both literate and introspective, the panellists could explain the internal conflict they faced and how they resolved it.

The emotions that some of the M-O panellists describe feeling when considering their behaviour or that of other people show that the illegality of their transactions posed a real dilemma for them. A few admitted feelings of guilt and shame. Typical of these was a middle-aged librarian who confessed that 'I have been guilty of augmenting my tea and milk ration by purchasing at usual prices from friends,

---

[7] M-OA, FR 2479, 'Report on New Statesman panel composition', May 1947.

[8] For a more detailed discussion of the sample see Roodhouse, 'Black Market Activity', 216–19.

[9] See Clive Emsley, '"Mother, what did policemen do when there weren't any motors?" The Law, the Police, and the Regulation of Motor Traffic in England, 1900–1939', *Historical Journal*, 36 (1993), 357–81.

but I should feel ashamed, I believe, if the charge were thrust in my face.'[10] One housewife recounted in detail her feelings of guilt after purchasing four handkerchiefs without surrendering the requisite number of clothing coupons.

> Alas, my husband has a public job. I am not free to be bad. Also I should very much dislike putting myself in the power of one I did not respect. I must admit I once bought 4 handkerchiefs for some of the children, and on proffering the clothing coupon book, I was told by the assistant that it wouldn't be right to take any coupons as I had so few. What with being taken aback, not wishing to appear ungrateful, and being glad anyway, I'm ashamed to say, I paid the ordinary utility price, and left without disputing his view. What made me feel most guilty was that we always have a good number of clothing coupons, as the children help, and my husband and I dress appallingly.[11]

The principal reason for her feeling of guilt was not that she was breaking the law nor undermining the Labour government's attempts to reconstruct the British economy, but that there was no need for her to evade the regulations. Her guilty feelings imply that she believed need alone could justify black market activity and that she was depriving others in need of the opportunity to buy clothes with or without coupons.

But dissonance need not prompt feelings of guilt or shame; it could also trigger the emotions of anger, hatred, contempt, and pride. Another housewife admitted to half-heartedly dealing in black markets, telling M-O, 'I am by temperament unfitted to do this kind of thing. I am, unfortunately, fundamentally law-abiding, even when I think the laws are unjust.' Anger masked the vague feeling of unease revealed in her statement. She railed against 'stupid regulation', blaming the government for testing her morals unnecessarily.[12] She was not alone in her anger. An unmarried middle-aged man working as a company secretary blamed 'Governmental stupidity' for the shortages that forced him to use black markets. By maintaining 'unnecessary' controls, the post-war Labour government had turned him into a criminal.[13] Such feelings were rare amongst the left-leaning panellists, but they reported the anger and contempt towards the authorities that they encountered amongst their friends and acquaintances.[14] Contempt was also something that the panellists who resisted temptation felt towards rule-breakers. This was often mingled with a sense of pride at their forbearance.[15]

That people could admire the moral restraint displayed by their law-abiding neighbours whilst evading the regulations themselves shows that they too had internalized the norms guiding their neighbours' behaviour. The behaviour of this 'moral minority' undermined the argument that the controls ran contrary to human nature, and reminded participants in black markets that illegal dealing was 'wrong'. Naturally, participants looked for signs of hypocrisy amongst the moral minority. But if they could not detect any hypocrisy, they would often respect and admire the will and determination of law-abiding people. One respondent wrote, 'I admire those people who rigidly accept all the rationing restrictions as necessary,

---

[10] M-OA, DR January 1948, DR 229.   [11] DR 55.
[12] DR 118.   [13] DR 160.   [14] DR 34.   [15] DRs 136 and 230.

but admit that they affect me the same way as very many other people. I think it rather clever to be able to get a bit more of this or that whenever you can.'[16] Admiration for the 'virtuous' was probably rarer than feeling angry or contemptuous towards the 'mugs' who considered themselves better than their fellows, as their restraint was an unwelcome reminder of the norms forbidding illegal dealing.[17] One respondent noted that 'The non-participant is most unpopular and it takes a great deal of resolution to keep free.'[18] Evaders might pressure non-participants to engage in black market dealing in order to remove the feelings of moral discomfort caused by their abstinence.[19]

The strength and variety of feelings triggered by the question about black market dealing points to the internal reality of the conflict that the respectable panellists experienced. It also shows that they acknowledged that evasion was in some sense wrong. If the panellists involved in evasion had no respect for the law, the government, or their fellows, then they would not have felt embarrassed, guilty, or ashamed about their actions. Technical offences aside, black market offenders were well aware that they were breaking the law. Most of the M-O panellists defined black market dealings as illegal economic transactions that contravened price and rationing regulations. Many of them went on to justify black market dealings—a tacit admission that such dealings were in some sense 'wrong'. These justifications resolved the internal conflict to which cognitive psychologists refer as 'cognitive dissonance' or 'self-discrepancy'.[20]

Rather than resolving internal conflict, some people managed to avoid acknowledging that it existed. Of course, it is impossible to identify those panellists guilty of wishful thinking or self-deception from their responses to the black market question. Fortunately, some of the panellists kept diaries for M-O which make it possible to compare their directive replies with less guarded records of their behaviour. In her written reply a retired nurse living in Steyning, Sussex, expressed her disapproval of black market dealings, which she defined as selling controlled goods, which might be stolen, for more than the ceiling price. She made her attitude clear when a rich woman complained that 'the Jews were getting all the food by scrounging around for things'. The nurse snapped back that 'if she was content with her rations and such things as she could get in the shops she would not run into Jews (or anyone else) scrounging'.[21] Wartime diary entries show that she held the same view six years earlier. In her entry for 17 September 1941 she noted:

> It is strange how some quite good, honest people will do terribly dishonest acts, and not realize how wrong they are. A neighbour told me her husband had brought home two army blankets, for which he had paid ten shillings. He would not tell her how, or where, he got them, but said she had better wash them. She is terribly shocked at him, and he is a fool, for that reason alone, if for no other.[22]

---

[16] DR 73.   [17] DR 61.   [18] DR 85.   [19] Ward, *War in the Countryside*, 79.
[20] Leon Festinger, *A Theory of Cognitive Dissonance* (Stanford, 1957); Tory E. Higgins, 'Self-Discrepancy: A Theory relating to Self and Affect', *Psychological Review*, 9 (1987), 319–40.
[21] M-OA, DR January 1948, DR 74.
[22] M-OA, War Diaries, September 1941, 'Adelaide Poole diary', 17 September 1941.

Her attitudes show remarkable consistency, but they were not always consistent with her behaviour. In a diary entry made nine days later, the nurse mentions a grey market deal that she struck with another neighbour: 'I let a neighbour have my cheese ration, because she has children, and I can do without it. She is able to get extra eggs, so told me she would get me some if I needed them.'[23] Granted the offence, for that was what it was, is no way as serious as the theft of blankets. But the diary entry, written to be read by M-O investigators, illustrates the way people defined 'Black Market dealings' to exclude their illegal transactions.

The housewife Nella Last also defined black market dealings so as to exclude her own illicit dealings. She did not admit to evading the regulations in her directive reply, recounting an incident when she turned down an offer of black market meat on the bus and expressing her disapproval of the selfish individuals who wangled bananas at the expense of 'weary mothers'.[24] Like many radio listeners, she poked fun at *The Brains Trust* panellist Cyril Joad for always prefacing his remarks with 'It all depends what you mean by', but her diary entries reveal that her directive reply might have been very different if she had begun in similar fashion. Last was an enthusiastic participant in the grey market, gifting rations, swapping coupons, and accepting paid favours. That these activities could be construed as black market dealing did not occur to her. These were the actions of a good wife, mother, friend, neighbour, or relative and nothing challenged her view. The M-O directive certainly did not. Nor did a direct appeal to 'shun black-market and spiv dealings, and help others to do the same' made by Lady Reading made to Last and fellow Women's Voluntary Services members at a meeting in Preston two months earlier. As far as Last was concerned, Barrow was not affected by 'real black market as much as fiddling'.[25]

The examples of Nella Last and the nurse show that the concept of grey marketing allowed many people to avoid or stave off any internal conflict remarkably effectively. It was a popular idea as the panellists' attempts to define 'Black Market dealing' revealed. For most panellists 'Black Market' was a moral category. A theological student had great difficulty in defining the term, agonizing over the practice of swapping unwanted rations and ration coupons. 'I can't make up my mind whether this is wrong—I equate "Black market" dealings with wrong.' A housewife explained that she used the term 'as a kind of adjective to describe any goods obtained by special favour, not necessarily rationed goods, or supremely expensive goods'.[26] One respondent was annoyed at such usage of the term black market. He reported 'a widespread habit of using the term as synonymous with profiteering'. The respondent considered 'the two as quite distinct' provided that the 'excessive' prices were within the law.[27] A wine merchant concurred, noting:

> In my own business the term 'Black Market' is rather loosely used. For instance, proprietary whisky is controlled by the Distillers as to distribution and price. But there is also a free market which is legal enough but the prices here are well over twice the

---

[23] M-OA, War Diaries, 26 September 1941.   [24] M-OA, DR January 1948, DR 58.
[25] Last diary, 5 November 1947, in Malcolmson and Malcolmson, *Last's Diary*, 203.
[26] M-OA, DR January 1948, DR 93.   [27] DR 290.

proprietary price and the general public usually call it 'Black market whisky' which of course it is not.[28]

A so-called 'black market deal' need not contravene regulations. According to the manager of a textile mill, 'Everything around here is called black market if one pays more than the usual price for something.'[29]

Illegality apart, two features of 'Black Market dealing' recur in the panellists' definitions: excessive pricing and getting more than your fair share. Of these two characteristics, obtaining more than your official entitlement was the more important. This is seen clearly in the response of a school medical inspector who explained that she understood black market to mean 'getting anything to which you are not legally entitled and usually above the controlled price'.[30] Many panellists shared her view including a commercial traveller who told M-O that he thought 'the essence of the offence is the unentitled share of the commodity, rather than the price'.[31] The stress they placed on entitlements in their definitions pointed to a deeper concern with the impact that illegal transactions had on others. A schoolmaster expressed this concern succinctly, telling M-O that he considered 'as Black Market any transaction, of whatever magnitude and at whatever price, if, by giving one person more than his entitlement, it reduces the quantity of goods available for others and so lowers the value or number of ration coupons'.[32] In many responses this attitude manifested itself as a concern with the value or quantity of goods involved.

Making high prices and negative impacts on third parties the defining characteristics of a black market deal excluded gifts, swaps, and paid favours from the category despite their illegality. A minority of panellists dissented from this view, branding all evasion black market. It was not a popular position. An insurance clerk who maintained that 'Anything illegal connected with controlled goods or services' was black market found herself without allies at work.[33] Like the majority of panellists, her colleagues disagreed with her. Majority opinion was, however, divided between those who considered all illegal monetary transactions black market and those who considered paid favours grey market. The writer Naomi Mitchison placed herself firmly in the second camp, telling M-O that she considered a deal 'Black when the object is money and Grey when it is an obligement or matter of friendship'.[34] A young married man from Eltham, south London, shared her opinion, although he expressed it differently. For him 'Black Market dealings' were 'operations by which someone either gets considerably more than their fair share of something in short supply (from eggs to tickets for the Danny Kaye show) or makes considerable amount of money by supplying the unfair demands of those with excessive buying power'.[35]

Thoughtful respondents recognized the self-serving nature of these definitions, which excluded everyday evasion. A commercial traveller explained that 'Black market dealings are the way the bloke down the road gets what he wants...when

---

[28] DR 189.   [29] DR 251.   [30] DR 88.   [31] DR 141.
[32] DR 144.   [33] DR 61.   [34] DR 65.   [35] DR 162.

the issue becomes more personal one notes a tendency for the colour of the trans-action to become Grey or even slightly Dirty White.'[36] A bank clerk who struggled to define 'black market dealings' acknowledged the subjectivity of any definition, writing 'It is not easy as what I buy, even a little underhand, is obviously not black market, it is what the other fellow buys that is really black mine is at the very worst only grey or off-white.'[37] Unsurprisingly, the 'other' was often a Jewish refugee or an American GI. Although remarkably effective in helping 'respectable' people to cope with the internal conflict that their evasion brought about, the grey market idea did not neutralize all feelings of discomfort. For self-aware panellists such as the clerk and the traveller, a palpable sense of unease remained which could only be assuaged in other ways.

Using obfuscatory language to describe illegal dealings was a less effective but equally important way of avoiding acknowledging dissonance. A company sec-retary close to retirement noted how 'In this village, they do not like the stigma and so, when discussing house repairs, they say: "Oh, no! You don't have to go on the Black Market; you can get it done privately".'[38] A fifty-something house-wife recounted how her neighbours talked about illegal dealing, telling her, 'Well my dear we pay a bit over the odds but we must have the stuff.'[39] Another woman, ten years her senior, described a local shopkeeper 'monkeying with pounds'.[40] Like the well known expression 'fall off (the back of) a lorry', the idioms 'get it done privately', 'pay over the odds' and 'monkey about' left the question of legality unanswered. Such ambiguous expressions proved useful as they allowed people to broach an illegal deal with a stranger in a roundabout and non-incriminating way. The circumlocutions also kept the issues of legality and morality at a distance. Dodges, favours, fiddles, gifts, swaps, tips, and wan-gles fell outside many respondents' definition of black market dealings. These terms, taken from the existing British exchange repertoire and applied to deal-ings in controlled goods, overlooked or minimized the related legal and moral issues. The minority who steered clear of illegal dealing saw through these lin-guistic manoeuvres. In the eyes of one married man the packets of cigarettes and 10-shilling notes given to milkmen, coalmen, and other roundsmen as tips were disguised bribes.[41]

VOCABULARIES OF MOTIVE

To retain one's self-respect and the respect of others, the panellists used an array of justifications which the American sociologists Gresham Sykes and David Matza were to make familiar. They identified five 'techniques of neutralization' that juve-nile delinquents used to shield themselves from 'internalized values and the reac-tions of conforming to others'. The delinquents denied responsibility for their actions, denied the existence of a victim, condemned their condemners, appealed

---

[36] DR 161.   [37] DR 291.   [38] DR 233.
[39] DR 52.   [40] DR 50.   [41] DR 178.

to higher loyalties, or pleaded ignorance.[42] Examples of each neutralization technique appear regularly in the directive replies, but the most popular techniques with the respondents were to deny the existence of a victim and condemn the condemners. Clearly, official campaigns explaining the need for regulation and the impact of petty evasion on others addressed the right issues but were too tentative and infrequent to challenge most people's views. Denying responsibility for one's action proved popular with producers and distributors, but had limited appeal to consumers. Few of the well-to-do panellists appealed to higher loyalties, but they excused the behaviour of people poorer than themselves who felt compelled to break the rules.

The panellists denied responsibility for their actions in various ways. Consumers blamed the authorities for imposing economic regulations that went against natural and irresistible human impulses, though they made least use of this excuse.[43] Others blamed traders for tempting them with black market goods which they found hard to resist because of 'natural' desires. Frequently, such accounts singled out Jewish traders.[44] Illegal dealers denied responsibility for their actions more frequently than their customers.[45] Retailers who overcharged customers blamed wholesalers for demanding above-ceiling prices for controlled goods, while the wholesalers redirected retailers' anger to greedy producers. The producers could not use the excuses that retailers and wholesalers employed, and instead they blamed impersonal market forces or the government for not controlling costs.

A poultry-farmer's wife, who was a rural district councillor and an active member of the Women's Institute, outlined the case for the producer in her reply to the M-O directive.

> The only respect in which we, as poultry farmers, touch the fringe of the Black Market is that when we send old hens to market, we know very well that the price they fetch is not the controlled price per pound for table poultry. This is the market's responsibility, not the poultry farmer's, and everyone knows it is a ramp. We profit by it, because it just doesn't pay to sell at the Government controlled price. It would be far better if the Government were to decontrol table poultry altogether. The controlled price doesn't pay the producer and is evaded right and left by the markets.[46]

She did not extend this justification to cover farm-gate sales of eggs.

> We are constantly badgered to sell eggs at the door—'I don't mind what I pay'—and consistently refuse, partly because my husband carries honesty to a fault, partly because he is an Accredited Poultry Breeder and has to be like Caesar's wife![47]

Clearly, it was harder to deny responsibility for an illegal deal if it was a face-to-face transaction between producer and consumer.

Denying the existence of a victim was far more common than denying responsibility for one's actions. A handful of suppliers and consumers refused to believe

[42] Gresham M. Sykes and David Matza, 'Techniques of Neutralization: A Theory of Delinquency', *American Sociological Review*, 22 (1957), 664–70.
[43] M-OA, DR January 1948: DRs 20, 65, and 118.   [44] DRs 74, 87, 103, and 174.
[45] DRs 182 and 220.   [46] DR 12.   [47] DR 12.

that shortages existed. They argued that there were more supplies to go round than the government acknowledged. In the circumstances getting a little bit extra could not deny others their ration. Nella Last wrote in her diary of her surprise when her sister-in-law used this argument to defend wangling a few extra eggs.

> Several times, she spoke as if to get more than she was entitled to was a *grand* game. I said, 'But Beat, if you take someone else's share, they will have to do without'. She said, 'Nonsense—there is plenty of food about. There must be, or else a place could not get it in such quantities. It's only a matter of organising properly'.[48]

Last's sister-in-law refused to believe she was taking someone else's allotment of eggs if she got some on the black market.

It was more common for consumers of black market goods to argue that obtaining a little bit extra could not possibly harm the war effort or post-war reconstruction. Speaking for many panellists, one man refused to acknowledge that his infrequent petty dealings could harm anyone.

> These have always been isolated instances and while I would not wish to claim that the offences were any more excusable because they were only little ones I feel that they cannot have had a bad effect on the state of the nation (as distinct from my character!). I really do disapprove of the large-scale black, or grey, market dealings of which I hear quite a lot. Mainly, I think, this is because I feel that the extensive black marketing prolongs and intensifies the shortages for everyone outside it, but it is also because I fear that if the scale of operations grows too big it will bring down the whole carefully constructed rationing scheme unless severely dealt with.[49]

Swapping ration and coupons was the most frequently cited example of a victimless offence. In his reply to the directive, a young civil servant challenged the view of his superiors that swapping rations and coupons was a crime.

> I don't see as 'Black Market' a deal in which someone's unwanted margarine ration is sold to a neighbour at the regulation price, although the Ministry of Food will not agree with me. In the same way I did not refuse when a garage offered me a gallon of petrol on a half-gallon coupon, at the standard price. No rationing system can take all demands accurately into account, and here obviously was a slight over-assessment of demand resulting in a surplus of supply. No one else went short, and I benefited.[50]

Others echoed his views. A manager wrote, 'I am not at all petty and consider swapping say clothing coupons for, say, a desired item of food no major crime.' He considered such a 'small breach of regulations, if nobody suffers thereby' acceptable.[51] Another panellist considered all evasion black market with the exception of barter. As far as they were concerned, 'one person may voluntarily give away or barter some of his or her rations with another willing person'.[52]

Condemning one's condemners proved popular with dealers and users alike. There were enough high-profile black market offenders to make this a feasible

---

[48] Last diary, 28 April 1942, in Richard Broad and Suzie Fleming (eds.), *Nella Last's War: A Mother's Diary, 1939–45* (Bristol, 1983), 201.
[49] DR 309.   [50] DR 179.   [51] DR 217.   [52] DR 306.

argument despite attempts to hush up some cases.[53] Given extensive press coverage of these cases and the derisory sentences imposed on public figures convicted of black market offences, it is not surprising that participants and non-participants believed that rich, famous, and powerful people evaded the regulations with near impunity. Buying seven or eight clothing coupons did not 'trouble the conscience' of an RAF corporal for he knew 'that the fair share rationing schemes never apply equally to 100% of the population'.[54] The behaviour of local notables also allowed participants to condemn their condemners or would-be condemners. The illegal dealings of magistrates and councillors gave participants the opportunity to undermine the credibility of the local committees responsible for administering and enforcing control at a local level while the illegal dealings of Church of England priests, Methodist preachers, and approved schoolteachers weakened the case of public moralists who denounced black market dealing.[55]

Appealing to higher loyalties was something that the overwhelmingly middle-class panellists did rarely. When they did, it tended to be on the behalf of mothers with young families struggling to maintain a decent living standard. Several male respondents to the directive approved of housewives obtaining black market goods to support their families.[56] Only one mother justified her illicit dealings in this way.[57] This is not surprising given that the middle-class mothers on the panel could not make a convincing case on the grounds of necessity. But many of them knew and sympathized with working-class women who sold clothing coupons to boost their household income.[58] The understanding of the working-class mother's plight, revealed in the replies, points to another facet of the panel: its support for Labour policies. This explains the absence of sustained political attacks on controls. The panellists who denied responsibility for their actions came closest to launching such attacks, but they did not build on their belief that economic controls ran counter to human nature. There is no attempt to portray evasion as an act of resistance to creeping state control—a reassertion of individual liberty.

Pleading ignorance of the regulations was also rare despite its popularity with defendants in court. In black market cases the accused pleaded ignorance regularly. Although ignorance was not a legally recognized defence, many courts, particularly magistrates' courts, took a defendant's pleas of ignorance into account when sentencing. In fact, the MoF accepted the plausibility of this defence, albeit reluctantly, in 1944, distinguishing between technical and black market offences.[59] Some of the directive respondents admitted that they did not know or understand all aspects of control. In doing so they revealed wilful ignorance of the regulations that left courts unimpressed. Preparing a directive reply prompted some to give serious consideration to black marketing for the first time. At the end of his reply,

[53] Cecil King diary, 27 October 1944, in King, *With Malice toward None: A War Diary* (London, 1970), 276–7.

[54] M-OA, DR January 1948, DR 249.   [55] DRs 67, 79, 224, and 299.

[56] DRs 167, 196, and 250.   [57] DR 113.

[58] DRs 14, 40, 84, and 100. Morris, *Crime and Criminal Justice*, 18; Addison, *Now the War is over*, 46–8.

[59] See Ch. 5.

a young schoolmaster noted that 'On considering all this, I find that my knowledge of the laws relating to the use of other peoples [rations] is very small. I must find out more about it.' But he did not use his ignorance as an excuse for participating in the coupon traffic.[60] Likewise, a housewife in her mid-twenties confessed that she would 'swap ½ lb tea now and then for 2 lb sugar with cash adjustment but don't know if this is Black Market dealing'.[61]

It is difficult to say whether these justifications prompted or legitimated evasion. The fact that the schoolmaster and the housewife did not plead ignorance is suggestive. What their comments show is the importance of wishful thinking and self-deception in avoiding dissonance. Rather than acknowledge the gap between their thoughts and deeds, people avoided unpleasant information, intentionally or unintentionally, and pleaded ignorance. This forced their critics to consider what it was reasonable to expect people to know about the regulations. But other excuses could motivate as well as justify action. A reply from a 71-year-old retired railwayman brings us closest to the decision-making process. In his reply, the former railwayman vented his spleen at his inability to buy a new suit.

> I need, not merely want, a new suit but cannot get one. I have one coupon left. When I get my 24 in March, I shall be short of the 26 required for a suit. What am I to do? I'll bet there is no member of the Cabinet or Government in such a plight, nor any member of the Royal Household.[62]

The retired railwayman was contemplating getting his new suit illegally. In this context, his belief that the clothing regulations did not apply to public figures probably reduced his moral inhibitions to black market dealing. Regardless of whether the justifications came before or after people participated in their first illegal deals, these excuses made it easier for them to excuse subsequent evasion— the rationalizations, like the deal itself, disinhibited them from making further deals. But what were the values that the panellists had to bypass or overcome to do so? The answer can be found in the folk category of grey market.

The mental effort that panellists spent on distinguishing technical offences from black market crimes testifies to the strength of the social norm to obey the law amongst 'respectable' people at the start of 1948. This rule-of-law norm meant people who had internalized conventional values had to find a plausible reason why the norm did not apply in their case. That all five of Sykes' and Matza's neutralization techniques cropped up in the directive replies suggests that conventional society accepted that this norm could be disregarded in specific circumstances. If the authorities or the population at large ignored the rules, the individual did not have to obey. The same was true if a person had no control over their actions. If breaking a law harmed no one, that law did not bind the individual. Nobody could be held to account for contravening regulations if they could not be reasonably expected to know them. This implied that the authorities needed to keep laws simple and communicate them effectively. If obeying the law conflicted with a more important norm, that norm trumped the rule of law.

---

[60] M-OA, DR January 1948, DR 144.   [61] DR 36.   [62] DR 267.

Although the authorities dismissed the excuse that everyone fiddles, they recognized the power of the norm that underpinned this defence and the danger it presented to respect for the law. The norm was that of conditional cooperation to which the sociologist Jon Elster attributes a quasi-moral status. Put simply, the norm enjoined a person to cooperate only if others did too.[63] That the norm of conditional cooperation lurks behind the ploy of condemning the condemners suggests that it was another way of appealing to higher loyalties rather than a justification in its own right. This would explain the norm's peculiar hold over the public and policymakers' determination to avoid giving the impression of widespread evasion. It is also why senior police officers and judges pressed for either harsher enforcement or rapid decontrol after the war when they felt evasion had reached a tipping point. But there was more to the popularity of condemning one's condemners amongst panellists than whether others followed the rules or not. Not only did the powerful have to follow the rules, but they also had to administer them fairly. Enter procedural justice. Following the rule-of-law norm in a particular instance was contingent on the consistent application and enforcement of a rule. Any hint that there was one rule for the rich and another for the poor weakened the grip that the rule-of-law norm had in that instance. This focus on due process reveals the existence of other norms that trumped the rule of law: fairness norms.

The regularity with which 'fair' and related words occur in the directive replies testifies to the importance of conventional notions of justice to the 'respectable', especially in terms of outcome. Interestingly, the panellists did not excuse their illicit dealings by appealing to fairness norms, although they exercised a powerful influence over their thinking about evasion. As one probation officer told M-O, 'In every case of black market I have come against I found that the people concerned who are buying the goods do it with the feeling that this is something to which they are entitled and of which they are being deprived.'[64] This is no surprise given the way that the authorities framed the issue of control. The sense of entitlement that the officially sanctioned language of fair shares encouraged can be seen in many other responses. Depriving others of their ration of essential goods was unacceptable, as it contradicted fairness norms invoked by government rhetoric. This, combined with respect for the law and unease about profiteering, ensured the moral unacceptability of black marketing to many, setting limits to its growth. But the same norms of fairness could also encourage evasion, as they led some to challenge the official definition of what constituted a fair price, fair profit, or a fair share. If they could achieve their fair share without depriving others, their actions did not break any norm. The panellists' replies show a disregard for the niceties of intellectual discourses of justice when it came to determining what their fair share

---

[63] Jon Elster, *Explaining Social Behaviour: More Nuts and Bolts for the Social Sciences* (Cambridge, 2007), 104.
[64] M-OA, DR January 1948, DR 86.

was. Ideas of equality, merit, and need mingled, as they continued to do at the end of the century.[65]

When discussing the rights and wrongs of black market dealing, one term is noticeably absent from the panellists' replies: sacrifice. It does not appear once. This would not have been the case had M-O posed the question three years' earlier. Several of the panellists who admitted post-war black marketing said that they complied with regulations during the war. A company secretary explained:

> With regard to my personal knowledge of it, I should first like to make it clear that I do differentiate between 'during the war' and 'after the war'. During the war I never made the slightest attempt to get any extra petrol, but on the contrary was as economical as possible, both personally and in the RAF, because seamen were risking their lives, and running the risks of terrible deaths to bring petrol here. Since the war, when the shortage is entirely due to Governmental stupidity, I frankly do not look at it in at all the same light, and if I had the opportunity of getting extra, had not the slightest compunction in taking it.[66]

Wartime propaganda aimed at bolstering support for economic control stressed the sacrifices made to feed, clothe, and fuel the people. It proved very effective. The company secretary and others like him felt obliged to comply with the regulations in return for the sacrifices made by the uniformed services. Peace ended this obligation, removing one normative constraint on evasion.

Victory changed the moral environment in other ways not captured in the directive replies. Reporting on feelings amongst the panel during the fortnight after the Japanese surrender, M-O noted that many felt that 'peace meant the end of communal effort, neighbourliness, and belief in a common cause. Many others felt...that the sense of purpose had gone, that private insecurities were increasingly monopolizing their own lives and those of their acquaintances.'[67] This was not an exhaustive list of responses to victory. Others included relief, boredom, survivor's guilt, a desire to return to normalcy, a rejection of collectivism, and a vigorous reassertion of individuality.[68] The desire to reassert one's individuality and the craving for action encouraged many people to engage in illegal dealing for the first time. Several of the respondents to the M-O directive wrote about the buzz that black market dealing gave them.[69] Demobilized servicemen felt the need to express their individuality and the yearning for action most strongly. A significant minority of demobbed soldiers dabbled in black market goods giving rise to the cultural trope of the disgruntled former serviceman sucked into a life of crime.[70]

---

[65] David Miller, 'Distributive Justice: What the People think', *Ethics*, 102 (1992), 555–93.

[66] M-OA, DR January 1948, DR 160.

[67] M-O, *Peace and the Public* (London, 1947), 9–10.

[68] See Paul Fussell, *Wartime: Understanding and Behaviour in the Second World War* (Oxford, 1990).

[69] M-OA, DR January 1948, DRs 34, 73, and 230.

[70] *The Times*, 6 May 1947 and 13 March 1951. D. Phillipson, *Smuggling: A History 1700–1970* (Newton Abbot, 1973), 127–35, 175–85. See Geoffrey Household, 'Brandy for the parson' in Household, *Tales of adventure* (London, 1952), 146–68; John Boland, *The League of Gentlemen* (London, 1958), and Nicholas Monsarrat, *The Ship that Died of Shame, and Other Stories* (London, 1959) for fiction inspired by the black market exploits of ex-servicement; and *The Ship that Died of Shame* (May 1955) and *The League of Gentlemen* (April 1960) for films inspired by these stories.

For some, these moral shifts led to a post-war black market boom. According to David Hughes:

> When the war finished Britain expected, not perhaps the lap of luxury, but at least bananas, a few more cigarettes, a range of cloths to choose suits from, a car maybe or a trip abroad, the odd bottle of whisky to celebrate the expanding horizons that had already started closing in. No arguments from the front bench ever quite persuaded people that they could not be given these things; somewhere, sadists were at work, or puritans.[71]

But there was no dramatic boom. Increasing evasion had more to do with the tightening of control than the return of peace. The disappearance of wartime moral imperatives made it marginally easier to overcome one's moral scruples about black marketing. This is not to deny the power of wartime solidarity, but its impact varied more than is usually allowed for. Inhibitions to illegal dealing differed according to the level of personal identification with the war effort, which was partly a function of one's proximity to the war. A strong sense of British identity allowed civilians to imagine that the war was their war. But direct experience of bombing or loss was more effective than national identity in personalizing the conflict with the result that remote communities disapproved less of evasion. This isolation need not have been the result of physical distance; it could be the result of close identitification with a distinct occupation or community. Liverpool dockers, who experienced heavy bombing and knew the human cost of imports, pilfered cargoes and supplies througout the war, while Northern Ireland, host to numerous military garrisons and naval bases, gained a reputation in Whitehall for being the Wild West of the black market.

Whatever the normative constraints on behaviour, the question remains as to whether 'respectable' people could factor moral opprobrium into their calculations of the costs and benefits of evasion. Due to the norms that black marketing infringed, the topic of evasion generated strong feelings amongst panellists. These emotions must have made calculation difficult as they affected the desires, beliefs, and information on which people based their decisions. But the norms and values of respectable society did not bind everyone as tightly as they did the panellists. Being part of a group that shared distinctive norms and values could insulate its members from the conventional norms of wider society and their usual interpretation. Transport workers, for example, had few qualms about stealing controlled goods, as they could construct this as one of the customary perks or fiddles of their jobs.

Once placed in this social context it is easy to mistake pilfering for an act of resistance but doing so ignores the material self-interest driving this 'social crime'. Transport workers were not rejecting conventional norms by redefining their actions. If anything, their behaviour confirms that the influence of conventional

---

[71] David Hughes, 'The Spivs', in Michael Sissons and Philip French (eds.), *Age of Austerity 1945–1951* (2nd edn., Harmondsworth, 1964), 92; see Rayne Minns, *Bombers and Mash: The Domestic Front 1939–45* (London, 1980), 161; Smithies, *Crime in Wartime*, 203; Smithies, *Black Economy*, 85; Addison, *Now the War is Over*, 41; Zweiniger-Bargielowska, *Austerity*, 60.

norms extended beyond the confines of middle-class society. Truly oppositional cultures or subcultures were rare and increasingly hard to maintain in the context of a 'people's war' that fostered a sense of common identity and shared endeavour. The social network of career criminals and their associates, referred to as the 'underworld', constituted a peculiarly stubborn subculture, but even some of its members could not resist the patriotic call to the colours.[72] National and ethnic minorities that did not necessarily define themselves against conventional British society were another grouping who were not easily constrained by its norms and values. Rich in social capital, villains, aliens, Irish nationalists, and Ulster unionists found that the bonds of convention rested lightly upon them, making it easy to throw them off and justify evasion.

[72] Ben Macintyre, *Agent Zigzag: The True Wartime Story of Eddie Chapman, Lover, Betrayer, Hero, Spy* (London, 2007).

8

Thieves' kitchens: local markets for local people

When researchers attempted to explain black market crime in wartime America, they turned to the new theory of differential association. The idea was simple: keeping bad company made it more likely that you would be bad too. Edwin Sutherland, whose theory it was, put it less succinctly. He thought that 'criminal behaviour is learned in association with those who define such behaviour favourably and in isolation from those who define it unfavourably, and that a person in an appropriate situation engages in such criminal behaviour if, and only if, the weight of favourable definitions exceeds the weight of the unfavourable definitions'.[1] The sociologist and one-time US OPA official Marshall Clinard found this theory helpful in understanding the black markets that he spent much of the war trying to prevent. He found that 'Most black market violations appear to have their origin in behaviour learned in association from others, unethical and illegal practices being conveyed in the trade as part of a definition of the situation and rationalizations to support these violations of law being similarly transmitted by this differential association.'[2]

Much criticized for its banality, the idea that those around you can lead you astray continues to feature prominently in explanations of white-collar crime, though it tends to be discussed in terms of occupational and organizational cultures.[3] That some trades and workplaces were more prone to evasion than others is borne out by the British experience of economic control. Locality, not discussed in contemporary American studies of black markets, was also important in the British setting. What links these patterns of differential association is the idea of community. Strong identification with a community that was detached or semidetached from conventional society facilitated evasion by providing its members with moral support and practical advice. From a government perspective these social ties were dysfunctional. They are a good example of what Robert Putnam dubbed 'bonding social capital', which works to the advantage of the individuals and groups concerned but to the disadvantage of wider society.

[1] Edwin H. Sutherland, *White-Collar Crime* (New York, 1949), 234; Frank E. Hartung, 'A Study in Law and Social Differentiation: As Exemplified in Violations of the Emergency Price Control Act of 1942 and the Second War Powers Act, in the Detroit Meat Industry' (Ph.D. thesis, University of Michigan, 1949) and his 'White-Collar Offenses in the Wholesale Meat Industry in Detroit', *American Journal of Sociology*, 56 (1950), 25–34.

[2] Clinard, *Black Market*, 298–9.

[3] Hazel Croall, *Understanding White Collar Crime* (Buckingham, 2001), 79–101.

NATURALIZING VOCABULARIES OF MOTIVE

In some instances, residential communities—the basis of most personal social networks—taught and reinforced the justifications that locals used to excuse illicit dealing. The same social networks that circulated information enabling people to make deals could also provide their members with the resources to overcome moral inhibitions to evasion. Here, social capital worked to promote delinquency and create local variations in the vocabulary of motive. Evidence of local communities legitimating evasion can be found in districts associated with 'social crimes' such as poaching and rustling in the countryside, wrecking on the coast, and pilfering in working-class neighbourhoods. Wartime shortages prompted resurgence in these classic social crimes that historians associate with the criminalization of custom as English society made its great transition from an eighteenth-century 'moral economy' to a nineteenth-century free-market economy.[4] Of these communities, working-class neighbourhoods are the best-documented.

In Salford's working-class districts—the setting for the novel *Love on the Dole* and much of L. S. Lowry's artwork—attitudes towards the traffic in coupons and rations resembled older social crimes such as workplace theft and street betting. In summer 1943 this illicit trade came to national attention after Salford's stipendiary magistrate imprisoned fourteen people for dealing in clothing books in a fortnight. Street prices ranged from £1 to £2 per book.[5] This spike in prosecutions was the result of a drive initiated by a local police superintendent. During July and August the Salford police prosecuted more than forty people for clothing offences. By the campaign's end the magistrate had convicted thirty-five people, imprisoning twenty of them for terms ranging from fourteen days to twelve months, and fining the remaining fifteen sums ranging from £3 to £80 plus costs.[6] Police uncovered a thriving trade in merchant seamen's clothing vouchers centred on the docks in Salford's Ordsall district that extended to the neighbouring districts of Pendleton, Broughton, and Hulme. The vouchers allowed a pedlar from Manchester's Cheetham Hill to supply a draper in the nearby town of Atherton with enough coupon-free cloth to run her shop for two months.[7] The traffic in Salfordians' clothing books extended into middle-class districts, including Prestwich, to the north of Manchester. Giving evidence in one of these cases a Detective Inspector informed the magistrate that many locals were under 'the impression that clothing books were the property of the people to whom they were issued'. But this was not the case, as 'They were the property of the Government and were issued only for use, the ownership remaining at all times with the Government'.[8] Local criminals had

---

[4] Hobsbawm, 'Distinctions between Socio-Political and other Forms of Crime', 5–6; E. P. Thompson, *Whigs and Hunters: The Origin of the Black Act* (London, 1975); John Rule, 'Social Crime in the Rural South in the Eighteenth and early Nineteenth Century', *Southern History*, 1 (1979), 35–53.

[5] *News Chronicle*, 24 August 1943.

[6] *Salford City Reporter and Chronicle*, 3 September 1943.

[7] *Manchester Guardian*, 25 August 1943.

[8] *Manchester Guardian*, 24 August 1943.

exploited this moral atmosphere a year earlier, flooding the market with thousands of clothing coupons printed in a house in the middle of an arts-and-crafts-style terrace.[9]

Like many civilians, local residents considered trading in surplus coupons and rations as a 'grey market' activity. Traditional notions of working-class respectability bolstered this belief. Independence was one marker of working-class respectability in both traditional inner city communities such as Salford's Hanky Park and newer suburban ones such as Manchester's Wythenshawe. Being beholden to another was avoided, while privacy was treasured. Household income and housing stock limited the expression of these 'Victorian values', which the working class shared with the middle class. In slum districts, reluctance to ask for help when in distress was deemed admirable but foolish, while refusing to help those in need, even if you yourself did not seek help in straitened times, was judged vicious and beneath contempt. Keeping yourself to yourself could also offend your neighbours, who interpreted such behaviour as unfriendly and judgemental.[10] This was less the case in lower-density suburban estates. In either setting, property—especially pawnable possessions—both displayed and maintained economic independence. Quick to recognize the exchange value of rations and coupons, people used them to maintain their independence—which was especially important for women with husbands serving in the armed forces—or to secure a little extra to make life more tolerable. That they were yours by right ensured that they were free from the taint of charity. As in rural communities, not-for-profit exchanges of coupons or rations, whether as a gift, a swap, or a paid favour, expressed and drew moral support from the practice of mutual aid that continued on suburban estates despite the threat that new neighbouring practices, which placed a premium on privacy and self-reliance, posed to it.

Attitudes that made gambling for small stakes an acceptable working-class hobby helped to legitimate 'black market' deals too. As well as knowing how to run an illicit retail business, bookmakers, the runners, and look-outs who worked for them, and to a lesser extent their clients, learned how to justify illegal street betting.[11] Like the bookmaker, the black marketeer enriched working people's lives. Dealers in coupons and rations provided both suppliers and customers with a 'bit extra' or the means to 'have a good time'. In the British context of limited evasion, the illicit trade was socially progressive, redistributing income from the more to the less affluent. Inflation did not off-set working-class gains from the traffic in official entitlements. Initially, workers considered any gain from this trade an unexpected

[9] *The Times*, 9, 19 February, 13, 14, and 16 May 1942.

[10] See Joanne Klein, '"Moving On": Men and the Changing Character of Interwar Working-Class Neighborhoods: from the Files of the Manchester and Liverpool City Police', *Journal of Social History*, 38 (2004), 407–21, for a recent view of the complexities of neighbouring in working-class districts.

[11] Andrew Davies, 'The Police and the People: Gambling in Salford, 1900–1939', *Historical Journal*, 34 (1991), 87–115; Andrew Davies, *Leisure, Gender and Poverty: Working-Class Culture in Salford and Manchester, 1900–1939* (Buckingham, 1992), 142–67; Mark Clapson, 'Playing the System: The World of Organised Street Betting in Manchester, Salford and Bolton, *c.*1880 to 1939', in Andrew Davies and Steven Fielding (eds.), *Workers' Worlds: Cultures and Communities in Manchester and Salford, 1880–1939* (Manchester, 1992), 156–78.

bonus, and over time they came to view such gains as their right. Seen from either of these perspectives, attempts to end the trade denied working people the opportunity to improve their lot, albeit marginally and temporarily. Police and ministry inspectors who enforced control were on the same side as those killjoys who sought to deny working people a smoke, a pint, or a flutter. This was the closest that most workers' rationalizations of evasion came to the type of overt resistance to authority associated with 'protest crime'.

In both urban and rural areas a local tradition of wrecking, pilfering, poaching, or rustling helped people to legitimize evasion, and reinforced the sense that what they were doing was grey market rather than black market. After the introduction of economic control, dockland families continued to frame workplace theft as one of a job's perks or fiddles, drawing no distinction between stealing controlled and uncontrolled goods. In docklands and elsewhere with a history of tolerating certain social crime, these local traditions were as important as those of mutual aid. The fate of the SS *Politician* and its cargo of whisky—a story that inspired Compton Mackenzie to pen his comic novel *Whisky Galore!*, which formed the basis for the Ealing comedy of the same name—is the best-known example of wartime wrecking. Residents of South Uist in the Outer Hebrides pillaged the ship's cargo holds after it ran aground off the island's coast in 1941. The local customs officer tried to stop the islanders' salvage operation and recover the whisky, with limited help from the police and none from the islanders.[12] Similar events took place around the UK throughout the war as bodies and wreckage from Atlantic and Arctic convoys washed up on the coastline, and continued in peacetime, albeit at a lower level.[13] Looting of bombed-out business premises was the urban equivalent of wrecking, proving difficult to control in blitzed cities and alarming the authorities. There was little stigma attached to salvaging goods from shops, factories, and warehouses by comparison to looting of personal possessions from bomb-damaged houses.[14] The cellar of a bombed-out customs warehouse supplied East-Enders, including the Met officers at the Isle of Dogs Police Station, with rough tobacco until the Port of London Police discovered where the tobacco came from.[15]

ON THE MARGINS

The tighter, closer social networks that characterized the worlds of the lumpen poor, the criminal underworld, or alien immigrants made oppositional subcultures both possible and stable. Their social isolation ensured that people from these urban groups were rarely exposed to outside influences. Wider society had little understanding of, or sympathy for, out-groups who inverted or ignored conventional norms and values. When Customs and Excise officers found nylon stockings

[12] Roger Hutchinson, *Polly: The True Story behind Whisky Galore!* (Edinburgh, 1990).
[13] *The Times*, 4 January 1947.
[14] Thomas, *An Underworld at War*, 76–85.
[15] IWM, Dept. of Doc., 81/10/1, H. F. Grey, 'The Reflections of A War Time Constable, or Me and My Bike' (unpublished memoir), 65–6.

in 128 parcels of matzos sent from the US to members of an east London Jewish congregation, the *Daily Express*, which broke the story, portrayed the congregation as a 'Big Nylon Gang', the source of most smuggled nylons.[16] Investigations by both Customs and Excise and the Jewish Trades Advisory Council uncovered a more complex story involving Holocaust survivors from Nitra, Slovakia.[17]

The scheme itself was simple. Smugglers in New York sandwiched pairs of nylon stockings between matzos or chocolate bars which they parcelled up and sent to London. The parcels contained either seventy-two or forty-eight pairs of nylons, which would be sold to hawkers and pedlars. To avoid arousing suspicion, the smugglers sent the parcels to people whom their British co-conspirators knew. By filling out customs declaration forms in the name of residents of the Williamsburg district of Brooklyn, the smugglers disguised their tracks further. Having received a list of consignees in advance, the British smugglers sent teenage boys to collect the parcels from addresses in Stoke Newington. The operation worked smoothly until customs officers conducting a routine check of US mail found 128 of the parcels.

When questioned, the consignees—all of whom were ultra-orthodox 'Jews of Continental origin'—maintained their innocence. What they had in common was a connection to the Agudath Israel movement that was helping Haredi youths who survived the Holocaust to emigrate to London, where they received a religious education. Some of these students collected the parcels, proving their bona fides by describing a parcel's contents and telling the consignee that it had been misaddressed. If questioned about the stockings, the students explained that 'Mere mus haben a poor fundt' ('We need a couple pounds').[18] Interviews conducted by an official of the Jewish American Congress revealed that the consignors were also connected to the Agudah.

The Trades Advisory Council and Customs concluded that two rabbis, who had survived the Holocaust and emigrated to New York, set the scheme in motion as a way to fund the Agudah's relief work. Both men, who had taught at a rabbinical college in the Slovakian town of Nitra before the war, had been involved in the Jewish underground during the war, organizing relief for Slovakian deportees in Poland and, through bribery, attempting to prevent further deportations.[19] Having left Nitra for Brooklyn, the two rabbis set out to rebuild their Yeshiva and the community it served.[20] Their primary loyalty was to their surviving students, fifty of whom they brought with them to the United States, and members of Nitra's Hasidic community who they wanted to resettle in Brooklyn, or failing that, London, where they had friends and family.[21] This required money—something of which the refugees had little. The nylon-smuggling operation was an ingenious, albeit illegal, way of raising funds quickly. If rumours circulating amongst the Chief Rabbi's court are to be believed, this was one of two smuggling operations—the

[16] *Daily Express*, 22 August 1949; see *Daily Mail*, 22 August 1949.
[17] TNA: PRO, CUST 49/3030, 'Report on Smuggling in Food Parcels', 20 August 1949.
[18] LMA, ACC/3121/E04/0274/1432, 'Note', 6 May 1949. Thanks to Ghil'ad Zuckermann for translating the Yiddish phrase 'Mere mus haben a poor fundt'.
[19] *New York Times*, 24 May 1961.
[20] *New York Times*, 17 November 1948.
[21] *New York Times*, 12 December 1946.

other involving jewellery hidden in boxes of tephilim sent from Brooklyn.[22] That these schemes contravened British regulations counted for nought. The refugees did not identify with the British, and had good reason to distrust the British state after their experiences at the hands of the Slovakian government, a German puppet state.

Northern Ireland's nationalist and unionist communities felt a similar sense of detachment from British austerity policies. British visitors to the province found its population apathetic and resentful of austerity measures. The atmosphere made one visitor feel guilty. 'It seemed, somehow, as if one was getting out of the war, and having too easy a life.'[23] Conscription—which ensured that every family in Great Britain had a personal stake in the war effort whether bombed or not—was not introduced in Northern Ireland for fear of inflaming nationalist feeling, making the war feel distant.[24] Although the unionist government at Stormont Castle supported the British war effort, the threat of German invasion seemed remote and food shortages unlikely. Sectarian politics continued unabated, and efforts to mobilize the province for war were compromised by attempts to preserve the unionist state. The lack of urgency about mobilization so infuriated J. E. Warnock, Parliamentary Secretary for Home Affairs, that he resigned from the Stormont government in protest, commenting that 'the government has been slack, dilatory, and apathetic'.[25] The situation changed a little after the bombing of Belfast and the arrival of American troops in 1941 and 1942, but the war continued to seem a remote affair.[26]

This Ulster outlook, condoned by the British authorities for the sake of domestic stability, minimized the effect of sectarian politics on the war effort. The effect was still noticeable, however. According to a senior civil servant working at Stormont, 'Anything in the shape of a call to duty or an appeal for national service evoked a readier response from them [the Protestants] than from Catholics, since they identified themselves more fully with the British state than many Catholics did.'[27] Nationalist opposition to the Stormont and British governments meant that few nationalists identified with the British war effort. Northern nationalists took an active role in civil defence and tolerated the crime-fighting activities of the RUC, as bombs and criminals did not distinguish between unionists and nationalists; but they saw no reason to obey economic controls unless shortages affected them. This mirrored attitudes towards control in southern Ireland.[28]

The nationalist sense that this was not their war, and its remoteness, for many unionists made it easier for evaders from either side to justify black market dealing. But the nationalists' hostility or ambivalence towards the state meant that they could better resist official attempts to label their dealings as unpatriotic, greedy,

[22] LMA, ACC/3121/E04/0274/1432, 'Note', 6 May 1949.
[23] M-OA, FR 1309, Tom Harrisson, 'Ulster Shipping Situation', 12 June 1942.
[24] St John Greer Ervine, *Craigavon, Ulsterman* (London, 1949), 554–5.
[25] David Harkness, *Northern Ireland since 1920* (Dublin, 1983), 89.
[26] M-OA, FR 2101, Tom Harrisson, 'Ulster outlooks', 20 May 1944.
[27] John Andrew Oliver, *Working at Stormont* (Dublin, 1978), 67.
[28] TNA: PRO, DO 130/28, Elizabeth Bowen, 'Notes on Eire', July 1942.

selfish, or criminal. In Northern Ireland such dealings almost always involved smuggling goods subject to control in the UK from Éire, where they were cheaper or unrationed. Unionists found it easy to square import smuggling with their political views, as they were not depriving fellow citizens of goods. Smuggling could even be construed as a patriotic act to increase Ulster's supplies in time of war—an argument that would have found favour with mercantilist thinkers.[29] Such arguments stilled any moral qualms that northern holidaymakers and daytrippers in Dundalk had about smuggling silk stockings, butter, eggs, tomatoes, and tinned food onto the Belfast train.[30] The same reasoning justified import smuggling of flour south of the border. The Éireann authorities came close to legalizing the trade when they removed all controls on the importation of flour, much to the annoyance of the MoF.[31]

Patriotism played differently in the predominantly Catholic and nationalist communities that straddled the border. Smuggling, especially of cattle, became an important and socially acceptable part of life in these communities soon after partition.[32] The new boundary did not respect physical or human geography, separating communities and disrupting local economies, and it was also hard to police. Customs officers controlled ten rail crossings and sixteen roads, 9 am to 5 pm, Monday to Saturday, leaving one hundred RUC officers to patrol them outside these hours and the remaining 174 cross-border roads.[33] Local people exploited price differences between north and south to improve their standard of living into the war years. In spring 1942 the independent TM James Dillon, voicing an opinion that chimed with those of his Monaghan constituents, called the Irish Minister of Supply Seán Lemass 'the father and mother of the Black Market', berating him for calling 'poor women in the country criminals for getting flour on the Black Market to feed children' and demanding he introduce flour rationing.[34] Dubliners and others distant from the border resented the ability of Dillon's Monaghan constituents to avoid shortages by exploiting their connections across the border in Fermanagh, Tyrone, and Armagh.[35] The trade could be highly organized and run on commercial lines. In March 1940, Garda and Irish customs officers confronted more than one hundred smugglers leading a donkey train carrying two tons of flour across Cuilcagh Mountain from the north, in the 'Battle of Dowra'.[36]

Hostile or ambivalent attitudes towards the border and the states it divided both justified and encouraged smuggling. Catholic hostility towards British naval personnel and American troops stationed in Derry encouraged the use of boats to smuggle Donegal poteen across the border. This flourishing trade, alongside others,

---

[29] *Irish Times*, 15 March 1941.   [30] *Irish Times*, 22 September 1941 and 19 July 1943.

[31] TNA: PRO, MAF 100/7, G. H. E. Parr to L. Maclean, 5 April 1941.

[32] D. S. Johnson, 'Cattle Smuggling on the Irish Border, 1932–38', *Irish Economic and Social History*, 6 (1979), 42–3.

[33] TNA: PRO, CAB 66/18/15, WP (41) 192, Herbert Morrison, 'Control of the Northern Ireland Border', 15 August 1941.

[34] *Irish Times*, 13 May 1942.

[35] *Irish Times*, 22 September 1941.

[36] *Irish Times*, 29 and 30 March, and 28 September 1940.

was a cause of serious concern for the Stormont and British governments.[37] MoF inspectors, customs officers, and police tried to prevent export smuggling of flour, bread, tea, coffee, cocoa, rice, tapioca, and cornflour to Éire.[38] The authorities also had problems with farmers smuggling fat and store livestock from Éire, as they fetched a higher price in Ulster's cattle marts.[39] Despite the best efforts of the British and Irish authorities, the cross-border trade continued into the 1950s.[40] With limited resources at their disposal, civilians found it easier to evade the customs officers. There was little need for more sophisticated methods such as concealing goods inside the stomach of dead animals destined for the knacker's yard. Weight of numbers meant that the crudest methods of concealment—such as loose tea in a bicycle frame, a fake pregnancy, or a false-bottomed basket—were usually succesful. When British customs officers walked through trains travelling from Donegal to Londonderry, women returning from cross-border shopping trips hung their bags on the outside handles of carriage doors facing away from the train platform.[41]

Smuggling across the Irish border was a unique black market offence, as border communities condoned it and nationalists could portray the traffic as a political protest against partition.[42] The only other social groups in which evasion was seen as a socially acceptable act of resistance were the criminal underworld and the lumpen poor from which the underworld recruited. Amongst the poorest, stealing to survive was acceptable, if not respectable, behaviour.[43] Several years after the war ended, residents of Liverpool's 'Ship Street' considered stealing 'normal so long as it takes place outside the individual's group'. Stealing from friends or relatives was wrong. Locals expressed their disapproval by describing this as 'robbing', distinguishing it from 'thieving' from 'stores or the like'.[44] This was a phenomenon found in other deprived working-class neighbourhoods in Liverpool and elsewhere.[45] During the war, children living on 'Branch Street' in north London held similar views, refusing to inform on one another and sanctioning anyone who broke silence.[46] The same was true of Campbell Bunk, centred on Campbell Road in Islington, north London.

[37] TNA: PRO, CAB 75/7, HPC (42), 112, 10 July 1942. John W. Blake, *Northern Ireland in the Second World War* (Belfast, 1956), 98, 100–1; Graham Smith, *Something to Declare: 1000 Years of Customs and Excise* (London, 1980), 169–70; Brian Barton, *The Blitz: Belfast in the War Years* (Belfast, 1989), 45, 48–9; Brian Barton, *Northern Ireland in the Second World War* (Belfast, 1995), 10–11, 127; Chris Ryder, *The RUC: a Force under Fire* (4th edn., London, 1997), 84.

[38] TNA: PRO, MAF 100/7, 'Note of meeting with North of Ireland Country Master Bakers' Associations', 31 July 1941.

[39] TNA: PRO, MAF 88/45, 'Minute', 12 January 1946.

[40] TNA: PRO, MAF 88/45, 'Minute', 20 October 1953.

[41] Phil Cunningham, *Derry Down the Days* (Londonderry, 2002), 132–3. Listen also to 'Border smuggling during the war', 'Robbie Crockett and memories of cross-border smuggling', 'Paddy Gillespie and cross-border smuggling', and 'Nell Traynor's border trips', on the Northern Ireland Museums Council's *Second World War* website, http://www.secondworldwarni.org.

[42] Rule, 'Social Crime', 138–9.

[43] Stephen Humphries, 'Steal to Survive: the Social Crime of Working Class Children 1890–1940', *Oral History*, 9 (1981), 24–33.

[44] Kerr, *Ship Street*, 119, 126.

[45] Mays, *Growing up*, 117–18, 122–3.

[46] Marie Paneth, *Branch Street: A Sociological Study* (London, 1944), 69.

Residents of the Bunk resented attempts by the police and organized religion to impose conventional morality in the neighbourhood. Policemen who tried to enforce the ban on betting and gaming in the street were likely to be assaulted. Residents would also help one another to escape the police, hiding the hunted or providing them with alibis.[47] Theft—a common crime for Bunk residents—was motivated by more than need or greed. Reflecting on their criminal careers, some locals explained their actions in terms that the sociologist Robert Merton, originator of strain theory, would have recognized. Albert Quinn—a young thief who lived in the Bunk during the 1930s—was typical. He did not see why his family should struggle to subsist while others prospered. Encouraged by the prevailing egalitarianism and economic individualism of the Bunk, he turned to crime to redress the balance. As he put it, 'I used to take things as a right.'[48]

Balmore Street, Highgate, and the Nichol district of Bethnal Green bred similar attitudes amongst their residents. After leaving school, Sid Day—a Balmore boy with an uncle who lived in the Bunk—followed the familiar career trajectory of a young man from one of London's 'Tiger Bays' or 'Thieves' Kitchens', drifting from one unskilled job to another, and supplementing his earnings with petty theft and penny capitalist enterprise. Like his father before him, Day worked as a jobbing builder once he married, while continuing a part-time criminal career.[49] Involved in black marketing of cigarettes, cloth, holly, pigs, and potatoes throughout the austerity years, Day, like Quinn, portrayed himself as a rogue who took only things from those who could afford it in order to provide for his family who could not.[50] This Robin Hood mentality, combined with the belief that everyone was at it, informed petty thefts of coal, timber, and food by children and young people from the poorest working-class families both in London and the provinces, and in urban and rural areas.[51] In most cases their nascent careers as thieves were cut short by securing a steady job—until the idea of companionate marriage took hold, as starting a family did little to domesticate youthful delinquents.[52] Entering regular employment, however, marked a shift from petty theft to pilfering—a less visible crime and a socially acceptable one for adults. What made these crimes acceptable was that they did not involve stealing from your own. This was rarely a problem until the late 1950s, as there was little incentive to steal from neighbours with few valuable possessions.[53]

Unlike Sid Day and Albert Quinn, crime provided Arthur Harding—a product of Bethnal Green's Nichol district—with a living. Harding was a Brick Lane wardrobe-dealer who made his living through theft and violence as a young man, and was involved in the clothing black market, trafficking in stolen clothes and clothing

---

[47] White, *Worst Street*, 118–21.　　　[48] *Worst Street*, 128.

[49] Day, *London Born*, 81–5.　　　[50] *London Born*, 129–45.

[51] Stephen Humphries, *Hooligans or Rebels? An Oral History of Working-class Childhood and Youth 1889–1939* (Oxford, 1981), 150–73.

[52] Barry S. Godfrey, David J. Fox, and Stephen Farrall, *Criminal Lives: Family Life, Employment and Offending* (Oxford, 2007), 107–8.

[53] Roger Hood and Kate Joyce, 'Three Generations: Oral Testimonies on Crime and Social Change in London's East End', *British Journal of Criminology*, 39 (1999), 142–50.

coupons. He bought immunity from prosecution by supplying detectives with information about other criminals.[54] Older than both men, he shared their lumpen background, discovering a flair for crime as a young man in the 1890s. Like many children from the Nichol, his criminal career began with petty thefts of coal and food, which he brought home or sold for cash.[55] His cunning and willingness to use violence distinguished him from other young thieves, establishing his reputation as a local 'terror' and earning him the respect of the professional villains and detectives with whom he began to associate, and by 1907 he was a well-known figure in the East End underworld.[56] It was bad to be good amongst fellow villains. Instead of justifying bad behaviour like M-O panellists and even the lumpen poor, they had to excuse behaviour that contradicted underworld ethics such as helping the police or avoiding a violent confrontation rather than conventional morality.[57] Freddie Foreman—a promising young thief in the post-war years—summarized this ethos as one of professionalism, fair dealing with one another, toughness, and secrecy. This sat easily with the lumpen poor's code that 'You would never steal from neighbours or your own, or from people as badly off as yourself', and the cardinal rule that 'you never trusted a policeman or told them anything'.[58]

Although not bound by conventional values, Harding and other underworld figures were not unaware of them, portraying themselves as social bandits who did not steal from the poor when criticized by their working-class peers, or trotting out justifications used by the M-O panellists when in court. Harding enriched his vocabulary of motive through his interactions with older criminals, both in and out of prison, and practised using it in court. As these 'old-timers' saw it, Harding needed to tell the court the good reasons for his actions rather than the real reasons for them. Through his court appearances he came to know the local magistrates and judges, learning who would listen to his pleas and how best to appeal to those who did. Defence lawyers also coached Harding and his associates in the best things to say when appearing in court.[59] Pleading ignorance of the regulations, accusing the authorities of entrapment, or planting evidence were common ploys. Such mitigating pleas infuriated prosecutors, as they played well with magistrates and juries.[60]

The closed social networks that characterized the underworld insulated habitual criminals from conventional values. Before the war the tiny number of persistent offenders in the railway town of Crewe, Cheshire, knew each other well, 'offending with and against one another'. Held together by neighbourhood, family, and business ties, they formed a hardcore around which other offenders clustered, substantiating contemporary views of a criminal fraternity.[61] Contact with 'respectable' society was limited and often antagonistic, reducing the hard core's exposure to

[54] Samuel, *East End Underworld*, 259–61.   [55] *East End Underworld*, 43–6.
[56] *East End Underworld*, 66–83, 106–24.   [57] Murphy, *Smash and Grab*, 2–5, 24–5.
[58] Freddie Foreman as told to John Lisners, *Respect: Autobiography of Freddie Foreman—Managing Director of British Crime* (London, 1997), i, 17.
[59] Samuel, *East End Underworld*, 71–2, 166, 193–4, 202–3, 253–5, 271–2.
[60] Faulks, *No Mitigating Circumstances*, 118; 'Interview with Glyn Hardwicke', 19.
[61] Godfrey *et al.*, *Criminal Lives*, 63.

conventional values. Security fears reinforced their aversion to the law-abiding.[62] As a result, moral dissonance was avoided or minimized, making a criminal sub-culture both possible and stable, and continuing unchanged into the 1960s. Few villains in London's underworld confessed to feeling pangs of remorse when re-flecting on their criminal careers. Arthur Harding did not, nor did younger genera-tions of thieves active during the austerity years. Billy Hill, self-proclaimed boss of the London underworld, and even Jack Spot, the man he ousted, seemed content with the life they had chosen and experienced no feelings of guilt.[63] The same was true of Frank Fraser and Freddie Foreman—two villains who built their reputa-tions stealing things to sell in the capital's underground economy.[64] The career criminal 'Robert Allerton', who considered himself the underworld equivalent of a Surbiton bank clerk, had no regrets about his life and no desire to reform. Aged thirty-three when interviewed in 1962, this one-time coupon trafficker hoped to retire on the proceeds from a big job and start a small business—a vision that Arthur Harding realized.[65]

Any moral discomfort prompted by contact with 'respectable' society was soon forgotten by villains. The thief Ruby Sparks experienced one of these unwanted epiphanies on his return to Dartmoor prison in summer 1940 after a successful escape attempt.[66]

> All the railway platforms and the other carriages of this train I was on were packed with sailors bound for Bristol and Plymouth. Faces like kids, and yet you knew what some of them must have seen. And most of them all joking and eager. I couldn't help thinking: 'Ruby, this is a shabby mess you're in, boy. Chained up and going back to prison.' It was the first time it dawned on me that all I'd done with my life was qualify to be treated like a mad animal. I didn't like it.[67]

Despite having these thoughts and being given the chance to put his talents to use in the army, Sparks deserted and resumed his criminal career, stealing goods and coupons.[68]

ONE OF THE BOYS

The London underworld, of which Sparks was a member, was an occupational community much like that of the CID. Members of both groups socialized with fellow villains or detectives who possessed similar skills and shared each other's values. Their work set them apart from their neighbours. Locality was more impor-tant in the construction of occupational communities in docklands, coalfields, or

---

[62] Parker and Allerton, *Courage of His Convictions*, 110–12.
[63] Billy Hill, *Boss of Britain's Underworld* (London, 1955); Janson, *Jack Spot*.
[64] Fraser and Morton, *Mad Frank*, 328–30; Foreman as told to Lisners, *Respect*, 316–18.
[65] Parker and Allerton, *Courage*, 186–9.
[66] *Daily Express*, 29 June 1940.
[67] Ruby Sparks and Norman Price, *Burglar to the Nobility* (London, 1961), 142.
[68] Murphy, *Smash and Grab*, 82.

farming country, and less so amongst members of the distributive trades and lorry drivers. Each of these occupational communities facilitated evasion by its members, as they provided them with information about how to get round the regulations and arguments legitimating such dodges. Yet more diffuse communities organized around formal associations and trade journals were just as effective at removing their members' moral inhibitions as these physically bounded communities were.

Footloose occupational communities that focused on particular places such as Smithfield Market in Manchester provide the clearest examples of the effects of differential association. According to Salford's food executive officer, Smithfield Market, which came under his control, was 'at least unclean' if not black. In December 1941 there were wholesalers 'who will not supply invoices with goods and who make the sale of certain goods conditional on the sale of others'.[69] Newspapers reported similar practices at wholesale markets around the country, the most numerous emanating from London's Covent Garden. Here, conditional or tie-in sales, discounts, kickbacks, and quality deterioration were normal business practice before the war. This gave rise to social jealousy that cut across class divisions. Some, like 'Mrs Jerrold', the wife of an optical instrument repairer in London, resented the easy money and perks picked up by 'Covent Garden porters earning £20 a week'.[70]

Fiddles in the hotel and catering trade, common in larger kitchens before the war, also thrived during austerity. Hoteliers, restaurateurs, and chefs had few qualms about obtaining black market food or drink. Cases involving caterers overcharging their customers or buying black market foodstuffs were a staple part of magistrates' diets during austerity. 'Operation Fiddler'—the largest case that MoF inspectors unearthed—involved a small family business supplying £83,410-worth of meat to West End clubs and hotels during a three-year period. The two brothers, whose firm it was, promised caterers a regular supply of poultry if they paid a black market premium. Ciro's Club off the Charing Cross Road, the London branch of an exclusive chain of restaurants and cabarets, was the firm's biggest customer, paying £41,000 for the firm's produce between 1945 and 1948. In court, Ciro's general manager and its catering managers found themselves in the company of the head chefs from the Park Lane Hotel, Piccadilly, the Mount Royal Hotel, Marble Arch, and the Ladies' Carlton Club, Grosvenor Place, as well as the owners of the Soho restaurant La Coquille. The Earls Court Restaurant and the Dorchester Hotel, Mayfair, were also implicated in the case, but the ministry chose not to prosecute them. All these businesses helped the brothers to conceal the illicit transactions by accepting spurious invoices and paying in cash.[71]

The import–export trade was another occupational community whose business practices conflicted with regulations. The post-war export drive, conducted at the expense of domestic consumption, made the re-export trade to Britain a lucrative

[69] *Manchester Guardian*, 24 December 1941.

[70] Bott, *Family and Social Network*, 181–2.

[71] Faulks, *No Mitigating Circumstances*, 122; *The Times*, 21 January, 10, 23, 24 February, 14 May, 21 September, 14, 21 October, and 10 December 1949.

prospect. Home demand for Staffordshire pottery and nylon stockings, both of which sold well in overseas markets, was strong, but controls limited the amount that British manufacturers could sell domestically, keeping demand artificially high. International traders recognized that they could exploit the situation by re-exporting export-only goods to Britain. The re-export or entrepôt trade had been a familiar part of the London trading scene since the eighteenth century, later taking root in the port cities of Liverpool and Hull. Re-exporting goods to evade British or foreign taxes was normal, albeit illegal, practice before the war. The post-war export drive made it possible to practice such scams once more.

One of the largest re-export scams involved the illicit trade in nylon stockings, which centred on Gibraltar, Malta, Tangier, Spanish Morocco, Hong Kong, and Éire. Traders in these places imported nylons made in Britain or elsewhere before re-exporting them to Britain disguised as gifts. Maltese and Gibraltarian traders were particularly active, placing advertisements in the British press and posting circular letters inviting Britons to purchase nylons for themselves or as gifts for friends.[72] Unable to tell whether a gift parcel was genuine or not, British customs officials opted to levy duty or purchase tax on any gift.[73] By colluding with foreign firms, British traders could compete with established continental mail-order businesses. The largest of these conspiracies that the authorities discovered involved the re-export of £50,000-worth of British-made nylon stockings from Belgium to the UK. The stockings never left Britain, as the London traders who bought them on behalf of various Belgian firms sold them to wholesalers and retailers in Wales, Yorkshire, and elsewhere.[74]

International traders were also active in supplying black market pottery. The need to earn hard currency meant that the BoT ordered the Staffordshire potteries to export all their decorated porcelain after the war. Export rejects and frustrated exports apart, it was impossible to obtain decorated china and earthenware legally in Britain—conditions which gave rise to a thriving illicit re-export trade. By 1950 the leakage of export china into the domestic market was so large that it was undermining the export drive.[75] One of the biggest black market operations that the authorities uncovered involved twelve businessmen and two firms diverting British-made porcelain worth at least £66,000 from overseas export markets to the home market from 1947 to 1950. The basic idea was simple but complex to execute, as it involved falsifying documents, creating fictitious companies, and using false identities. The traders placed orders with British suppliers for export-only pottery, which was crated, marked, and dispatched to a London wharf. Carriers removed the crates from the wharf using release notes that shuffled the goods from one dummy company to another. Having covered their tracks, the traders sold the pottery on the domestic market.

[72] TNA: PRO, CUST 49/4338, 'Tarachand Viroomal circular', n.d.; *Daily Telegraph*, 16 December 1949 and 3 January 1950; *The Star*, 31 January 1950.
[73] TNA: PRO, CUST 49/4338, A. G. Bottomley, 'Report on Nylon Stockings', 6 December 1950.
[74] Faulks, *No Mitigating Circumstances*, 151; *The Times*, 21–5 and 28–30 April, and 1 and 7 May 1953.
[75] *Manchester Guardian*, 30 March 1950.

This highly sophisticated conspiracy took the police three years to unravel, result-ing in an Old Bailey trial that lasted for forty-one days—up to that point the longest trial in the Central Criminal Court's history. The instigator of the conspiracy worked with established suppliers, exporters, and buyers whom he befriended, promising them a good return while entertaining them at London nightclubs and lavishing them with gifts.[76] Each link in the distribution chain was aware that the company at the centre of the operation with whom they dealt bent or broke the regulations governing their transactions with it, accepting incomplete or inaccurate paperwork without comment. According to the prosecution counsel, the attitude of the de-fendants, all of whom were found guilty, was 'If we can appear either not to break a regulation or, at the highest only be guilty of a technical breach, then we do not really mind what lies are told, or what dishonest practices follow. What we want are the profits that are coming in easily.'[77] Passing sentence, the judge took a similar view, remarking that this was a 'bad case' of 'grave commercial dishonesty'.[78] Like the trial judge, the appeal judges who heard the case portrayed it as a case involving a few rotten apples, ignoring the number of traders involved, some of whom left to work for other firms before police discovered the conspiracy, and ignoring similar cases featuring different people from a few years earlier.[79]

The import–export trade, as well as the hotel and catering trades, were not the only occupational communities to insulate their members from the values of con-ventional society. The same was true of other trades. The trade press, suppliers, competitors, lawyers, and accountants communicated values and beliefs that helped to justify evading regulations as well as circulating information about how to do so. These were the negative aspects of commercial cultures that shaped busi-ness practices, and which have received little attention from historians until re-cently.[80] Other forms of community, based on residence, shielded members from conventional society or added weight to the justifications used by 'respectable' people. In only a few cases, such as communities of non-integrated migrants like the Hasidim and the lumpen poor, did this amount to a genuine oppositional subculture. But, as we shall see in the next chapter, community was not the only source of moral support for individuals contemplating a black market deal. Politi-cians and journalists did much to legitimate popular justifications for black marketeering.

---

[76] Sir Harold Scott, *Scotland Yard* (London, 1954), 120–1; Faulks, *No Mitigating Circumstances*, 142–4; *R. v. Newland and Others* (1953) 3 WLR; *Manchester Guardian*, 13 January 1953.

[77] *The Times*, 21 March 1953.

[78] *The Times*, 4 April 1953.

[79] *R. v. Newland and Others* (1953) 3 WLR; *The Observer*, 16 November 1947; *Manchester Guard-ian*, 5 January 1950.

[80] See Mark Bevir and Frank Trentmann (eds.), *Markets in Historical Contexts: Ideas and Politics in the Modern World* (Cambridge, 2004); James Taylor, 'Commercial Fraud and Public Men in Victorian Britain', *Historical Research*, 78 (2005), 230–52; and Taylor, *Creating Capitalism: Joint-Stock Enterprise in British Politics and Culture, 1800–1870* (Woodbridge, 2006); as well as Paul Johnson, 'Civilizing Mammon: Laws, Morals, and the City in Nineteenth-Century England', in Peter Burke, Brian Har-rison, and Paul Slack (eds.), *Civil Histories: Essays presented to Sir Keith Thomas* (Oxford, 2000), 301–19; and Johnson, *Making the Market* (Cambridge, 2010).

9

'No basic, more spivs': public endorsement

Addressing a protest rally in Coventry from the back of a flatbed lorry in autumn 1947, Sir Miles Thomas, President of the Society of Motor Manufacturers and Traders, lambasted the Labour government for withdrawing the private motorist's basic petrol ration. The cut was part of a package of measures introduced to reduce dollar imports in the wake of the balance of payments crisis earlier that year. To sell this cut to drivers, the Minister of Fuel and Power Hugh Gaitskell had explained that his ministry would issue more supplementary rations. This would not erode savings from cutting basic as withdrawing the ration would lead to a slump in demand for black market petrol amongst 'pleasure' motorists. Petrol that would otherwise be lost to the black market would cover the increase in supplementary issues. Gaitskell earned the admiration of colleagues for his adroit presentation of the ration squeeze, while his opponents such as Sir Miles did their best to challenge the way he framed the cuts.[1]

Considering the black market argument in his speech, snippets of which appeared in British Movietone News and British Paramount News, Sir Miles agreed with Gaitskell that 'we don't want any long-distance black market joy-riding, but I submit to you that that kind of thing will become worse now, more than better, because the more you attempt to control and restrict the people's freedom unreasonably, the greater lengths they will go to evade those restrictions'. Applause and cries of 'hear, hear' met his words. Later, when Sir Miles returned to the theme, uttering the phrase 'No basic, more spivs' the crowd laughed and applauded.[2] The speech lent credence to those evaders who excused their behaviour by denying responsibility for their actions or appealing to higher loyalties. It was one of many post-war speeches made by politicians and businessmen that portrayed economic control as unnatural, unjust, and unnecessary, challenging the way the Labour government and its predecessors framed the issues of control and black marketing.

Sir Miles' speech points to the importance of politics in shaping the way individuals framed the issue of evasion once the war ended, but the newsreel reports of it alert us to the importance of the media in this process. In the British Paramount News item about the rally, the commentator summarized the speech for cinema audiences, describing Sir Miles as mentioning 'the unfairness to thousands of ex-soldiers who saved hard to buy a car, only to find now that they've got to lay it up

---

[1] Philip M. Williams, *Hugh Gaitskell: A Political Biography* (London, 1979), 185–7.
[2] 'No Basic More Spivs Cameraman Dope Sheet', *British Paramount News*, 23 October 1947, BUFVC, ID 040772, <http://bufvc.ac.uk/newsonscreen/search/index.php/story/40772>.

in the garage'. This chimed with the belief, fostered by the opposition, that the post-war Labour government had reneged on its moral obligation to reward wartime sacrifice with a peacetime dividend, prolonging control unnecessarily—one of the lines that the M-O panellists used to justify evasion. A short extract from the speech focusing on the black market issue followed, ending with Sir Miles' catchphrase, 'No basic, more spivs'. The message that control bred crime and that it, not the criminal, was to blame was another popular excuse with the panellists. No mention was made of the difficulties that Sir Miles thought this posed for mothers making the school run or going shopping, and no mention of his reassurance that the motoring lobby accepted the need for some petrol ration cuts. The report simplified Sir Miles' views, giving the impression that he did not consider evasion a crime. This was a hazard that public figures appreciated as they struggled to set the post-war political agenda and frame the items on it. But crime news and fiction had already exerted considerable influence over evasion before the resumption of party politics. The media's wartime focus on serious black market offences, which were often attributed to non-British elements, provided supporting evidence for the excuses made by the panellists and others.

CRIMINAL ELEMENTS

The language used to discuss non-compliance with the price and rationing regulations came from the news media. Prior to the war, journalists coined the expressions 'black market' and 'grey market' to refer to currency dealings conducted outside official channels, and in spring 1941 they also extended their meaning to include unofficial or illegal dealings in controlled goods. As spring gave way to summer, reporters and columnists ceased to discuss evasion in terms of 'profiteering' and 'hoarding'. These concepts of Great War vintage had dominated public discussion of non-compliance until that point. Once war broke out, cartoonists such as David Low resurrected the stock image of the rotund besuited profiteer sporting cigar and homburg hat.[3] Opinion polls and secret morale reports revealed that the public also saw the issue through the lens of profiteering, affecting individuals in unforeseen ways.[4] Muriel Green, who helped out at her family's Norfolk garage, worried that school friends would think she was married to a profiteer when the fat, middle-aged mechanic drove her to King's Lynn on a shopping trip.[5] Now 'black marketeering' entered vogue, suggesting kinship between the 'black marketeer' and the 'racketeer' of Prohibition-era America. This association encouraged journalists and their readers to think of the black market as an organized

---

[3] *Evening Standard*, 16 September and 14 October 1939.

[4] Gallup, *Opinion Polls*, i, 22–3; TNA: PRO, MEPO 2/3434, Home Office, 'Summary of Reports received from Chief Officers of Police and Regional Police Staff Officers', 29 October 1939, 26 October, and 9 November 1940.

[5] Muriel Green diary, 12 March 1940, in Dorothy Sheridan (ed.), *Wartime Women: An Anthology of Women's Wartime Writings for Mass-Observation 1937–45* (London, 1990), 86.

underworld. Britons were not alone in making this mental link, and Americans and Canadians imagined their black markets in similar fashion.[6]

Several journalists drew explicit parallels between bootleggers and black marketeers. Under the heading 'Rations and Racketeers' *The New Statesman* reported allegations of widespread black marketeering in London during spring 1941. Reviewing the food situation for the magazine a few months later, another writer commented on the growth in 'food bootlegging' and the emergence of 'food speakeasies' to feed the 'black market'.[7] Always careful to include some reference to the moral complicity of those who bought goods illegally, feature writers and columnists discussed black marketeers in greater detail. The suppliers' stories—especially those social outlaws who made a living through crime—were inherently more interesting than those of their respectable customers. The popularity of American gangster films and hardboiled detective fiction with British audiences exaggerated the effect. Here was a news story that twinned Sheffield terraces with New York tenements. British readers of Dashiell Hammett, Raymond Chandler, and others, or fans of James Cagney's and Edward G. Robinson's films could reimagine their cities as dangerous places populated by gangsters.[8]

News editors were quick to appreciate the romantic allure that the black marketeer had for their audiences, reinforcing the view that serious and organized criminals ran black markets. Crime was a staple topic of news at mid-century. Its role in the commercial success of the popular press—particularly mass-market tabloids such as the *Daily Mirror* and the *News of the World*—is well known. When the Royal Commission on the Press analysed the content of the nine London-based national daily newspapers in 1947, it found that the *Daily Mirror* carried the most crime reports, devoting 34% of its news space (minus advertisements, editorials, and features) to crime stories. Its nearest rival in terms of crime coverage, the *Daily Express*, devoted a mere 13% of its space to crime reports.[9] Potentially, papers like the *Express* or the *Mirror* could influence people's attitudes towards black market dealing greatly. This influence was eclipsed by mass-market Sunday papers such as the *News of the World*, which contained more crime reports and enjoyed a wider circulation than any daily newspaper.[10] As war altered the pattern of crime, black market offences came to dominate crime news, which continued to feature heavily in newspapers due to paper restrictions.

---

[6] Clinard, *Black Market*, 14; Jeff Keshen, 'One for All and All for One: Government Controls, Black Marketing and the Limits of Patriotism, 1939–47', *Journal of Canadian Studies*, 29 (1994), 111–43.

[7] 'Rations and Racketeers', *New Statesman and Nation*, 29 March 1941; Ritchie Calder, 'The Food Situation', *New Statesman and Nation*, 26 April 1941.

[8] Mark Roodhouse, 'In Racket Town: Gangster Chic in Austerity Britain, 1939–1953', *Historical Journal of Film, Radio and Teleision*, 31 (2011), 523–41.

[9] Report of the Royal Commission on the Press 1947–1949 (PP 1948–9 Cmd.7700 xx, 1), app. vii, table 9.

[10] Cyril Bainbridge and Roy Stockdill, *The News of the World Story: 150 Years of the World's Best-Selling Newspaper* (London, 1993); Jean Ritchie, *150 Years of True Crime Stories from the News of the World* (London, 1993); David Butler and Gareth Butler, *Twentieth Century British Political Facts 1900–2000* (Basingstoke, 2000), 538–9.

Editors of the popular press saw another opportunity to boost circulation figures in the black market story. By crusading against black marketeers and their wealthy customers, their papers proved themselves to be defenders of 'ordinary people' who could not afford to supplement their meagre food rations with black market goods nor avoid the strictures of rationing. From February 1941 onwards the black market provided regular exercise for the righteous indignation of *Daily Mirror* and *News Chronicle* writers. Bill Connor—better known as Cassandra in the *Daily Mirror*—was something of a pioneer in this regard. During the Blitz, Connor used his column to criticize racketeering and profiteering in food, which he considered selfish and unpatriotic, alongside his more familiar attacks on political and military leaders.[11] His personal campaign reached its apogee in a 'Gutskrieg' on wealthy individuals eating coupon-free in expensive restaurants.[12]

Coverage of individual black market crimes followed the conventions of crime-reporting. Journalists deemed a crime newsworthy if it was unusual, fitted into the press cycle, involved well-known people and places, occurred close to home, or marked crime reaching a significant level.[13] Editors gave more space to reports of serious crimes, crimes involving a high status offender or victim, or those involving whimsical, sentimental, or dramatic circumstances.[14] This led the nationals to focus on murder, robbery, and juvenile delinquency in their crime coverage.[15] By concentrating on serious violent crime and youth crime, the papers inverted the picture that emerged from official statistics, giving the impression that the incidence of particular crimes was greater than it was, and that the chances of being caught and punished were higher too.[16] BBC radio news bulletins shared press news values, often reporting the same crimes, but bulletin length meant that radio news covered crime stories in less detail. News readers reported the facts of a case to the exclusion of any analysis. While crime reporters made some attempt to contextualize crime, their focus was also on the individual incident. Rarely did the press feature articles about the causes of crime or its underlying patterns, preferring to editorialize about the moral state of the nation. These tendencies manifested themselves in coverage of evasion too.

Disproportionate newspaper coverage of serious offences fostered an impression of widespread, organized, and large-scale black market dealing. The organization of crime reporting, as well as news values, made this inevitable. Drawing on

---

[11] Cassandra, *The English at War* (London, 1941), 19–20.

[12] Hugh Cudlipp, *Publish and be Damned! The Astonishing Story of the Daily Mirror* (London, 1953), 148.

[13] Colin Seymour-Ure, *The British Press and Broadcasting since 1945* (2nd edn., Oxford, Blackwell, 1996), 148; Stanley Firmin, *Crime Man* (London, 1950); Percy Hoskins, *Street of Disillusion* (London, 1958); and William Veitch, 'The Reporter—II', in Kemsley Newspapers, *The Kemsley Manual of Journalism* (London, 1950), 232–3.

[14] Bob Roshier, 'The Selection of Crime News by the Press', in Stanley Cohen and Jock Young (eds.), *The Manufacture of News* (London, 1973), 40–51; Robert Reiner, 'Romantic Realism: Policing and the Media', in Frank Leishman, Barry Loveday, and Stephen P. Savage (eds.), *Core Issues in Policing* (2nd edn., London, 2000), 52–66.

[15] Steve Chibnall, *Law-and-Order News: an Analysis of Crime Reporting in the British Press* (London, 1977), 228–9.

[16] Reiner, 'Romantic Realism: Policing and the Media'.

contacts with police, lawyers, and criminals, crime correspondents focused on major police investigations and the resultant prosecutions, glossing court reports from agencies and staff as well as securing exclusives with those involved in a case.[17] As a trade, crime reporting centred on London, with journalists following Scotland Yard detectives to the provinces when local police requested the Yard's help. Setting aside a press room for members of the newly formed Crime Reporters' Association in 1945 cemented the already close relationship with Yard detectives.[18] No such relationship existed with ministry enforcement agencies, coverage of whose activities was left to others. When the *Daily Express* conducted a black market investigation in spring 1942, the editor directed the food, crime, and women's reporters to work together with a special correspondent to produce a comprehensive picture of the problem.[19] This was a unique and short-lived experiment, with the result that most major black market crime stories concerned the activities of known criminals—the type of offender whom the ministries left to the police.

When it came to reviewing the state of black market crime, the opinions of senior officers at the Yard weighed more heavily with crime reporters than those of ministry officials, the exception being a handful of seconded and retired detectives working for the ministries. After one of the Metropolitan Police's assistant commissioners remarked at a press briefing that black marketeering centred on three cities—naming Leeds and Liverpool, which he knew nothing of, having never served there, alongside London—the papers began to talk authoritatively about the 'L-triangle', much to the annoyance of the Leeds and Liverpool police.[20] This idea, touted with authority, had itself come from a report in the *Daily Mail* a month earlier.[21] It has also shaped recent historical discussion of black markets, much of which unwittingly recreates the crime reporter's view of evasion by focusing on celebrated cases of theft and coupon forgery, lavishly covered in the press and discussed in some detail in reporters' and detectives' memoirs.[22]

Wartime reporting of black market crime, which itself was influenced by interwar American crime fiction, fed British writers' imaginations. Like prohibition, economic control provided a rich subject for crime fiction. Reviewing *Black Market* by Bernard Newman—one of the first detective novels to base its plot around black market dealing—the critic Maurice Disher noted: 'There is plainly as much scope for crime investigation in the black market as there is in murder.'[23] The subsequent flurry of crime stories featuring black marketeers cooperating with Axis agents to sabotage the war effort or murdering people who knew too much about their operations proved him right.[24] The bestselling British crime

---

[17] George Scott, *Reporter Anonymous: The Story of the Press Association* (London, 1968), 158; Duncan Campbell, 'The Man in the Mac: A Life in Crime Reporting', *Guardian*, 5 September 2009.

[18] Scott, *Scotland Yard*, 83–5.   [19] *Daily Express*, 3 March 1942.

[20] *Evening Standard*, 4 January 1945.   [21] 'In Racket Town', *Daily Mail*, 6 December 1945.

[22] Robert Kee, *1945: The World We fought for* (Harmondsworth, 1995), 27; Thomas, *Underworld at War*, 154.

[23] 'Poison for the Painter', *Times Literary Supplement*, 16 January 1943.

[24] The attraction of black market crimes to writers working in both the classic and hardboiled traditions can be seen in Maurice Richardson's regular *Observer* column 'Crime Ration', which reviewed the latest crime fiction.

writers Peter Cheyney and John Creasy, busily anglicizing the American tough guy, recognized the narrative possibilities that evasion offered, setting their fictional creations on the trail of black market gangs.[25] In their efforts to update the classic English murder mystery, H. C. Bailey and others had their detectives solve black market murders.[26] These novels reached a wide audience as the reading public's appetite for crime fiction increased during the war—which took critics by surprise.[27] Black marketeers also appeared in literary fiction, with the war poet Alun Lewis and the novelist Elizabeth Bowen, amongst others, penning stories about them.[28]

The image of a violent, black market underworld was at its starkest in crime fiction aimed at children and young adults. Storylines in which detectives or children battled gangs who forged, smuggled, or stole controlled goods and coupons did not differ markedly from inter-war fictions about criminal masterminds and crime rings. John Hunter—a regular writer for *The Sexton Blake Library*—introduced the British detective to the wartime underworld in 'The Riddle of the Black Racketeers' (see Fig. 9.1), one to which Blake returned regularly, tangling with thieves, counterfeiters, and latterly spivs, in both his *Knockout* comic strip and the *Library* series.[29] His rivals Bulldog Drummond, Dick Barton, PC 49, and Harris Tweed did their bit to break the gangs too. Child protagonists also helped, with Enid Blyton's Famous Five and Richmal Crompton's William tackling vicious but witless crooks.[30]

Recast as a pantomime villain, the black marketeer surfaced in several British comedy films. The popular music hall characters Gert and Daisy exposed a black marketeer in *Gert and Daisy Clean Up* (1942), while their great rival Mother Riley helped police to catch a black market ring in *Old Mother Riley Detective* (1943) a year later. Other music hall performers poked fun at the black marketeer—notably the West Midlands comic Sid Field, whose fast-talking wide boy 'Slasher Green' auditions for 'an easy job in a new racket—the stage'.[31] It was the star turn in the 1943 revue *Strike A New Note*, one of the must-see West End shows during the war.[32] The character Slasher Green, rebranded as a spiv, featured in the musical *London Town* (1946), a Sid Field vehicle that flopped at the box office.

---

[25] Peter Cheyney, *You can Always Duck* (London, 1943); John Creasey, *The Toff Goes to Market* (London, 1942); Roland Daniel, *The Black Market* (London, 1943).

[26] H. C. Bailey, *Dead Man's Shoes* (London, 1942); Kathleen Hewitt, *Plenty Under the Counter* (London, 1943); H. C. Bailey, *Slippery Ann* (London, 1944).

[27] See Steve Chibnall, 'Pulp versus Penguins: Paperbacks go to War', and Stephen Knight, 'Murder in Wartime', in Pat Kirkham and David Thoms (eds.), *War Culture: Social Change and Changing Experience in World War Two Britain* (London, 1995), 131–49 and 161–71.

[28] See Alun Lewis, 'Night Journey', in Lewis., *In the Green Tree* (London, 1948), 69–75 written in 1942; and Elizabeth Bowen, 'Careless Talk', in Bowen. *The Collected Stories of Elizabeth Bowen* (London, 1980), 667–70 from 1941.

[29] John Hunter, *The Riddle of the Black Racketeers*, Sexton Blake Library, 3 (London, 1942), 28.

[30] Enid Blyton, *Five Go To Smuggler's Top* (London, 1945); Richmal Crompton, *Just William's Luck* (London, 1950).

[31] John Fisher, *What A Performance!* (London, 1975), 86.

[32] Raymond Mander and Joe Mitchenson, *Revue: a Story in Pictures* (London, 1971), 43.

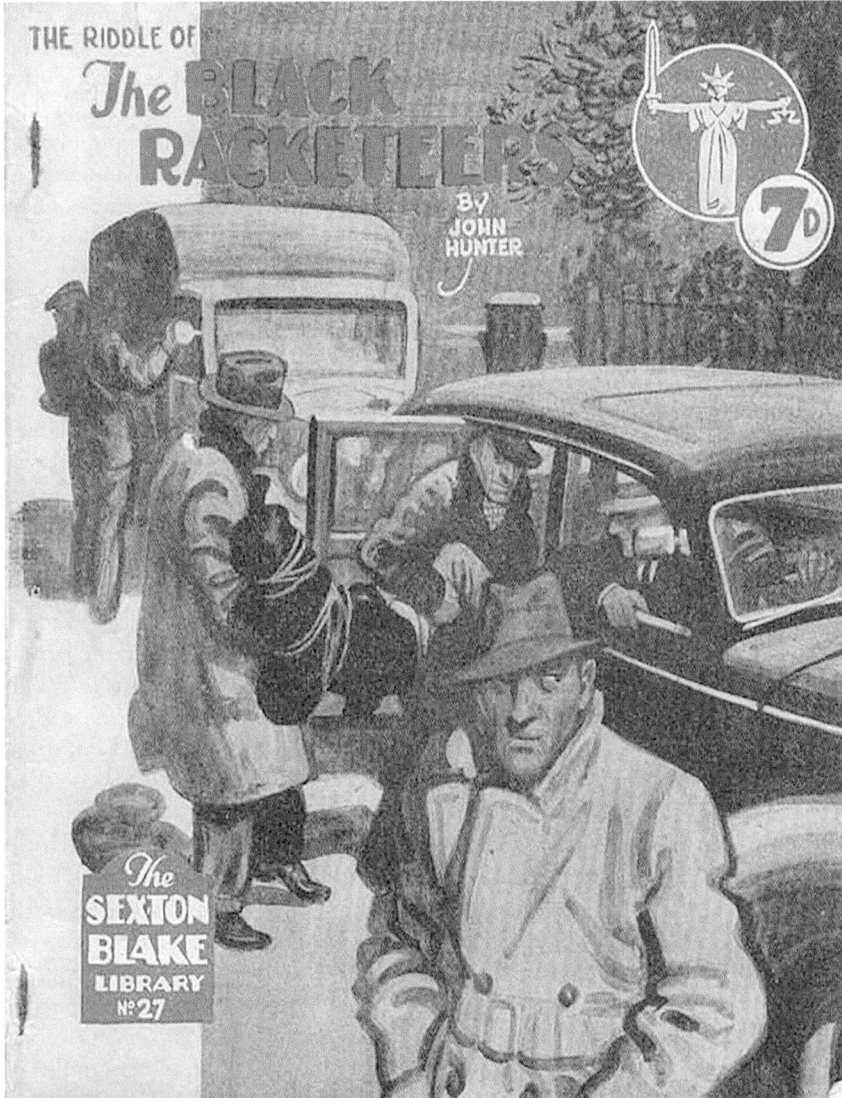

Fig. 9.1. Cover of *The Riddle of the Black Racketeers*, by John Hunter. © IPC Media 2010.

By equating black marketing with a criminal underworld, crime fiction and crime news encouraged people to distinguish between 'black' and 'grey' markets. This distinction was of great importance to people when excusing their fiddles. The image of the black marketeer led some M-O panellists to conclude that there was no black market dealing where they lived, as there was no evidence of a criminal underworld in their local area. There was no 'definitely criminal Black Market' in stolen goods and coupons, according to a Berkshire farmer's wife; but Londoners paying over the odds for her husband's old hens at auction was not connected to the black market in poultry.[33] Like many people, a female doctor assumed that the 'supply side of the business often involves criminal actions, since the goods often have to be stolen'. This allowed her to reframe the trade in coupons amongst members of the local Women's Institute as acceptable.[34] Respectable people like the doctor and the farmer's wife needed the black marketeer in order to maintain their self-image as respectable and law-abiding citizens. Media representations of evasion made this easier, providing them with evidence to support self-serving definitions.

Having established that a boss or syndicate controlled big black market operations, crime news and fiction suggested that the organizing genius was foreign in origin. This tendency was bolstered by official unwillingness to acknowledge the existence of organized crime. When faced with incontrovertible evidence of its reality, the authorities stressed the involvement of alien elements.[35] Press coverage of the 'Battle of Lewes' of 1936—one of a series of confrontations between London gangs struggling for control of on-course betting—fixed the image of organized crime as an Italian or Jewish affair.[36] This chimed with contemporary Hollywood portrayals of racketeers, the racetrack gangs' more glamorous Stateside counterparts, as Irish, Italian, or Jewish. Linking black marketeering to racketeering made the association between a foreign 'other' and organized crime both natural and inevitable. Of the two communities, Italians seemed more likely candidates for demonization due to their uncomplicated status as enemy aliens. The Italian mobster as enemy within appeared in some of the earliest crime novels about black markets, but internment, conscription, and imprisonment of Italian immigrants ensured that there was little on which to base these fictions.

The Jewish trader proved a more promising folk devil because of similarities between the images of the Jew and the black marketeer. According to Tony Kushner, the black marketeer was 'inevitably money-minded and unscrupulous in the way he made his fortune, corresponding neatly to the Shylock image', while the figure of the black marketeer recalled that of the First World War profiteer with its anti-Semitic overtones. Both the black marketeer and the Jew were seen as exerting a baleful and hidden influence on society.[37] Beliefs about Jewish criminality, rooted in the *fin de siècle* and represented in the figures of the prostitute and the trafficker, strengthened the association between Jews and the black market.[38] The pivotal role that small numbers of working-class Jews played in London's underground

[33] M-OA, DR January 1948, DR 12.   [34] DR 121.

[35] Philip Jenkins and Gary W. Potter, 'Before the Krays: Organized Crime in London, 1920–1960', *Criminal Justice History*, 9 (1988), 209–30; Heather Shore, 'Criminality and Englishness in the Aftermath: The Racecourse Wars of the 1920s', *Twentieth Century British History*, 22 (2011), 474–97.

[36] Murphy, *Smash and Grab*, 33–7.

[37] Tony Kushner, *The Persistence of Prejudice: Antisemitism in British Society during the Second World War* (Manchester, 1989), 119–20.

[38] Paul Knepper, 'British Jews and the Racialisation of Crime in the Age of Empire', *British Journal of Criminology*, 47 (2007), 61–79.

economy between the wars perpetuated these images as well as creating those of the long-firm fraudster and the spieler owner.[39]

Congruence between Jewish stereotypes and the figure of the black marketeer made Jews more likely scapegoats for evasion than Italians, but these were not the only reasons. There were more Jews, spread more widely, in Britain than there were Italians. Also, internment affected a smaller proportion of Jews than Italians. It is important to remember that the over-representation of Jews in food retailing and the rag trade—sectors subject to control—meant that the authorities prosecuted a disproportionate number of Jewish traders for black market offences given the community's size. Overpolicing of retailing at the expense of wholesaling and manufacturing exaggerated this effect, with the result that Jewish traders were three times more likely than non-Jewish traders to be prosecuted for deliberate offences than technical offences against price and rationing regulations. Jewish traders were also twice as likely as non-Jewish traders to be prosecuted for black market offences against the criminal law than technical offences.[40] Press coverage amplified these effects further. When covering a court case, crime reporters always included a defendant's name, address, and occupation to avoid actions for libel.[41] Using these facts, Jew-conscious readers surmised a defendant's ethnicity. It was common for a brief and formulaic report to include additional and unnecessary information, such as defendants' previous names if they had Anglicized them, their place of birth, or their nationality, to steer less sensitive readers towards a similar conclusion. 'Russian', 'alien', and 'refugee' were often code for Jew.[42] Another clue was to mention that defendants took the oath with their heads covered. The brevity of news bulletins did not prevent radio reports from including similar information.[43]

Concerned about biased coverage, the Jewish Trades Advisory Council monitored press reports. According to the council the national press covered forty of the 2,000 MoF prosecutions in May 1941. Half of the reported cases involved defendants with Jewish-sounding names, and 'These particular cases were given a prominence out of all proportion to their intrinsic news value.'[44] The findings prompted the council's statistical committee to investigate the problem in more detail. Using names to distinguish between Jew and gentile, the committee estimated the proportion of Jews whom the rationing ministries prosecuted between April 1942 and January 1944. This was compared to the proportion of black market cases involving Jews reported in a sample of newspapers and trade journals. It became apparent

[39] See Janson, *Jack Spot* for a fictionalized account of life of the East End Jewish gangster Jack 'Spot' Comer. See Samuel, *East End Underworld*, 128–31, on less well-known Jewish career criminals.

[40] LMA, ACC/3121/C13/3/7/37, 'Interim report of the Statistical Committee of the Trades Advisory Council', November 1944.

[41] Marjorie Jones, *Justice and Journalism: A Study of the Influence of Newspaper Reporting upon the Administration of Justice by Magistrates* (Chichester, 1974), 86.

[42] Andrew Sharf, *The British Press and Jews under Nazi Rule* (London, 1964), 179.

[43] Home News bulletin broadcast on the BBC Home Service 18:00hrs 19 June 1942; Board of Deputies of British Jews, C6/10/7/1 f2, S. Salomon to A. P. Ryan, 22 June 1942; LMA, ACC/3121/A031, Board of Deputies of British Jews minutes, 23 June 1942.

[44] LMA, ACC/3121/G4/1/1, Monthly Bulletin of the Trades Advisory Council, June 1941.

that a disproportionate number of cases reported in the national dailies and the trade press involved Jewish offenders. Of the four national papers studied, the *Daily Telegraph* and the *Daily Express* presented the most distorted view of Jewish involvement in evasion. The committee estimated that 11% of prosecutions for black market offences involved Jews during the study period, but reports in the *Telegraph* and *Express* gave the impression that the proportion was 25% and 29% respectively. When it came to trade journals, those for the textile and clothing trade gave the most distorted view, their reports doubling, and in the case of *The Outfitter* more than tripling, the actual prosecution rate of 11%.[45]

The effect of all this on crime news is best represented by the occasion in July 1942 when Lord Chief Justice Caldecote sentenced Sidney Seymour—one of ten London businessmen convicted of evading food regulations—to four years' penal servitude and fined him £2,000. This was national news, as Seymour received the heaviest sentence for a black market offence to date. Police and food inspectors investigating the ring found black market food stored in a shop storeroom that doubled as a synagogue on holy days, and in a Soho restaurant. The case, at the Old Bailey, revealed that Seymour supplied several Soho restaurants with black market food, including La Coquille and La Cigale, owned by Jean Alphonse Pages and patronized by Charles de Gaulle.[46] Reports stressed the foreign angle of the story. The *Daily Mirror* focused on the synagogue-cum-dump as well as the personal stories of Seymour, known to some as 'Skylinsky' and 'born in Russia', and Pages, a 'tall, good looking Frenchman'.[47] The Jewish Whitechapel side of the story received even more attention than the cosmopolitan Soho aspect. All the mass-market papers, with the exception of the Labour-supporting *Daily Herald*, which did not mention the synagogue, approached the story in this way. Only the *Manchester Guardian* failed to mention Seymour's name-change and place of birth.[48]

The *News Chronicle* and *Daily Express* placed most stress on Jewish involvement in the case. As well as emphasizing Seymour's Jewishness, the *News Chronicle* report dwelt on the 'small Jewish shopkeeper', 'a Jew by both blood and faith', who used the 'synagogue adjoining his shop' to store 'illicit foodstuffs'.[49] The *Express* carried the most tendentious account of the case, splashing its report across the front page with the headline 'Black Market Food hidden in Synagogue'.[50] The leader writer for the *Jewish Chronicle* thought that the article conveyed the impression 'to the multitude of the paper's readers that the Black Market was not merely the lucrative haunt of individuals but that it was an organized Jewish racket into which even the Synagogue itself had been drawn'.[51] Although most papers placed less stress on this than

[45] LMA, ACC/3121/C13/3/7/37, 'Interim report of the Statistical Committee of the Trades Advisory Council', November 1944.

[46] BL, BBC Sound Archive, LP44469 b02, Hugo Dunn-Meynell, 'The Five Bob Meal', BBC Radio 4, 23 September 1982.

[47] *Daily Mirror*, 11 July 1942.

[48] *Manchester Guardian*, 11 July 1942.

[49] *News Chronicle*, 11 July 1942.

[50] *Daily Express*, 11 July 1942.

[51] *Jewish Chronicle*, 17 July 1942.

the *Express* did, all included extraneous information identifying Jewish defendants—evidence that crime reporters believed that the defendants' Jewishness helped to explain their criminality. It was even rumoured that one press lord instructed his editors to play up Jewish involvement in black market cases.[52]

Crime news continued to link Jewish traders to black marketeering into the post-war years through the inclusion of odd bits of information in the shortest court reports that were so frequent that the Jewish Defence Committee did not have the resources to follow them up. If Jews featured in large black market cases, news reports, by stressing their Jewishness, implied that they were more likely to commit such crimes. Covering the trial of Henryk Malinowski and Marian Grondkowski for the murder of the 'stateless Russian' Reuben Martirosoff in November 1945, the *Daily Telegraph* crime reporter Stanley Firmin alleged that the two men killed Martirosoff, a Jewish gangster, in order to seize control of his rackets in diamonds, currency, and whisky. Harry Proctor—Firmin's rival at the *Daily Mail*—went further, including an interview 'with a handsome Jewess' who knew the victim. The story inspired at least one feature film.[53] The illegal currency dealings of 'Black' Max Intrator with wealthy British visitors to the Riveria in 1947, and the corrupt dealings of 'contacts man' Sidney Stanley with Labour ministers in 1948, followed a similar pattern.[54]

The image of the Jewish black marketeer, fostered by crime news, resonated with the public, influencing civilians' views of evasion and their illicit dealings. Nazi radio propaganda and British anti-Semites seized on crime reports, stressing Jewish responsibility for black marketeering.[55] Civilians did not need their encouragement to reach this conclusion. As early as July 1941, secret morale reports noted non-Jews blaming Jewish traders for black marketeering.[56] During the Blitz a few months earlier an East End air-raid warden's colleagues engaged in heated debate about the topic. One was adamant that the 'Yids' were behind the black market, while the other believed that this was a lie encouraged by the press.[57] Writing his diary in August 1941 during a break in talks about the future of Palestine, the diplomat Oliver Harvey noted: 'The Jews are their own worst enemy by their conduct in cornering foodstuffs.'[58] Hilda Neal, the owner of a London typing agency who took the *Daily Telegraph* and *Evening Standard* regularly, noted in a diary entry for April 1942 that 'The Black Market is still rampant, and every day there are prosecution cases, mostly against Jews'.[59] A month earlier Neal

[52] Keith Hutchinson, 'Everybody's Business: British Press Trusts', *The Nation*, 10 August 1946, 157.

[53] See *Daily Telegraph* and *Daily Mail* for 2 November 1945 and 14 February 1946. *Crime Reporter*, directed by Hal Wilson (Knightsbridge Films, 1947).

[54] Hughes, 'Spivs', 97–8; Mark Roodhouse, 'The Belcher Affair and Lynskey Tribunal', *Twentieth Century British History*, 13 (2002), 410–11.

[55] Alexander Ratcliffe, *The Truth about the Jews* (2nd edn., Glasgow, 1943); Joseph Goebbels diary, 6 March 1942, in Elke Fröhlich (ed.), *Die Tagebücher von Joseph Goebbels: Diktate 1941–1945*, 15 vols. (Munich, 1994), iii, 423; Willia A. Boelcke (ed.), *The Secret Conferences of Dr Goebbels, October 1939–March 1943*, trans. Ewald Osers (London, 1967), 220.

[56] TNA: PRO, INF 1/292 Pt. 1, Home Intel. weekly report No. 42, 16–23 July 1941.

[57] Barbara Nixon, *Raiders Overhead: A Diary of the London Blitz* (London, 1943), 89.

[58] Oliver Harvey diary, 7 August 1941, in John Harvey (ed.), *The War Diaries of Oliver Harvey* (London, 1978), 28.

[59] IWM, Dept. of Doc., PP/MCR/59, Hilda Neal diary, 30 April 1942.

cited court reports as evidence of Jews as the principal buyers and sellers of black market goods.[60] Several M-O panellists revealed their anti-Semitic prejudices when discussing black markets. A Yorkshire woman thought that Leeds must be the regional centre of illegal dealing because of 'its large Jewish community', disregarding its role as a centre for the wool industry.[61] A telephone engineer thought it remarkable that a local butcher, heavily involved in illicit markets, his associates, and his customers were not Jews.[62] Both panellists admitted minor fiddles. Another panellist—an electrician who had 'no scruples about where things come from really'—preferred to starve than buy black market food from 'a fat cigar-smoking Jew'.[63]

The press also devoted a surprising number of column inches to reports of cases involving public figures, such as the conviction of Major General Sir Percy Laurie, the Army's Provost Marshall, for ration-book fraud.[64] Readers learned about the misdeeds of aristocrats such as Lord Donegall, the Countess of Mayo, Sir Hamilton Westrow, Lady Elizabeth Clyde, and the daughter of the Duke of Bedford, all convicted of black market offences.[65] They could take pleasure in the misfortunes of celebrities who fell foul of the regulations. The conviction of Noël Coward, Victor Silvester, Jack Hyam, and Ivor Novello received extensive coverage.[66] Despite most prosecutions resulting in a conviction, news reports fed the belief that the wealthy evaded the regulations with impunity. Readers and listeners considered the sentences imposed unduly lenient. When in 1943 Lady Astor was found guilty of attempting to smuggle clothes into Britain from the United States, Home Intelligence noted that her prosecution had caused 'some sarcastic comment'.

> Her defence that she did not know she was committing a breech of the Regulations is ridiculed, and there was 'rather unholy glee over the magistrate's comments on her ignorance'. People say 'if this is the case she had no right to be in Parliament', and that 'if she had been an ordinary person she would have been treated much more harshly'.[67]

Assiduous reporting of a handful of corruption scandals touching on the administration of controls compounded the impression that politicians feasted in private whilst fasting in public.[68] Home Intelligence found this a common reaction to the news that a Tribunal of Inquiry was to look into rumours of corruption in Newcastle's fire, police, and civil defence services.[69] The 1947 corruption scandal involving the Brighton Food Control Committee provided yet more evidence for hypocrisy amongst politicians and administrators, as did the Lynskey Tribunal a

---

[60] Hilda Neal diary, 3 March 1942.   [61] M-OA, DR January 1948, DR 49.

[62] DR 174.   [63] DR 263.

[64] HC deb, vol. 386, 2 February 1943, col. 737; *The Times*, 30 March, 19 May, and 7 July 1943.

[65] Hughes, 'Spivs', 97.

[66] Philip Hoare, *Noël Coward* (London, 1995), 330–1; Paul Webb, *Ivor Novello* (London, 1999), 124–9.

[67] TNA: PRO, INF 1/292 pt. 3, Home Intel. weekly report No. 148, 27 July–3 August 1943. See *Evening Standard*, 30 July 1943; and Anthony Masters, *Nancy Astor* (London, 1981), 211, for more details of the case.

[68] *The Times*, 29 August 1942.

[69] TNA: PRO, INF 1/292 pt.4, Home Intel. weekly report No. 176, 8–15 February 1944; No. 179, 29 February–7 March 1944; No. 180, 7–14 March 1944; No. 181, 14–21 March 1944; and No. 188, 2–9 May 1944.

year later, which revealed that government ministers were happy to buy suits without surrendering clothing coupons.[70] Cynicism greeted these post-war scandals. In her diary a Sheffield housewife tired of exhaustive coverage of the Lynskey Tribunal proceedings wrote: 'We all know bribery and corruption goes on all the time, and when some break the Eleventh Commandment [thou shalt not get caught], punish them by all means, but don't go so haywire.'[71] Ministers appreciated the damage such allegations could cause, ensuring that due process took place while downplaying the seriousness of the offences involved. The strategy worked when the Director of Public Prosecutions instituted proceedings against a Labour minister, two Conservative MPs, and an admiral for coupon-free purchases of grain in 1942.[72] It did, however, leave suspicious newspaper editors with the impression of a cover-up.[73]

There were no official crime figures nor independent research to temper tendentious press coverage of black market crime during the war—a critical period in the definition of the problem. There was no news to challenge the image of gangsters dominating black market supply, nor to remind civilians of their moral complicity with suppliers. The public could, and did, dismiss official attempts to challenge the image, such as the MoF 'Black Sheep—Black Markets' campaign or the MoI *Partners in Crime* film, as propaganda. Attempts by the BBC to educate public opinion through the radio plays *Black Market* and *Rats* faced the same problem despite reaching 4 million and 4.3 million listeners respectively.[74] Judging by the sporadic coverage that monthly MoF enforcement data received, crime figures would have made little impact even if they had been available.[75] When in June 1944 the Metropolitan Police published its annual report for 1943—the first published annual report for four years—press coverage concentrated on the Metropolitan Police's efforts to close unlicensed West End nightclubs and deal with rising car-theft. No mention was made of the overall drop in crime, nor the changing pattern of crime in wartime.[76]

While attempts to educate public opinion failed to change the black market–underworld equation, propaganda and foreign news coverage led to exculpatory comparisons with Britain's continental neighbours. Allied pamphlets about conditions in occupied Europe gave the impression that black markets posed a bigger problem to the Axis powers than did the Allies, while foreign news coverage stressed

---

[70] 'The Brighton Food Office Inquiry', *News-sheet of the Bribery and Secret Commissions Prevention League*, October 1948; TNA: PRO, MAF 150/661, 'Report of enquiry into allegations of inefficiency, mal-practice, bribery and corruption among officials', 1948; Roodhouse, 'Belcher Affair'.

[71] M-OA, Diaries, November 1948, D 5474.

[72] TNA: PRO, CAB 65/27/9, WM (42) 93, 21 July 1942.

[73] King diary, 27 October 1944, in King, *With Malice toward None*, 276–7.

[74] BBC WAC, R19/92 C63, 'Black Market: The Story from the Documents', Home Service, 20:00 hrs, 7 October 1941; BBC WAC, Play Scripts, 'Rats', Home Service, 19:30 hrs, 16 April 1942; Vol. 5, General Listening Barometer—Week 41, 7 October 1941; Vol. 6, 'General Listening Barometer—Week 16', 16 April 1942.

[75] *The Times*, 31 January 1941.

[76] *The Times*, 28 June 1944; *Daily Mirror*, 28 June 1944; Report of the Commissioner of Police of the Metropolis for 1943 (PP 1943–4 Cmd.6536 iv, 507).

that black marketeering was rife overseas, even in British Malta.[77] Some of the earliest references to black markets in controlled goods, as opposed to currency, occurred in reports about life under the Nazis.[78] Relying upon information from the Ministry of Economic Warfare, the *Manchester Guardian* reported that the situation in France was dire, with black marketeers posing as food inspectors to obtain dead civilians' ration cards from their relatives.[79] Drawing on reports from neutral correspondents, *The Times* informed its readers that inadequate food rations left those Italians and Germans, without the means to buy food on thriving black markets, hungry.[80] Advantageous comparisons of British black markets with those of Continental Europe increased in number in the wake of the Allied invasions of Italy and France. In their dispatches from the Netherlands, BBC war correspondents chose to comment extensively on evasion.[81] At the same time, in overseas broadcasts BBC presenters downplayed the extent of domestic black marketeering.[82] Flattering comparisons with conditions in Continental Europe belittled fiddling and wangling. It also fed the belief that the British were a law-abiding people who had a greater degree of self-control than other peoples—a characteristic which meant that the British Bobby need not carry arms.

CONDEMNING CONTROL

With the resumption of party politics in 1945, public understanding of economic control and black markets changed dramatically. Arguments about the timing and extent of decontrol eroded the moral consensus that black markets were a bad thing in which others, especially foreign others, were involved. The main parties accepted the need for economic control in wartime and during the post-war transition. That evasion was an unmitigated evil was the corollary of this cross-party agreement. By retaining Conservative control of the rationing ministries in the coalition government, Churchill allayed Liberal and Conservative fears of 'war communism', thus preventing control from becoming a source of political controversy. When coalition politics forced him to give the Labour politician Hugh Dalton control of the Board of Trade in 1942, Conservative backbench opposition restricted Dalton's freedom of manoeuvre. Only the Communist Party of Great Britain (CPGB), which was not part of the coalition government, exploited control and black markets for political advantage. By rebutting allegations that black marketeering was a Jewish problem and calling on the authorities through public

---

[77] The Inter-Allied Information Committee, *Rationing under Axis Rule*, Conditions in Occupied Territories, 2 (London, 1942); BL, BBC Sound Archive, T5889, Queenie Lee, 'Life in Malta', 29 June 1943.

[78] 'German "Black Markets"', *Manchester Guardian*, 14 November 1940.

[79] *Manchester Guardian*, 8 May 1941.

[80] *The Times*, 19 May 1942.

[81] BL, BBC Sound Archive, 11546, 'Robert Dunnett despatch', 15 May 1945 and 'Matthew Halton despatch', 19 May 1945.

[82] W. J. West (ed.), *Orwell: The War Broadcasts* (London, 1985), 71–6.

meetings and deputations to enforce the regulations rigorously, the CPGB hoped to increase its electoral support in east London.[83]

The future of control became a defining issue in post-war politics. Both Conservatives and Liberals had supported control as a temporary measure to be removed as soon as economic conditions allowed. Rationing and price control were anathema to both parties. As premier, Churchill had accepted grumpily the need for economic control, privately resisting the imposition of new regulations during the war and urging ministers to ease restrictions early in 1945. Churchill and his Tory colleagues disliked the costly bureaucracy involved—especially the enforcement apparatus—and the restrictions control placed on individual choice. The resumption of party politics freed them to press ahead with dismantling the system. Under Churchill's leadership the caretaker government, formed after the wartime coalition's collapse, put this policy into action, relaxing regulations as the supply situation improved. By comparison, the Labour position on control lacked conviction. Publicly, Labour policy at the 1945 general election resembled that of its opponents, the aim being to float off control on a rising tide of supplies. The party distinguished its cautious pragmatic approach to decontrol in which the interests of working people came first from its opponents' hasty ideologically driven one. In his first election broadcast during the 1945 campaign, Churchill challenged this characterization of party difference, suggesting that Labour was ideologically committed to control for control's sake, and using this as an example of the threat that a Socialist government posed to individual liberty.[84] This was also the message in the election guide for Conservative party workers and speakers.[85]

Of limited significance at the polls in 1945, control assumed greater importance from 1946 onwards. Debates within the Labour government about retaining some regulations permanently, as well as the tightening and extension of control in some areas, led voters to see government policy as contradictory, ideologically driven, and unnecessary. Conservative rhetoric pushed swing voters towards this view. By 1947, Conservative Central Office had rationalized the party's instinctive opposition to control, building an intellectually coherent and persuasive case for bringing price control and rationing to a rapid end. The message played well in east London, where voters disliked black markets but no longer agreed with the CPGB that the solution was tighter control. The Chairman of the Mile End Conservative Association attracted a large and appreciative audience to an open-air meeting by attacking control. Engaging in hyperbole, he told them how there were 'more criminals to the thousand now than at any time in our history', many of whom were otherwise law-abiding respectable people. All 'sorts of people in all walks of life' were 'brought before the courts for all manner of offences which never before were considered as such'.[86]

---

[83] *East London Advertiser*, 23 January 1943; Henry Srebrnik, *London Jews and British Communism, 1935–1945* (Ilford, 1995), 66–8.

[84] Charles Eade (ed.), *The War Speeches of Winston S. Churchill*, 3 vols. (2nd edn., London, 1964), iii, 478–9.

[85] Conservative Central Office, *General Election 1945: Notes for Speakers and Workers* (London, 1945), 19.

[86] *East London Advertiser*, 13 June 1947.

The attack on controls as criminogenic gathered strength from autumn 1947 as the Labour government tightened regulations and tried to prevent rationed goods leaking into black markets. Viscount Hinchingbrooke laid out the Conservative case at the start of the parliamentary session.[87] Official investigations of corruption in the Brighton Food Office, the meat black market, and the petrol black market strengthened it further as they fed the impression of rampant evasion and corruption, providing further evidence and encouragement for Conservative attacks. The government kept two of the reports secret, which suggested that their contents were explosive. When set alongside newly released figures showing a post-war surge in recorded crime, the argument that controls bred crime seemed unanswerable. The investigation of alleged corruption at the BoT as the year ended justified this idea. With an election looming, Conservative Central Office issued a *Weekend Talking Point* encouraging party members to use the scandal to attack control.

> The vital issue involved is that a method of elaborate controls fosters irregularities and evasions of this type. It is the multiplicity of controls, which makes observance of little account to the unscrupulous. Their complexity tends to diminish respect for law and imposes a needless strain on the ordinary citizen and on government officials. Such evasion may bring into disrepute what Mr Churchill called, at the setting up of the Tribunal, 'the honour and reputation of the system by which we carry on Government,' in precisely the same way as prohibition in the USA encouraged law-breaking and bred a gangster society.[88]

The *Talking Point* likened control to prohibition—a powerful argument given the popular association of black marketeering with racketeering—and informed the section on 'Political Controls and Public Standards' in the 1950 general election campaign guide.[89] The Labour government recognized how persuasive the Tory case was, shelving plans for amending the Prevention of Corruption Act so they did not give their critics further ammunition.[90]

The Conservative message chimed with the views of a network of allied interest groups that formed a loose anti-Socialist coalition, which included the basic petrol campaign organized by the motoring lobby. When parliament discussed the results of the corruption investigation, Churchill echoed the campaign's slogan 'No basic, more spivs', arguing that 'If you destroy a free market, you create a black market. If you make 10,000 regulations, you destroy all respect for the law.'[91] Due to the efforts of the British Housewives' League during the austerity debates of 1946 and 1947, Churchill's rhetoric resonated with middle-class women. The League—a militant consumer organization at the outermost fringes of the Conservative's partisan network—organized resistance to unnecessary controls which it perceived as

[87] HC deb, vol. 443, 23 October 1947, cols. 303–4.

[88] Bodleian Library, Oxford, Conservative Party Archive, PUB 216/1, 'Weekend Talking Point', 5 February 1949.

[89] Conservative Central Office, *General Election 1950: The Campaign Guide* (London, 1949), 651–62.

[90] TNA: PRO, CAB 195/8, 'Cabinet Secretary's notebook', 23 November 1950.

[91] HC deb, vol. 460, 3 February 1949, col. 1862.

a totalitarian threat.[92] For the league's leadership, controls were un-British and the ministry inspectorates a form of Gestapo.[93] Cases of prosecutions for 'perfectly reasonable' transactions angered contributors to the league's newsletter, reinforcing their belief in ration book tyranny. In the circumstances, evasion was a patriotic duty. When the government made it illegal to lend or give coal to another person, the Merseyside branch organized a barter system for members. According to the League newsletter, 'The Ladies subscribe to the idea that what they have bought, they own. Short of waste or destruction, they maintain the right to dispose of their own possessions in accordance with their own wishes.'[94] Like the League, the Women's Institute, the Townswomen's Guild, and the Mothers' Union lobbied government for the relaxation and removal of unnecessary controls, but did so in a non-confrontational way. Avowedly non-partisan, these three women's organizations formed part of a Conservative network due to the social characteristics of their membership, serving as informal conduits for Conservative ideas about control.[95]

The business interest groups and large corporations that formed an important part of the Conservatives' partisan network made similar points throughout the late 1940s. Business leaders criticized control at company meetings and industry gatherings in the knowledge that economic correspondents, many of whom were hostile to Labour economic policy, would report their remarks. Bakers were some of the government's most vehement opponents after the surprise introduction of bread rationing in 1946.[96] Of those industries already subject to rationing, the meat and clothing trades proved the most vociferous in their calls for decontrol.[97] The business lobby also exploited official committees to publicize their ideas. When called to give evidence to the Millard Tucker Committee on taxation of trading profits, business interests urged the committee to recommend that fines and penalties for contravening regulations become tax-deductible. 'They pointed out that in modern conditions the mass of legislation is such that owners of businesses find it difficult to avoid committing technical breaches of the law.'[98] Witnesses such as the Federation of British Industry who wanted to preserve influence and avoid appearing partisan supported the organizations Aims of Industry and the Economic League in their campaigns against control.[99]

---

[92] James Hinton, 'Militant Housewives: the British Housewives' League and the Attlee Government', *History Workshop Journal*, 38 (1994), 128–56.

[93] 'A Food Ministry Raid', *British Housewives' League Newsletter*, August 1946.

[94] 'A Challenge', *British Housewives' League Newsletter*, April 1947.

[95] Mary Stott, *Organization Woman: The Story of the National Union of Townswomen's Guild* (London, 1978); Maggie Andrews, *The Acceptable Face of Feminism: The Women's Institute as a Social Movement* (London, 1997); Cordelia Moyse, *A History of the Mothers' Union: Women, Anglicanism and Globalisation, 1876–2008* (Woodbridge, 2009); Stacey, *Tradition and Change*; James Hinton, *Women, Social Leadership, and the Second World War: Continuities of Class* (Oxford, 2002).

[96] Ina Zweiniger-Bargielowska, 'Bread Rationing in Britain, July 1946–July 1948', *Twentieth Century British History*, 4 (1993), 57–85.

[97] *The Times*, 14 December 1948.

[98] Report of the Committee on the Taxation of Trading Profits (PP 1950–1 Cmd.8189, xx, 1).

[99] See Stephen Blank, *Industry and Government in Britain: The Federation of British Industries in Politics, 1945–65* (Farnborough, 1973).

In building a case against control the Conservative party drew on the arguments of public moralists. Increasing dishonesty associated with black marketeering was a common lament of religious leaders from 1941 onwards. In 1943, when reviewing the effects of war on the nation's morals, Archbishop Temple, speaking at Lambeth Palace, ranked dishonesty alongside sexual immorality as the biggest threats to morality, returning to the issue several times.[100] A year earlier Chief Rabbi Hertz had drawn attention to dishonesty when urging Jewish traders to maintain the highest standards of commercial morality.[101] Religious figures continued to express concern about the issue throughout the decade, but it came to the fore once again when the Archbishop of York launched an Honesty Campaign in autumn 1948. A popular and respected member of the House of Lords, Archbishop Garbett received support from senior Conservative politicans when he used his position in the Lords to launch his campaign.[102] His analysis was simple: the increase in crime was the direct result of declining religious observance.[103] When his first campaign showed few results, he mounted a second in 1951.[104] The Quaker Seebohm Rowntree devoted a chapter to the issue in his 1951 survey *English Life and Leisure*, noting that 'there is abundant evidence that a great many individuals, actuated by a desire to obtain goods or services without giving anything in exchange, are dishonest in many small ways'. Like Archbishop Garbett, Rowntree believed that lack of belief meant that people succumbed to temptation.[105]

The public comments of senior criminal-justice professionals bolstered the Conservative case. Like religious leaders, senior police officers, magistrates, and judges began to express concern about the effects of control during the war. With peace, their worries about the effects of unenforceable and now indefensible regulations strengthened. Successive Metropolitan Police Commissioners' concerns about black market crime received widespread coverage and occasioned much comment in Conservative newspapers. The same papers also reported similar opinions amongst legal professionals—especially the magistracy. Dominated by Tory appointees, the magistracy was drawn into the Conservatives' partisan web. The affiliation with the Tory party was strengthened by the appointment of the Conservative peer Lord Templewood as Chairman of the Magistrates' Association in 1947. Templewood used his position to promote the view, shared by many on the bench, that controls undermined respect for the law. In public Templewood linked evasion by adults to juvenile delinquency, and made common cause with Archbishop Garbett in autumn 1948.[106] Lord Chief Justice Rayner Goddard was more circumspect in his criticism, though his views about the pernicious effects

[100] *Manchester Guardian*, 24 April 1943.
[101] LMA, ACC/2805/6/1/179, Dr J. H. Hertz, 'Passover Letter', 19 March 1942.
[102] Charles Smyth, *Cyril Forster Garbett, Archbishop of York* (London, 1959), 433–9.
[103] Borthwick Institute of Historical Research, University of York, Bp C & P XIV/1, ' "Startling" Increase in Crime', 1 November 1948.
[104] York Minster Library, COLL 1973/1 Garbett J/6, 'The Increase in Crime', n.d. (1951).
[105] Rowntree and Lavers, *English Life and Leisure*, 226; Borthwick Inst., Rowntree Papers, LTE/11, 'Note on dishonesty', n.d.
[106] *Manchester Guardian*, 23 October 1948.

of control on public respect for the law were well known before he expressed them publicly in 1951.

The Conservative case against control, made by formal party organizations as well as groups and individuals who formed part of a loosely partisan network, echoed the points that M-O panellists and others made to justify evading the regulations. The post-war austerity debates made economic control and black markets subjects of political controversy. By contesting the official image of evasion, the Conservative party and its allies made it easier for evaders to disguise self-interested actions as principled acts of resistance. Control was unnecessary, unnatural, and unjust—a temporary wartime measure to be dispensed with as soon as economic conditions allowed. To underline this point, Conservatives pointed to the faster pace at which Allied governments relaxed and removed economic control—a process widely reported in the British press. Tory critics seized upon the fact that British control continued after former Axis countries removed theirs.[107] The Labour government did not counter such arguments by citing the inflationary consequences that rapid decontrol had in many of these countries.

MEET THE SPIV

The effect of the austerity debates on public understanding of evasion, which made evasion easier to countenance, is seen clearly in the Janus-faced figure of the 'spiv'—a penny capitalist flogging goods of unknown origin to a public hungry for controlled goods, who first came to widespread attention in autumn 1945. Throughout the late 1940s, gossip columnists recorded the antics of spivs with improbable names such as The Boy, Greeny, and Mac, alongside those of members of London society. The sudden rise to social prominence of the spiv prompted readers of the *Daily Telegraph* to debate the etymology of 'spiv' in the letters column.[108] The word had a meteoric linguistic career, moving from criminal cant to low slang to popular slang, displacing the term 'wide boy' by the end of 1946. The public readily accepted the word, as it was a handy label for the increasingly visible ranks of petty black marketeers.

Attitudes towards the spiv, however, were ambiguous, unlike those towards the black marketeer, reflecting shifting attitudes towards evasion. The black marketeer had no redeeming features, while the spiv secured the sneaking respect of a post-war public tired of constraints on personal consumption. In the austerity debates, politicians appropriated the spiv, casting him as a folk devil.[109] The Labour government used the term to castigate black marketeers and their customers whilst attempting to bolster support for tightening austerity in the wake of the 1947 balance of payments crisis.[110] In the eyes of their Conservative opponents the spiv represented

---

[107] *The Times*, 30 January 1950.

[108] See *Daily Telegraph* for 24, 29, 30 July, and 1 August 1947.

[109] 'What is a Spiv?', *Socialist Standard*, October 1947.

[110] Crofts, *Coercion or Persuasion?*, 45–7; Jim Tomlinson, *Democratic Socialism and Economic Policy: the Attlee Years 1945–1951* (Cambridge, 1997), 177–8.

the moral turpitude brought about by excessive economic control. Otherwise respectable people were 'forced' to evade 'unnecessary' regulations, bringing them into contact with spivs and undermining their respect for the law. The only way to restore support for the law and purge British society of spivvish tendencies was to remove direct controls.

The author and playwright Bill Naughton was responsible for alerting the British public to the spiv's existence. Before the war the spiv was linked to race-going and gambling in south-east England and the Midlands. In racing parlance a spiv was someone with no obvious means of support who made his living on the fringes of London's underworld.[111] This changed when the *News Chronicle* published Naughton's article 'Meet the Spiv' in September 1945. Although Peter Cheyney had introduced the public to 'Willie the Spiv' and other black marketeers in a series of articles for the *Sunday Dispatch* in June 1944, the crime writer's account of Willie's dealings did not capture the public imagination.[112] As a result, the editor of the *News Chronicle* felt it necessary to introduce readers to this unfamiliar character.

> Londoners and other city dwellers will recognise him, so will many city magistrates—the slick, flashy, nimble-witted tough, talking sharp slang from the corner of his mouth. He is a sinister by-product of big-city civilisation—counterpart to the zoot-suited youths of America.[113]

The newspaper article reported a conversation between a south London lorry driver and Naughton, the driver's mate. The driver vividly described the spiv's style of dress, mannerisms, language, and attitudes.

> 'Coo, he's a proper little Spiv', said my driver mate. We were unloading our vans at a depot in Bermondsey. 'See his Spivy coat—the width of the lapels, the padded-out shoulders and how it is curled round his backside? See his shirt with the little tight collar? And the big knot in his tie? (There's a dodgy way of doing that: you take the right-hand length over three times instead of twice when you're tying the knot.)
>
> 'Notice how his hair is parted in the middle, and the wave at either side? And how it was long at the back, with the four-noughts clippers brought up to meet it? Regular Spivy touch is that; not one barber in ten knows it.
>
> 'See the style he held his cig.? And the way he spoke out the corner of his mouth? Did you hear him going on about "bleeding red tape", "bleeding malarkey on the job", and how he's not going to be "turked around" by any guv'nor? Spivs, they always talk like that. It's because they feel that way, I should know, I'm one myself.'[114]

According to Naughton's narrator there was even a spiv walk:

> 'You stiffen the shoulders, and lift them a drop. And walk knowing you are walking. Fancy little style it is, and there's no other walk just like it. It's a mixture of pug and pansy.'[115]

---

[111] The Earl of Rosebery, 'Letter to the Editor', *Daily Telegraph*, 29 July 1947.
[112] *Sunday Dispatch*, 25 June, 2, 9, 16, and 23 July 1944.
[113] Bill Naughton, 'Meet the Spiv', *News Chronicle*, 13 September 1945.
[114] *News Chronicle*, 13 September 1945.
[115] *News Chronicle*, 13 September 1945.

Although he might be dressed by a Jewish tailor, Naughton's spiv was not Jewish. He liked to wear up-to-the-minute suits and jewellery, and he frequented pubs, night-clubs, dance-halls, races, and boxing matches. Although he might temporarily take a waged job, he preferred to be self-employed. According to the narrator, 'This nicking of loaded lorries: whisky, tobacco, butter and handy-selling cargoes like that—it's right up a Spiv's street.' Spivs were mainly single and in their twenties and thirties, retiring before they turned forty to take employment as a bookie's runner, a market help, or a barrow boy.

The *News Chronicle* article launched the spiv on his meteoric post-war career. Within a week of the article's publication, editors were taking Naughton out for meals and asking him for more articles and stories about spivs.[116] The spiv, as described by Naughton, was instantly recognizable. The term gave a name to the group of young working-class men who hawked and peddled coupons and controlled goods in city streets. According to Sir Ernest Gowers, author of the style guide *Plain Words*, it was a classic example of how slang words can sometimes 'gatecrash irresistibly because their sound is so appropriate to the meaning they are trying to acquire' and fill a 'vacant place' in the language.[117] The spiv captured the post-war flourishing of a metropolitan penny capitalist culture of sharply dressed working-class wide-boys that had long fascinated social investigators.[118] This was what Naughton intended. His article was a shorter version of his essay 'The Spiv', published by the sociologist Charles Madge in the first issue of his short-lived journal *Pilot Papers*.[119] Madge, who suggested the topic, called it a 'documentary account'.[120] It resembled the vignettes of London life that Naughton wrote for the London *Evening News* and had much in common with Henry Mayhew's and Charles Booth's portraits of street traders.[121]

When Naughton proved incapable of slaking the press thirst for the spiv—only returning to the topic with a short story about a spiv in 1947—editors encouraged their own staff to do so.[122] Cartoonists latched onto Naughton's careful description of spiv style—none more so than the *Daily Express* cartoonist Osbert Lancaster, who 'pinned' the spiv down 'like a butterfly' (see Fig. 9.2).[123] In Lancaster's hands the American Look, described by Naughton and pushed to demobbed servicemen and young men by working-class tailors such as Cecil Gee, with its double-breasted full drape lounge suit, pleated trousers with deep turn-ups, colourful shirts, handpainted kipper ties, trilby hat, and two-tone shoes became the spiv's uniform.[124]

[116] Bill Naughton, *On the Pig's Back: An Autobiographical Excursion* (Oxford, 1987), 49.
[117] Sir Ernest Gowers, *Plain Words: A Guide to the Use of English* (London, 1948), 26–7.
[118] Eric Partridge, 'Spivs and Phoneys', *Lilliput Magazine*, October 1947.
[119] Bill Naughton, 'The Spiv', *Pilot Papers*, 1 (1945), 99–108.
[120] Naughton, *Pig's Back*, 48.
[121] Charles Madge, 'Editorial', *Pilot Papers*, 1 (1945), 5–6.
[122] Bill Naughton, 'Spiv in Love', *Lilliput Magazine*, August 1947.
[123] Hughes, 'Spivs', 87.
[124] Francis Wyndham, 'Gee, but its great to be Gee!', *Sunday Times Magazine*, 19 January 1969; Nik Cohn, *Today there are no Gentlemen: the Changes in Englishmen's Clothes since the War* (London, 1971), 16–21.

'*Don't be so stuffy, Henry! I'm sure that if you asked him nicely the young man would be only too pleased to give you the name of a really* GOOD *tailor who doesn't worry about coupons!*'

Fig. 9.2. Osbert Lancaster pocket cartoon, *Daily Express*, 24 June 1947. © John Murray (Publishers) Ltd.

A slicked-back 'wave cut' with a rounded 'Boston neckline', a pencil thin moustache, and a cigarette drooping from the corner of his mouth completed the spiv.[125]

Although cartoonists helped people to spot a spiv in his urban habitat, columnists explained his behaviour and appearance. The most influential of these guides

---

[125] James Stevens Cox, *An Illustrated Dictionary of Hairdressing and Wigmaking* (2nd edn., London, 1989), 32.

to spiv behaviour was Arthur Helliwell. His weekly 'Follow Me Around' column for *The People* chronicled the lives of the 'Boys'. On his return from wartime service in South East Asia, Helliwell was struck by changes in British society. For him, the post-war streets of London's Soho with their throngs of spivs were as exotic as anything he had seen in Malaya. His vivid descriptions of the doings of flashily clothed Soho spivs with laughable nicknames were a 'must read' for the 5 million people who took *The People* every Sunday. His editor, recognizing the column's popularity, paid Helliwell a phenomenal £2,500 a year for his services, while his colleagues began to file spiv copy.[126] In July 1947, Charles Rowe reported the anger of coffee stallholders outside King's Cross station who were being closed down because of the night-time violence at 'Spivs' Corner'.[127] A few weeks later the paper carried an article by Peter Forbes describing the spiv.[128] That summer, the popular press was awash with spiv stories.[129]

The spiv was also the subject of numerous crime fictions. There was a veritable flood of books with titles such as *King Spiv* by Leo Gree, *Soho Spiv* by Ben Sarto, and *The Affair of the Spiv's Secret* by John Hunter. There was a stage play called *The Affair of the Demented Spiv*, and even a spiv ballet, *Paradise Row*, broadcast on BBC television in 1949. There was also a cycle of British 'spiv' films, concerned with the criminal underworld in which the spiv was a central character. Eight crime films with readily discernible spiv characters and plots centring on black market activity, including *Brighton Rock* (1947) and *The Third Man* (1949), were released between January 1947 and December 1949. Most of their action took place in cafés, street-markets, dog-tracks, railway sidings, pubs, and clubs.[130] Spivvish characters featured in other genres of British film—notably in comedies produced by Ealing studios such as *Hue and Cry* (1947), *Whisky Galore!* (1949), and *Passport to Pimlico* (1949). The criminal and the comic aspects of the spiv revealed in popular culture highlight the ambivalent status of this figure who became a site for the articulation of changing post-war attitudes towards evasion.[131]

As a valued provider of illicit goods and services, the spiv was an ambiguous figure who resisted moralists' attempts at vilification. Unlike the more recent term 'chav', calling someone a spiv was rarely an expression of class disgust. The lives of the spivs fascinated a wider public, who found their antics entertaining, reprehensible, and inevitable. Helliwell, who fixed the spiv image, considered the 'Boys' an unavoidable by-product of economic control. He had little time for their selfish hedonism, which contrasted starkly with the wartime camaraderie of the armed forces. Helliwell's feelings came out when sketching the character of the 'Perfect Spiv'.

[126] *Newsweek*, 14 August 1950.
[127] Charles Rowe, 'They're up in arms at Spivs' Corner', *The People*, 6 July 1947.
[128] Peter Forbes, 'Spivs', *The People*, 3 August 1947.
[129] Partridge, 'Spivs and Phoneys'.
[130] Robert Murphy, *Realism and Tinsel: Cinema and Society in Britain 1939–48* (London, 1989), ch. 8.
[131] See Andrew Spicer, 'The Representation of Masculinity in British Feature Films, 1943–1960' (Ph.D. thesis, University of Westminster, 1998) on these varieties of celluloid spiv.

Tilting his black Homburg to an even cockier angle and shifting his cigarette to the corner of his mouth, the incredible character they call the 'Perfect Spiv' summed up the situation for me yesterday in a few terse sentences.

'They'll never catch us', he boasted. 'Most of the boys were on the run all through the war. So what chance have they got of roping us in now? Ration books and identity cards don't mean a thing. They belong to the mug's world—and so far as we're concerned only mugs work.'

That little piece of 'spivosophy' is only too true of course. No laws or regulations made in Downing Street will ever trap the wide boy.[132]

Here, Helliwell, writing for a Labour-leaning paper, echoed the Conservative view that controls bred a spiv economy. The moral ambiguities of Helliwell's stance did not go unchallenged. When the *Daily Mail* printed an anonymous letter saying that cartoonists and columnists should thank the spiv for keeping them in work, Helliwell reacted angrily to the suggestion that he made his living through crime, albeit indirectly.[133]

A controversy surrounding the appearance of a spiv on the BBC radio programme *London Magazine* made the contrast between those like Helliwell, who viewed the spiv as an inescapable by-product of control, and those who saw the spiv as a selfish individual undermining fair-shares policies readily apparent. In September 1947 the producer booked Arthur Helliwell to talk about Soho for the 15-minute programme broadcast on the Home Service at 7.30 on Saturday evenings.[134] In his talk Helliwell described Soho as a major black market centre before introducing listeners to self-confessed spiv 'Jack Smith', whom he had met in a Lyons Corner House. Smith told Helliwell that he could obtain anything from nylons to smuggled cars before adding that Scotland Yard was too busy with murders and other crimes to clamp down on the spivs.[135] A small number of an estimated 2.1 million listeners complained to the BBC about the programme condoning spivvish activities, and the apparent ease with which Helliwell found a spiv to appear on the radio programme prompted many listeners to send letters to the commissioner questioning the competence of the Metropolitan Police. Detectives and ministry inspectors, embarrassed by the brouhaha, interviewed Helliwell and the producer of *London Magazine*.[136]

The controversy prompted an internal review of BBC policy towards the black market in its programmes at a time of national 'crisis' brought about by balance-of-payments problems. A week after Helliwell's appearance, the corporation's senior controller issued a directive banning light-hearted treatment of evasion. Like Labour ministers busily demonizing 'spivs, drones, and eels', the senior controller made it clear that the 'BBC does not consider that the Black Market is funny'. He acknowledged 'that it may not be possible to cut out entirely such jokes from OBs [Outside Broadcasts]', but thought 'it is desirable to do so as far as is

---

[132] *The People*, 12 October 1947.   [133] *The People*, 4 January 1948.
[134] *Daily Express*, 3 October 1947; *Newsweek*, 14 August 1950.
[135] BBC WAC, R34/279, Sir John Woods to Sir William Haley, 17 October 1947.
[136] BBC WAC, R9/12/3, Listening Barometer for 27 September 1947; *The People*, 5 October 1947.

reasonably practicable, and in addition they should be entirely banned from our own studio programmes'.[137] The burden of policing the directive fell on the director of variety, who sent a memo to producers explaining that the black market, 'fruitful though it may be for comedians' gags, is in fact anything but funny'.[138] This sentiment chimed with those members of the public, often from the provinces, who held London spivs responsible for the country's ills. Residents of Barnsley complained about a spiv invasion when London traders descended on the town's market, selling toy balloons and paper flowers in the run up to Christmas. 'Angry' housewives refused to buy, complaining instead about their husbands having to 'slave' at the coal-face to keep young men like 'those' in idleness.[139] According to Macclesfield gardeners, spivs on the other side of the Pennines were also fixing flower-show results by poisoning prize chrysanthemums.[140]

Despite some public support for its stance, the BBC found it difficult to control its output. The Western Brothers—a popular vaudeville act—broke the ban within two weeks of its coming into force by singing 'Alhambra of the Air' on the popular Saturday-night show *Music Hall*.[141] The BBC received no complaints about the brothers, who went on to defame the Minister of Fuel and Power the following year. Performers on the Light Programme's Friday-night variety show *Merry-Go-Round* flouted the ban regularly.[142] Unlike most comics who escaped with a mild reprimand, Leon Cortez was banned from broadcasting for six months after slipping in a joke considered too blue.[143] On his return to the airwaves in 1948 he continued to make spiv gags, but by this point BBC executives had ceased to enforce the ban. The radio comics' portrayal of the spiv as a hapless working-class rogue fitted the public perception that 'the spivs was just ordinary people going round wheeling and dealing and selling what they could', as one schoolboy described them.[144]

By 1948 the comic spiv was close to vanquishing the criminal spiv from the public mind. In March, two enterprising cartoonists published an edition of an imaginary *Spivs' Gazette*, lampooning the activities of the spivs and capitalizing upon the spiv's hard-won status as a loveable working-class rogue. Readers could enrol in the Spivs' Union for 1*s*, and in return they received a Membership and Rules Card bearing an official Union Number. Naturally, the rules of the union were tongue in cheek. The first of ten rules stipulated that 'All members must swear to uphold the best traditions of spivvery at all times.' Under rule four, 'Any member found doing honest work of any kind, or giving any client a square deal, will be chucked out of the Union forthwith.' Union members could also buy a Union badge or tie-pin featuring Ivor Racket, the President of the Spivs' Union.[145] There was even a 'Spivs' Anthem' sung to the tune of 'Side by Side'.

[137] BBC WAC, R34/279, Directive 78, 8 October 1947.
[138] BBC WAC, R34/279, Director of Variety to all producers, 27 October 1947.
[139] *Barnsley Chronicle*, 13 December 1947.
[140] *Washington Post*, 9 November 1947.
[141] *Music Hall*, Home Service, 18 October 1947, 20:00hrs.
[142] BBC WAC, R34/279, C. F. Meehan to Leslie Bridgmont, 29 October 1947.
[143] *New York Times*, 16 November 1947.
[144] Terry Alford, cited in Addison, *Now the War is Over*, 49–50.
[145] *Spivs' Gazette*, March 1948.

Oh, we've all made a barrel of money,
Maybe you think that we're funny,
As we travel along, singing a song,
Side by side.
It may be a little bit risky,
Driving a lorry of whisky,
But we travel the road, sharing our load,
Side by side.
We all have a racket.
It may be big or small,
But if we make a packet,
It doesn't matter at all.
Some people work for a living,
But we much prefer to keep spivving,
And we travel along, singing a song,
Side by side.

The *Spivs' Gazette*, intended as a one-off, proved so popular that the Exeter-based cartoonists began to publish an edition every quarter (see Fig. 9.3). By February 1949 there were 1,300 members of the Spivs' Union, including the comic Sid Field and the actor Dirk Bogarde. A handful of readers set up Spivs' Clubs. The Hull Spivs' Club, with a membership of forty, arranged an annual trip to the seaside, social evenings, and dances—and even staged a pantomime.[146] The success of the *Spivs' Gazette* allowed the two cartoonists to found a regular adult comic, *Comic Life*, which featured regular reports of the activities of the Spivs' Union.

By 1952 spivs had ceased to be portrayed as a social menace. Cartoons depicted their reduced circumstances as they struggled to make a living hawking red Santa hats on city streets in the run up to Christmas, or queuing outside the Labour Exchange to find gainful employment. St Trinian's provided refuge for Flash Harry, one of their number. The social stigma attached to spivvish antics disappeared as controls floated off on a rising tide of supplies, reducing the opportunities for evasion, and the changing understanding of the spiv reflected the declining importance of the black market. In the immediate post-war years, evasion had figured prominently in the austerity debates between the Labour government and its political opponents. Then, the image of the criminal spiv, not the comic spiv, dominated public discourse.

Thanks to Conservative politicians, it became increasingly popular to see evasion as the inevitable product of 'unnatural' regulations. This notion, pushed by a Conservative partisan network, facilitated evasion by members of conventional society as it legitimated the exculpatory tactic of condemning one's condemners. By going on to question the very need for the continuation of control, the Conservative critique allowed evaders to present their offences as principled resistance to unjust, unnecessary, and unnatural regulations. During the war years, before the all-party consensus on control broke down, crime fiction and crime news had

---

[146] *Spivs' Gazette.*

THE BIGGEST LAUGH OF THE CENTURY !

PUBLISHED EVERY CRISIS ——— BLACK-MARKET PRICE 6ᴰ

SPIVS' GAZETTE

incorporating

THE BARROW-BOYS' BULLETIN

CONTENTS:—

JOIN THE SPIVS' UNION!
(with Rules in full and Coat of Arms)

THE FIRST SPIV

NERO, who "fiddled" while Rome was burning

LATEST BLACK MARKET PRICES

"DOWN SPIVVY-ST."
(Two Pages of Cartoons)

SPIV GLOSSARY

A DAY IN THE LIFE OF A BARROW-BOY

60 CARTOONS

AND OTHER ITEMS OF INTEREST TO ALL SPIVS, DRONES, EELS AND BUTTERFLIES

OUR PRESIDENT
IVOR RACKET

Fig. 9.3. Front page of the *Spivs' Gazette*, March 1949. British Newspaper Library.

shaped public understanding of evasion. By portraying black market offences as a form of serious and organized crime, the media justified the distinction that people drew between acceptable grey market dealing on the one hand and reprehensible black market dealing on the other. The press made it even easier for the majority of the public to define their illicit transactions as illegal but acceptable by associating

Jewish traders with black marketeering. Although the media and latterly politicians did not condone evasion, they made it much easier for the 'law-abiding' to justify while reinforcing the moral support that some communities afforded their members.

***

The moral economy that underpinned compliance and non-compliance with control disappeared as austerity haltingly gave way to affluence. This moral economy, which made evasion possible and determined its shape, emerged during the war and proved remarkably stable. By framing evasion as criminal, selfish, and unpatriotic, government bolstered public support for temporary control by invoking norms of obedience to the law and norms of fairness in exchange, distribution, and use. Any would-be evaders had to overcome their moral inhibitions to illicit dealing before breaking the law. There were clear bounds to self-interest. Familiar techniques of neutralizing moral dissonance, such as condemning one's condemners or appealing to higher loyalties, made it possible to do this. They also drew strength from popular notions of fair treatment and fair shares which clashed with official definitions. Over time these found durable expression in the idea of a grey market, which reduced the mental effort required for an individual to justify evasion. For conventional society the boundary between grey market and black market was clear. With their national reach, the news and entertainment media played a critical role in circulating and legitimating the conventional values and beliefs that made evasion possible. In some residential and occupational communities the boundary between grey market and black market differed slightly from that drawn in conventional society. Only a handful of communities, opposed or indifferent to conventional mores, did not recognize the distinction.

Conclusion: a fair trade

Black markets were everywhere and nowhere in austerity Britain; socially significant yet economically unimportant. Billy Hill, the self-proclaimed boss of Britain's underworld, who thought black markets were 'the most fantastic side of civil life in wartime', and Lord Woolton, the former Minister of Food who thought it a tribute to the British that 'there was little or no black market', were both right.[1] But there is no paradox here, as most evasion involved non-monetary exchange of supplies earmarked for civilian consumption. Gifting and swapping of unused coupons and rations—the most common fiddles—did not feed inflation or divert resources from the war effort or latterly the export drive. When money crossed palms, the black market premium was low or non-existent, as considerations of profit were of limited importance to most traders. Even when profit was uppermost in traders' minds, they were more likely to concern themselves with a satisfactory rather than an optimal illegal return as they sought to bolster dwindling legal earnings. Only the blackest of illicit deals that involved the traffic in stolen or counterfeit goods and coupons resembled the classic monetary transactions of contemporary price theory. Criminal entrepreneurs such as Billy Hill who made these deals were the only black market operators whose behaviour approached that of economic man.

Despite widespread evasion of price control and rationing, economic control was a success. Policymakers aimed to mobilize and demobilize the economy so as to avoid the mistakes of the First World War. In this they were successful: inflation was contained, a post-war slump was avoided, and class conflict was minimal. Although popular support for the continuance of the system fell after the war, it remained surprisingly high into the 1950s. As late as March 1953, just over two-fifths of adults opposed the Conservative government's plans to remove controls—controls which had ensured that working-class households received a fair share of consumer goods at a fair price, improving living standards and public health.[2] Comparisons with the experience of other combatant nations flatter the British system further. Polls show that British public opinion was consistently more favourable towards control and more hostile towards black markets than public opinion in Allied countries such as Australia, Canada, or the USA.[3] For British

---

[1] Hill, *Boss of Britain's Underworld*, 73; Woolton, *Memoirs*, 231.

[2] Frank Trentmann, 'Bread, Milk and Democracy', in Martin Daunton and Matthew Hilton (eds.), *The Politics of Consumption: Material Culture and Citizenship in Europe and America* (Oxford, 2001), 156, n. 97.

[3] Hadley Cantril and Mildred Strunk (eds.), *Public Opinion 1935–1946* (Princeton, 1951), 45–6, 654–64, 729–35.

civilians the war was not a distant reality, which made it easier to identify with the war effort and accept the link that politicians made between winning the war and the need for control. That controls rationed scarcity not abundance helped too. As a result, evasion was less of a problem for the British than it was for their allies.[4] When the International Penal and Penitentiary Commission studied the war's impact on member countries' criminal-justice systems, black market crimes were of much less concern in the UK than elsewhere.[5]

Evasion posed less of a threat to economic control in the UK because much of it involved what Britons held to be 'grey' as opposed to 'black market' dealing. In popular usage 'grey market' referred to the non-market exchange of controlled goods and ration coupons whether money changed hands or not. Equating barter and monetary exchange with market exchange—a category error to which historians seem prone—hides the significance of the paid favour. Fair-shares policies had led government to intervene in the informal economy—an aspect of economic life that the state ignored during the inter-war period as it was associated with household production and non-market exchange. Controls—the instruments for implementing these policies—guided goods from importers and producers through 'official channels' to consumers, those channels being the supply and distribution chains associated with the formal economy before the war. Measures to prevent the development of shadow supply chains and secondary retail markets regulated small-scale producers, many of whom were self-suppliers, and banned all exchanges outside official channels with the exception of transfers within the household.

These rules, which outlawed gifts, swaps, loans, and paid favours between households, criminalized community exchange networks and eroded any distinction between the legal and illegal sectors of the underground economy. But the shortages that prompted these regulations also promoted a boom in the underground economy as civilians shored up declining living standards through a mixture of self-help and mutual aid, both longstanding and respectable social practices. Government encouraged this trend through 'grow your own' and 'make do and mend' campaigns. Communally sanctioned and condoned by government at least in part, illegal production and exchange associated with the grey market were archetypal social crimes.

Illicit markets in smuggled, stolen, and counterfeit goods, less reputable but equally long established community exchange networks, expanded, diversifying into controlled goods and coupons. Some legitimate businesses—the principal retailers of black market goods—sourced goods and coupons from these markets, but most developed shadow supply chains paralleling official ones. This was a simpler and less risky option for established traders than involvement in the 'traditional' crimes of theft, forgery, and fraud, building upon their knowledge and experience of inter-war sharp practice. Selling black market goods through legitimate retail outlets increased the number of potential buyers, as it insulated

---

[4] Mills and Rockoff, 'Compliance'; Keshen, 'One for All or All for One'; Milward, *War, Economy and Society*.

[5] All nine country studies appear in IPPC, *Effects of the War*.

customers from the crimes that made under-the-counter deals possible. The adage that 'If something sounds too good to be true, it probably is' still held, but the patron of a Soho restaurant could enjoy dishes containing scarce ingredients without having to acknowledge their probable source. Consumer fraud ceased to be a problem for traders as new and established fraudsters exploited the system to get extra ration books. The naked or thinly disguised greed that contemporaries believed drove these activities—associated with the illegal side of the inter-war underground economy—set them apart from grey market deals.

The types of evasion associated with the grey market created social capital by strengthening existing social ties and creating new ones within local communities. Contrary to the myth of the Blitz, 'pulling together' could, and often did, involve participating in forms of community exchange outlawed by Whitehall officials. The increasing importance of self-provisioning and mutual aid to the middle class, who had long avoided dependence upon their neighbours, enriched ties between middle-class friends and acquaintances, while it also encouraged them to forge ties with the working class, especially in smaller mixed communities and workplaces. As well as promoting community cohesion, grey marketing increased the efficiency of economic control by allowing people to bring official allocations into closer alignment with individual preferences. This shuffling rewarded thrift and promoted social justice when it involved rationed goods and coupons. By granting everyone the right to consume a certain quantity of goods, rationing gave the poor and the prudent a new entitlement that they could exchange for cash or goods. Illegal transfers of these entitlements are a hitherto unacknowledged factor that may have contributed to a levelling of class during the austerity years.[6]

Given that most evasion involved grey market deals, the popularity of these socially acceptable transactions undermines the easy notion that a high level of non-compliance with the regulations 'casts doubt on the myth of shared sacrifice'.[7] Such deals were rarely crimes of protest, unlike in Nazi-occupied Europe, where evasion constituted an act of resistance against an illegitimate authority. The British government's legitimacy was not seriously questioned outside Northern Ireland. Most social groups accepted conventional morality, quibbling about its interpretation and application rather than opposing it. Would-be moral statisticians looking for a barometer to gauge social solidarity and support for austerity policy needed to distinguish between the black market deal and the grey market deal as contemporaries did.

Of course, the boundary between grey and black marketing was unclear. For some, money use marked the point at which grey became black, while for others it was the desire to make a profit that defined the line. Both attempts at demarcation distinguished between legitimate need and illegitimate greed. A dislike of monetary transactions signalled a belief that monetary exchange and commodity exchange were synonymous. Focusing on the issue of profit, as most people did,

---

[6] Summerfield, 'Levelling of Class'; Ian Gazeley, 'The Levelling of Pay in Britain during the Second World War', *European Review of Economic History*, 10 (2006), 175–204.
[7] Zweiniger-Bargielowska, *Austerity*, 151.

indicated a more subtle understanding of money's meaning than historians have allowed for. Cash could be used legitimately to satisfy the desire for a reasonable standard of living. There was one proviso, however: no third party should suffer at your expense. So long as this was observed, obtaining a little extra illegally was excusable as well as understandable. Feelings of entitlement and ownership, fostered by fair-shares rhetoric, bolstered consumers' view that transferring controlled goods and coupons was acceptable. By helping them to obtain a few home comforts that made austerity bearable at nobody else's expense, people considered grey marketing to be socially beneficial. In stark contrast, black marketing was anti-social as it denied other people their fair share.[8]

Such definitions were frequently self-serving, characterizing one's illegalities as excusable attempts to satisfy basic needs, keep a business afloat, or secure a few home comforts. But the issue of ownership and entitlement was harder to evade than that of greed. Goods and coupons diverted from official channels denied others their fair share. Thanks to media portrayals of evasion, the public, and on occasion officials, came to associate this 'Black Market' with organized crime, though most black marketing involved established businesses developing an illicit sideline. Despite occasional coups that posed temporary threats to individual control schemes, neither criminal entrepreneurs nor business sideliners nor ration fraudsters could rival grey market networks as a means for securing a little extra. This mid-century boom in the underground economy had no lasting effects. The community exchange networks central to grey market dealing shrank in extent and importance as austerity gave way to affluence. Small independent businesses that dabbled in black market dealing survived austerity, but such illegal dealing did not leave them better placed to cope with renewed competition from their larger and more modern rivals after decontrol. Fears of permanent demoralization and diminution in respect for the law proved unfounded. At austerity's end, social surveys found that the British held their law-and-order bureaucracy in high regard, which chimed with the experience of those enforcing the law.[9] If there was any effect, it was on criminal entrepreneurs. But this paled in comparison to the effects of pro-hibition and economic control on serious and organized crime in the United States and Japan.[10]

Means, motive, and opportunity provide a partial explanation of this peculiar pattern of evasion. Shortages were never as acute as elsewhere in Europe. In the UK evasion was a way of improving an acceptable standard of living, not a means for securing it. Opportunities for evasion were also limited. Dependence upon imports made it comparatively easy to control the distribution of goods flowing through port bottlenecks.[11] Import dependence meant that the problem of domestic

---

[8] See Jonathan P. Parry and Maurice Bloch, *Money and the Morality of Exchange* (Cambridge, 1989) and Caroline Humphrey and Stephen Hugh-Jones (eds.), *Barter, Exchange and Value: An Anthropological Approach* (Cambridge, 1992).

[9] Gorer, *Exploring English Character*, 213–28; Gabriel A. Almond and Sidney Verba, *The Civic Culture: Political Attitudes and Democracy in Five Nations* (Princeton, 1963), 106–14; Emsley, *English Police*, 169–70.

[10] Griffiths, 'Need, Greed and Protest'.   [11] Milward, *War, Economy and Society*, 283.

producers withholding goods from official markets was much smaller than it was in much of continental Europe, and thus was easier to monitor. British farms were also comparatively large and therefore relatively few in number, so there were fewer people to control and the problem of domestic consumption on the farms was smaller. Due to a very large urban population there was less contact between consumers and farmers, which meant that there was less opportunity for petty black marketing in Britain than in continental Europe.[12] Finally, a well-staffed system of vertically and horizontally integrated controls left fewer loopholes for evasion.[13] But these explanations ignore the ease with which even a comparatively well-designed and well-resourced system of control could be evaded. Despite possessing a clear motive, Britons did not seize every opportunity that presented itself to evade the regulations. Lack of means is not a sufficient explanation for this. Many civilians could recognize their opportunities, as press reports and word of mouth provided them with plenty of information about illegal dealing in their locality.

Enforcement did not tilt the balance of risk and reward sufficiently in favour of risk to explain the failure of evasion to fulfil its potential. Manpower shortages meant that the chance of being caught was low, while the challenge of policing 'victimless' crimes and the rivalries between and within agencies exacerbated the problem. Anyone unlucky enough to be caught found it difficult to calculate their chances of being punished and working out what that punishment might be. In theory, penalties for breaking the rules were severe, but the courts did not enforce them consistently. The social composition of the lay magistracy who handled most cases ensured that there was, if anything, a tendency towards lenient sentencing. Despite their criminal jurisdiction, the behaviour of the magistrates' courts bears comparison with that of the county courts. Like county court judges, some lay magistrates saw themselves as enforcing norms that did not always coincide with the law.[14] Government publicity attempted to disguise these realities of enforcement, but the bluff was easy to see through. That the regulations could be evaded easily with limited risk was readily apparent to civilians, yet many chose not to do so. Even the economist Gary Becker, whose work inspired economic analyses of crime and punishment, concedes that 'many people are constrained by moral and ethical considerations, and did not commit crimes even when they were profitable and there was no danger of detection'.[15] Two obvious but unsatisfactory explanations for this reluctance to break the law offered by contemporaries and historians are patriotism and respect for the law.

Patriotism is a powerful but ephemeral motive for action—something which Tom Harrisson and other contemporary commentators recognized. They feared that the public would grow tired of patriotic appeals as the war dragged on. Independent studies of the effectiveness of such campaigns bore out concerns

---

[12] Blagburn, 'Control of Marketing', 71.

[13] Mills and Rockoff, 'Compliance'.

[14] Peter Scott, 'The Twilight World of Interwar Hire Purchase', *Past and Present*, 177 (2002), 220–1.

[15] Gary S. Becker, 'The Economic Way of Looking at Life', in Torsten Persson (ed.), *Nobel Lectures, Economics 1991–1995* (Singapore, 1992), 41–2.

about patriotic fatigue.[16] This became a chronic problem once the war, which had given the patriotic appeal an edge, ended. Although publicity emphasizing that you could 'do your bit' by consuming less was partially successful in framing discussion of consumption, it had a limited effect on consumer behaviour, much like the 1931 'Buy British' campaign.[17] Most traders provided their customers with few cues to remind them of their patriotic duty when making a purchase. In fact, the only requirements that the authorities placed on traders were to display an official price list in a prominent position and fix price tickets to goods; but judging by the number of warnings and prosecutions for failure to display price lists and tickets, this was frequently ignored. Few traders chose to paste posters on walls and windows as an additional reminder of shoppers' patriotic duty. When it came to rationed goods there was a second cue in the form of the ration book, prompting traders and customers to recall their patriotic and legal obligations. But none of these reminders prevented patriotic fatigue.

For complying with the regulations, a motive more enduring than patriotism was respect for the rule of law. The accounts gathered by M-O from members of its national panel in 1948 testify to the power that the rule-of-law norm exerted over conventional society, but they also reveal its limits. Many panellists did not feel bound by the regulations if they considered them unfair—something which the tax authorities had long appreciated.[18] This concern with fairness included the administration of control schemes as well as their effects: due process mattered as much to the panellists as did the outcomes of that process. Also important was that other people obeyed the rules. By accusing others of fiddling, panellists trying to maintain an image of themselves as respectable citizens appealed to a quasi-moral norm of conditional cooperation. They argued that they did not have to comply with the regulations if others did not, and that it was unfair to expect them to cooperate in such circumstances. By framing controls in terms of equality of sacrifice and fair shares, official rhetoric encouraged civilians to think about illegal dealing in this way, but bureaucratic notions of what constituted a fair price, a fair profit, or a fair share did not always accord with individual notions of distributive justice.

The officially sanctioned language of fairness had the curious effect of both limiting and enabling evasion. Government led civilians to believe that they were entitled to a reasonable standard of living, which the state guaranteed. If the official distribution fell short of a person's expectations, some felt justified in breaking the law to obtain 'a little bit extra'. Such mismatches occurred because controllers ignored one of three distributive principles: desert, equality, and need. Officials determining retail prices and ration levels attempted to strike a balance between efficiency on the one hand and equality and need on the other. Rewarding people

---

[16] M-OA, FR 1149, Tom Harrisson, 'Some Thoughts on Greyhounds and National Unity', 10 March 1942.

[17] Stephen Constantine, 'The Buy British Campaign of 1931', *European Journal of Marketing*, 21 (1987), 44–59.

[18] Martin Daunton, 'How to Pay for the War: State, Society and Taxation in Britain, 1917–24', *English Historical Review*, 111 (1996), 882–919.

in proportion to their contribution to the national effort played no part in their calculations. Government anxiety about economic incentives should not to be confused with concern about just deserts. Yet considerations of desert were, and remain, a central feature of popular notions of fairness across all classes. Craft unions invoked this principle during the war when resisting attempts to erode pay differentials.[19] Many civilians, like Ivor Novello, felt that they deserved as well as needed more than economic control allowed them. Obtaining a little bit extra was excusable as long as it did not rob somebody else of their legal entitlement—a qualification that had as much to do with property rights as it did considerations of fairness.

This moral position found stable expression in the related concepts of white, grey, and black markets. Civilians colour-coded economic transactions according to their legality and morality: white for legal and moral, grey for illegal but moral, and black for illegal and immoral. The idea found ready acceptance because it meant that people could avoid the costly mental gymnastics needed to work out what was right and wrong every time they contemplated breaking unfamiliar and complex economic regulations. Instead, they could economize on the effort associated with moral reasoning by invoking a rule or citing a precedent that allowed them to paint their actions as grey. This was necessary when their moral intuitions about what was right and wrong pointed in different directions. Of course, even the rules and precedents that constituted black market morality were not always easy to apply, especially in novel situations which occurred frequently as government introduced new control schemes or revised existing ones, forcing civilians to reason for themselves, take advice from those they considered 'moral experts', or comply with the regulations.

Of course, the moral atmosphere in which people made economic choices shifted during the fourteen years of austerity. At the war's outset the public accepted the need for temporary rationing and price control without question. This was the lesson which most drew from collective memory of economic control ending the rampant inflation, shortages, and social unrest that characterized life on the Home Front during the middle years of the Great War. Thanks to this successful precedent and the state's hard-won reputation for class neutrality, the public trusted the authorities to ensure a fair distribution of goods in short supply. Comparison with the difficulties encountered by 'illegitimate' authorities in German-occupied Europe underlines the importance of the reserves of legitimacy on which initial public support for control was based. These reserves needed to be renewed as patriotic fervour waned once it became apparent that this would be another great war. Concerns about the fairness of control, one of the key antecedents of legitimacy, which in turn inspired trust and compliance, came to the fore from 1941 onwards. As Ina Zweiniger-Bargielowska has shown, the politics of sacrifice took centre stage with interest groups lobbying government to ensure that they shouldered what they considered their fair share of the burden of cuts and no more.

---

[19] Gazeley, 'Levelling of Pay'; Miller, 'Distributive Justice'.

At the individual level, perceived procedural and distributive injustices prompted grumbling, avoidance, and evasion, but the rhetoric of equality of sacrifice and fairness kept it within bounds.

This moral economy, which gave rise to a thriving 'grey' market and a limited 'black' market, crumbled but did not collapse after the war. At first glance, 1945, the year war ended, is an obvious break point, as public acceptance of economic control was predicated on its being a temporary measure for the duration of the emergency. But people did not expect immediate and total decontrol with victory—another lesson drawn from the Great War—while the authorities anticipated a manageable rise in the number of 'graver offences' as the result of increased 'irritation and resistance' to control.[20] The consensus of opinion was that there should be a gradual transition from war to peace. Politicians bickered over the pace of decontrol—a sign of the return to normalcy—but all parties accepted the need for decontrol. Although renewed partisanship led more people to question the need for some regulations, it did not delegitimize control. The austerity debates of 1946 and 1947, not the end of the war, proved a decisive turning point in this regard. Successive economic crises forced the Labour government to temporarily reverse the policy of gradual decontrol, lending credence to Conservative charges that the government had no intention of relinquishing control. Labour stood accused of reneging on the bargain that control would be temporary, to be ended as soon as possible, which it and its wartime coalition partners had struck with the public. The government struggled to persuade the middle class, who felt that they had sacrificed most, that the country faced Keynes' 'financial Dunkirk', which necessitated tightening not relaxing control, reversing a policy followed since late 1944. Appeals to their patriotism and enlightened self-interest fell flat.

This shift in opinion, nurtured by Conservative rhetoric and elements in the press, had a destabilizing effect on support for control and the level of compliance that flowed from it. It made it possible to portray non-compliance as regrettable but natural, as well as irresistible and excusable. It also legitimated those who justified evasion as an act of political defiance. Nevertheless, support for a transitionary period of control remained high. The post-war increase in the level of non-compliance reflected the expansion and tightening of control rather than a lowering of moral inhibitions to evasion amongst the public. Many accepted the Labour case for temporarily tightening control, and even welcomed the suggestion that some regulations should be retained permanently. Despite weakening one of its pillars, the critique of control left the moral economy, forged in war, largely intact. The ending of the political truce, which muted public criticism of wartime control, exaggerated the deficiencies of peacetime control, fooling some but not all contemporaries. A legitimate and competent authority operated a fair and transparent system that achieved a fair distribution of goods in short supply, albeit not as effectively as during the war. A general sense of obligation and willingness to obey the law—the rule-of-law norm—as long as others did—the norm of conditional

---

[20] TNA: PRO, MAF 67/174, 'Food Enforcement Officers' Circular 992', 14 December 1944.

cooperation—continued to inhibit people who saw no need for control from participating in black markets.

Although criticism of control challenged the government's fair-shares rhetoric, it continued to influence people's choices after the war. The fact that even those who rejected the austerity policy felt it necessary to argue that nobody lost out because of their illegal deals is testimony to the lingering appeal of this rhetoric. It was the improving supply situation that killed off the moral economy of austerity and not Conservative attacks on control, which only drew attention to the return of abundance. Concerns about fairness mattered less to the public once there seemed to be plenty to go around. The invocation 'Fair shares for all'—a slogan that the Labour movement had made its own since 1945—had ceased to connect with norms of fairness in increasingly affluent times. Although, as Jim Tomlinson shows, fairness continued to figure prominently in discussion of economic matters as policymakers became increasingly aware that the public viewed the economy in ethical terms, this masked a change in public understanding of what social justice meant.[21] In an expanding economy the principle of just deserts mattered more than ideas about equality and need, which remained central to Labour thinking. Labour's opponents, who had helped to coin a wartime language of fair shares with which they felt uncomfortable, found it easier to speak to affluent voters who wanted a fair deal or a just reward for their efforts. This renewed emphasis on 'fair play' threatened to limit the Labour movement's electoral appeal, just as it had done in the inter-war period.[22] But this focus on the changing meaning of distributive justice obscures continuity in popular understanding of procedural justice. Observing due process in arriving at and administering a policy could reconcile some people to outcomes that they might otherwise consider unfair.

Beyond providing us with an insight into an aspect of everyday ethics at mid-century, just before permissiveness changed the moral landscape, grey and black markets challenge our ideas about economic life in modern Britain. The distinguishing feature of the modern economy is the rhetorical dominance of market relations over other forms of exchange. By the mid-nineteenth century the market ideal was ascendant, exerting a near monopoly over economic thought. Accounts of this 'great transformation' tend to focus on the penetration of market relations into economic life, which is portrayed as advancing swiftly on all fronts, even entering the household. According to Avner Offer, 'What is less noted is the persistence of non-market exchange.'[23] Recent work on credit and debt during the long nineteenth century and into the inter-war period supports this view.[24] Non-market exchange was not an archaic survival; it continued to fulfil an important albeit subsidiary role in economic life at mid-century. Not only did it allow people

---

[21] See Jim Tomlinson, 'Managing the Economy, Managing the People: Britain *c*.1931–70', *Economic History Review*, 58 (2005), 555–85 and Tomlinson, 'Re-inventing the "Moral Economy"'.

[22] McKibbin, 'Why was there no Marxism?'

[23] Avner Offer, *The Challenge of Affluence: Self-Control and Well-Being in the United States and Britain since 1950* (Oxford, 2006), 75.

[24] Finn, *Character of Credit*; and Scott, 'Twilight World'.

to satisfy their need for regard though gift exchange, as Offer argues, but it also helped some to secure a decent standard of living using an exchange repertoire that included swaps, paid favours, tips, and loans. In austere times, non-market exchange increased in economic importance, as did illicit market exchange. While market relations dominated the modern economy after the 'great transformation', spheres of exchange continued to ebb and flow as the fortunes of the formal market economy waxed and waned.

The continued importance of non-market exchange to economic life at mid-century reminds us that all forms of exchange—market exchange included—retained a moral dimension. The idea of a 'disembedded' modern market economy, inherited from Karl Polanyi, is a misnomer.[25] In fact, Polanyi's notion of 'embedd-edness' on which this argument rests perpetuates the idea that economic activity is in some subtle and fundamental way distinct from social life. People selected a form of exchange from the British repertoire which they considered socially and morally acceptable as well as suitable for their purposes. At mid-century, consid-erations of fairness were central to individuals' judgements about the moral and social appropriateness of an economic act—and the same was true in other coun-tries.[26] British politicians who invoked popular notions of procedural and distribu-tive justice in order to bolster public support for control succeeded in framing individual economic choice as a moral choice.

The principles of 'fair play' and 'fair shares' on which Lord Woolton sought to base a 'national food code' were not innate nor the product of an archaic social contract. Rather, they were the product of earlier public debates about taxation and social welfare, which were themselves informed by the ruminations of econo-mists and political philosophers. But neither 'practical men' like Woolton nor the wider public were, as Keynes believed, 'the slaves of some defunct economist'. John Stuart Mill said much about equality of sacrifice when it came to taxation, but he said nothing about applying the principle to rationing and price control. As discur-sive constructs, norms of fairness left plenty of room for interpretation, as they could not specify what to do in every instance, especially in novel situations such as those created by economic control. Without clear guidance from respected legal or moral authorities, individuals had to make up their own minds as to what they should do or to whom they should listen. Poorly understood principles and incomplete codes of behaviour placed constraints on their interpretation while allowing for great variety in their application. In such conditions of uncertainty it was far from clear which interpretation would become the dominant one.

Calls for fair shares, fair prices, and fair profits, as opposed to calls for a fair deal or a just reward, resonated with fewer people in more affluent times, dropping out of mainstream political debate in the 1950s. Considerations of just deserts displaced ideas of need and equality. When it came to black market dealing in austerity

[25] Kurtuluş Gemici, 'Karl Polanyi and the Antinomies of Embeddedness', *Socio-Economic Review*, 6 (2008), 5–33.
[26] Matthew Hilton and Martin Daunton, 'Material Politics: An Introduction', in Daunton and Hilton, *Politics of Consumption*, 17.

Britain, an idea of fairness, based on equal treatment and satisfying individual needs, was a critical factor in deciding whether or not one should circumvent the regulations. In certain circumstances, popular notions of fairness trumped moral inhibitions to illicit dealings, dictating what form of exchange to use. Black market morality meant that dealers and their customers considered themselves fair traders and ethical consumers. Although it continued to inform the economic practices of the poor, this morality was increasingly irrelevant to the beneficiaries of affluence whose ideas of justice centred on the notion of a fair deal rather than a fair share. Once common currency, the vocabulary of motive associated with black market morality slipped out of popular usage to become an argot associated with tax-dodgers and benefit cheats.

Bibliography

ARCHIVAL COLLECTIONS

BBC Written Archives Centre, Caversham Park, Reading
  Administrative and Programme Files
  Play scripts
  Talk scripts
Board of Deputies of British Jews, London
  Jewish Defence Committee (C6)
Bodleian Library, Oxford
  Conservative Party Archives
Borthwick Institute for Historical Research, University of York
  Papers of Benjamin Seebohm Rowntree
  Papers of Cyril Foster Garbett
BP Archive, Modern Records Centre, University of Warwick
British Library, St Pancras, London
    BBC Sound Archive
    Millennium Memory Bank
    National Life Story Collection
    National Sound Archive
British Library of Political and Economic Science, London
  Papers of William Beveridge
British Universities Newsreel Database, British Universities Film and Video Council
Churchill Archives Centre, Churchill College, Cambridge
  Papers of Winston Churchill
Imperial War Museum, Lambeth, London
  Documents
    Diary of Hilda Neal
    Notebook of PC Walter Atkin
    Papers of Geoffrey Lloyd
    Papers of Stephen Pena
    Unpublished memoir of H. F. Grey
  Sound Archive
    Military Operations, 1939–45
    Naval Operations, 1939–45
    A People's War
    West Country at War
ITN Source, London
  British Paramount News
  Gaumont British News
London Metropolitan Archives
  Board of Deputies of British Jews files (ACC 3121)
  Office of the Chief Rabbi files (ACC 2805)
Mass-Observation Archive, University of Sussex, Falmer
  Diaries
  Directive Replies

File Reports
Topic Collections
Metropolitan Police Archives
Museum of London
  Museum of Docklands Oral History Project
The National Archives: Public Record Office, Kew
  British Transport Commission files (AN)
  Board of Trade files (BT)
  Cabinet Office files (CAB)
  Dominions Office files (DO)
  Foreign Office files (FO)
  HM Customs and Excise files (CUST)
  HM Treasury files (T)
  Home Office files (HO)
  Lord Chancellor's Department files (LCO)
  Metropolitan Police files (MEPO)
  Ministry of Food files (MAF)
  Ministry of Fuel and Power files (POWE)
  Ministry of Information files (INF)
  Ministry of (War) Transport files (MT)
  Prime Minister's Office files (PREM)
  (Wartime) Social Survey files (RG)
The National Archives of Scotland, Edinburgh
  Scottish Home Department (HH)
UK Data Archive, University of Essex, Colchester
Centre of South Asian Studies, University of Cambridge
  Papers of Charles Augustus Tegart
York Minster Library
  Papers of Archbishop Cyril Foster Garbett

OFFICIAL PUBLICATIONS

Periodicals
  Annual Abstract of Statistics
  Economic Trends
  Hansard, *Parliamentary Debates*, fifth series
  Labour Gazette
  Public and General Statutes
  Statutory Rules and Orders

Parliamentary Papers
Annual Report of the Prisons Department for Scotland for the Year 1938 (PP 1938–9
  Cmd.5967 xiv. 467).
British Transport Commission: First Annual Report: Statement of Accounts and Statistics
  for the Year ended 31st December 1948 (PP 1948–9 (235) xii, 1).
Criminal Statistics: England and Wales, 1939–1945 (PP 1946–7 Cmd.7227 xv. 781).
Eighty-fourth Report of His Majesty's Inspector of Constabulary for Scotland for the Year
  ended 31st December 1946 (PP 1947–8 Cmd.7247 xiv. 311).
Employment Policy (PP 1943–4 Cmd.6527 viii, 119).

First Report of the Departmental Committee of Inquiry into Statutory Smallholdings (PP 1965–6 Cmnd.2936 vii, 255).

Fuel Rationing (PP 1941–2 Cmd.6352 iv. 275).

Report of the Commissioner of Police of the Metropolis for 1943 (PP 1943–4 Cmd.6536 iv. 507).

Report of the Commissioner of Police for the Metropolis for the Year 1944 (PP 1944–5 Cmd.6627 v. 427).

Report of the Commissioner of Police for the Metropolis for the Year ended 29th September 1946 (PP 1946–7 Cmd.7156 xiii, 563).

Report of the Commissioners of Prisons and the Directors of Convict Prisons for the Year 1938 (PP 1939–40 Cmd.6137 v. 261).

Report of the Commissioners of Prisons and the Directors of Convict Prisons for the Year 1945 (PP 1946–7 Cmd.7146 xiv. 155).

Report of the Committee of Enquiry on the Evasions of Petrol Rationing Control (PP 1947–8 Cmd.7372 xiv. 187).

Report of an Enquiry upon the Proceedings at the Hearing of Two Informations before Justices of the Aberayron Division of the County of Cardigan on 24th April 1946 (PP 1946–7 Cmd.7061 xiii, 51).

Report of His Majesty's Inspectors of Constabulary for the Year ended 29th September 1946 (PP 1946–7 (134) xiii, 541).

Report of HM Inspectors of Constabulary for the year ended 29th September 1945 (PP 1945–6 (168) xiv. 193).

Report of the Committee of Privy Counsellors appointed to inquire into the Interception of Communications (PP 1956–7 Cmd.283 xv. 125).

Report of the Committee on Poaching and Illegal Fishing of Salmon and Trout in Scotland (PP 1950 Cmd.7917 xi, 219).

Report of the Committee on Cruelty to Wild Animals (PP 1950–1 Cmd.8266 viii, 245).

Report of the Committee on Horticultural Marketing (PP 1956–7 Cmnd.61 xiv. 241).

Report of the Committee on the Taxation of Trading Profits (PP 1950–1 Cmd.8189 xx, 1).

Report of the Departmental Committee on Export and Slaughter of Horses (PP 1950 Cmd.7888 xii, 9).

Report of the Royal Commission on Police Powers and Procedure (PP 1928–9 Cmd.3297 ix, 127).

Report of the Royal Commission on the Press 1947–1949 (PP 1948–9 Cmd.7700 xx, 1).

Report of the Tribunal appointed to inquire into the Administration by the Council of the City and County of Newcastle-upon-Tyne and its Committees and Officers of their Functions in relation to the Fire, Police, and Civil Defence Services (PP 1943–4 Cmd.6522 iv. 315).

Report on Prisons in Scotland for the Years 1939–1948 (PP 1948–9 Cmd.7747 xx, 635).

Royal Commission on Justices of the Peace 1946–1948: Report (PP 1947–8 Cmd.7463 xii, 733).

Statement by His Majesty's Government on Price Stabilisation and Industrial Policy (PP 1940–1 Cmd.6294 viii, 311).

Non-Parliamentary Publications

Board of Trade, *Restraint of Trade* (London, 1931).

Board of Trade, *Third Report of the Retail Trade Committee* (London, 1942).

Home Office, *Report of the Departmental Committee on Detective Work and Procedure* (5 vols. London, 1938).

Ministry of Agriculture and Fisheries, *Agricultural Statistics: United Kingdom, ii: Output and Utilisation of Farm Produce in the Agricultural Years 1943–1944 to 1949–1950* (London, 1953).

Ministry of Agriculture and Fisheries, *Agricultural Statistics: England and Wales.*

Ministry of Agriculture, Fisheries and Food, *Output and Utilization of Farm Produce in the United Kingdom, 1946–47 to 1955–56* (London, 1958).

Ministry of Food, *Lectures on the Administration of Food Control, Rationing and Distribution, arranged at the request of the British Council, and given at the Carlton Hotel* (London, 1944).

Ministry of Food, *The Market Square: The Story of the Food Ration Book 1940–1944* (London, 1944).

Ministry of Food, *How Britain was fed in War Time: Food Control, 1939–1945* (London, 1946).

Ministry of Food, *The Urban Working-Class Household Diet: First Report of the National Food Survey Committee* (London, 1951).

Ministry of Information, *Civilian Supplies in Wartime Britain* (London, 1945).

Ministry of Labour and National Service, *Industrial Relations Handbook, 1944, Supplement No. 2, January 1948* (London, 1948).

Ministry of Transport, *Petrol Stations: Report of the Technical Committee* (London, 1949).

Ministry of Transport, *Road Traffic Census, 1950* (London, 1952).

NEWSPAPERS, PERIODICALS, AND REPORTS

Newspapers
Barnsley Chronicle
Cambridge Daily News
Daily Express
Daily Mail
Daily Mirror
Daily Telegraph
East London Advertiser
Evening News
Evening Standard
Irish Times
Jewish Chronicle
Manchester Guardian
New York Times
News Chronicle
Norfolk and Suffolk Journal and Diss Express
The Observer
The People
Salford City Reporter and Chronicle
Scotsman
Sunday Dispatch
Sunday Express
Sunday Times
The Times
Washington Post
Western Mail

Periodicals

British Housewives' League Newsletter
The Economist
The Field
Justice of the Peace and Local Government Review
Lilliput Magazine
The Magistrate: The Bulletin of the Magistrates' Association
Monthly Review of the Incorporated Society of Inspectors of Weights and Measures
The Nation
News-sheet of the Bribery and Secret Commissions Prevention League
New Statesman and Nation
Newsweek
Police Journal
Punch
Socialist Standard
Spectator
Spivs' Gazette
Times Literary Supplement
Tribune

Reports

Annual Report of the Chief Constable of Leeds City Police
Magistrates' Association Annual Report
Metropolitan Police Fund Annual Financial Statement and Estimate

FILMS

Brighton Rock, directed by John Boulting (Associated British Picture Corporation, 1947)
Crime Reporter, directed by Ben R. Hart (Knightsbridge-Hammer, 1947)
Hue and Cry, directed by Charles Crichton (Ealing Studios, 1947)
The League of Gentlemen, directed by Basil Dearden (Allied Film Makers, 1960)
Partners in Crime, directed by Frank Launder and Sidney Gilliat (Gainsborough Pictures, 1942)
Passport to Pimlico, directed by Henry Cornelius (Ealing Studios, 1949)
A Private Function, directed by Malcolm Mowbray (HandMade Films, 1984)
San Demetrio—London, directed by Charles Frend (Ealing Studios, 1943)
The Ship that Died of Shame, directed by Basil Dearden (Ealing Studios, 1955)
The Third Man, directed by Carol Reed (London Films, 1949)
Whisky Galore, directed by Alexander Mackendrick (Ealing Studios, 1949)

OTHER PUBLISHED WORKS

For reasons of space only works cited more than once are listed here.
Addison, Paul, *Now the War is over: A Social History of Britain, 1945–51* (London, 1985).
Allen, C. K., Sir, *Law and Orders: An Inquiry into the Nature and Scope of Delegated Legislation and Executive Powers in English Law* (2nd edn., London, 1956).
Becker, Gary S., 'Crime and Punishment: An Economic Approach', *Journal of Political Economy*, 76 (1968), 169–217.
Beveridge, Peter, *Inside the CID* (London, 1957).

Bott, Elizabeth, *Family and Social Network: Roles, Norms, and External Relationships in Ordinary Urban Families* (2nd edn., London, 1971).

Brassley, Paul, and Potter, Angela, 'A View from the Top: Social Elites and Food Consumption in Britain, 1930s–1940s', in Frank Trentmann and Flemming Just (eds.), *Food and Conflict in the Age of the Two World Wars* (Basingstoke, 2006), 223–42.

Chibnall, Steve, 'Whistle and Zoot: The Changing Meaning of a Suit of Clothes', *History Workshop Journal*, 20 (1985), 56–81.

Clinard, Marshall B., *The Black Market: A Study of White Collar Crime* (New York, 1952).

Colquhoun, Robert, *Life begins at Midnight* (London, 1962).

Court, W. H. B., *Coal* (London, 1951).

Croall, Jonathan, *Don't You know there's a War on? The People's Voice 1939–45* (London, 1988).

Crofts, William, *Coercion or Persuasion? Propaganda in Britain after 1945* (London, 1989).

Day, Sidney, *London Born: A Memoir of a Forgotten City* (London, 2006).

Dennis, Norman, Henriques, Fernando, and Slaughter, Clifford, *Coal is Our Life: An Analysis of a Yorkshire Mining Community* (London, 1956).

Devlin, Patrick, Sir, *Trial by Jury* (2nd edn., London, 1966).

Dow, J. C. R., *The Management of the British Economy, 1945–60* (Cambridge, 1964).

Emsley, Clive, *The English Police: A Political and Social History* (2nd edn., London, 1996).

Faulks, Neville, Sir, *No Mitigating Circumstances* (London, 1977).

Finn, Margot C., *The Character of Credit: Personal Debt in English Culture, 1740–1914* (Cambridge, 2003).

Foreman, Freddie, with Lisners, John, *Respect: Autobiography of Freddie Foreman—Managing Director of British Crime* (London, 1997).

Fraser, Frankie, as told to Morton, James, *Mad Frank: Memoirs of a Life of Crime* (London, 1994).

Gallup, George H. (ed.), *The Gallup International Public Opinion Polls: Great Britain 1937–1975*, 2 vols. (New York, 1976).

Gardiner, Juliet, *Over Here: The GIs in Wartime Britain* (London, 1992).

Gazeley, 'The Levelling of Pay in Britain during the Second World War', *European Review of Economic History*, 10 (2006), 175–204.

Godfrey, Barry S., Fox, David J., and Farrall, Stephen, *Criminal Lives: Family Life, Employment and Offending* (Oxford, 2007).

Gorer, Geoffrey, *Exploring English Character* (London, 1955).

Green, F. H. W., 'Urban Hinterlands in England and Wales: an Analysis of Bus Services', *Geographical Journal*, 116 (1950), 64–81.

Griffiths, Owen, 'Need, Greed and Protest in Japan's Black Market, 1938–1949', *Journal of Social History*, 35 (2002), 825–58.

Hammond, Richard J., *Food*, 3 vols. (London, 1951–62).

Hancock, W. K., and Gowing, M. M., *British War Economy* (London, 1949).

Hargreaves, E. L., and Gowing, M. M., *Civil Industry and Trade* (London, 1952).

Hill, Billy, *Boss of Britain's Underworld* (London, 1955).

Hobbs, Dick, *Doing the Business: Entrepreneurship, the Working Class and Detectives in the East End of London* (Oxford, 1988).

Hughes, David, 'The Spivs', in Michael Sissons and Philip French (eds.), *Age of Austerity 1945–1951* (2nd edn., Harmondsworth, 1964), 86–105.

International Penal and Penitentiary Commission, *The Effects of the War on Criminality* (Berne, 1951).

Janson, Hank (Stephen D. Frances), *Jack Spot: Man of a Thousand Cuts* (London, 1959).

Jefferys, J. B., *Retail Trading in Britain, 1850–1950* (Cambridge, 1954).

Joyce, Stephen, 'The Black Economy in the Soar Valley, 1945–1971', *Transactions of the Leicestershire Archaeological and Historical Society*, 82 (2008), 245–54.

Kerr, Madeline, *The People of Ship Street* (London, 1958).

Keshen, Jeff, 'One for All and All for One: Government Controls, Black Marketing and the Limits of Patriotism, 1939–47', *Journal of Canadian Studies*, 29 (1994), 111–43.

King, Cecil H., *With Malice toward None: A War Diary* (London, 1970).

Klockars, Carl B., *The Professional Fence* (New York, 1974).

Levy, Hermann, *The Shops of Britain: A Study of Retail Distribution* (London, 1947).

Lewis, Roy, and Maude, Angus, *The English Middle Classes* (London, 1949).

Longmate, Norman, *The GIs: The Americans in Britain, 1942–1945* (London, 1975).

Malcolmson, Patricia, and Malcolmson, Robert (eds.), *Nella Last's Peace: The Post-War Diaries of Housewife 49* (London, 2008).

Malcolmson, Robert, and Mastoris, Stephanos, *The English Pig: A History* (London, 1998).

Marquis, Frederick James, 1st Earl of Woolton, *The Memoirs of the Rt. Hon. the Earl of Woolton C.H., P.C., D.L., Ll.D.* (London, 1959).

Mars, Gerald, *Cheats at Work: An Anthropology of Workplace Crime* (London, 1982).

Maude, Angus, *The Black Market*, Current Affairs 56 (London, 1948).

Mays, John Barron, *Growing up in the City: A Study of Juvenile Delinquency in an Urban Neighbourhood* (1954; Liverpool, 1964).

McKibbin, Ross, 'Why was there no Marxism in Great Britain?', *English Historical Review*, 99 (1984), 297–331.

Meynell, Francis, *My Lives* (London, 1971).

Miller, David, 'Distributive Justice: What the People think', *Ethics*, 102 (1992), 555–93.

Mills, Geofrey, and Rockoff, Hugh, 'Compliance with Price Controls in the United States and the United Kingdom during World War II', *Journal of Economic History*, 47 (1987), 197–213.

Milward, Alan S., *War, Economy and Society, 1939–1945* (1977; Berkeley, 1979).

Morris, Terence, *Crime and Criminal Justice since 1945* (Oxford, 1989).

Mullins, Sam, and Stockdale, David, *Talking Shop: An Oral History of Retailing in the Harborough Area during the Twentieth Century* (Stroud, 1994).

Murphy, Robert, *Smash and Grab: Gangsters in the London Underworld* (London, 1993).

Naughton, Bill, *On the Pig's Back: An Autobiographical Excursion* (Oxford, 1987).

Parker, Tony, and Allerton, Robert, *The Courage of His Convictions* (London, 1962).

Partridge, Eric, and Beale, Paul (eds.), *A Dictionary of Catch Phrases: From the Sixteenth Century to the Present Day* (2nd edn., London, 2005).

Payton-Smith, D. J., *Oil: A Study of War-time Policy and Administration* (London, 1971).

Rawlings, William, *A Case for the Yard* (London, 1961).

Reddaway, W. B., 'Rationing', in D. N. Chester (ed.), *Lessons of the British War Economy* (Cambridge, 1951), 182–99.

Robbins, Lionel, *The Economic Problem in Peace and War: Some Reflections on Objectives and Mechanisms* (London, 1947).

Rollings, Neil, 'Whitehall and the Control of Prices and Profits in a Great War, 1919–1939', *Historical Journal*, 44 (2001), 517–40.

Roodhouse, Mark, 'The 1948 Belcher Affair and Lynskey Tribunal', *Twentieth Century British History*, 13 (2002), 384–411.

——'Black Market Activity in Britain, 1939–1955' (Ph.D. thesis, University of Cambridge, 2003).

——'The "Ghost Squad": Undercover Policing in London, 1945–49', in Gerard Oram (ed.), *Conflict and Legality: Policing mid-Twentieth Century Europe* (London, 2003), 171–91.

——'In Racket Town: Gangster Chic in Austerity Britain, 1939–1953', *Historical Journal of Film, Radio and Television*, 31 (2011), 541–59.

Rowntree, B. Seebohm, and Lavers, G. R., *English Life and Leisure: A Social Study* (London, 1951).

Rule, J. G., 'Social Crime in the Rural South in the Eighteenth and Early Nineteenth Centuries', *Southern History*, 1 (1979), 135–53.

Samuel, Raphael, *East End Underworld: Chapters in the Life of Arthur Harding* (London, 1981).

Scott, Sir Harold, *Scotland Yard* (London, 1954).

Seymour, Victoria, *Court in the Act: Crime and Policing in WWII Hastings* (St Leonards on Sea, 2004).

Sheridan, Dorothy (ed.), *Among You taking Notes: The Wartime Diary of Naomi Mitchison 1939–1945* (London, 1985).

Simonds, Lord, 'Law', in Ernest Barker (ed.), *Character of England* (London, 1947), pp. 112–35.

Skyrme, Thomas, Sir, *History of the Justices of the Peace*, 3 vols. (Chichester, 1991).

Smithies, Edward, *Crime in Wartime: A Social History of Crime in World War II* (London, 1982).

—— *The Black Economy in England since 1914* (Dublin, 1984).

Stacey, Margaret, *Tradition and Change: A Study of Banbury* (London, 1960).

Steale, Jess (ed.), *A Working Class War: Tales from Two Families* (London, 1995).

Summerfield, Penny, 'The "Levelling of Class"', in H. L. Smith (ed.), *War and Social Change: British Society in the Second World War* (Manchester, 1986), 179–207.

Sutton, Mike, with Johnston, Katie, and Lockwood, Heather, 'Handling Stolen Goods and Theft: A Market Reduction Approach', *Home Office Research Study*, 178 (1998).

Thomas, Donald, *An Underworld at War: Spivs, Deserters, Racketeers and Civilians in the Second World War* (London, 2003).

Tindall, Gillian, *Two Hundred Years of London Justice: The Story of Hampstead and Clerkenwell Magistrates' Courts* (London, 2001).

Visram, Rozina, *Asians in Britain: 400 Years of History* (London, 2002).

Ward, Sadie, *War in the Countryside, 1939–45* (London, 1988).

Weinberger, Barbara, *The Best Police in the World: An Oral History of English Policing from the 1930s to the 1960s* (Aldershot, 1995).

White, Jerry, *The Worst Street in North London: Campbell Bunk, Islington, between the Wars* (London, 1986).

Wilson, Harold, Baron Wilson of Rievaulx, *Memoirs: The Making of a Prime Minister 1916–1964* (London, 1986).

Zweiniger-Bargielowska, Ina, *Austerity in Britain: Rationing, Controls, and Consumption, 1939–1955* (Oxford, 2000).

Index